The Rock House® Method

Presents

Learn BASS

MASTER EDITION

Written & Method By:
John McCarthy

Adapted By: Jimmy Rutkowski
Supervising Editor: John McCarthy
Music Transcribing & Engraving: Jimmy Rutkowski
Production Manager: John McCarthy
Layout, Graphics & Design: Jimmy Rutkowski
Photography: Jimmy Rutkowski, Rodney Dabney
Copy Editors:
Cathy McCarthy & John McCarthy

Cover Art Direction & Design:
Jimmy Rutkowski

MP40020360
ISBN 979-8-9985228-1-9
Produced by McCarthy Publishing®

Table of Contents

Steaming Video, Backing Tracks & Worksheets

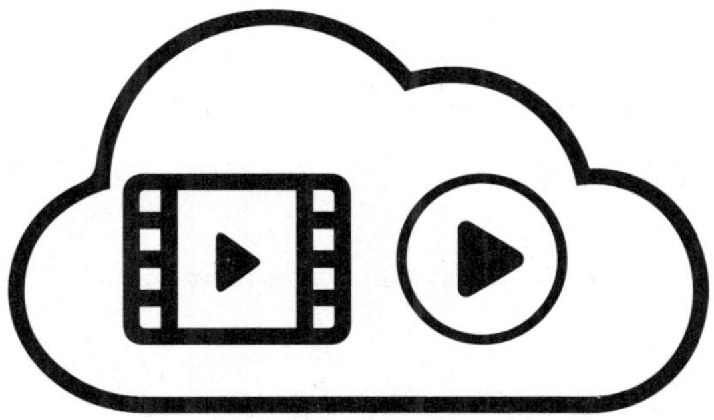

Book 2
Audio & Video
Page 73

Words from the Author

Playing music is a rewarding art form that will last you a lifetime, I discovered that fact shortly after I was given my first instrument. I have spent my career sharing the passion I have for music with others. With my teaching method, I truly believe you too will enjoy years of fun and will pass on the passion you discover. If you follow the method step-by step you will be successful and enjoy playing bass for years to come. When I designed The Rock House Method®, my mission was to create the most complete and fun way to learn. I accomplished this by developing and systematically arranging a modern method based on the needs and social demands of today's players. I not only tell you where to put your fingers, I show you ways to use what you learn so that you can make music right from the start. I know it is hard to imagine, but even the all-time greats started somewhere, there was a time when they too didn't even know what a chord was. As you progress as a bass player, keep your mind open to all styles of music. Set-up a practice schedule that you can manage, be consistent, challenge yourself and realize everyone learns at a different rate. Be patient, persistent and remember music is supposed to be fun!

NOW, GET EXCITED, this is it. YOU are going to play bass!

John McCarthy

Take Your Quiz

Each level of the curriculum contains multiple quizzes to gauge your progress. When you see a quiz, go to the lesson support on **RockHouseMethod.com** using member number **WWT-28P-HPC** or **AmpliTeach.com** if you are a member.

Worksheets

Throughout this book you will see the worksheet icon letting you know that there is a worksheet available to use for that lesson. By using worksheets you will make sure you understand and excel on the most important topics for learning guitar. **Use the QR codes** to access these worksheets.

Steaming Video, Backing Tracks & Worksheets

Streaming Video

There are video tutorials that correspond with most the lessons in the book. They include close up views of both hands and examples played slowly to guide you through each lesson with ease. Scan the bar code or use the link below to access these videos.

Audio Backing Tracks

We created audio backing tracks and examples that correspond with many lessons in this book. These tracks demonstrate how each lesson should sound. There are also full band backing tracks that allow you to apply what you have learned in a musical band format. This will help prepare you to play in a band. **Scan the QR code** below or use the link to access these tracks.

Book 1 Videos

bit.ly/41OWddP

Book 1 Audio

bit.ly/4kLI21U

Book 1 Worksheets

https://bit.ly/4is0fA2

Parts of the Bass

A bass is made up of three main sections: the body, the neck and the headstock. All of the other parts of the bass are mounted on these three sections.

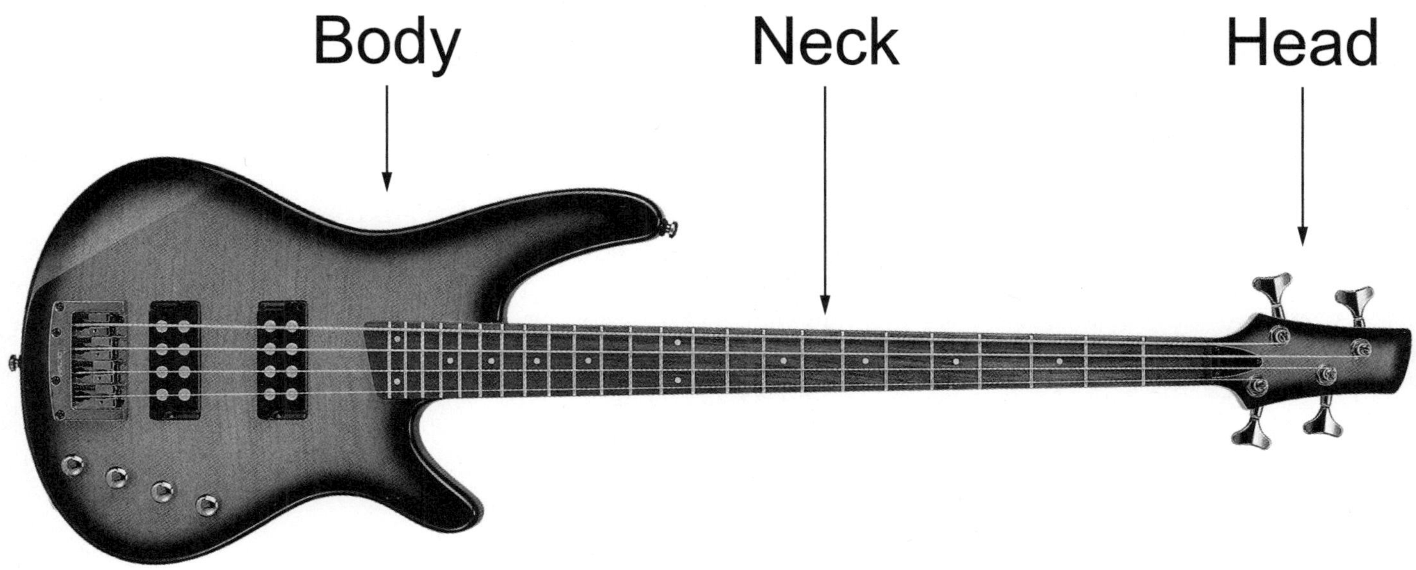

The bridge is the assembly that anchors the strings to the body. Pickups are also mounted to the body and work like little microphones that pick up the sound from the strings. A cable is plugged into the bass's input jack to send the signal into the amp. Most bass guitars will also have a pickup selector switch along with volume and tone knobs. A strap can be attached to the strap buttons to play the bass standing up.

The metal bars that go across the neck are called frets. The dots between certain frets are called position markers and help you know where your hand is on the neck while playing. At the end of the neck is the nut which guides the strings onto the headstock and keeps them in place. On the headstock, the strings are wound around the tuning posts, and the tuners (also called machine heads) are used to tune the strings to pitch.

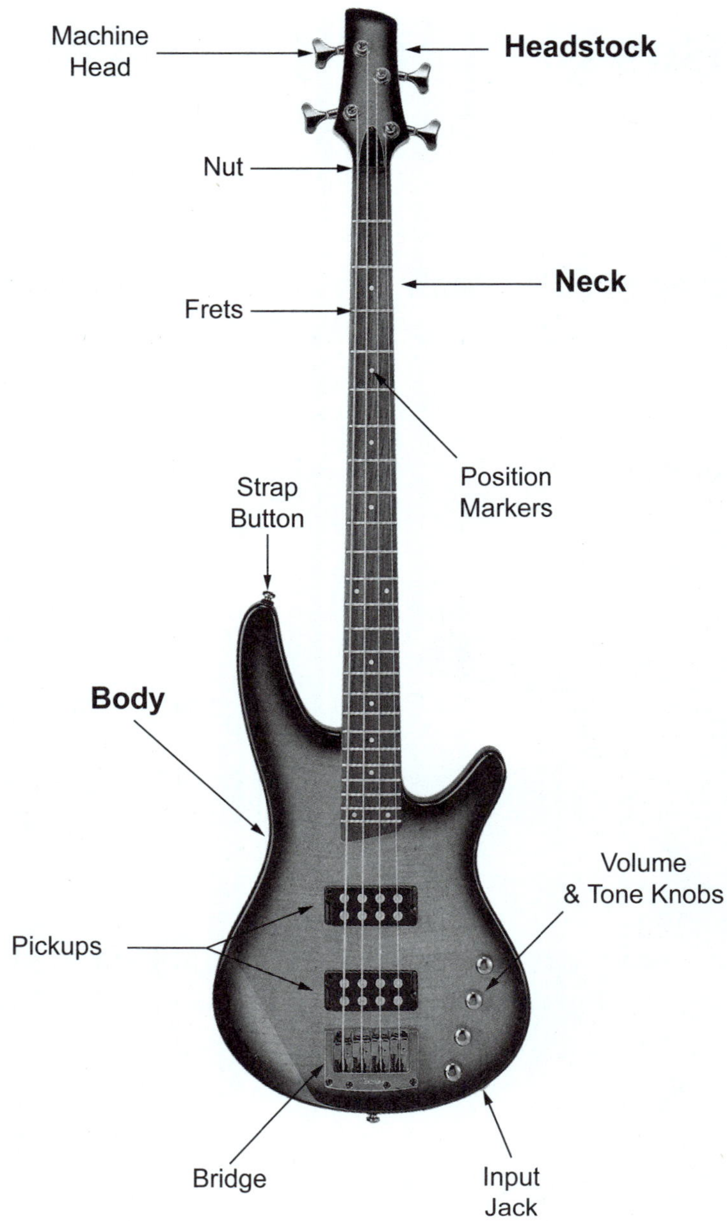

Holding the Bass

Throughout this book, we will refer to the picking hand as your right hand, and the hand fretting the notes as your left hand. When sitting find a comfortable chair with no arms and make sure you can sit with your feet planted flat on the ground. Hold the bass neck up at a 30 degree angle.

Right Hand Position

Drape your arm and hand over the strings almost parallel with the bridge. Keep your thumb planted either on top of the pickup or thumb plate if your bass has one.

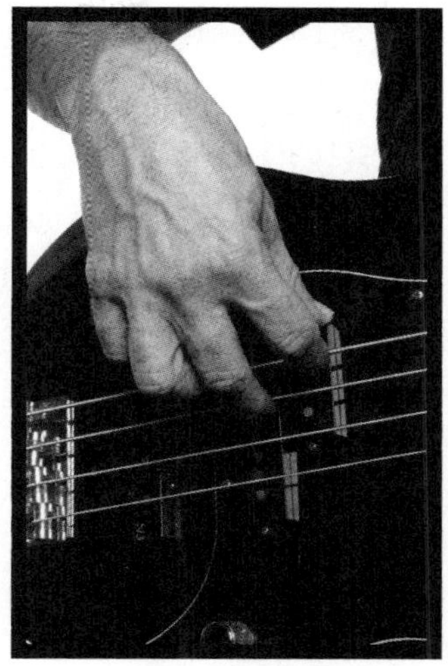

Left Hand Position

Hold your left hand out in front of you with your wrist straight and your fingers curled in to make a "C" shape with your hand.

Place the first joint of your thumb against the back of the neck. Don't bend or contort your wrist; only the tips of your fingers should touch the strings.

Attaching Your Strap

To stand up and play you must attach a strap to your bass. Most bass guitars have strap buttons on both sides of the body of the bass. Simply attach the strap to each side of the bass at these buttons.

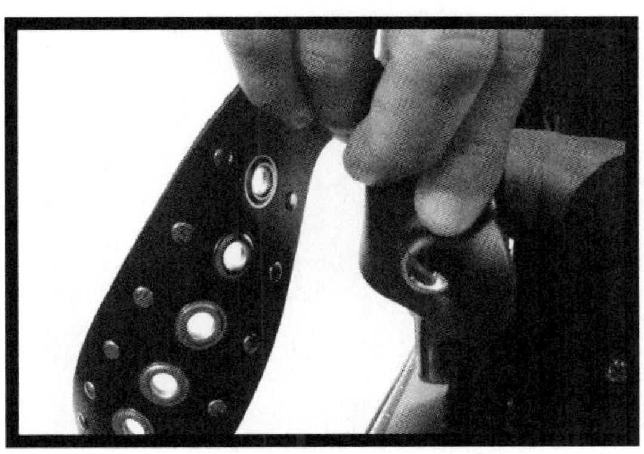

Most straps are adjustable and should be set to a comfortable height. A good starting point is to look at how the bass rests against your body when sitting down and duplicate this position when you stand up. You may think it looks cooler to have the bass positioned lower (like some of your favorite bassists) but at this stage it will make learning more difficult. Remember that you should always have the neck of your bass pointed up at about a 30 degree angle (sitting or standing) to ensure proper hand position.

Finger Numbers

As you progress through this book I will be referencing your left hand fingers with numbers. It is very important for you to memorize these now so you can follow along with ease. To the right are the numbers that correspond with your fingers.

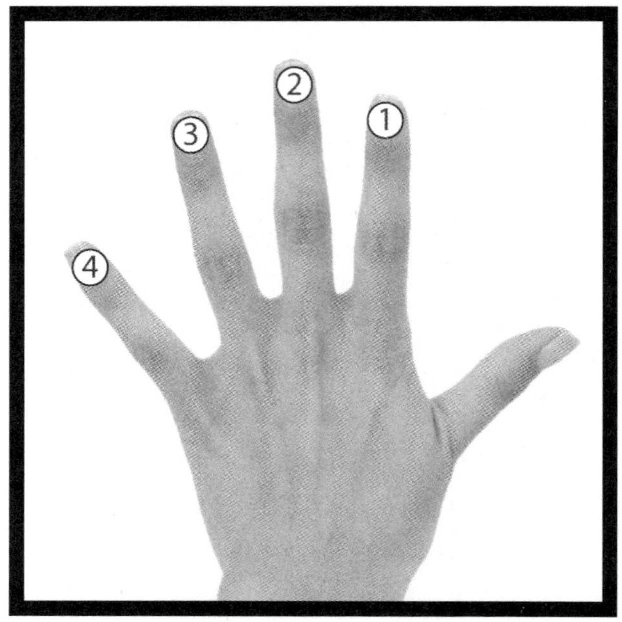

Fretting hand:

Index finger = 1 Middle finger = 2
Ring finger = 3 Pinky finger = 4

Muting

Muting is a technique that helps you control the strings from unwanted notes and string noise. The basic concept is to lightly touch your hand on the strings that you are not playing. You can do this with your left or right hand. Play the next exercise and as you switch strings mute or deaden the other strings so only the string you are playing is sounded.

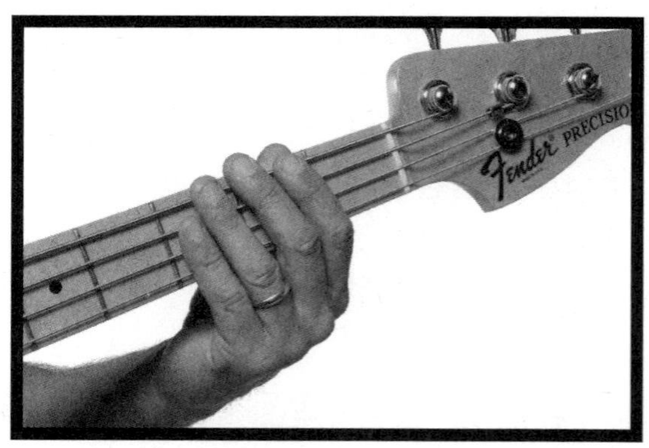

Names of the Open Strings & Tuning

The fattest string is the 4th string and the thinnest is the 1st string. A great way to remember the open strings is to use an acronym creating a word for each letter name. The following is an acronym I created: Good – Days – Are – Exciting. Make up you own saying for the open strings.

(Thinnest) 1st String	2nd String	3rd String	(Thickest) 4th String
G	**D**	**A**	**E**
Good	**Days**	**Are**	**Exciting**

Tune your bass using the machine heads on the headstock. Turn the machine heads a little bit at a time while plucking the string and listening to the change in pitch. Tighten the string to raise the pitch. Loosen the string to lower the pitch. The easiest way to tune a bass is to use an electronic tuner.

Reading Tablature

Tablature (or tab) is a number system for reading bass sheet music. The four lines of the tablature staff represent each of the strings on the bass. The top line is the thinnest (highest pitched) string. The bottom line is the thickest (lowest pitched) string. The numbers placed directly on these lines are the fret number to play each note. Underneath the staff, is a series of numbers. These numbers tell you which left hand finger to fret the notes with.

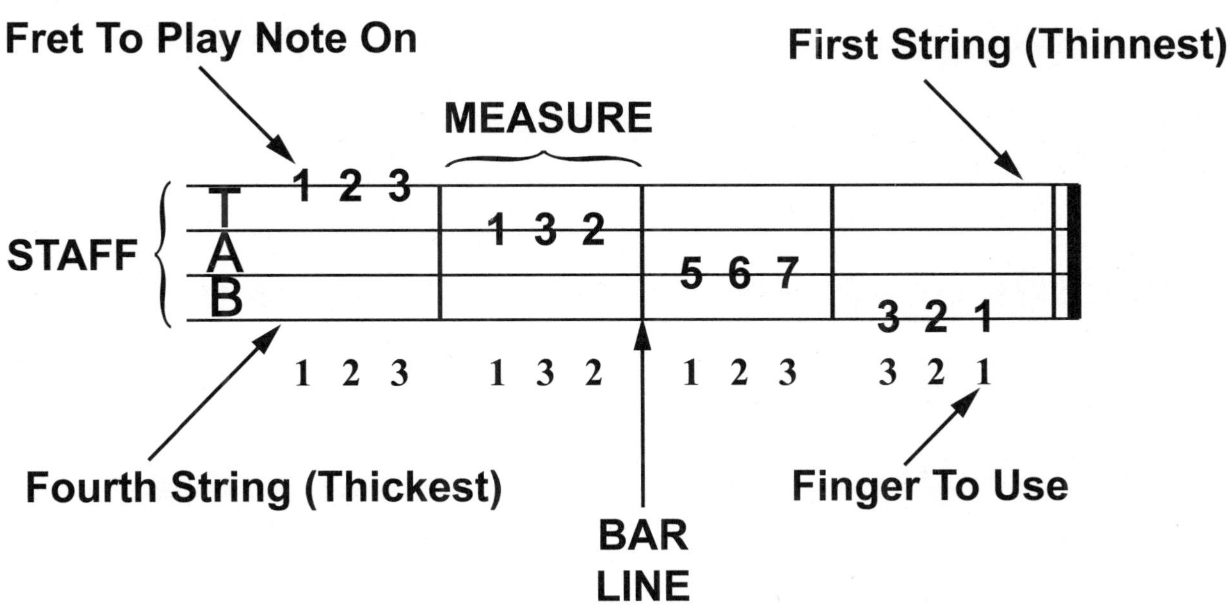

Repeat Sign Brackets

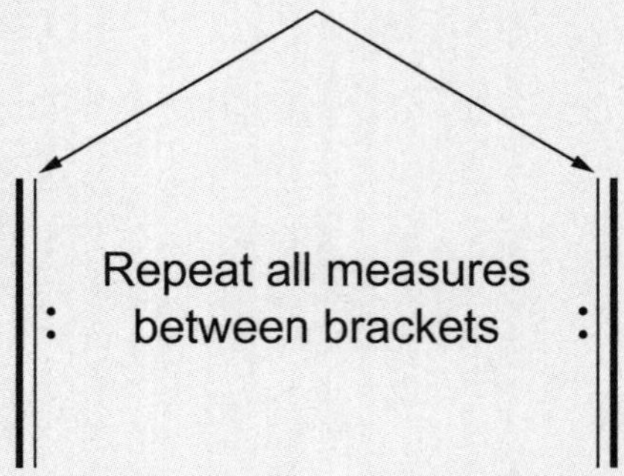

Plucking Symbols

⊓ = Index Finger

V = Middle Finger

Alternating

Alternating is picking (plucking) with your index and middle fingers repetitively. You can play notes effectively and with speed by using your fingers in this manner. Play through the exercise below using open strings in four note patterns:

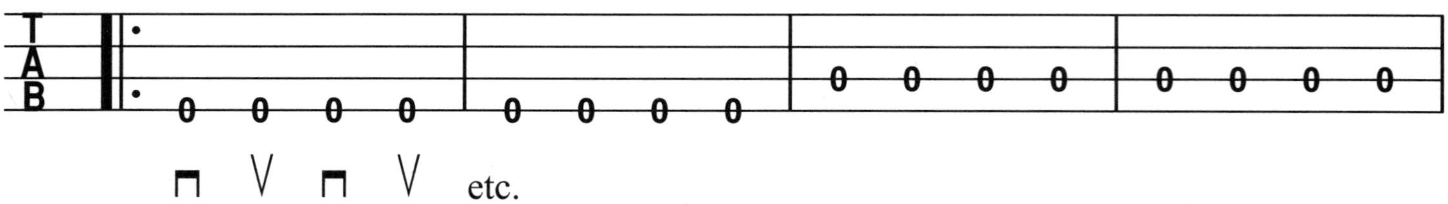

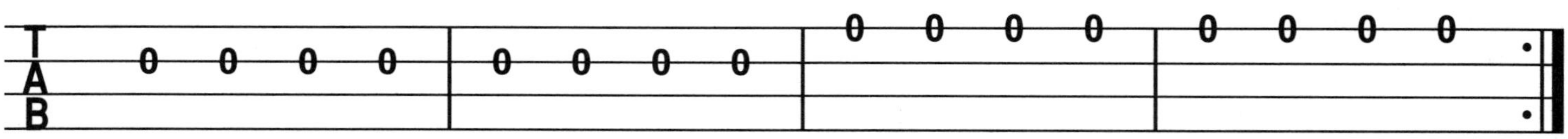

Timing Explanations – Note Values

The Parts of a Note

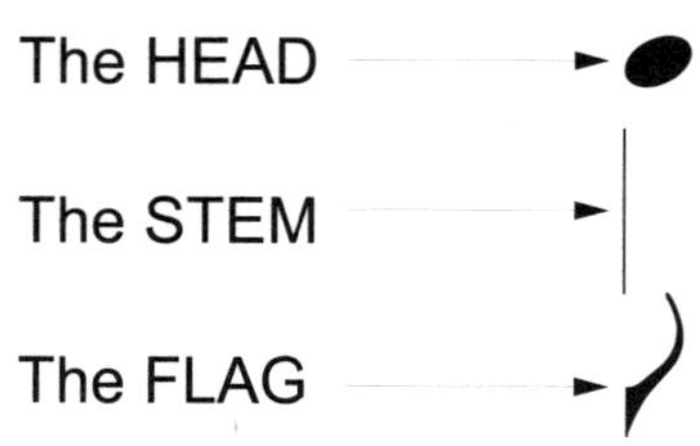

The Types of Notes

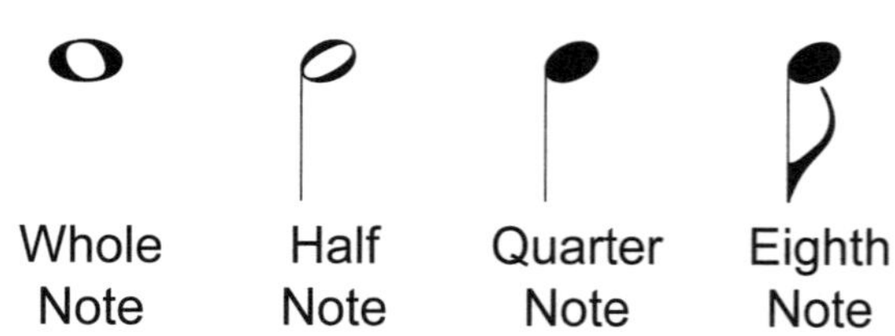

Rhythm Tab

Throughout this book you will see that many of the tablature staffs have rhythms written with the notes. These will tell you how long each note should ring. Here is what the rhythmic notations look like on the tab staff.

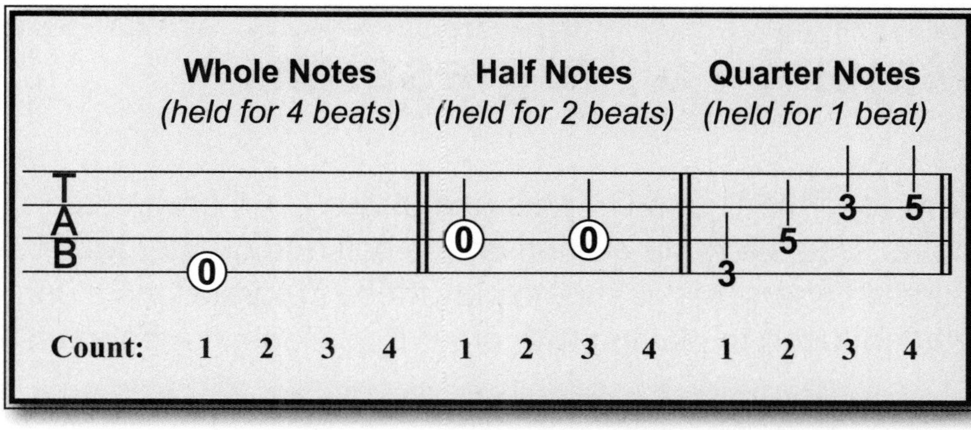

The Metronome

A metronome is a device that clicks at an adjustable rate you set. It will help you develop a sense of timing and gauge your progress. By playing along with the "clicking" sound you get the sense of playing with another musician. Each click represents one beat. I will note the best times to use a metronome throughout this program with a metronome icon.

The Musical Alphabet

The musical alphabet consists of seven letters A through G. After G the letters loop back to A and start over again. There are no letter names in the musical alphabet higher then G.

A - B - C - D - E - F - G

Numbers for Chord Progressions

When progressions are presented in music numbers are used that corresponds with the position the chord has in the scale. For example the Major 1 – 5 Progression in the next lesson goes from C to G chords. Starting with C the G is 5 letter names higher.

C - D - E - F - G
1 5

Major 1 - 5 Progression

Now take the C and G notes and play a 1 – 5 progression using whole, half and quarter notes. Use alternate picking on the half and quarter note variations using your index and middle fingers. Make sure to play these progressions along with the backing track to help you get used to playing with other musicians in a band fashion.

Whole Notes

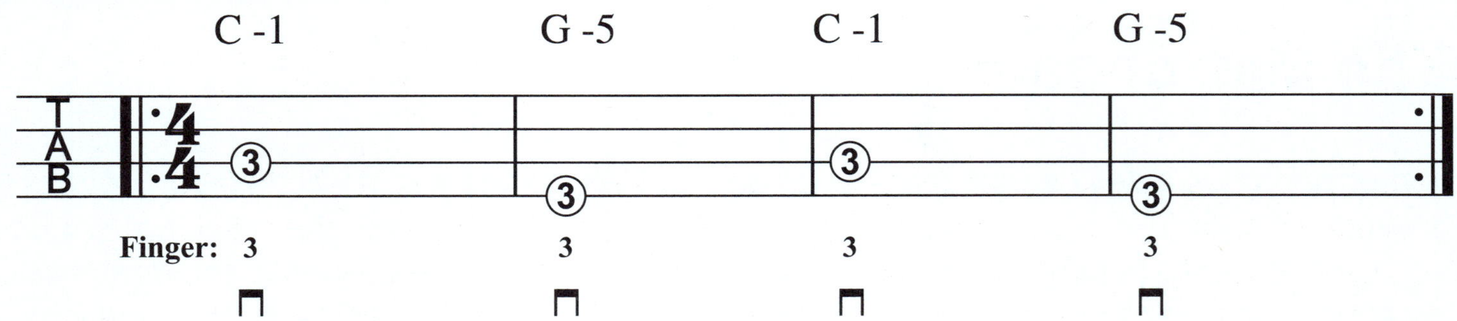

Half Notes

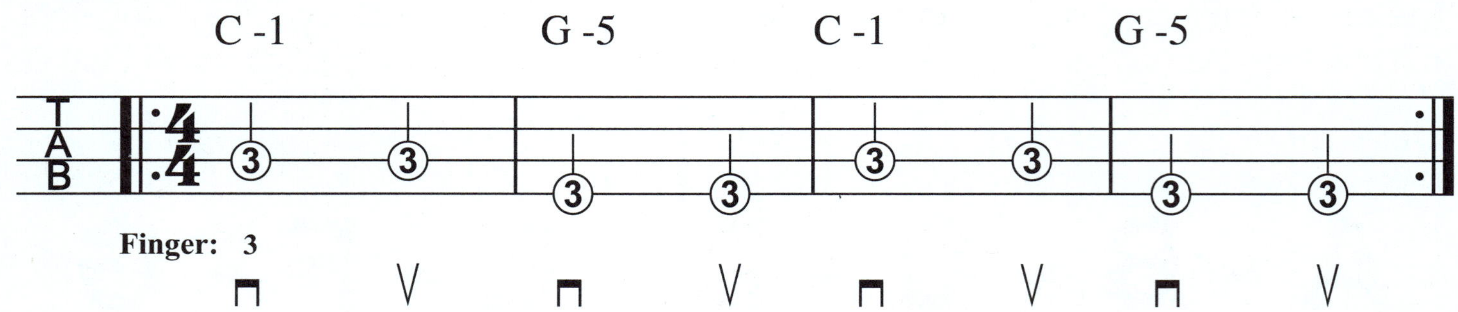

Quarter Notes

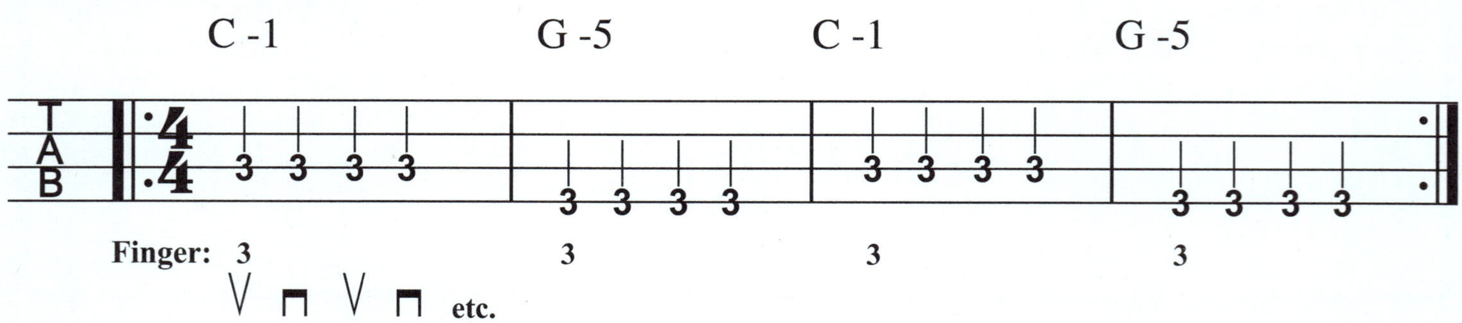

Your First Bass Line

Get excited! It's time to learn your first bass line. This bass line is played using alternate plucking in steady quarter notes. Follow the tablature below and be sure to use the proper finger for each note. Once you can play this without hesitation play it along with the backing track to create a full band sound.

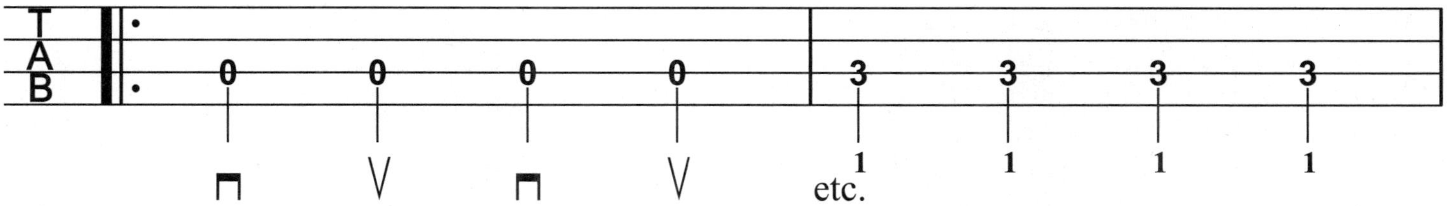

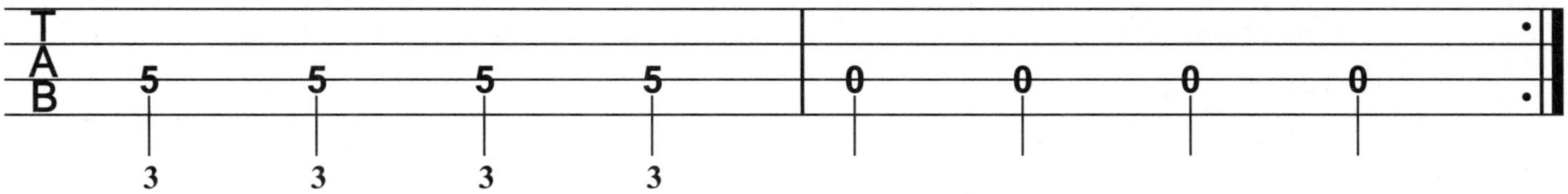

Time Signatures

Time signatures are written at the beginning of a piece of music. The sole function of a time signature is to tell you how to count the music. The top number tells you how many beats there are in each measure and the bottom number tells what type of note receives one beat. Time signatures will be used where specific timing is indicated in this book.

4 = Number of beats per measure.
4 = A quarter note receiving one beat.

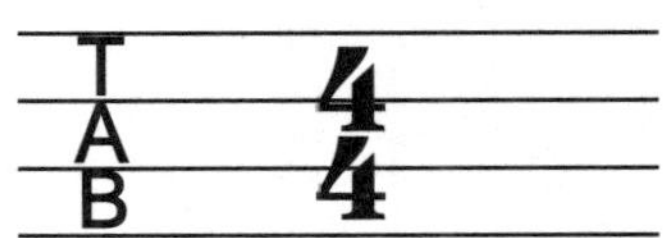

Indicates four beats per measure.

Indicates three beats per measure.

Counting Beats

A beat is the basic unit of time in music. A common way to count beats is to tap your foot. One beat would equal tapping your foot down-up. Tap your foot and count 1 – 2 – 3 – 4 repetitively, say each number as your foot hits the ground. You will learn different note types that tell you how many beats to let notes ring.

Foot Down

Foot Up

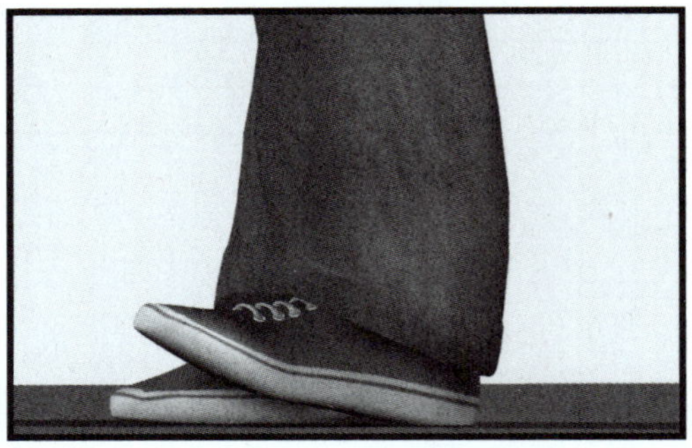

Counting with a Drum Beat

Now you will count along with a drum beat. The drum beat used for this lesson is the most common timing 4/4. This means it is divided into four beat sections (or measures). Notice the 4/4 at the beginning of the staff below, this will be on all music that is in this time signature. As the drum beat is playing count 1 – 2 – 3 – 4 and repeat this count. The 1 & 3 are counted when you hear the bass drum which is the big bass toned drum; while 2 & 4 are counted on the snare drum which is the higher pitched drum that has a bit of rattle to its sound.

Count:	1	2	3	4	1	2	3	4
Drums:	Bass Drum	Snare Drum	Bass Drum	Snare Drum	Bass Drum	Snare Drum	Bass Drum	Snare Drum

1 - 4 - 5 Progressions

The 1 – 4 – 5 progression is one of the most popular in music over the past 60 years. This progression can be found in countless hits from the 60's like Wild Thing to the 80's in songs by the Ramones and more recently in many songs by bands such as Green Day. Below is this progression in the keys of E and C.

KEY OF "E"

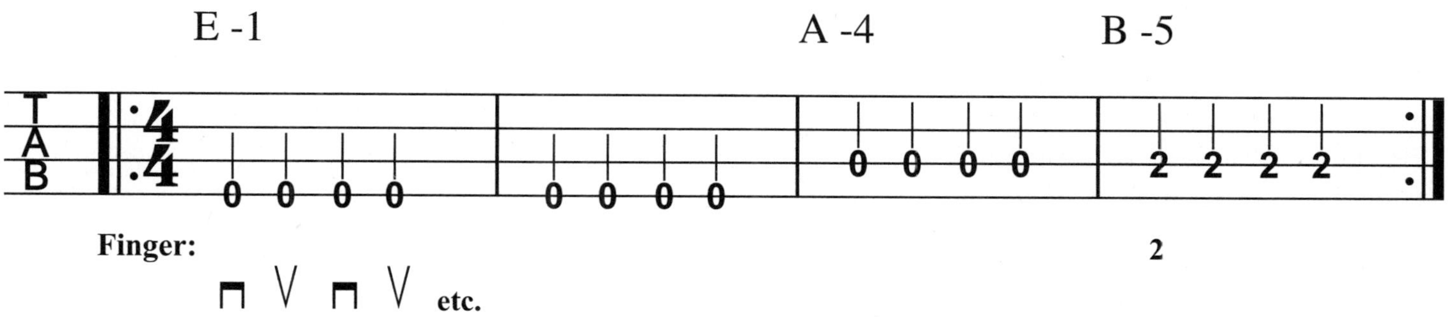

KEY OF "C"

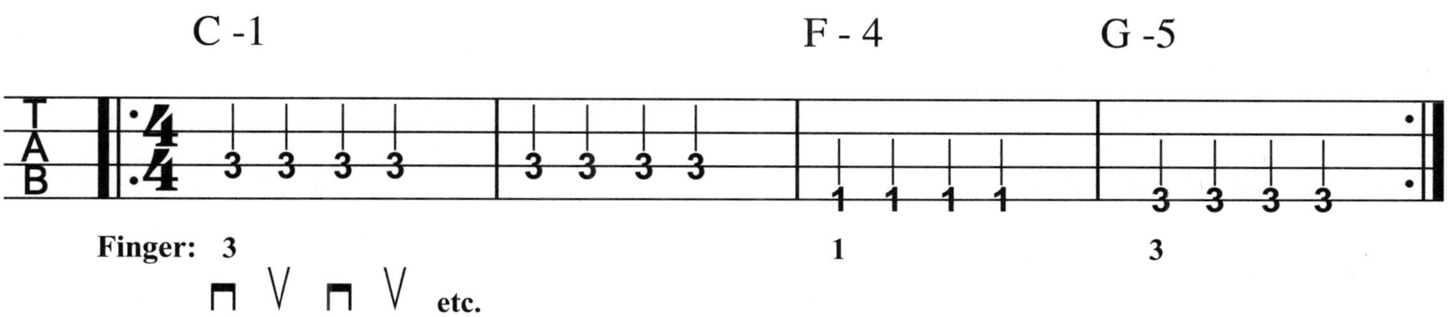

Rhythm – Playing with the Drums

In a drum beat the bass drum and snare drum are the back bone of the beat. You must learn the sound of these drums because you will play along with them to create a solid foundation for songs.

You will play along with the bass and snare drum. The bass drum hits on beats 1 and 3 while the snare drum hits on beats 2 and 4.

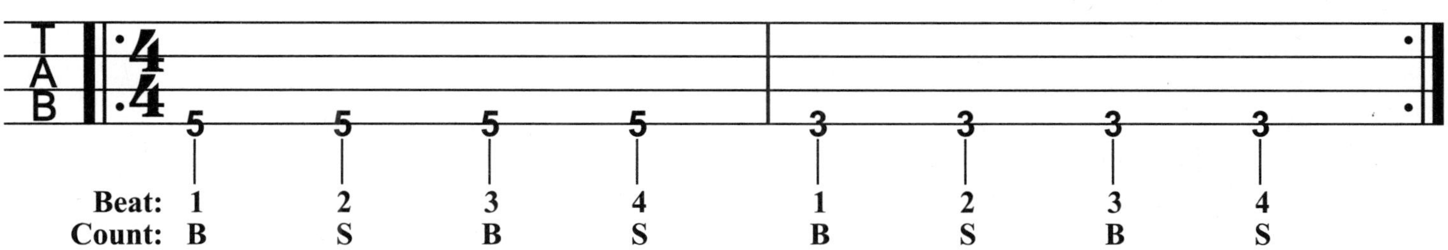

Blues In A

Blues has influenced almost every genre of music. A basic understanding of the blues will give you a great advantage as a bassist. The following blues progression is played using a series of open strings. This is a 12 bar blues progression which means it consists of 12 measures. This progression should sound familiar; it's the foundation for many rock and blues songs.

First play through the progression with a straight feel, which is an even steady pattern. Make sure to use alternate plucking.

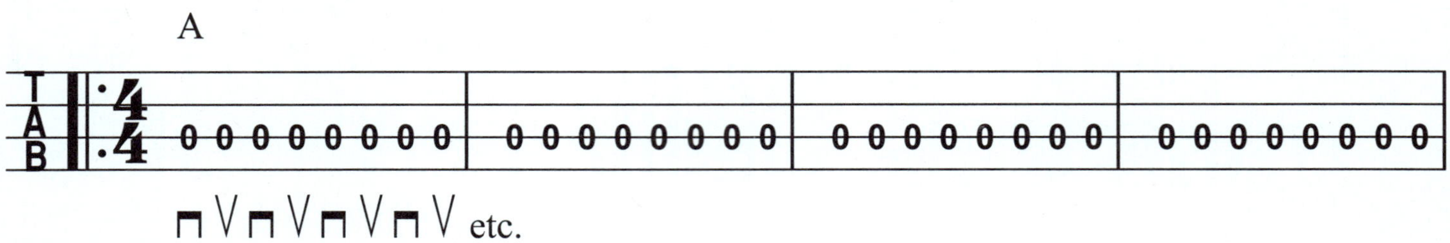

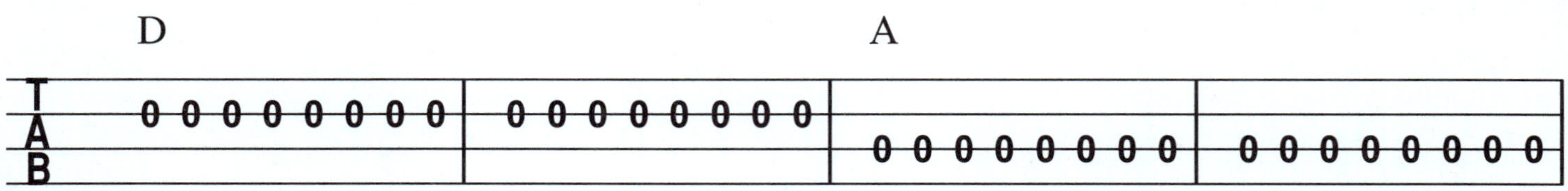

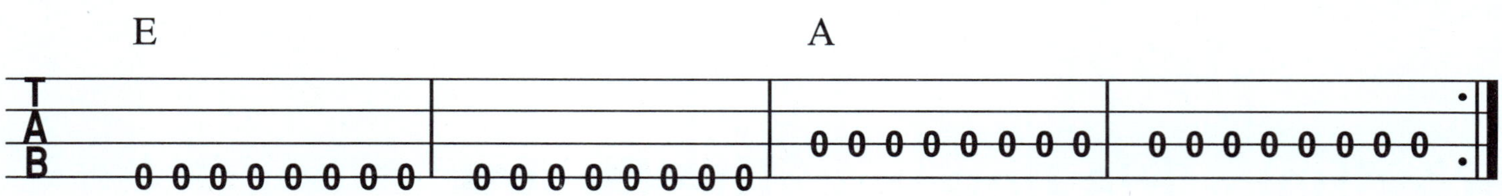

Shuffle Feel

The shuffle feel is an uneven rhythm that creates a sway to a song. This rhythm is found in countless blues and rock songs. Play the measure below using the open 3rd string to get familiar with this rhythm feel, the way the notes are spaced depicts the timing.

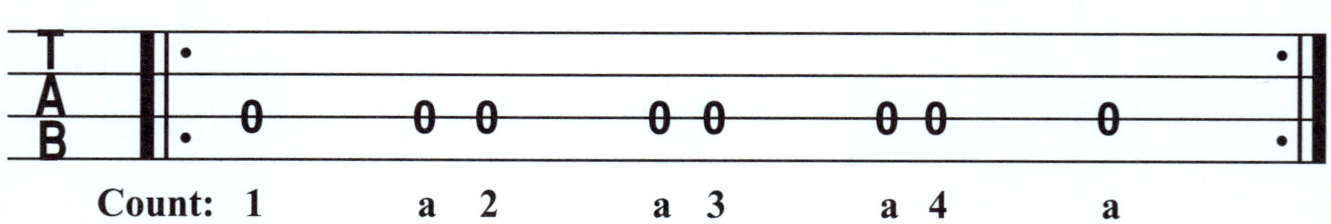

Blues Shuffle Progression

Now apply the shuffle feel to the blues progression. The shuffle feel is also called the swing feel. Pay close attention when going to each new measure, the last note of each measure should flow to the first note of the new measure seemlessly.

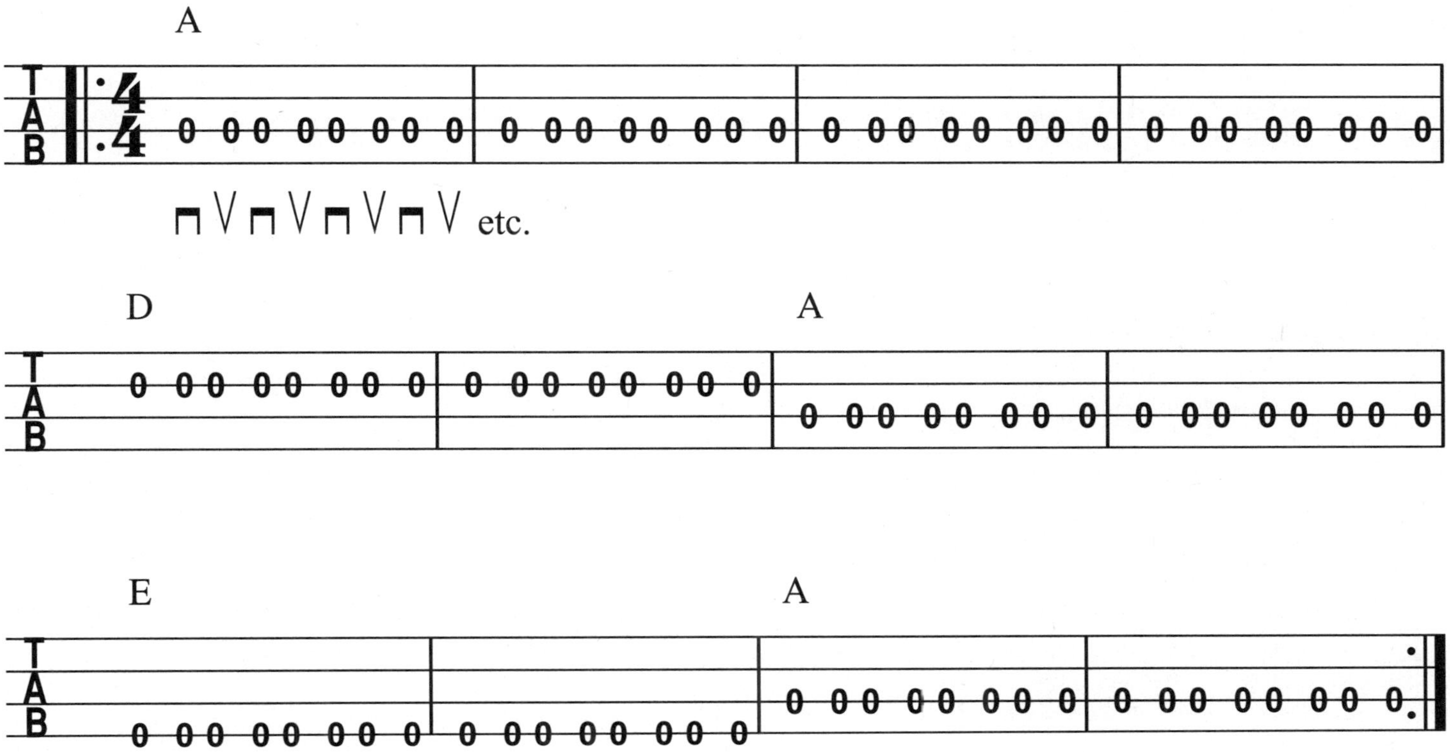

Music Assignment

Listen to your favorite music and try to hear the blues influence. There is a blues influence in almost every genre of music. After you play this rhythm with both a straight and shuffle feel you will easily play the blues feel in songs you learn in the future.

Bass 1 Quiz #1

You're ready to take your next quiz now! Please review all the lessons in the previous section then go to page 4 to see where to take your quiz.

Gear Shifter

The following is a quarter note bass line. Make sure to use alternate plucking.

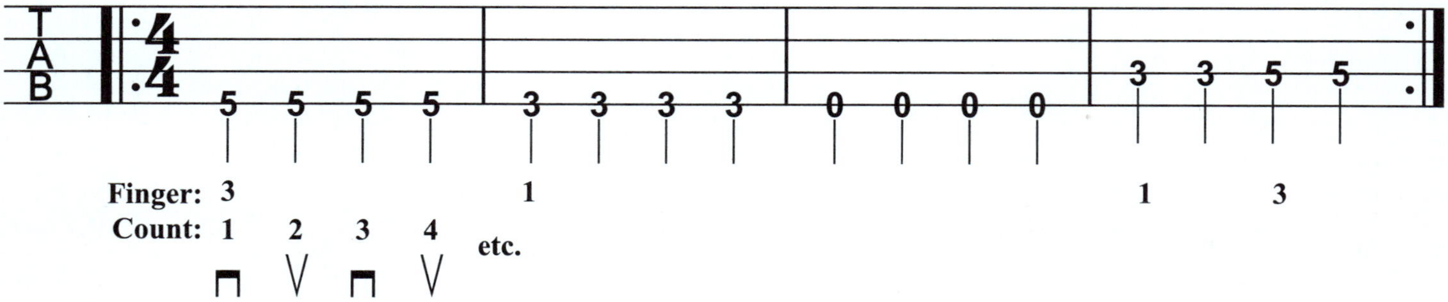

Finger Flexing

Here is an exercise that will help develop the strength and coordination of your hands. This exercise is a 5 – 7 – 6 – 7 fret pattern repeated on each string. You should use alternate plucking continuously. There are two plucking patterns below the staff. Make sure to practice both patterns. Take your time and increase your speed in small increments. This would be a great lesson to play along with a metronome.

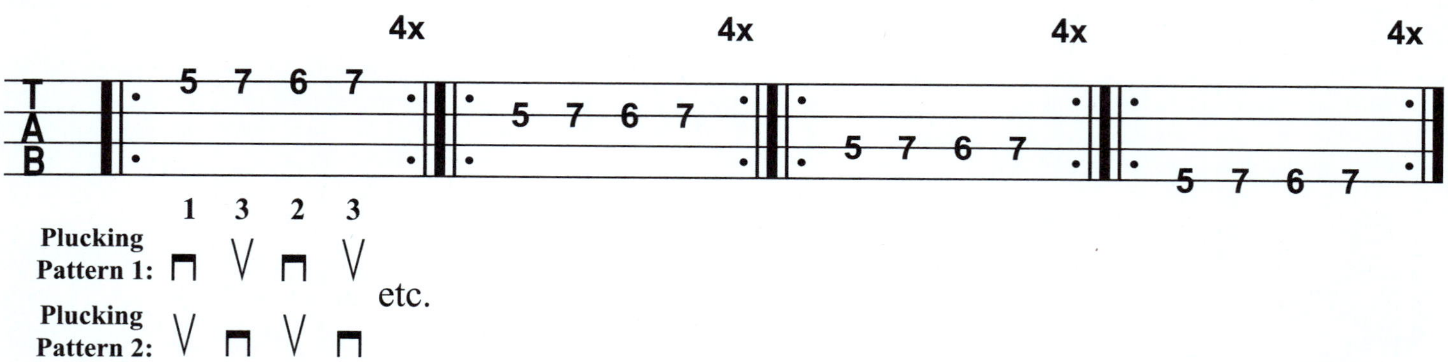

Music Assignment

Once you can play this pattern smoothly across all four strings move it one fret lower starting on the 4th fret and playing frets 4 – 6 – 5 – 6 down each string. The distance between the frets gets wider as you move toward the nut; this will help stretch your hands reach to play difficult passages in songs. Keep moving it down as you feel comfortable with the fret position until you reach the first fret.

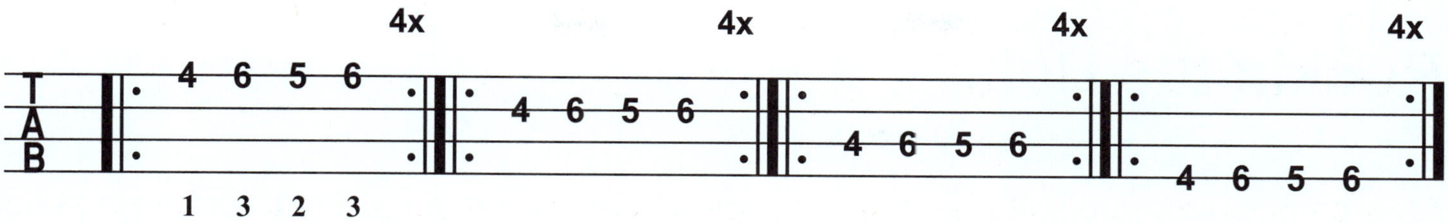

Hit it Hard

Here is another bass line to challenge your fingers. Once you can play this steady all the way through play it with the backing track to apply it in a band fashion. Again there are two plucking patterns below the staff. Both patterns are alternate plucking, the difference is that one begins with your index finger and the other with your middle finger.

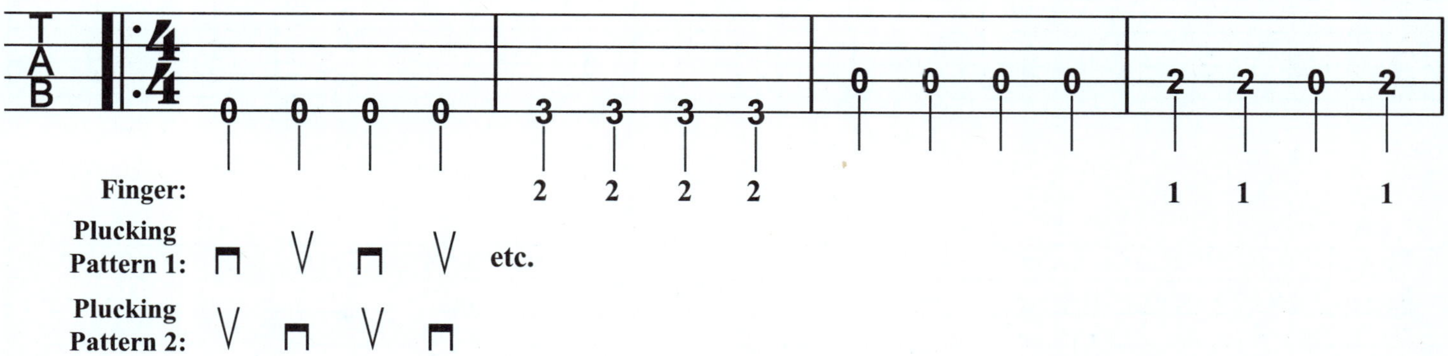

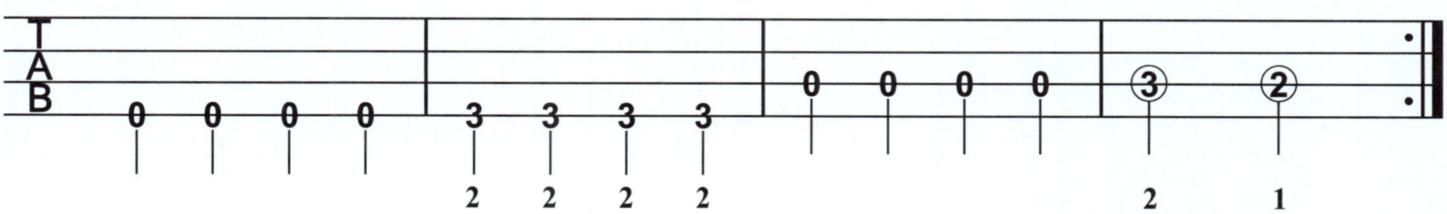

Inspirational Quote

"The biggest room is the room for improvement."

Chinese Proverb

Rockin the Bells

As a bass player you will play many songs where your main job is to create a solid foundation and rhythm for a melody. In this song you will be doing this for the popular melody Jingle Bells. Make sure to use the backing track that contains the melody to create a full sounding song structure.

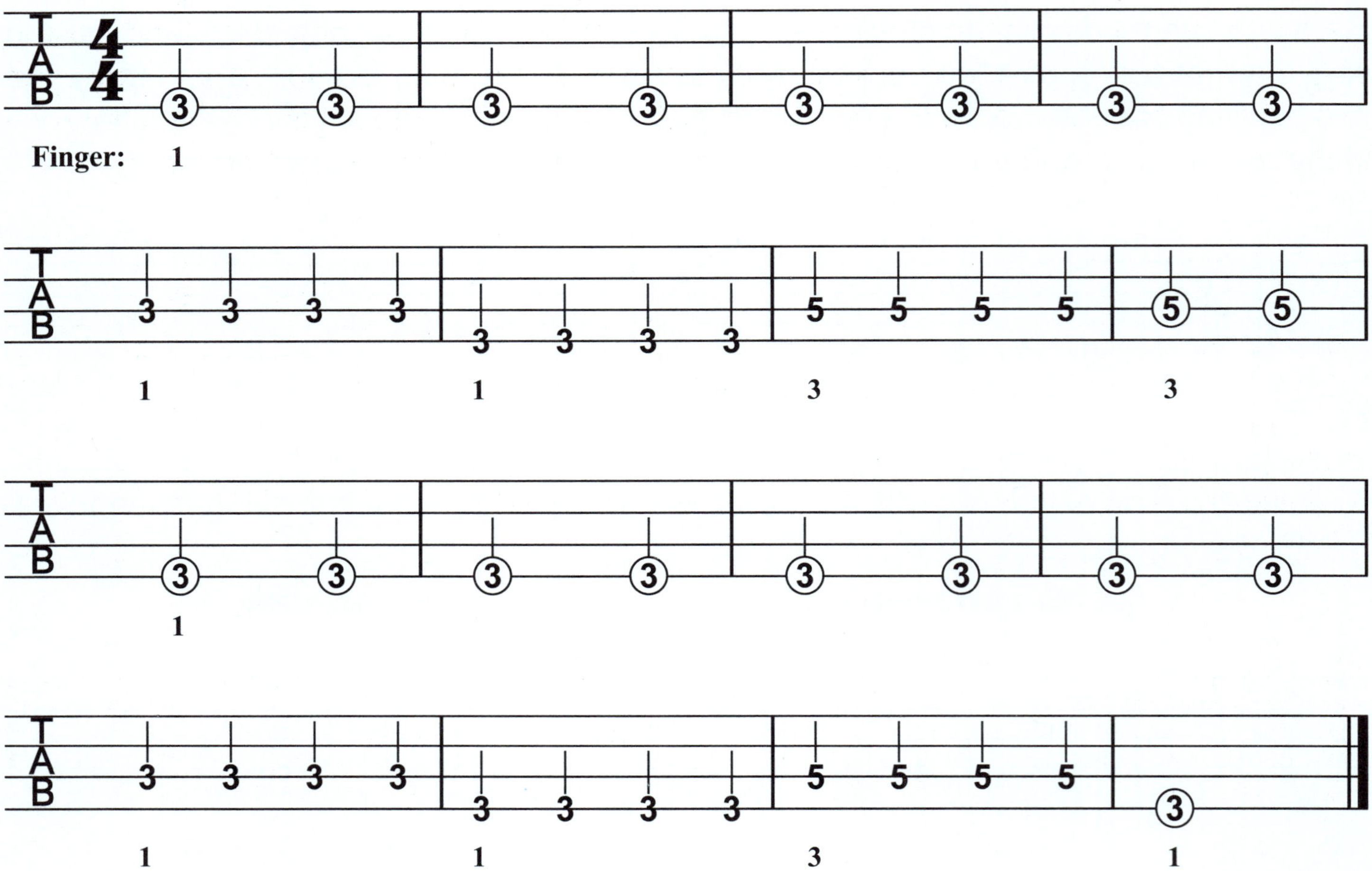

Inspirational Quote

"Obstacles are those frightful things we see when we take our eyes off our goals."

Chinese Proverb

Eighth Notes

An eighth note receives ½ beat of sound and divides a quarter note in half. For every one beat you will hit two notes. You will also use a different kind of counting. Instead of one, two, three, four, sub-divide that in half and count one & two & three & four &. The one, two, three and four are when your foot hits the ground, each "&" is when your foot goes up in the air.

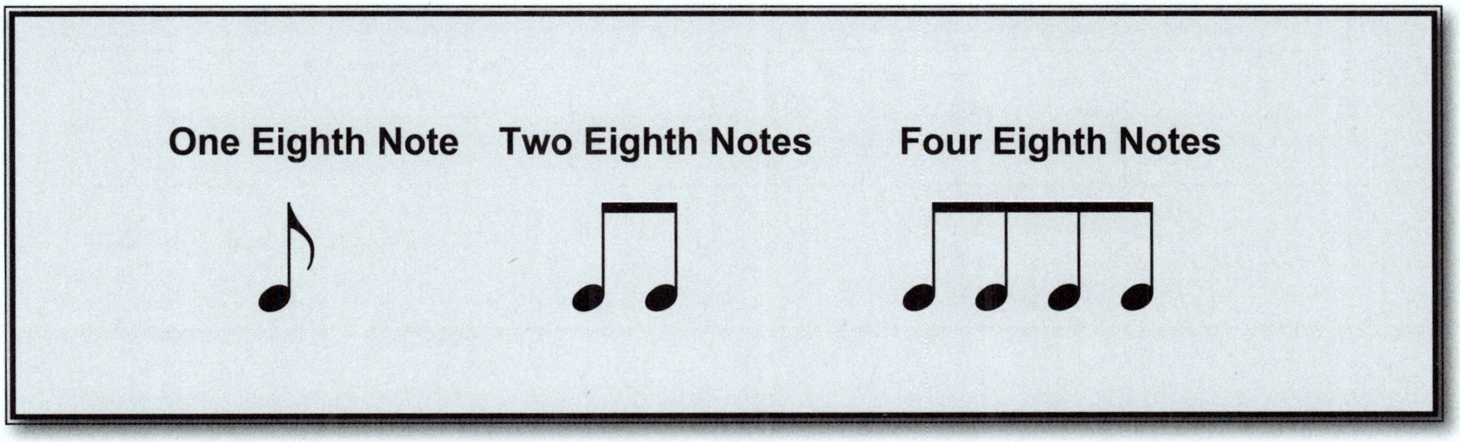

Here is an exercise playing eighth notes. While plucking your 3rd string open tap your foot and play it in eighth notes. Use alternate plucking while you do this to get speed and fluidity.

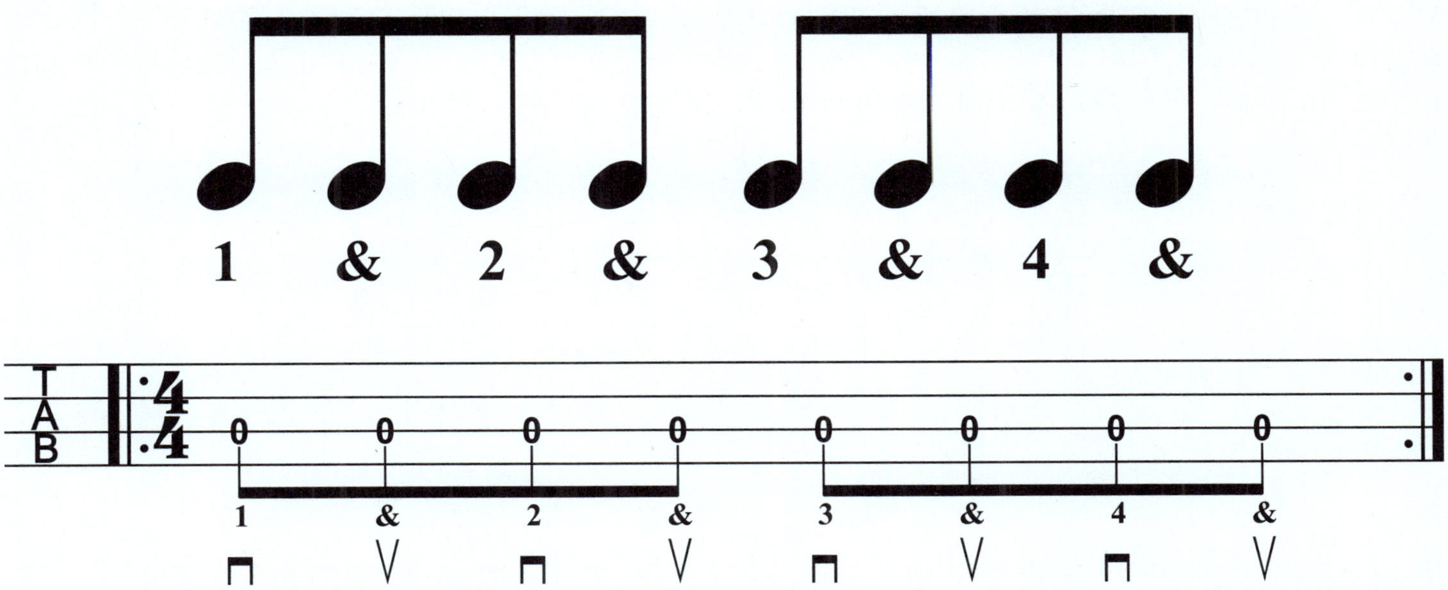

MUSIC ASSIGNMENT

Now that you are playing eighth notes play them along with the drum beat used in the "Counting with a Drum Beat" lesson. While the drum beat is playing, pick eighth notes starting on the low E string and then down all four strings. Make sure to tap your foot along to get your body clock into motion. Use alternate plucking.

Rests

The following examples contain your first rests. A rests is a period of silence. Like whole, half and quarter notes you keep time only there is no sound. See what each rest looks like below:

Whole Rest 4 Beats	Half Rest 2 Beats	Quarter Rest 1 Beat	Eighth Rest 1/2 Beat

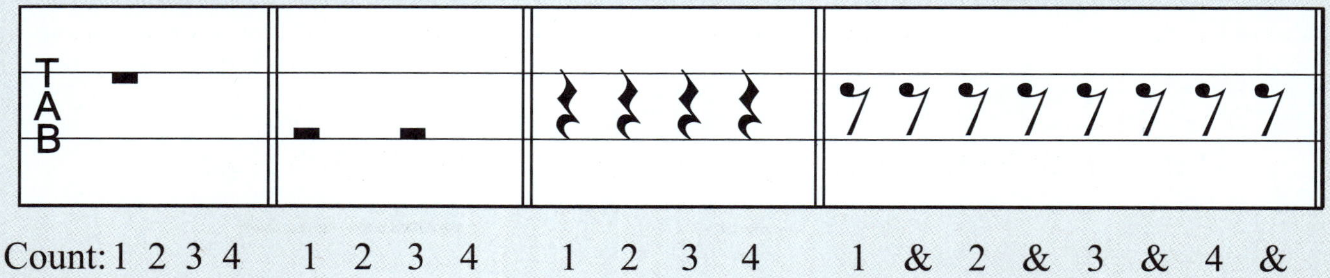

Rhythm – Playing Eighth Notes

When playing eighth notes in a bass line you can create syncopated rhythms. These rhythms contain notes played on the up beat or "&" count. In example 1 you will play notes on the 1 – 3 – & counts along with the drum backing track.

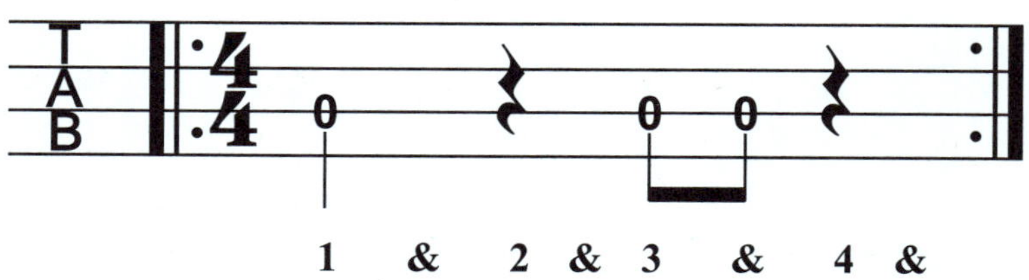

In example 2 you will play on the 1 count followed by three up beat notes played on the "&" counts. This creates a very syncopated rhythm.

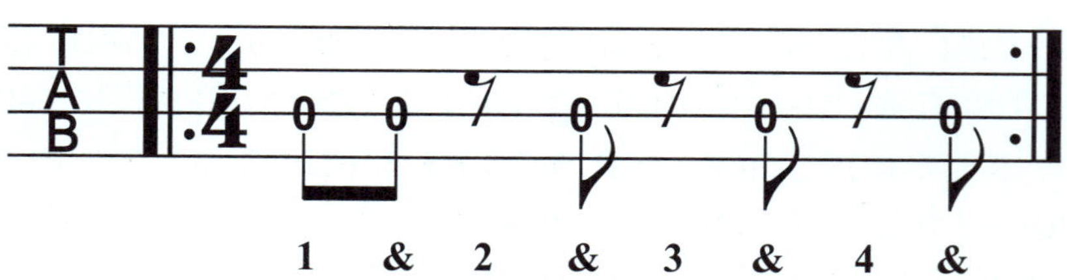

Open String Bass Progression

This rock song contains all open strings. Even though you are not fretting notes you will still have to use your hand to control the strings and mute all the strings you are not playing. Make sure to play this along with the backing track. There are a lot of layers in the backing track so keep focused on your part and keep a steady bass pulse.

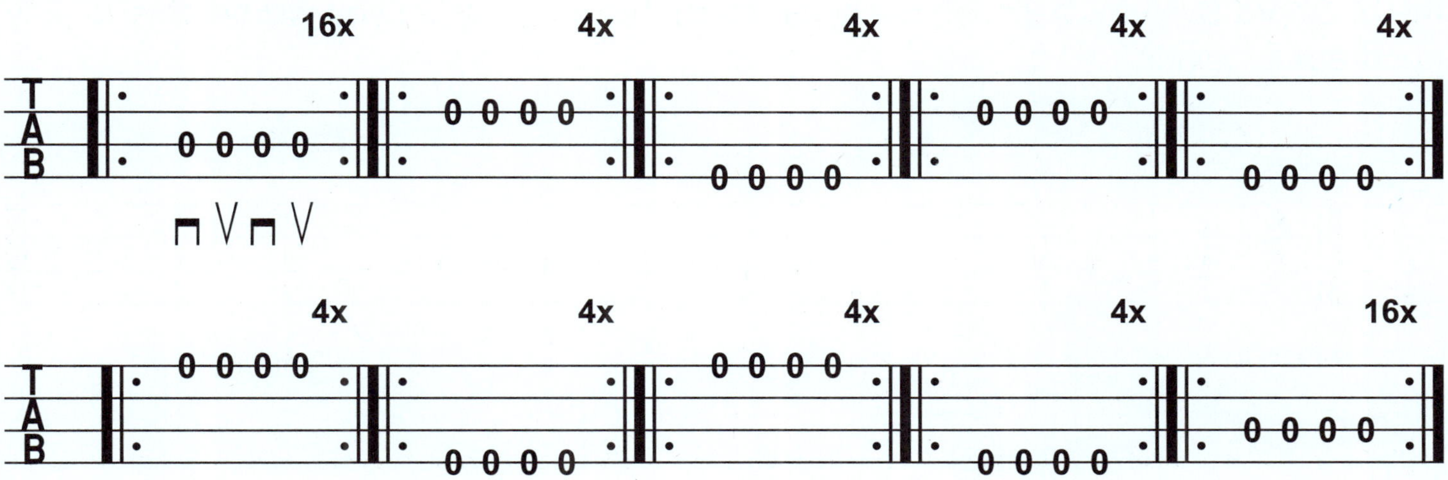

Riff Challenge

Here are two fun riffs to challenge your fingers. Pay attention to the fingering on both hands to make sure you play the notes correctly.

Example 1 - Pete's Gun

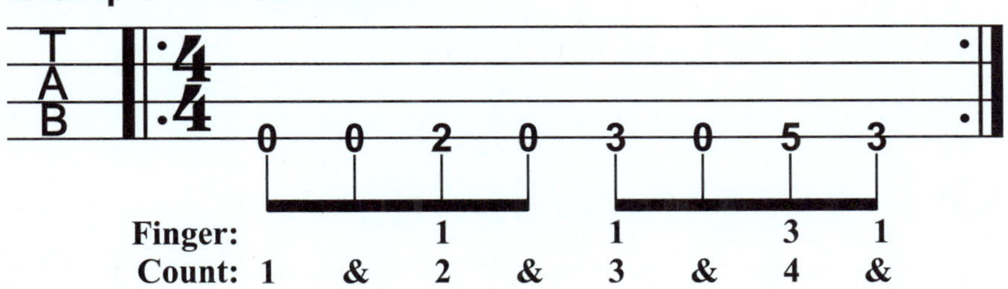

Example 2 - How Many Timez

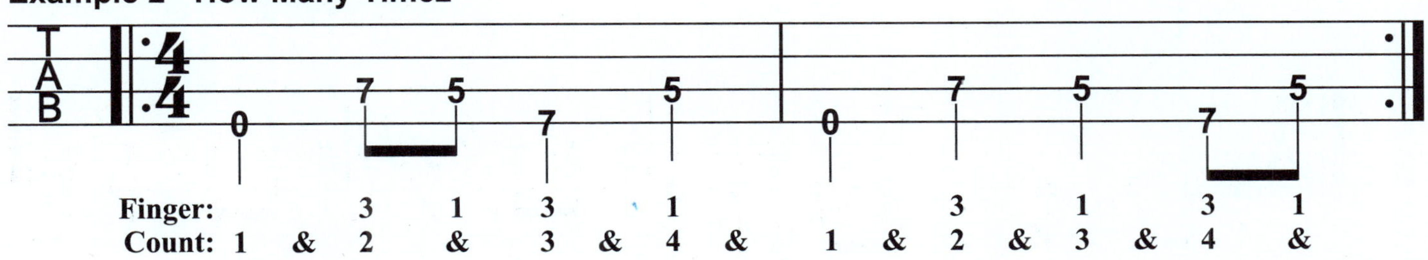

Royal Rock

The 4 Chord Song 1 - 5 - 6 – 4 Progression

The 1 - 5 - 6 – 4 progression is today's most popular chord progression being used in thousands of songs. I have listed a few examples in various styles and genres. I call it the "4 Chord System" because once you learn this progression you will be able to play hundreds of songs.

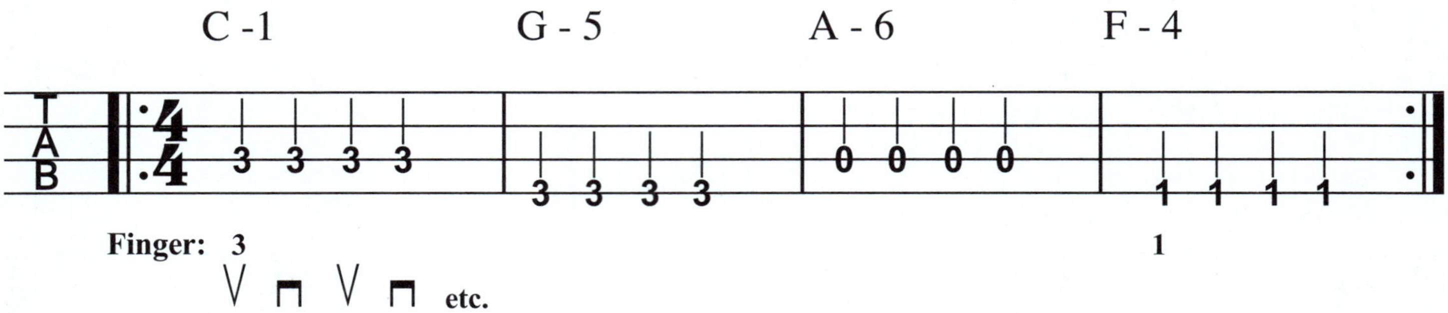

> **Songs Using the 1-5-6-4 Progression**
>
> **Glycerine - Bush**
> **With or Without You - U2**
> **Man In The Mirror - Michael Jackson**
> **Hey Soul Sister - Train**
> **No Woman No Cry - Bob Marley**
> **Apologize - One Republic**
> **It's My Life - Bon Jovi**
> **Beast of Burden - Rolling Stones**
> **Don't Stop Believing - Journey**
> **When I come Around - Green Day**

A Day At the Beach

1 - 4 - 5 Progression In G

In this song progression you will apply an eighth note rhythm into the progression. Make sure to count the timing as you play to help you get the rhythm quickly and effectively.

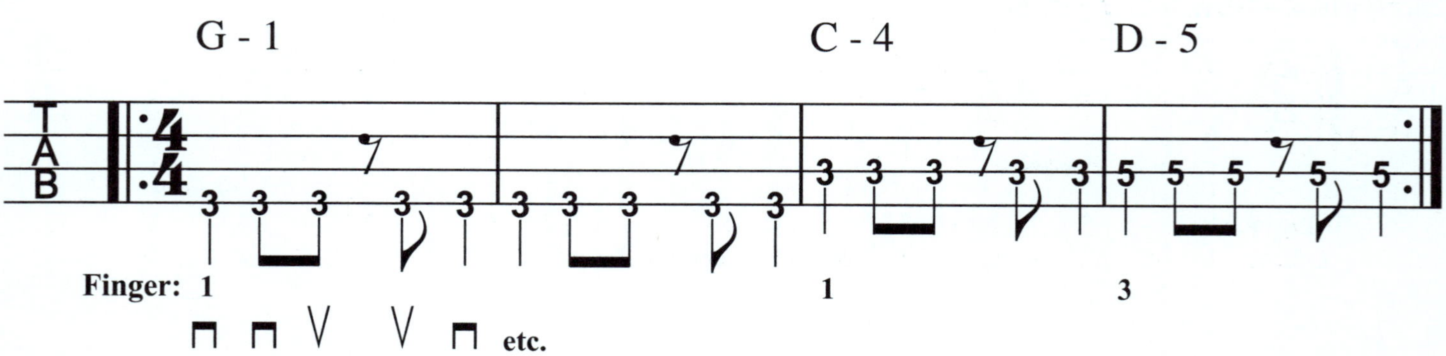

Intervals – The Half Step

An interval is the distance between two notes. Intervals come in different sizes gauged by the distance between the notes. If the notes are sounded in a row, it is a melodic interval. If sounded together, it is a harmonic interval. The smallest interval in music is the half step. A half step would be the distance of one fret on the bass. If you play any note and then play the note at the next fret you are playing a half step. A whole step is made up of two half steps.

Sharps and Flats

A sharp "#" means higher in pitch by a half step or one fret. A flat " ♭ " means lower in pitch by a half step or one fret. Sharps and flats are used in music when creating chords and scales and are also referred to as accidentals.

♭ = Flat **# = Sharp**

The Chromatic Scale

All the music we listen to is derived from a group of 12 notes known as the Chromatic Scale. These 12 notes are all a half step (one fret) apart. There are two natural half steps in music: B to C, and E to F. There will not be a sharp or a flat between these notes. Study and memorize the Chromatic Scale below:

Natural Half Steps (B–C, E–F)

A   A#/B♭   B   C   C#/D♭   D   D#/E♭   E   F   F#/G♭   G   G#/A♭   A

Notice that there is a common flat and sharp note, one note with two different names such as A#/B♭. This is because if you start with an A note and raised it a half step it would be called A#. If you start with a B note and lower it a half step it would be called B♭. Same note, different name. These are called Enharmonic notes.

Music Assignment

Write out the chromatic scale on a piece of paper starting from A and going back to A. Be sure to put the enharmonic sharps and flats on the paper. Next if you feel courageous, try writing it backwards from A to A. The better you have this memorized, the easier you will be able to follow this book.

Notes in the First Position

It's important to learn the names of the notes on your bass so you can communicate with other musicians effectively. The first position is considered the first four frets of the bass. Starting with the names of the open strings you will use the chromatic scale to learn all the notes on your bass.

Start with the 4th string open E and go up the chromatic scale from there: F first fret, F♯ second fret, G third fret, G♯ fourth fret. Next, do this same process on the other three strings. It is important to practice each string without looking and memorize the note names.

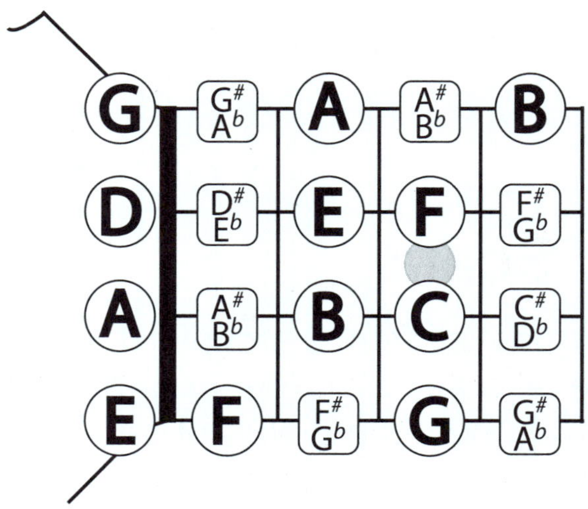

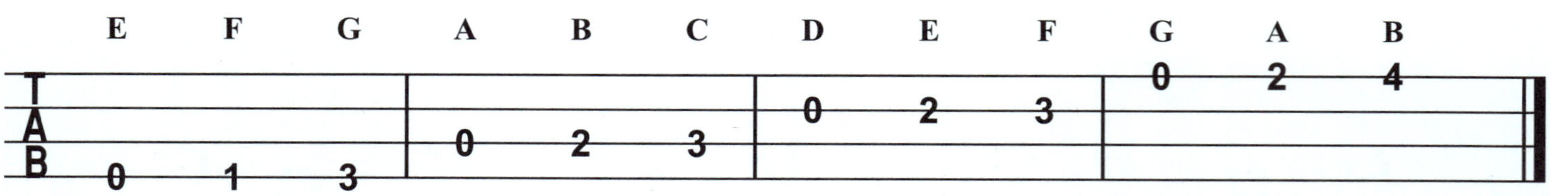

Music Assignment

Use the chromatic scale to learn the names all the way up each string. This will be a great way to better understand your instrument.

5ths

5ths are commonly used in bass lines. They are created using the root note and 5th degree of a major scale. There are five shapes that you will learn starting on the 4th, 3rd and 2nd strings. When playing the root 4th, 3rd and 2nd shapes, you will use your first and third fingers and the first finger will always be the name or root note. These are movable shapes and can be played anywhere across the neck.

The open 4th and 3rd shapes are played using your first finger and the open string will give the shape its name. Since these are open position shapes they are not moveable. Play the 5ths below:

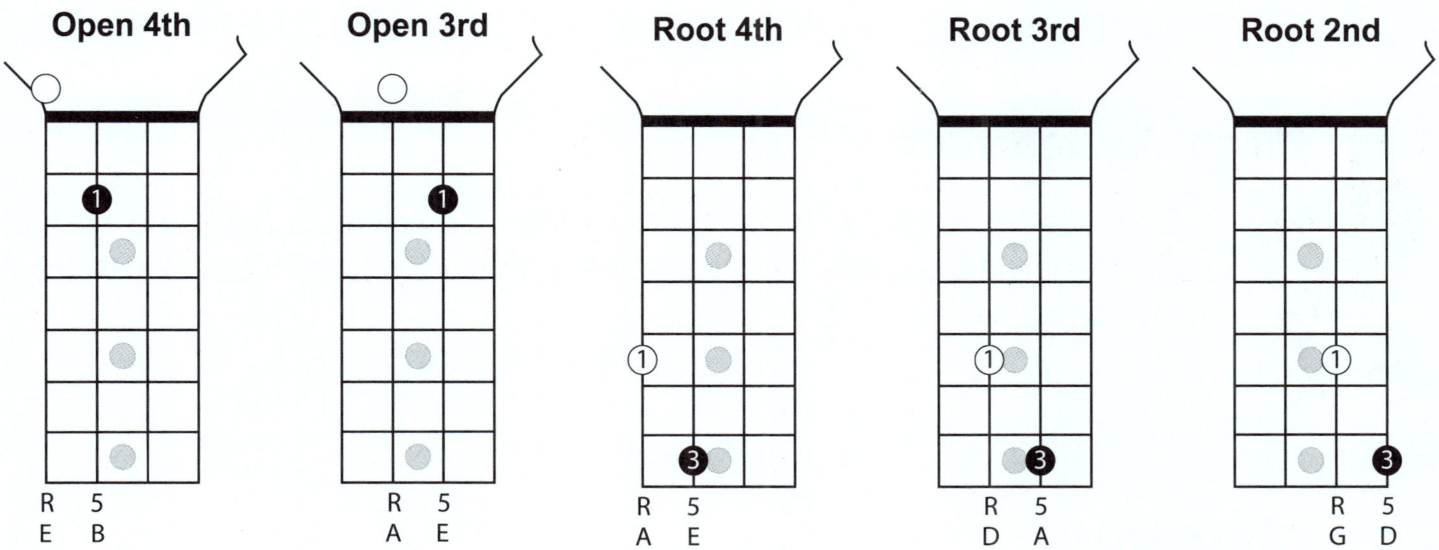

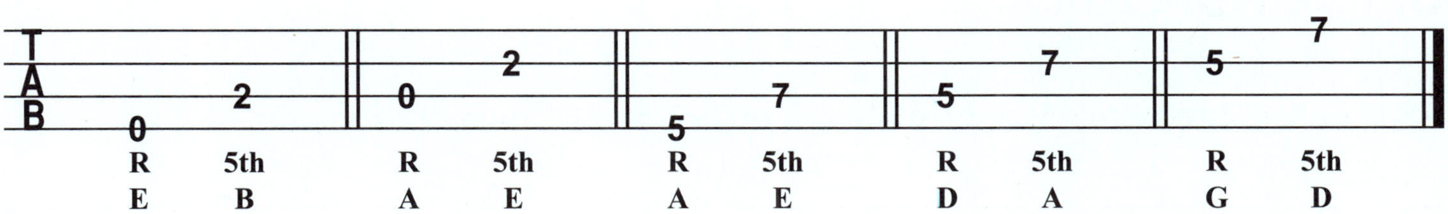

Music Assignment

Take the 5th shapes and move them around the neck to different frets. Make sure that you know the note played with your first finger will be the root note. Call out the name of each root note as you play these across the neck.

Rock Climbing

Applying 5ths

Here is a bass line that will show you how to apply 5ths in a bass line. Notice how they follow the chord change. Many times the bass line will coordinate with the chord changes in this fashion.

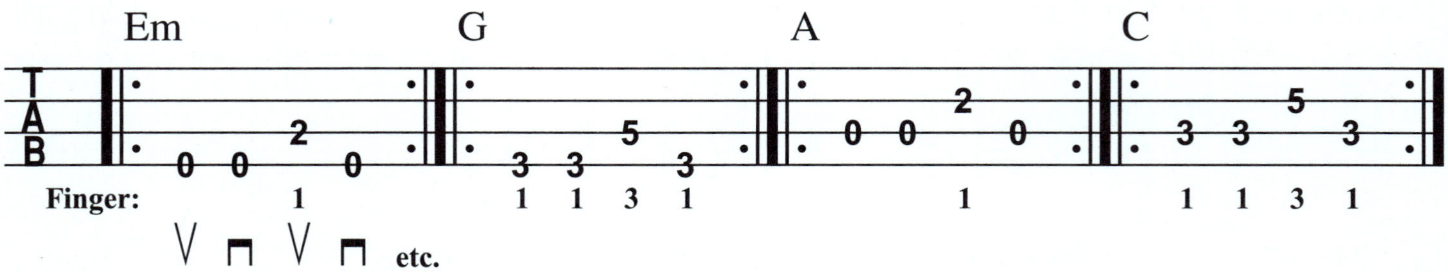

Music Assignment

Play the bass line with the backing track to create a full band sound. Concentrate on where the changes are, this will help you develop a great ear for music.

The Mission

Single Note Riff

Play the last two notes of each measure quickly to get the proper rhythm.

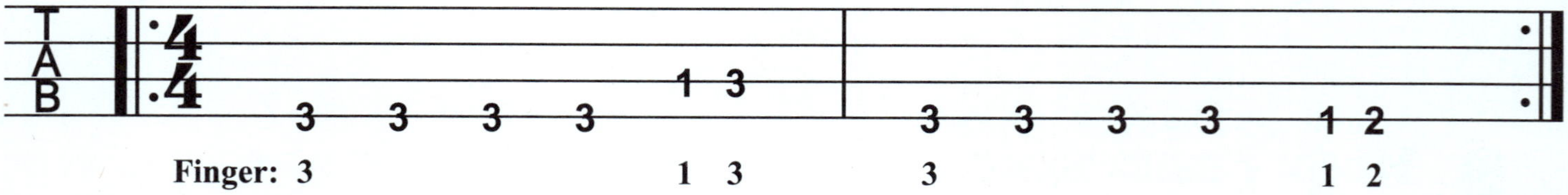

Bass 1 Quiz #2

You're ready to take your next quiz now! Please review all the lessons in the previous section then go to page 4 to see where to take your quiz.

How to Read a Scale Diagram

Scale diagrams are used to visually show you a scale pattern on the neck of a bass. The four lines that go horizontally from left to right represent each of the four strings. Like with tablature, the top line is the thinnest (highest pitched) string and the bottom line is the thickest (lowest pitched) string. The lines running vertically from top to bottom are the frets. The dots placed directly on a string show you the specific fret to play each note and the letters inside indicate what note you are playing. The fret markers on the neck in the diagram indicate where on the neck the scale is located, in this diagram the scale begins at the 5th fret.

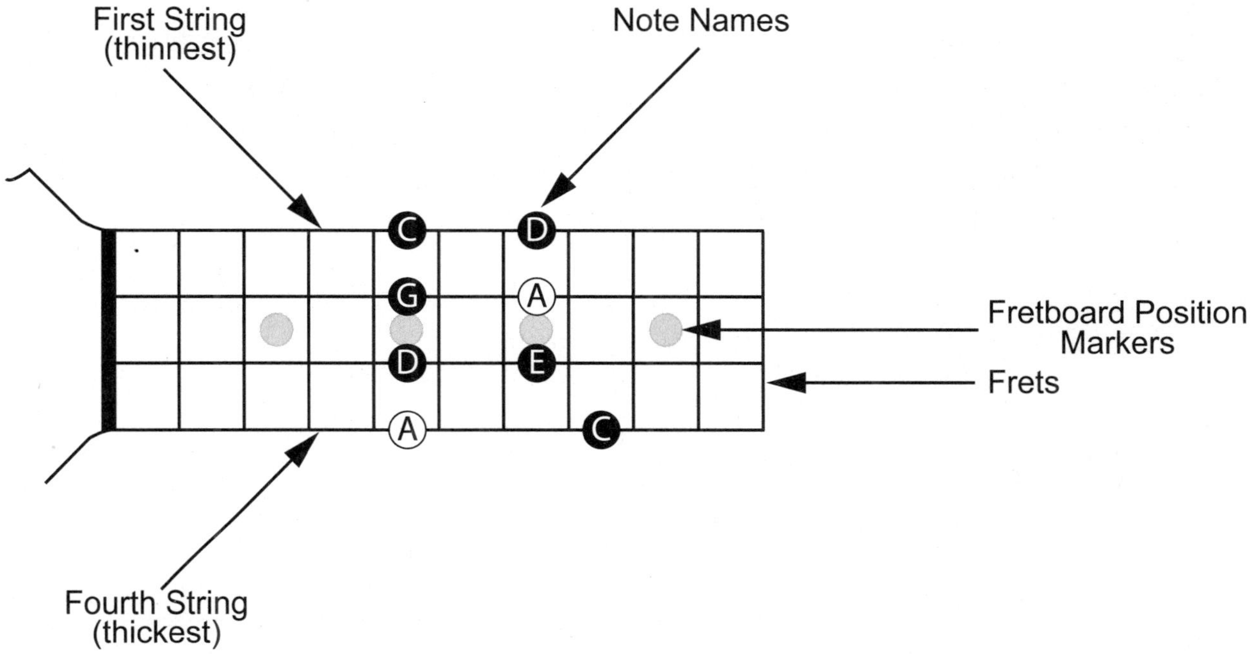

Notice how the diagram above is a mirror image of the bass neck. Below see how this scale pattern looks on the bass. In the diagram above the top line is the thinnest string and the bottom is the thickest string like a tab staff.

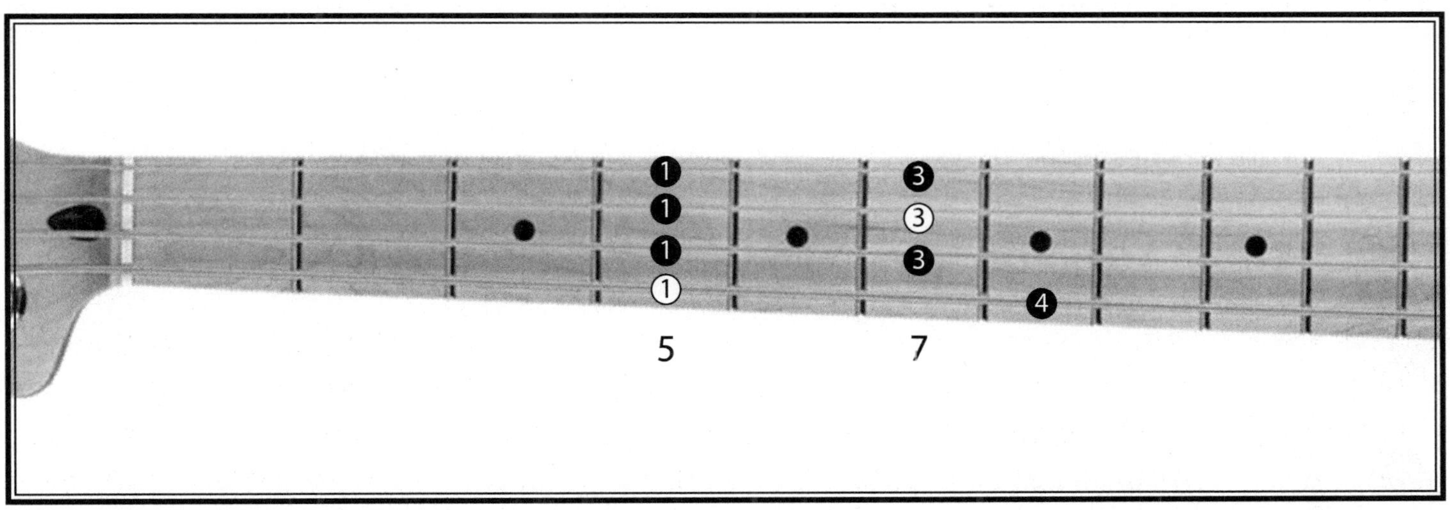

Minor Pentatonic Scale

First Position Key of "A"

SCALE PROFESSOR

Minor pentatonic scales are the most widely used scales in rock and blues music. This is a five note scale, which means that it repeats after five notes back to the beginning note (root note) in a circle-type fashion. The notes of the A minor pentatonic scale are A – C – D – E – G, then it repeats back to A. Notice that the A notes (or root notes) are in white.

Scales are your alphabet for creating bass lines and melodies. Just like you learned your alphabet in school and then expanded into words, sentences and complete stories you will learn scales for bass then expand to melodies, bass lines and complete songs. Practice this scale with a metronome using whole, half and quarter notes.

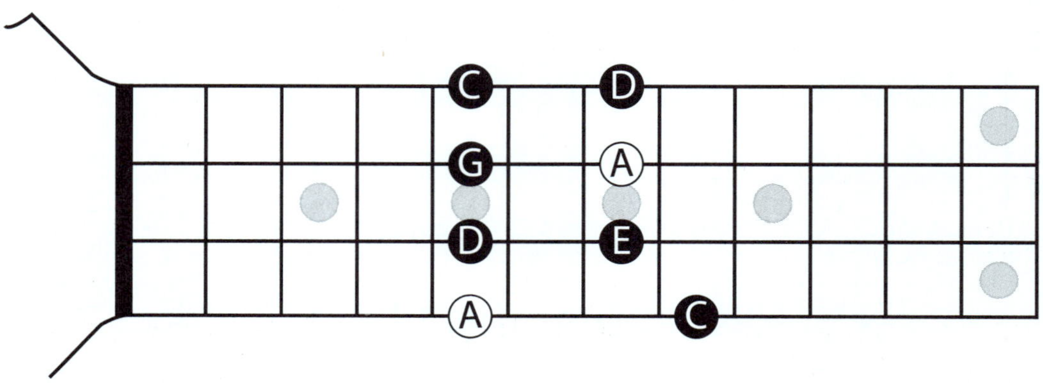

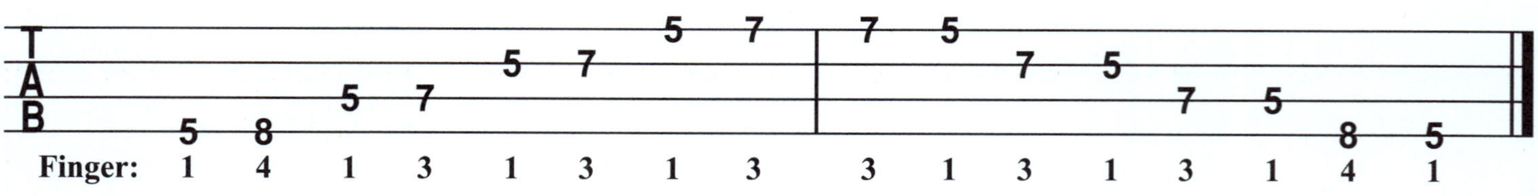

MUSIC ASSIGNMENT

After you can play this scale easily forwards and backwards, play through it, mix the notes up and see how the notes fit together perfectly. Think of this scale as a creative tool not just a group of notes forming a scale. You can even create your own bass lines within the confines of the scale notes by mixing the order and listening for interesting combinations.

Minor Pentatonic Single Note Pattern

This doubling pattern comes directly from the first minor pentatonic scale. This is a great exercise to help develop the coordination of your hands and help you use the scale in a creative manner.

As you play through the scale the pattern will be to double the 3rd and 2nd strings going forward and backwards. Be sure to use alternate plucking consistently and build up your speed gradually. I recommend using a metronome to help gauge your progress.

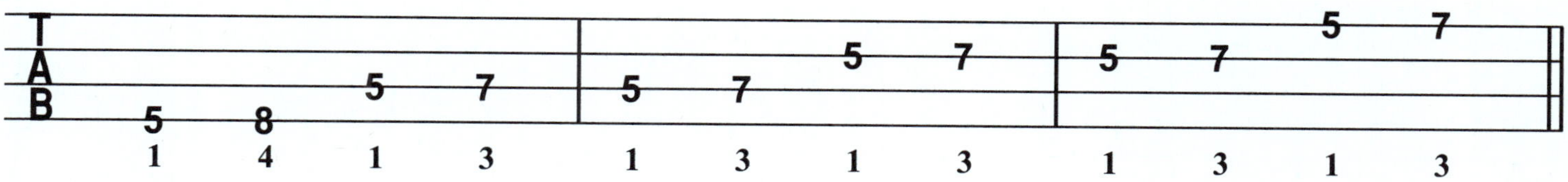

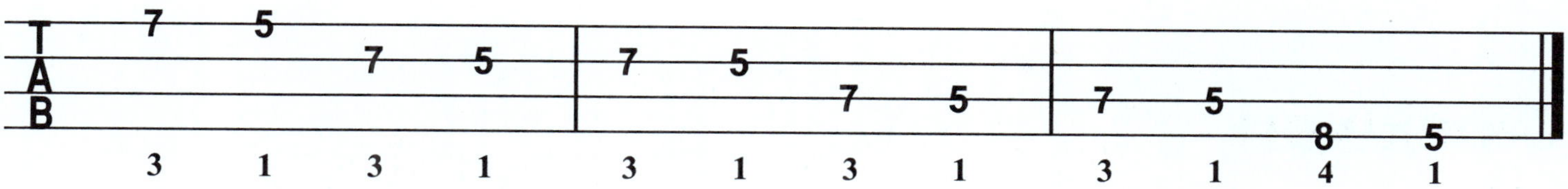

Music Assignment

Be sure to tap your foot along with the pattern to get your body clock ticking and really feel the pattern. Start by playing this pattern as quarter notes giving each note beat. Next, play each note in eighth note timing playing two notes for each beat.

Practice Tips

- **Make sure to review previous lessons. A good idea is to review the past songs as a warm up before you start your new lesson.**
- **Use a metronome when practicing. Always start at a slow speed and increase your tempo once you can play the speed you are at comfortably.**
- **Record yourself if you have the capacity. When you listen back you will be more objective to any inconsistencies. Learn to be your own biggest critic.**

The 4 Chord Song Progression Part 2

1 - 6 - 4 - 5 Progression

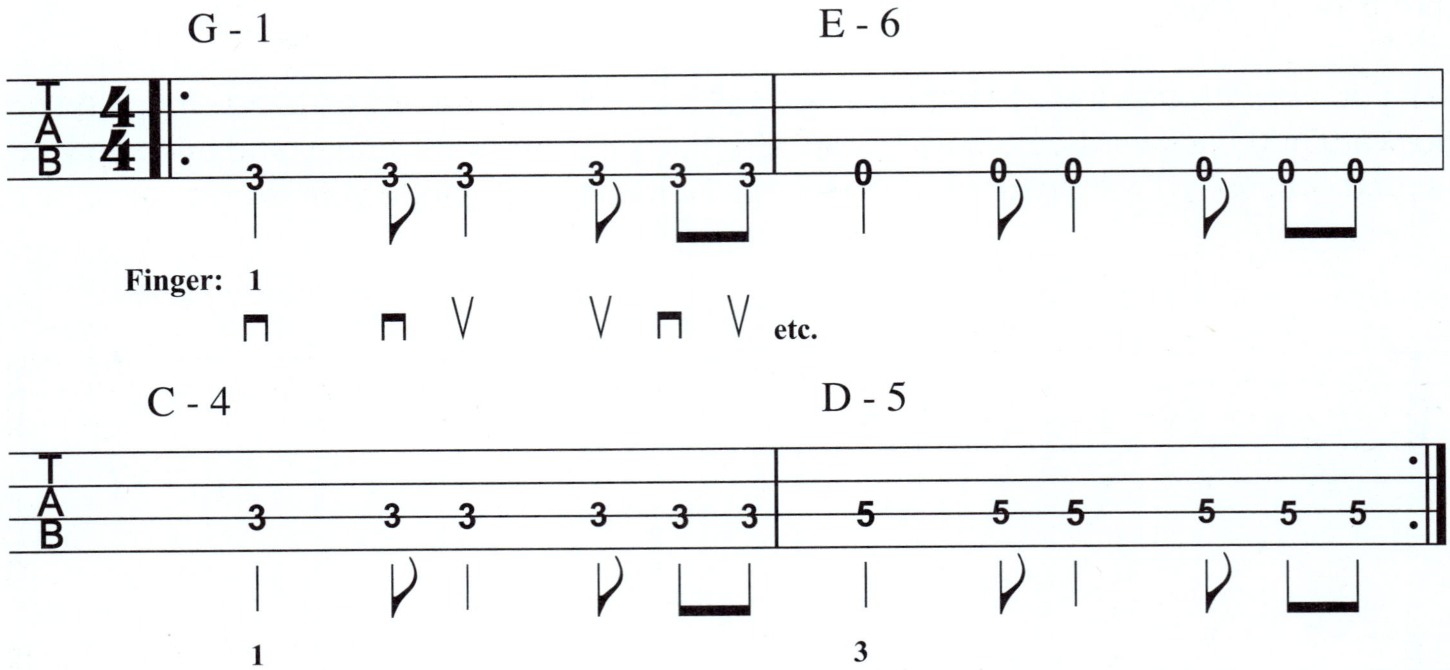

Clockwork

Complete Song Progression

In this lesson you will learn a complete bass song progression in eighth note timing. Notice how many of the notes come from the minor pentatonic scale you just learned. Use consistent alternate plucking and build speed gradually.

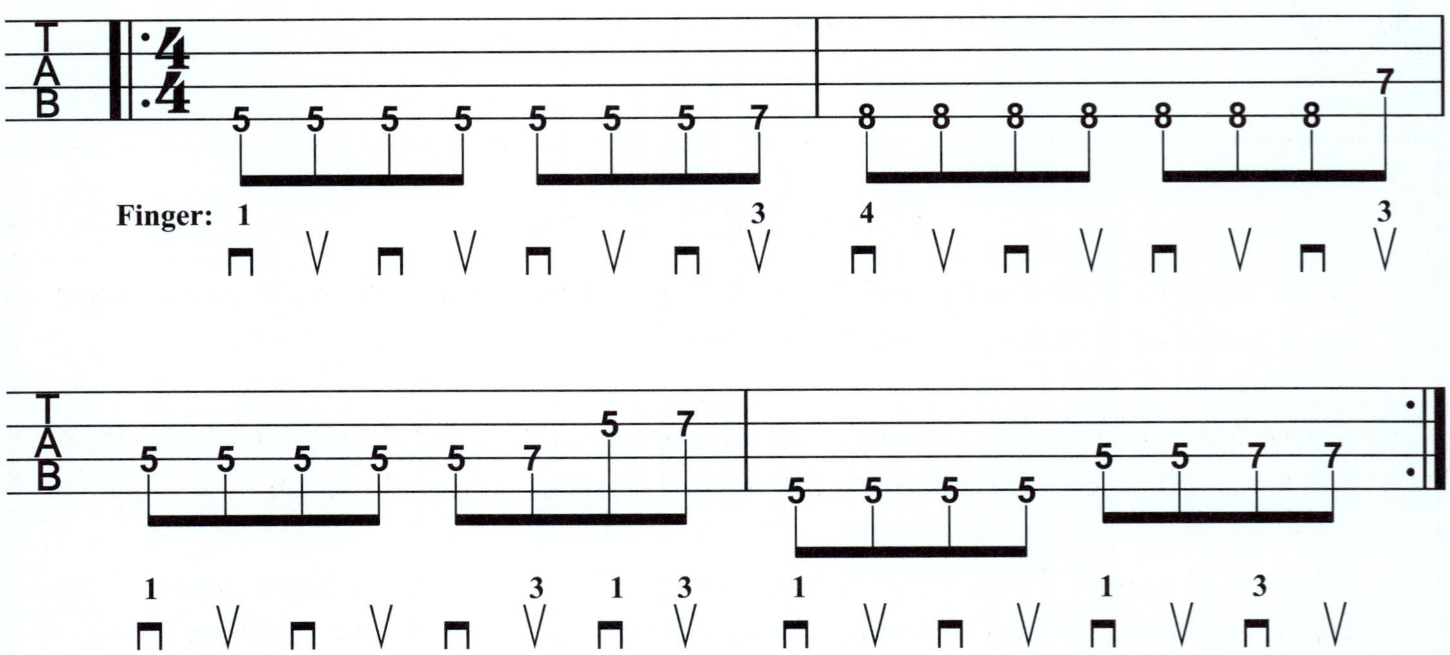

Minor Pentatonic Scale

Positions 2 & 3

With the first minor pentatonic scale in the key of "A" you learned the names of the five notes that make this scale: A, C, D, E and G. The word pentatonic is "penta" meaning five and "tonic" meaning first note. In this lesson you'll learn the 2nd and 3rd positions of this scale. These are the same exact notes played at different places on the neck.

When learning scales a great way to memorize them is to find the finger pattern (the fingers you use on each string). The finger pattern for the second position scale is 2 – 4, 1 – 4, 1 – 4, 1 – 3 always keep your fingers in a one finger per fret alignment. Play through this position and get familiar with the pattern. Again, notice that the root notes are in white.

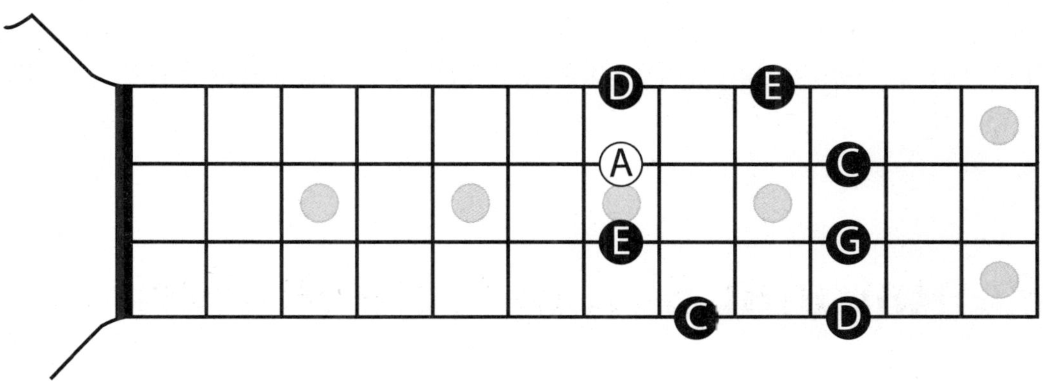

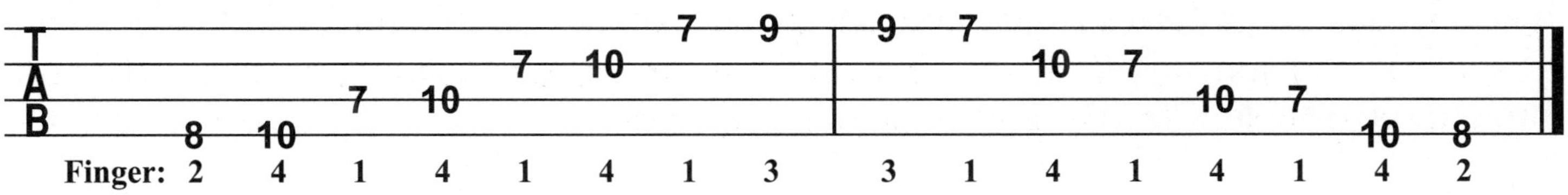

The 3rd scale position starts on the 10th fret, and the finger pattern is 1 – 3, 1 – 3, 1 – 3, 1 – 4. The tricky part here is on the 1st string you have to shift down to the 9th fret to get the first note, then stretch your fourth finger to the 12th fret to get the second note.

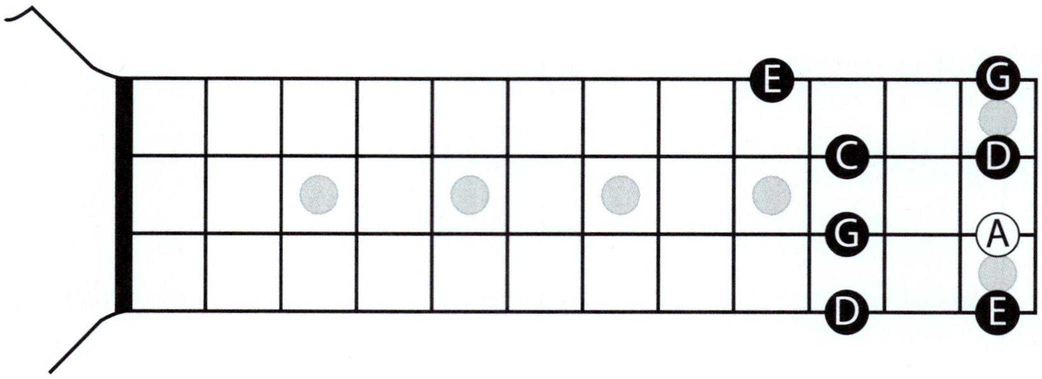

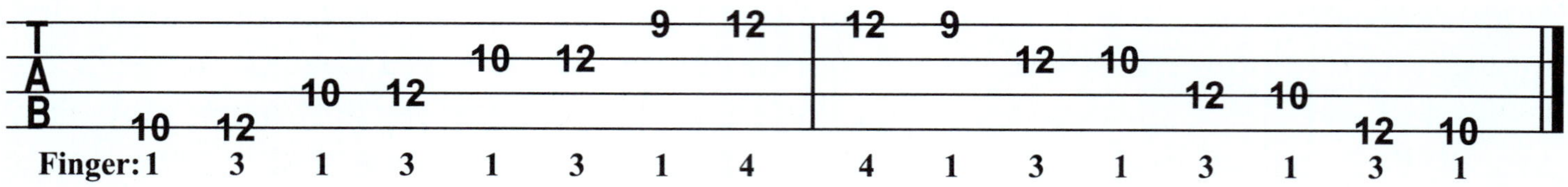

Make sure to use alternate plucking as you build up speed with these scales. Memorize the patterns so that you could play them easily and effectively. Also try to memorize the locations of the root notes within the scale patterns. In the coming lessons I will show you patterns that use these scales, so get excited!

Minor Pentatonic Single Note Pattern

Positions 2 & 3

Take the double pattern you learned earlier and apply it to the scales in the previous lesson. Double the notes on the 2nd and 3rd strings going forward and backwards through each scale. Play the 2nd scale position below:

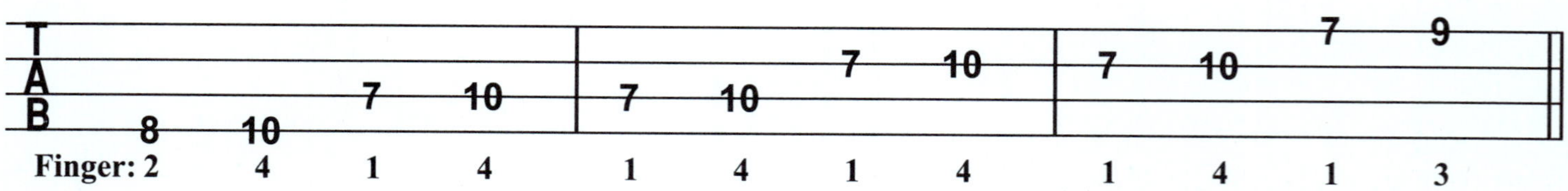

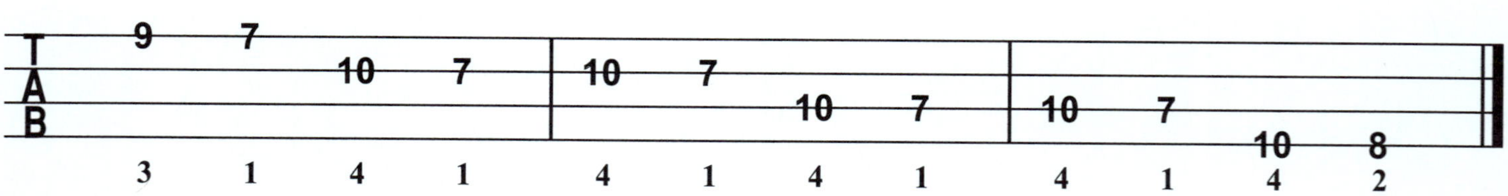

Next apply this pattern to the 3rd scale position, starting on the 10th fret.

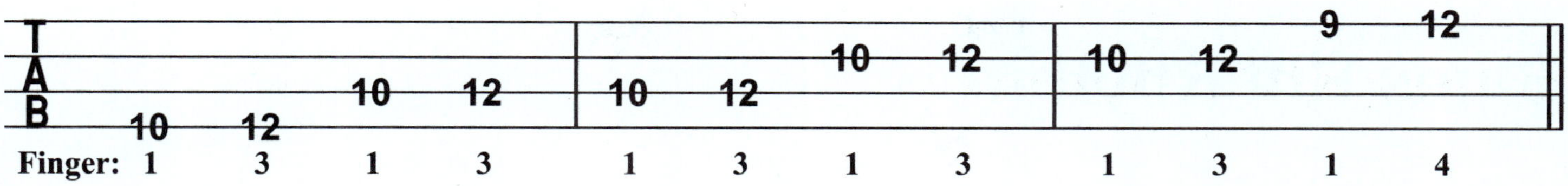

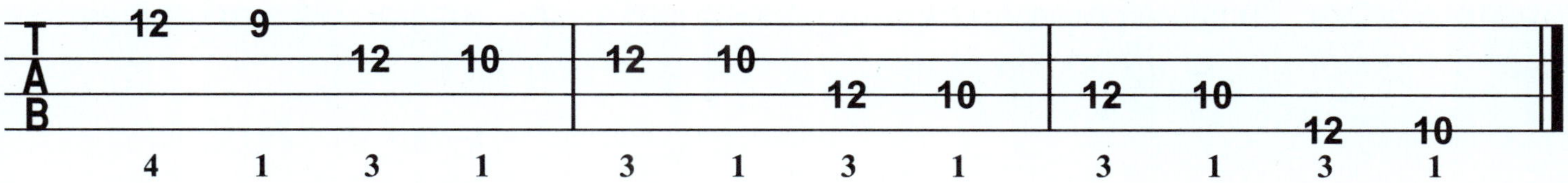

Music Assignment

Once you're comfortable with this pattern, practice along with a metronome to gauge your progress. Start at a slow tempo and increase the tempo each time you practice. Keep clean technique, plucking each note clear and distinct, while alternating consistently. To make this pattern more challenging pluck each note twice as you play through the pattern sequence.

Ode to Joy

Here is another song progressions where you must support the melody with a solid bass line. Be sure to practice this with the backing track that includes the melody.

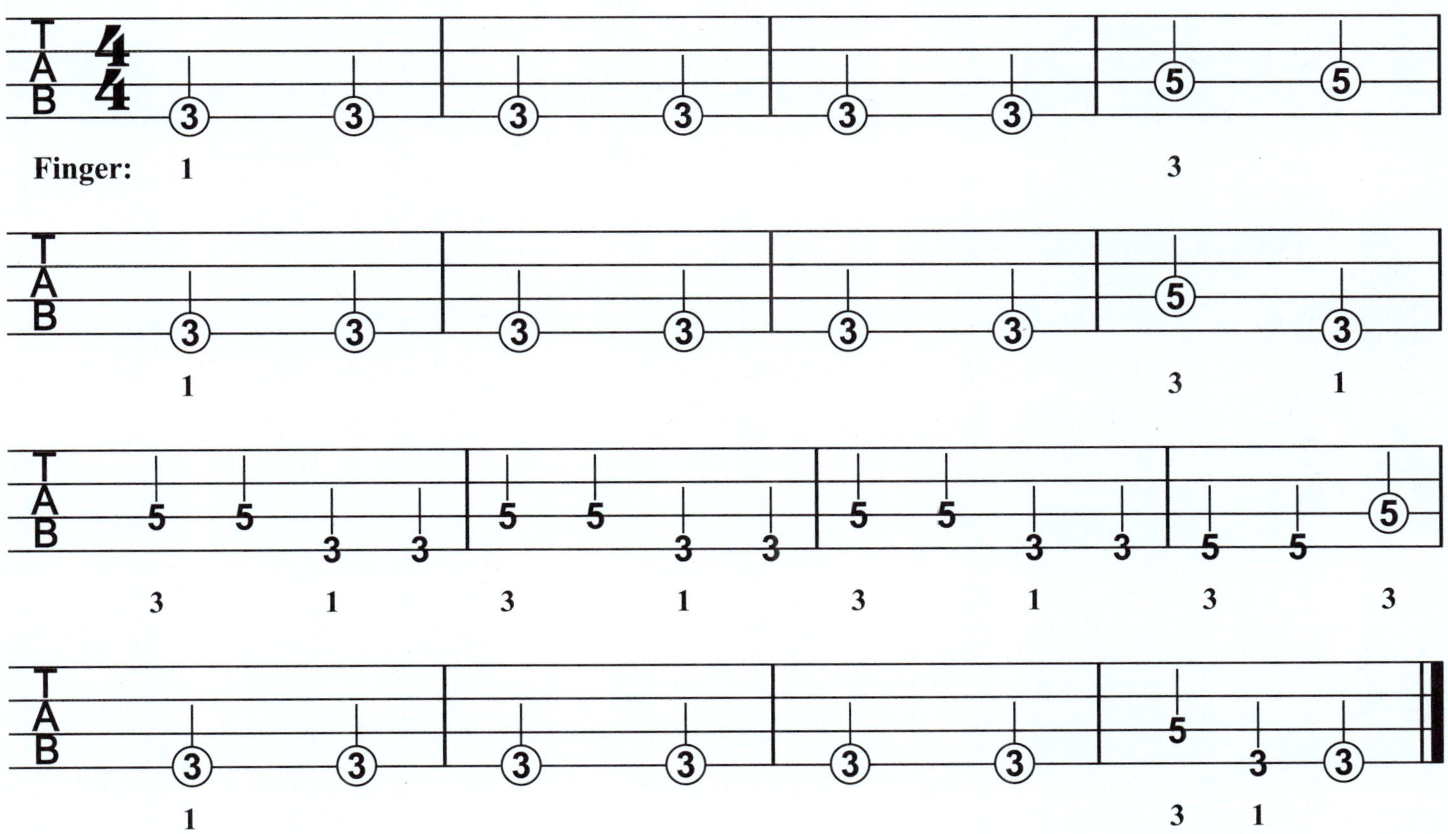

Blues Riff Rhythm

The following is a single note blues riff rhythm. There are many times in music where a rhythm for a song will be constructed using single notes played with the bass and the guitar together. This is a common rhythm so it should sound familiar. Be sure to play this over the guitar and drum backing track.

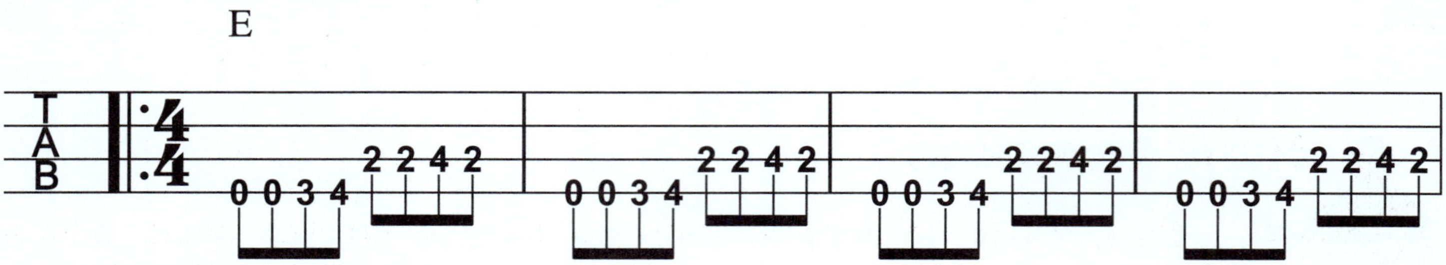

Finger: 2 3 1 1 3 1 etc.

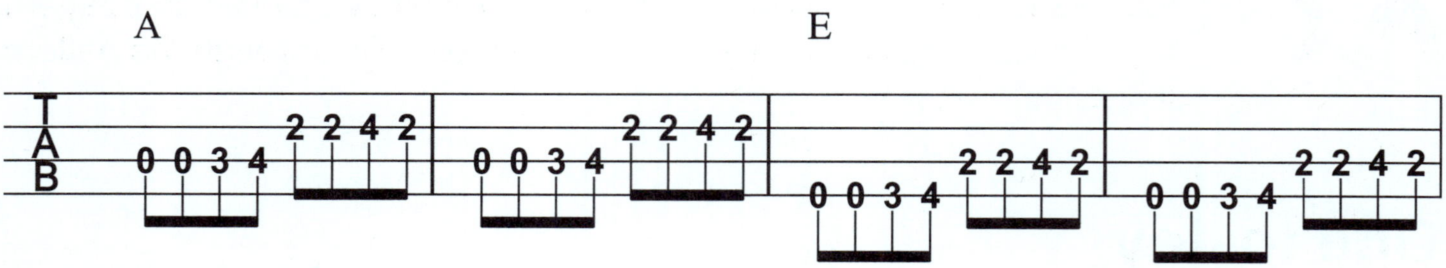

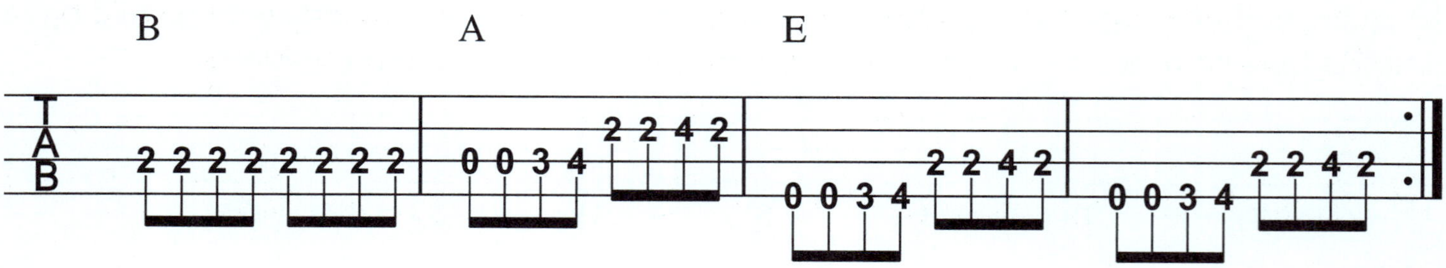

Music Assignment

This rhythm can be played with the shuffle feel that you learned in the Blues Progression lesson. Below are the first few measures with the shuffle feel rhythm to get you started:

Blue Velvet

1 - 6 - 3 - 5 Progression

The rhythm pattern for this song is: 2 quarter notes followed by 4 eighth notes. Play this plucking pattern once for each chord. Keep your hand, arm and shoulder loose and relaxed at all times. Never tense or tighten up your arms. Once you can play this progression use the backing track and play along with the guitar and drums.

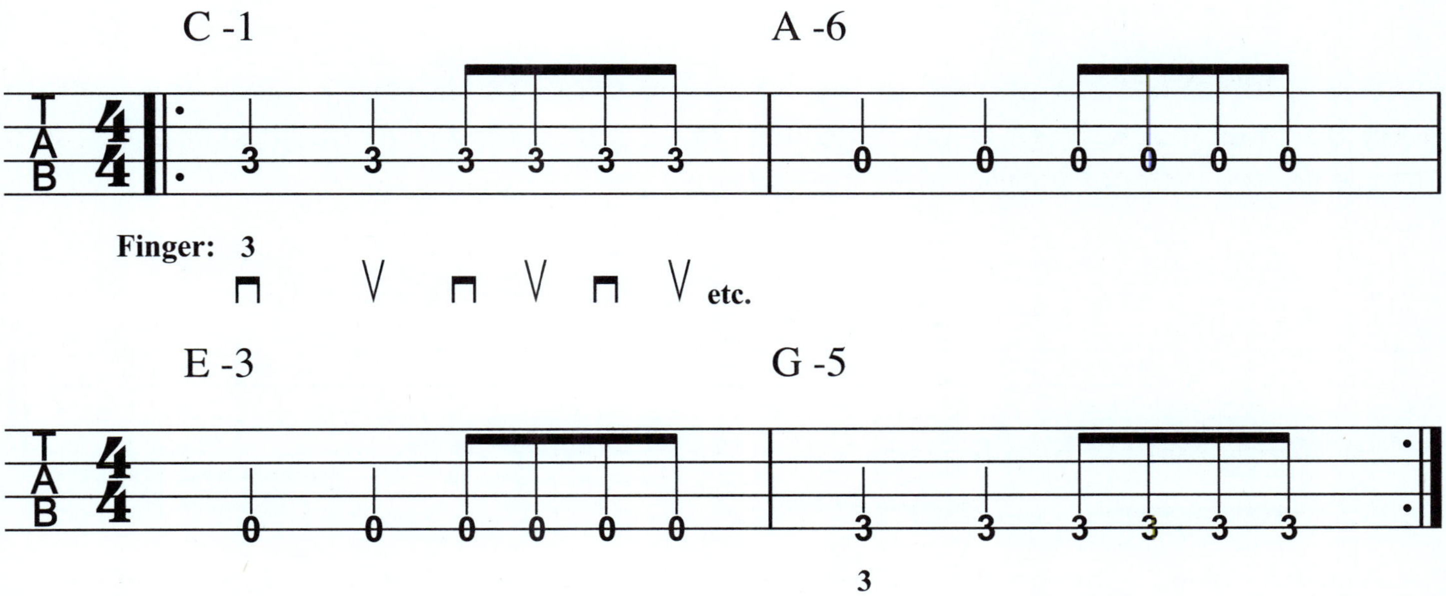

Triplets

Eighth and sixteenth notes subdivide a beat in half and quarters. These are even number breakdowns of 2 and 4. Triplets subdivide a beat into threes. For every one beat, you're going to play three notes. Count triplets like this:

1 – trip – let, 2 – trip – let, 3 – trip – let, 4 – trip – let

Next play the open 4th E string in triplets following the tablature and feel the triplet timing:

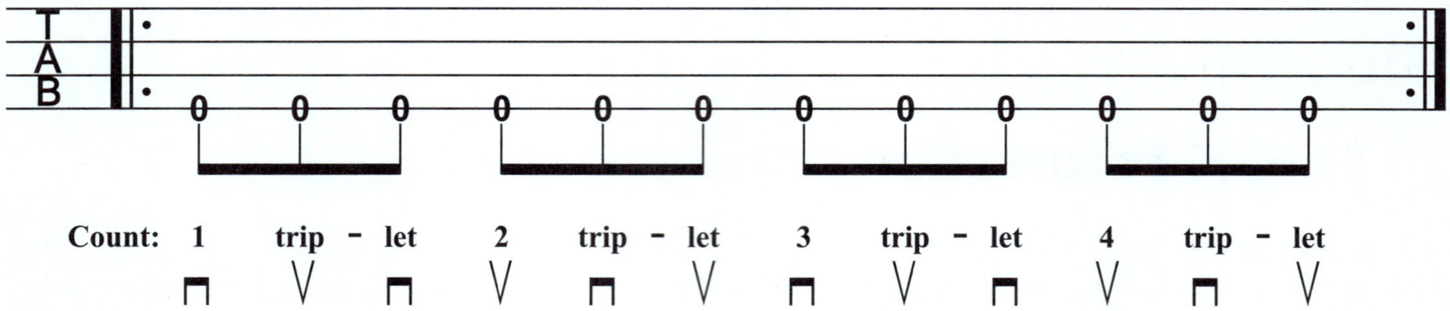

Triplet Pattern

Here is a triplet pattern applied to the first three minor pentatonic scales. This pattern goes up three notes from each degree of the scale. Below I've outlined the first two strings so you can get familiar with the pattern:

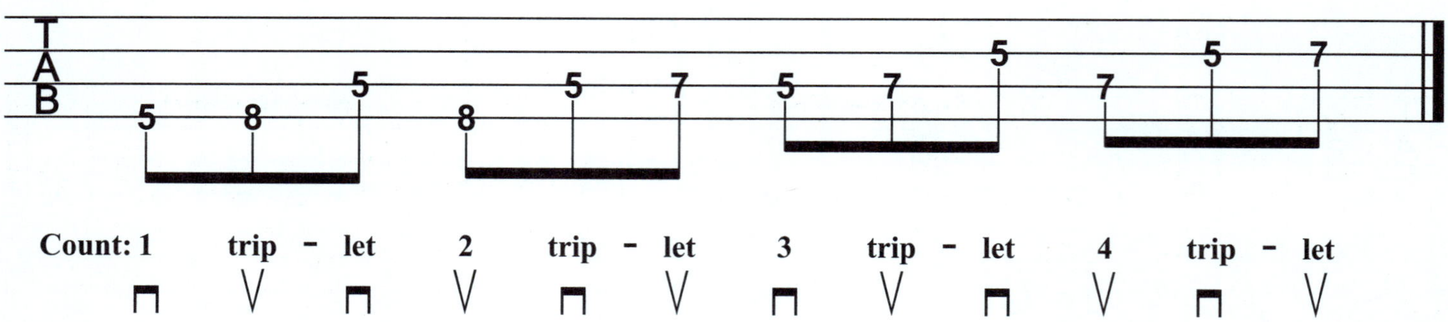

Now play the triplet lead pattern with the first three minor pentatonic scales:

1st Position

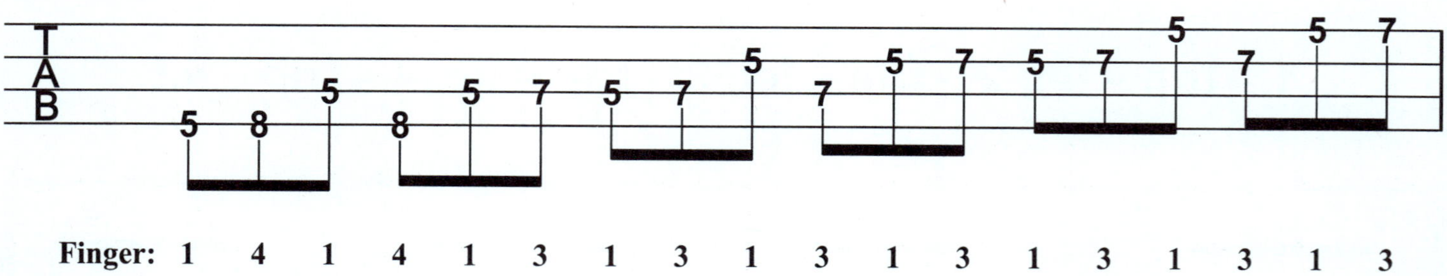

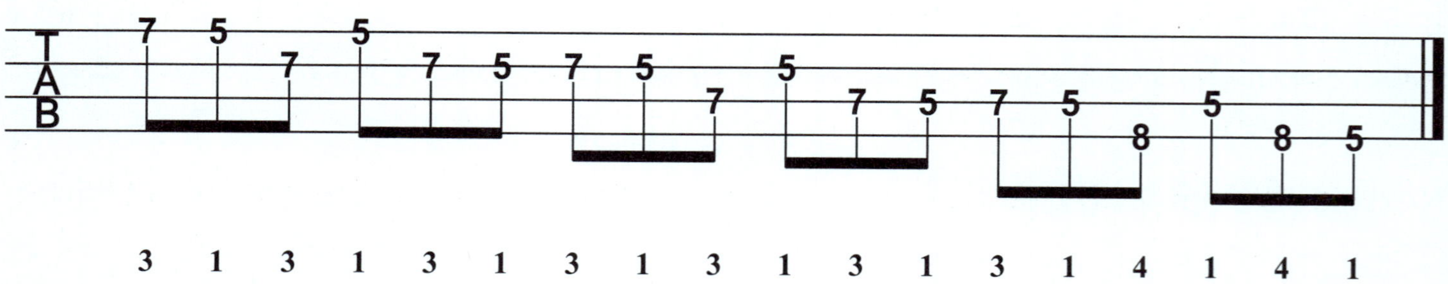

2nd Position

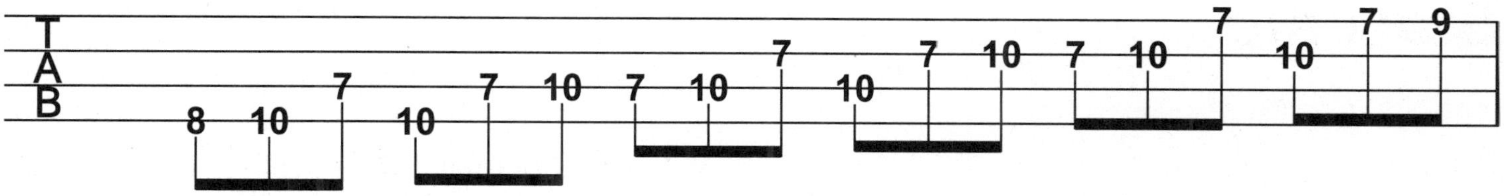

Finger: 2 4 1 4 1 4 1 4 1 4 1 4 1 4 1 4 1 3

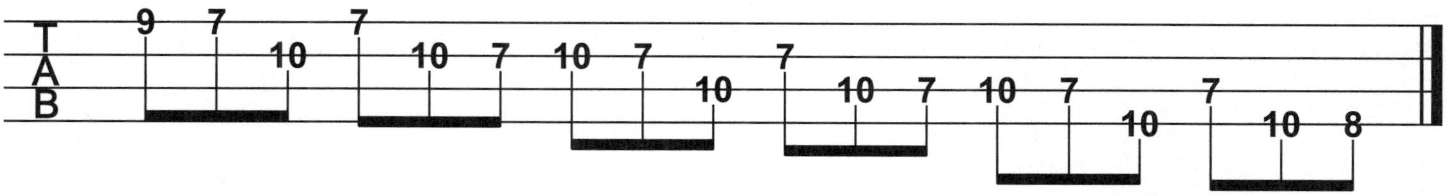

3 1 4 1 4 1 4 1 4 1 4 1 4 1 4 1 4 2

3rd Position

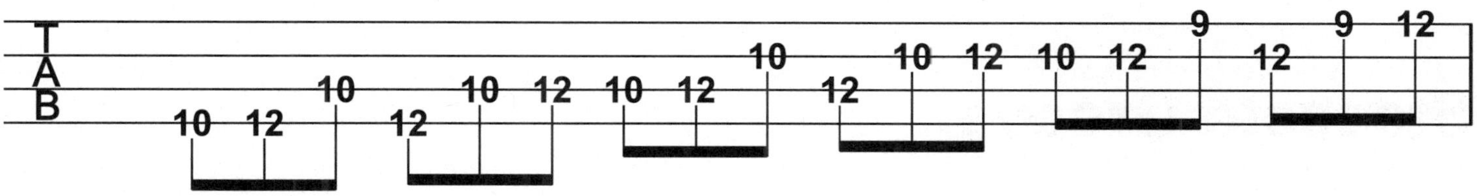

Finger: 1 3 1 3 1 3 1 3 1 3 1 3 1 3 1 4 1 4

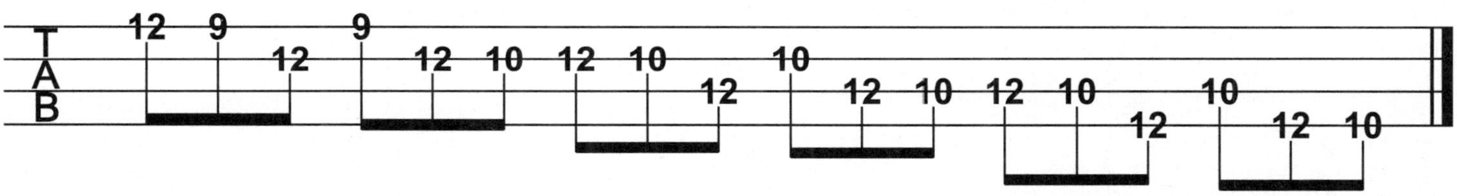

4 1 4 1 3 1 3 1 3 1 3 1 3 1 3 1 3 1

Music Assignment

Vary this pattern and play each note of this triplet pattern two times. Then transpose this pattern forwards and backwards with all three scale positions.

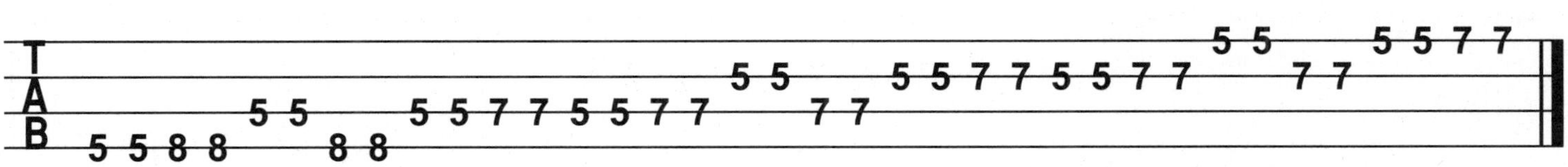

Staccato

Staccato by definition means short and detached. A note separated by silence. To attain this you must use both hands to mute the sound. With your fretting hand you simply lift the pressure off a note and with your plucking hand use the side of your hand to touch the strings as they come off the bridge. Notes that are to be played with staccato will have a dot placed over the note. Play the following notes using the staccato technique.

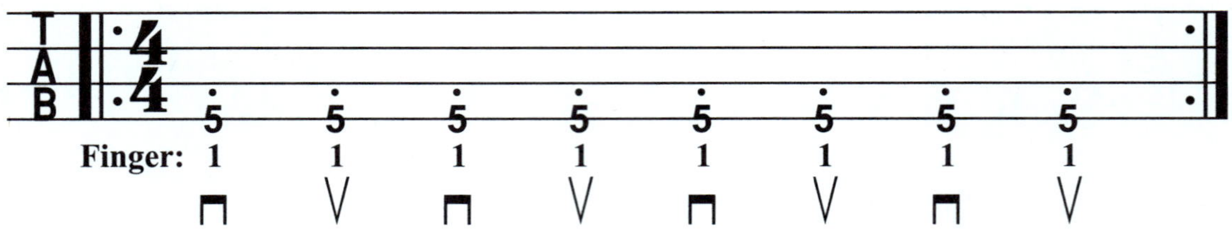

Staccato Groove

Below is a staccato groove bass progression. Make sure to use the mute technique and also lift the pressure off each note to get the staccato sound.

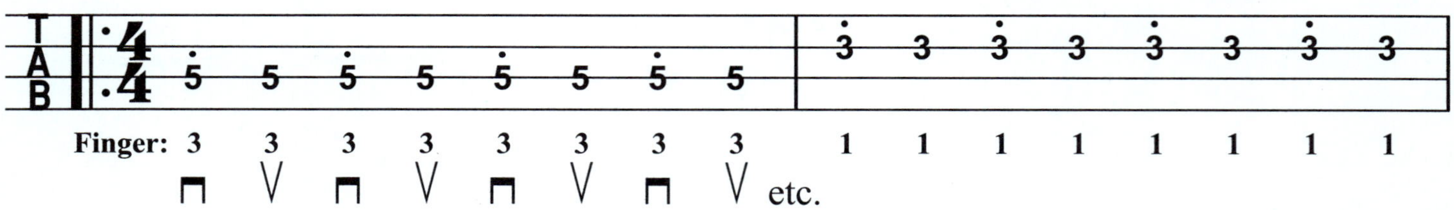

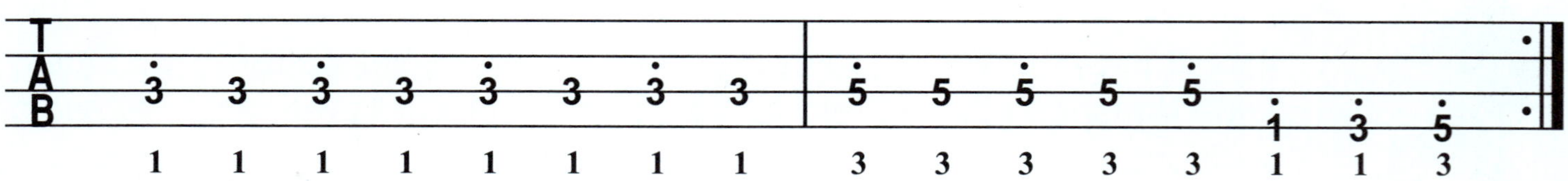

Bass 1 Quiz #3

You're ready to take your next quiz now! Please review all the lessons in the previous section then go to page 4 to see where to take your quiz.

Street of Dreams

2 - 4 - 1 - 5 Progression

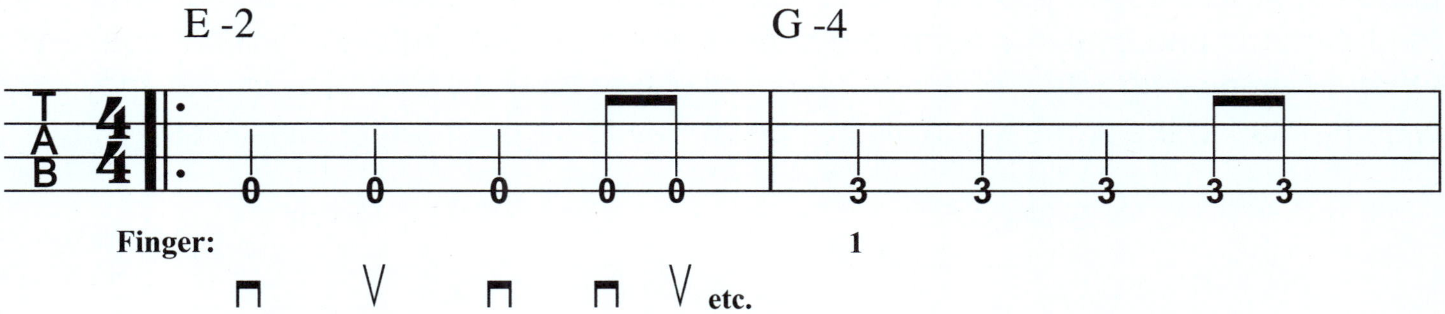

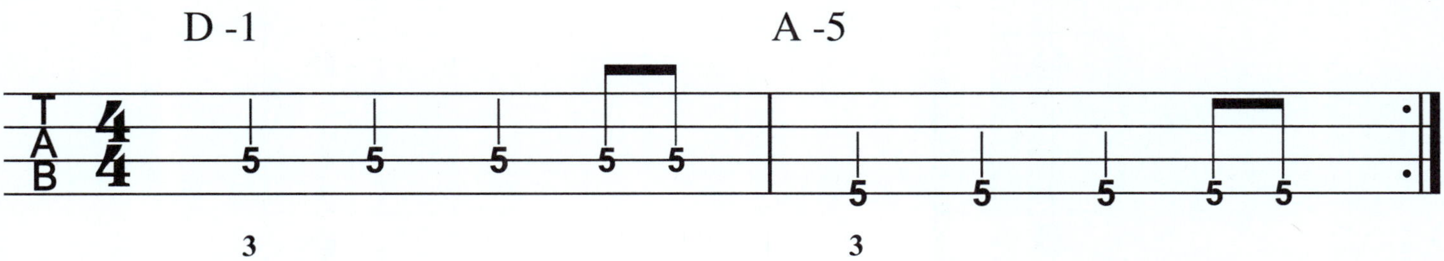

The Major Scale

Key of "G"

SCALE PROFESSOR

The major scale is the mother of all music. All scales and chords are created by altering this scale and isolating certain notes within them. The first note of the scale is the name of the key or root note. This is a G major scale starting with a G note on the 4th string 3rd fret. Pay close attention to the fingering and keep your fingers lined up, one finger per fret.

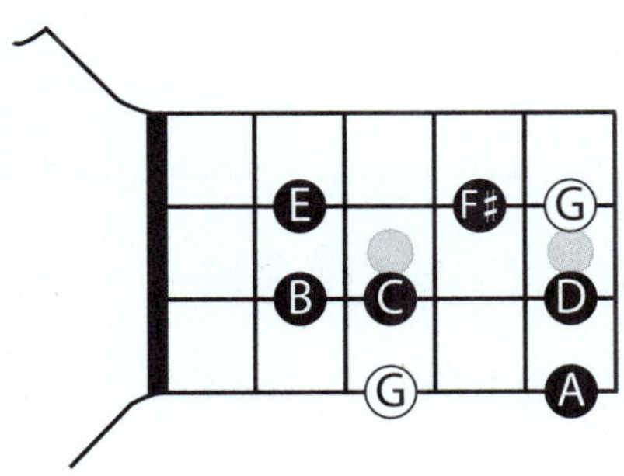

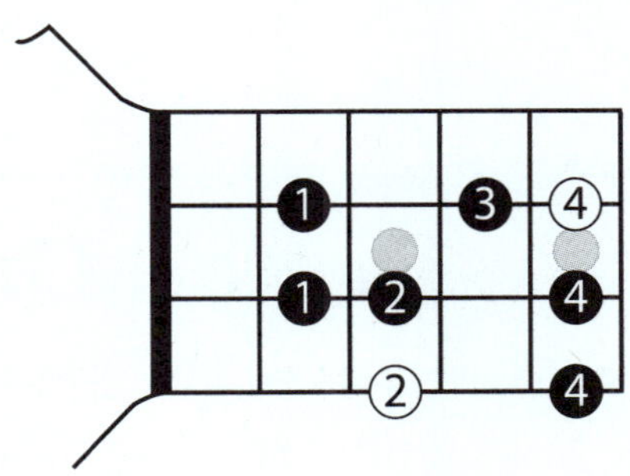

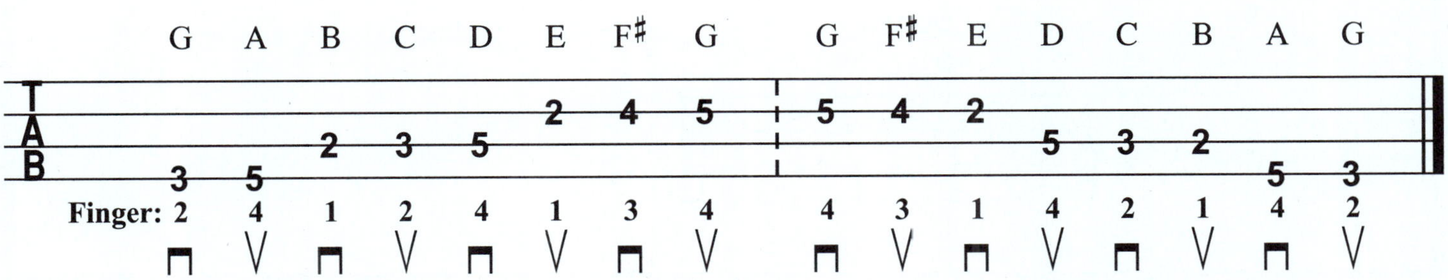

Major Triads

A triad is the three notes that make a chord. Many bass lines are written using triad patterns. In this lesson you will learn a common major triad pattern. These are movable triad patterns and by just playing the same pattern at other frets you will change keys. Often when playing with a guitar or keyboard player you can follow the chords they play with the triad of the same key. This is a great way to begin creating bass lines.

G Major

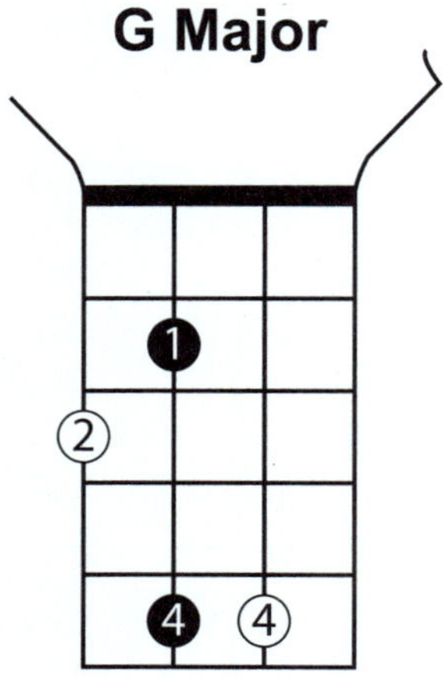

C Major

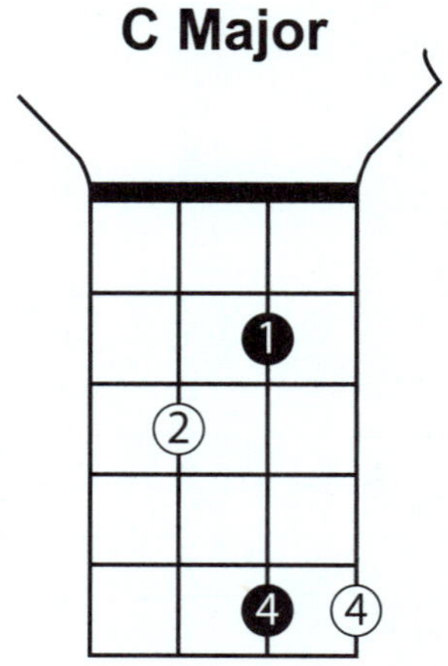

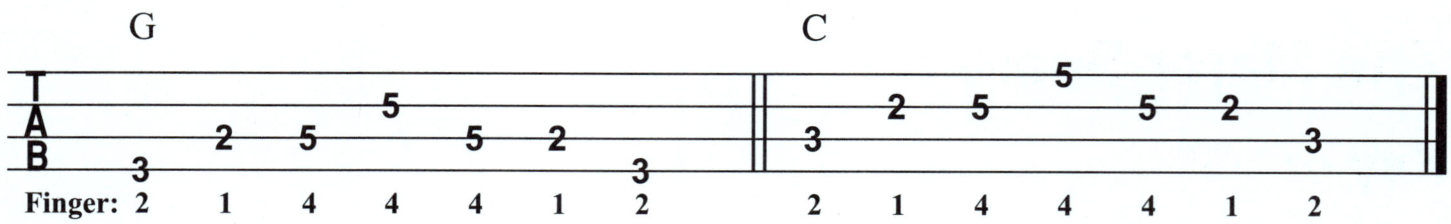

Music Assignment

Take the triad shapes from this lesson and move them around the neck. You need to become familiar playing these anywhere on the neck. Remember that the first note is the name of the triad.

Dotted Quarter Notes

The dot after a note increases the duration of the note by half of its original value. A dotted quarter note would receive 1 ½ beats or counts.

Dotted Quarter Note

1 1/2 Beats

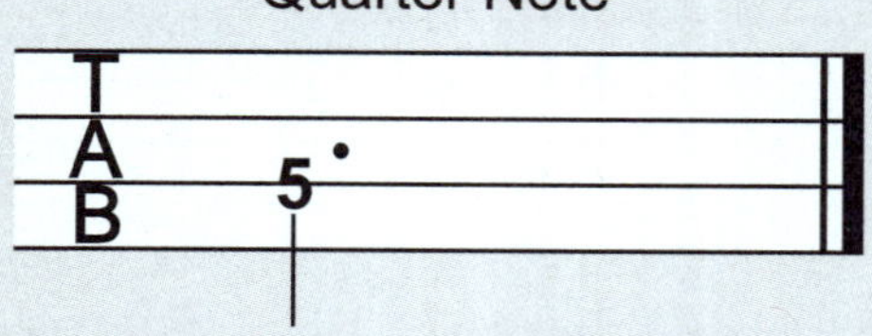

Dotted Quarter Note

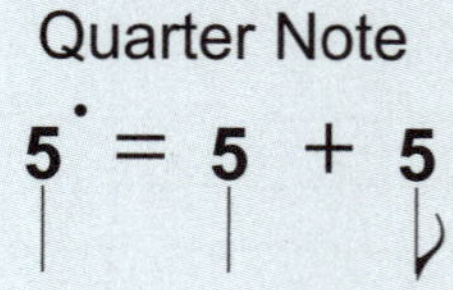

Cherry Sky

Major Triad Progression

Let's put the major triads into a progression and form a bass line. The following is a four chord progression formed with the chords G, C, A and D. You will play major triads for these four chords within this bass line.

First Groove

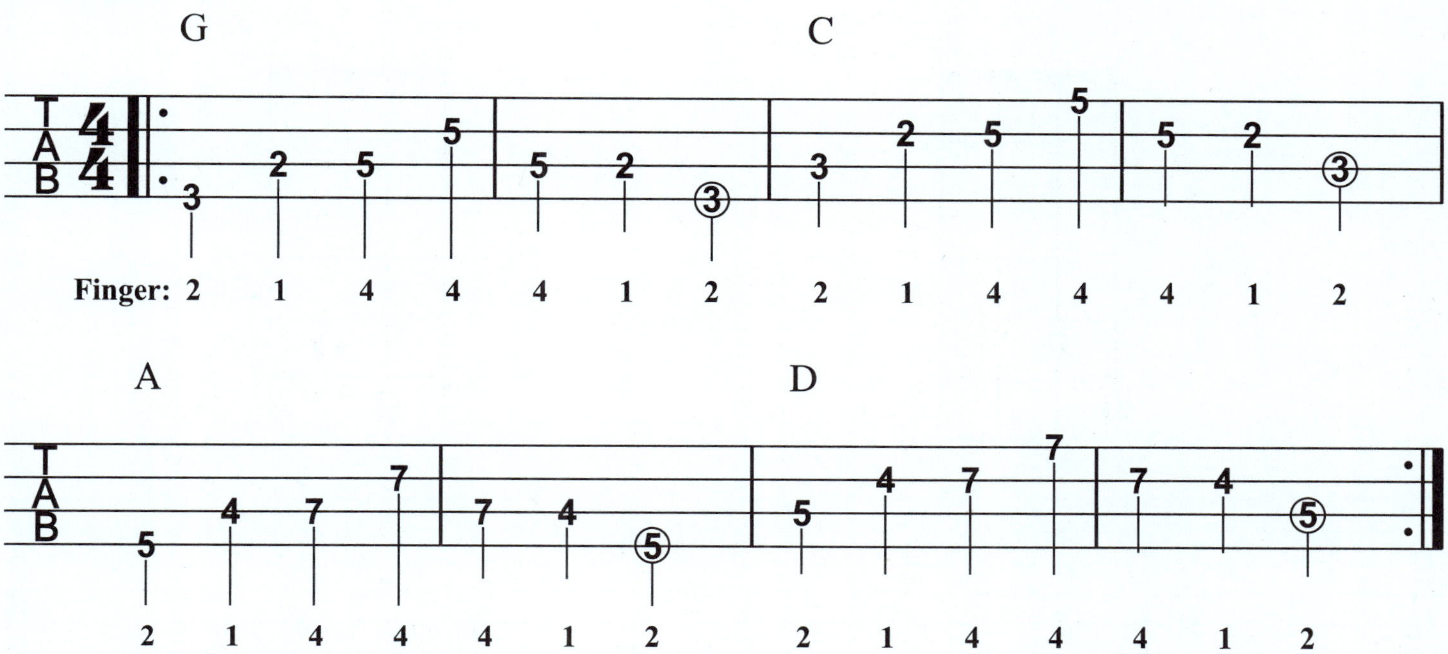

Second Groove

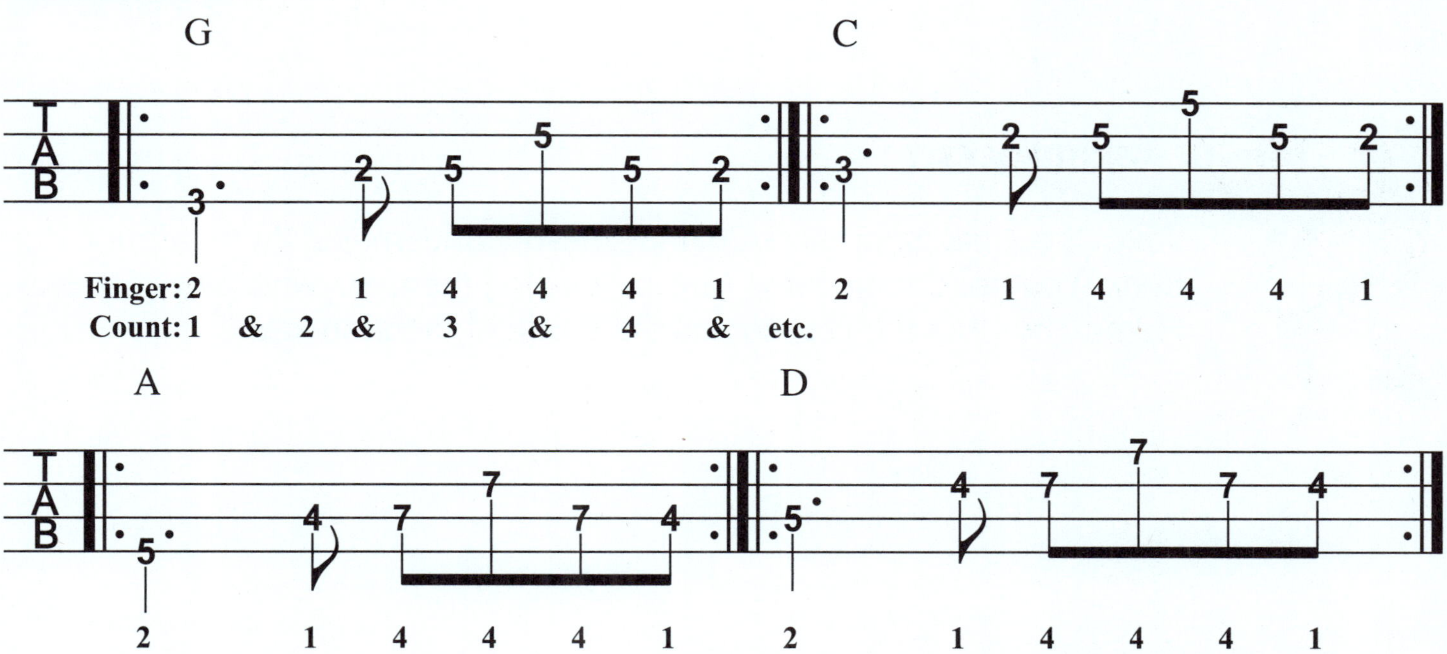

Minor Triads

A minor triad is similar to the major triads you learned only they contain the three notes that form a minor chord. These patterns are also movable and can be played in other keys by moving them to different frets across the neck. Get familiar with these minor triads.

G Minor

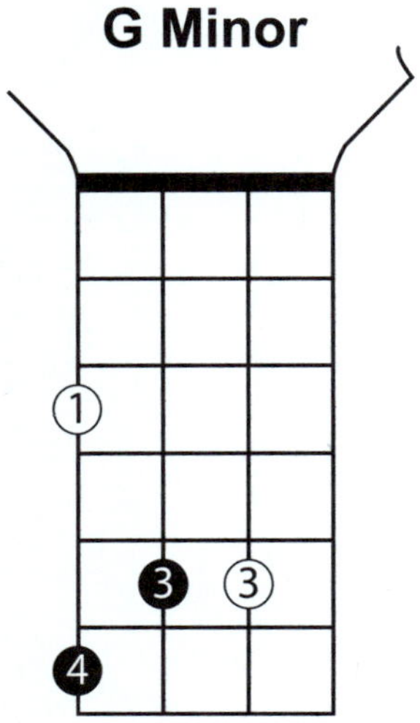

C Minor

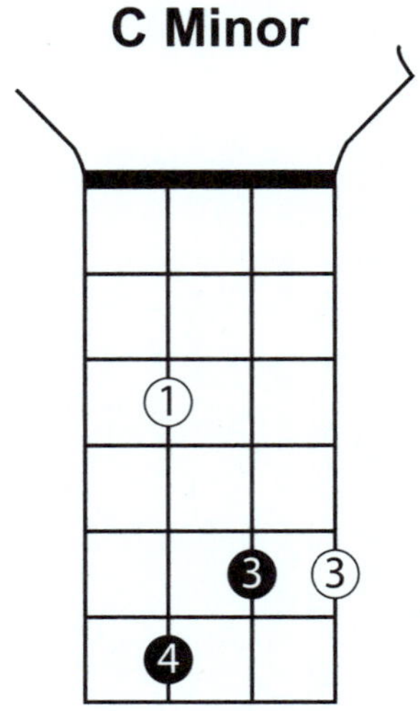

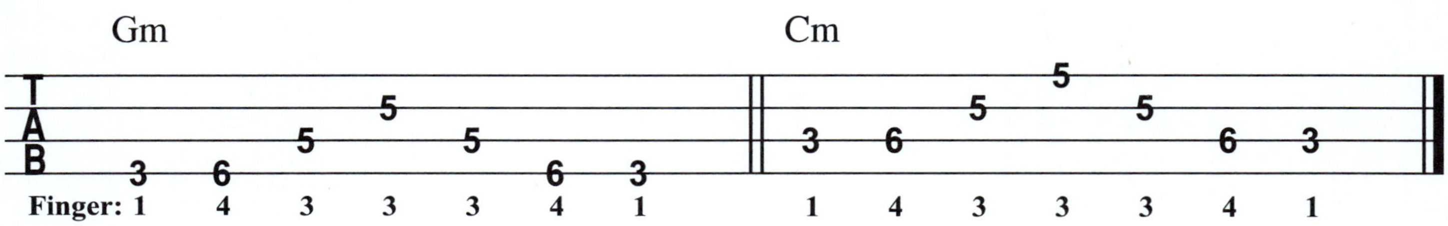

Music Assignment

Take the triad shapes from this lesson and move them around the neck. You need to become familiar playing them anywhere on the neck. Remember that the first note is the name of the triad key.

Unbreakable

Minor Triad Progression

Let's put the minor triads into a progression and form a bass line. You will use the same four chord progression from the major triads formed with the G, C, A and D chords. You will play minor triads for these four chords within this bass line. Make sure to play this over the band backing track.

First Groove

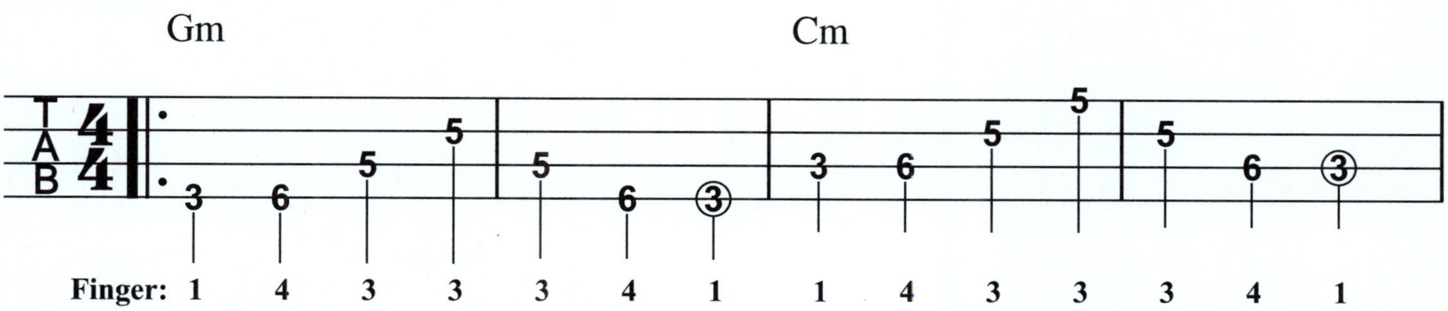

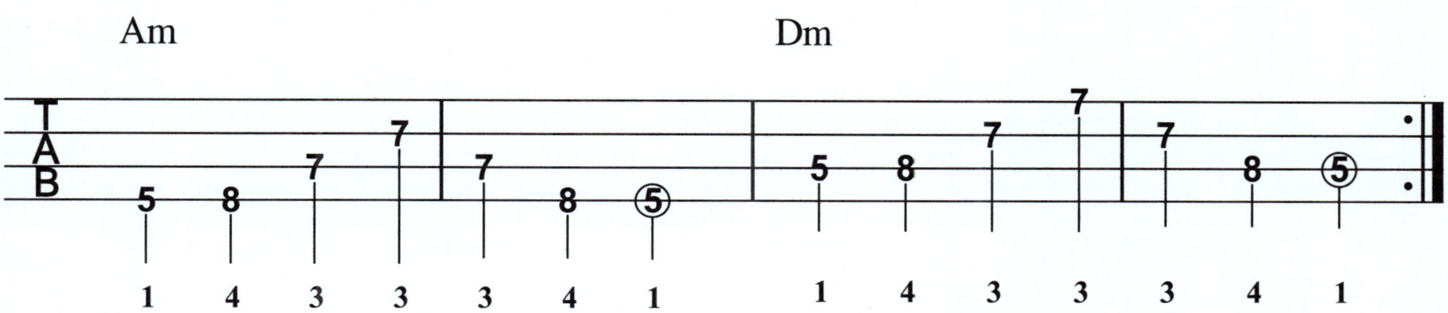

Second Groove

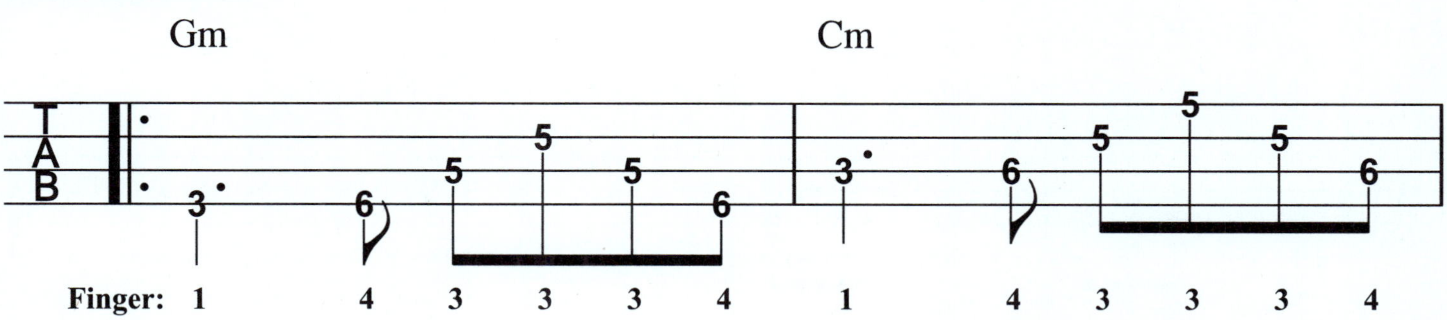

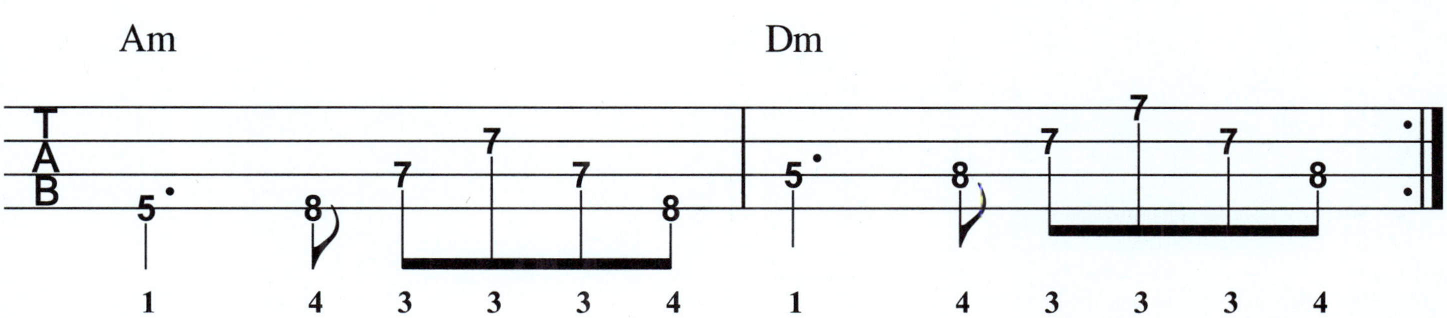

Major & Minor Triads

A Spell on Me

Many times you will combine both major and minor triads to form a bass line. The following is a great example of this in a two part song progression. This first section is a verse and the second section is the chorus. Make sure to play this along with the backing track after you can play it up to speed.

Part 1

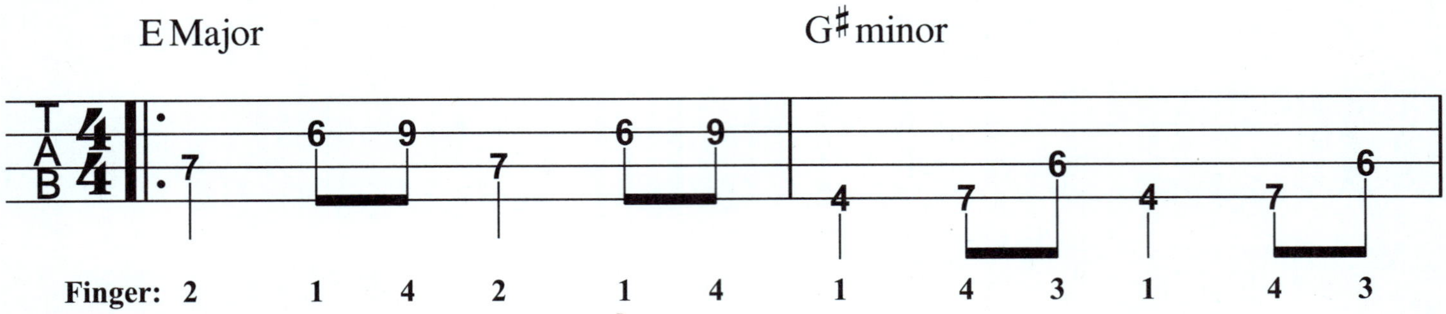

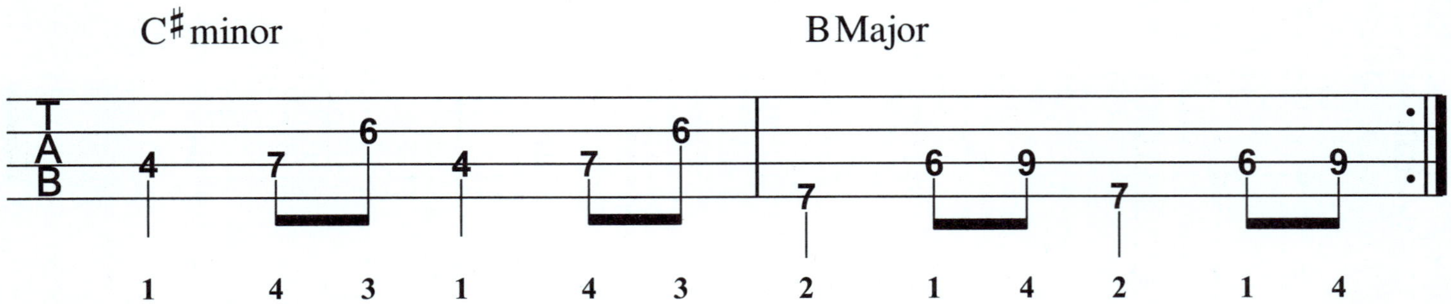

Part 2

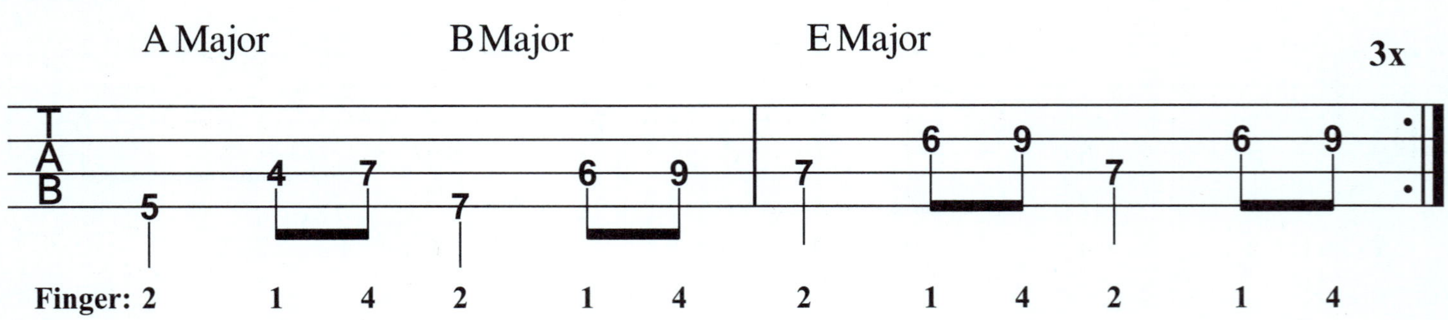

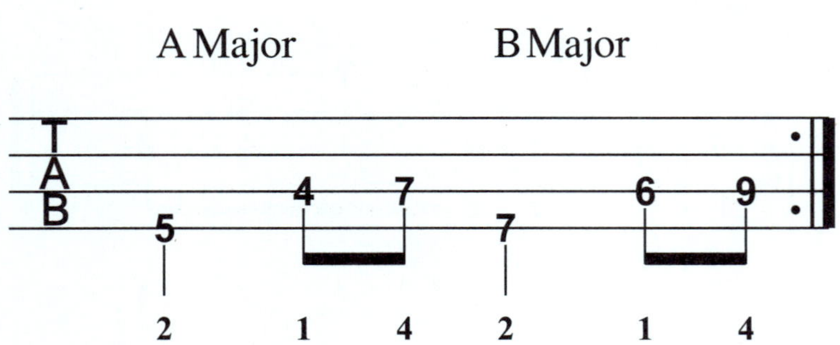

Octaves

Octaves are a common intervallic technique used in all genres of music. Octaves are formed by taking a root note and finding the same root note 8 scale degrees higher creating a higher pitched root note. There are a few shapes that are most characteristic that I am going to show you. These shapes incorporate a string skip where you have to play a note two strings away. Many players use octaves in bass lines as a technique. Play through the following octave shapes and move them around the neck to different frets.

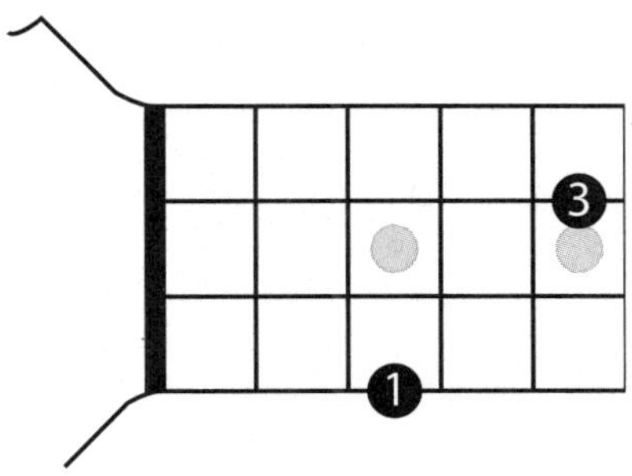

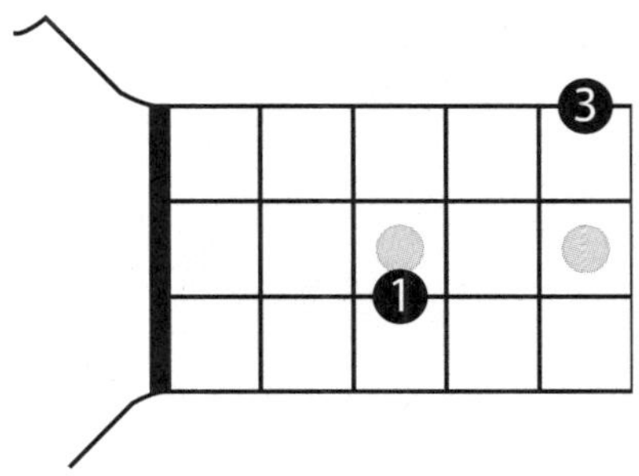

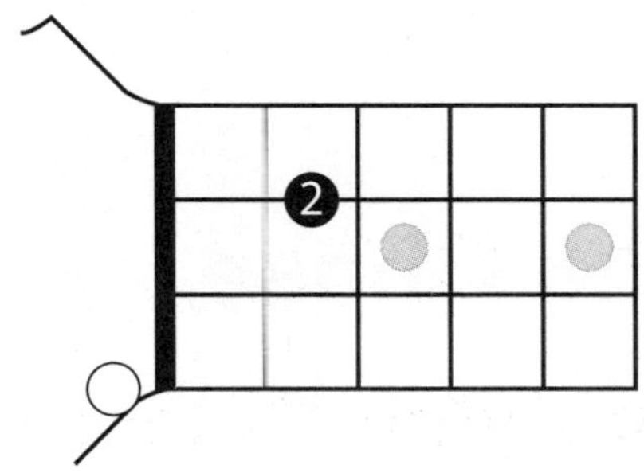

Example 1 - G **Example 2 - C** **Example 3 - E**

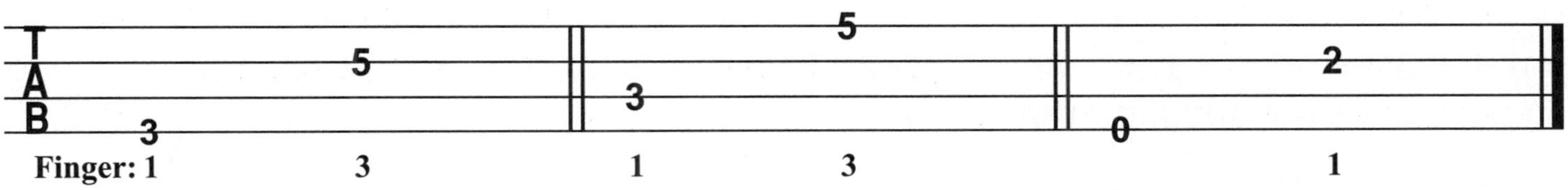

MUSIC ASSIGNMENT

Start at the 2nd fret and move these patterns one fret at a time all the way up and down the neck. It's important to be comfortable playing these octaves anywhere on the neck so you can use them to play songs.

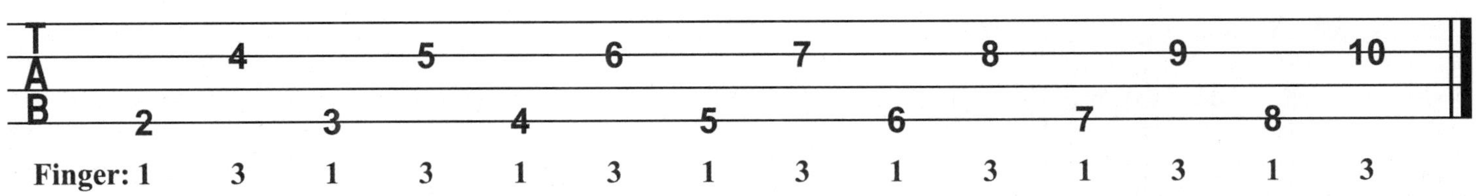

Octave Rock Progression

The tablature notes are spaced to help you with the timing. Pay close attention to the plucking, the pattern repeats but is not consistent alternate plucking.

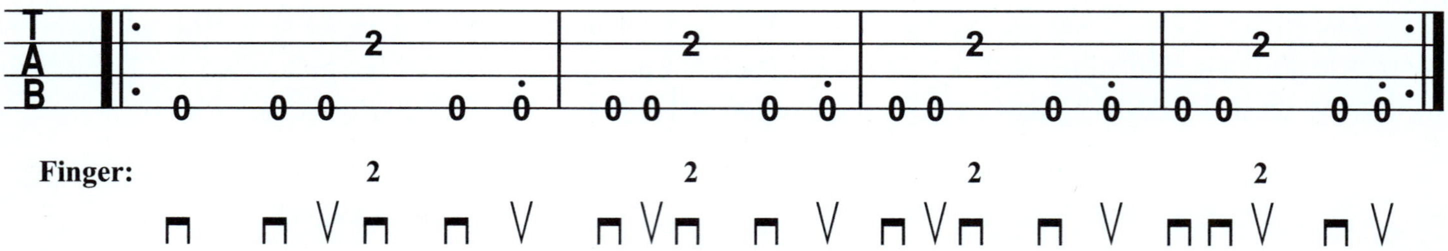

The Chase

Applying Octaves

Here is an example of how you can use octaves to create a bass line. The chord changes here are G – F – Bb – C. For this song the octave shapes will be played with the first and fourth fingers, this is a common fingering variation. Make sure to use alternate plucking consistently throughout this bass line.

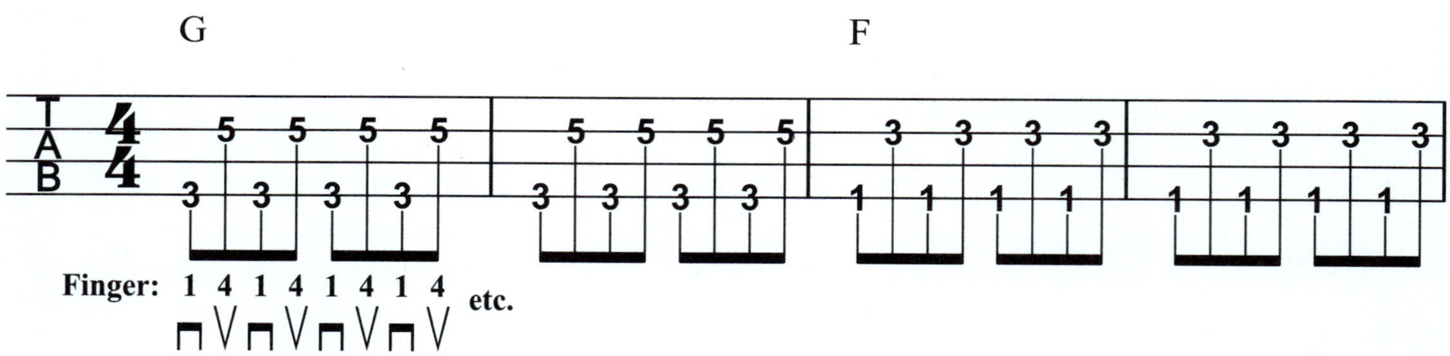

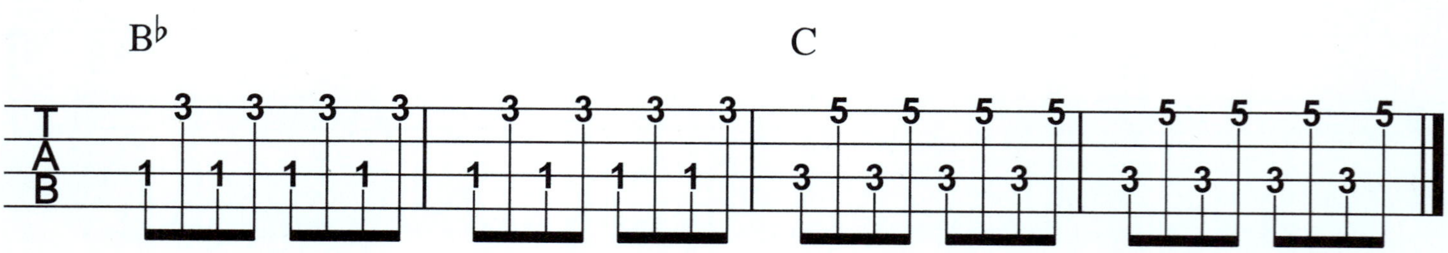

Minor Pentatonic Scale

Positions 4 & 5

Up to now you've learned three minor pentatonic scale patterns in the key of "A." Now it's time to learn the last two. The 4th scale position starts on the 12th fret with your first finger. Play through this scale position below:

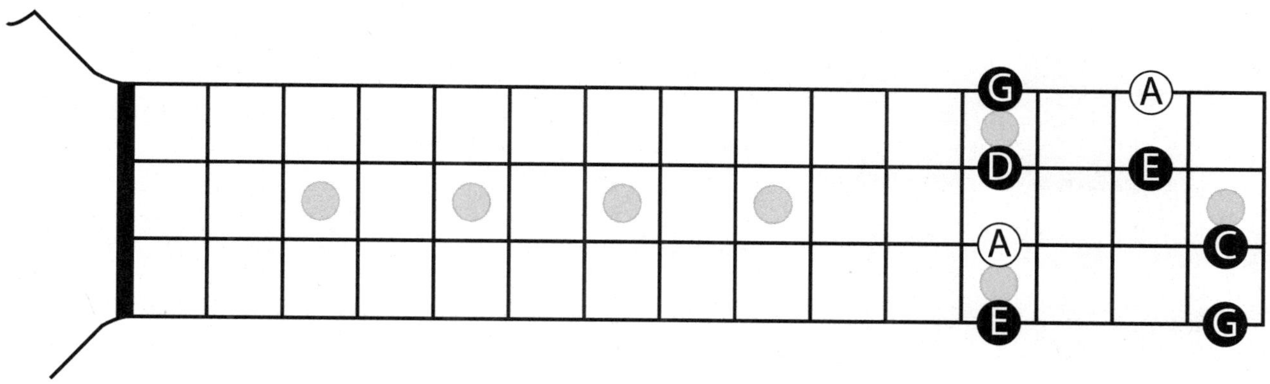

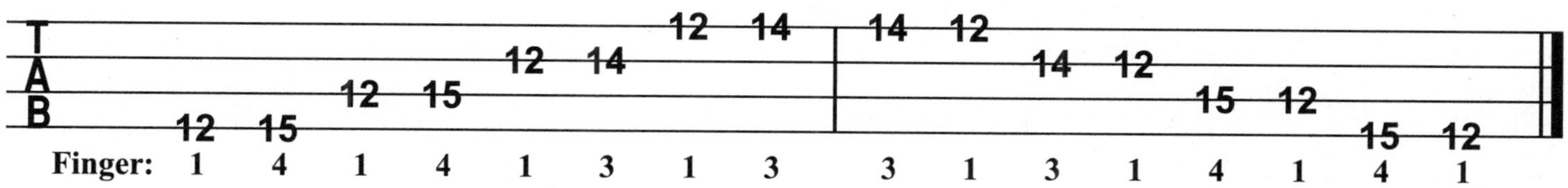

The 5th scale position starts on the 3rd fret with your second finger. This pattern is pretty easy to memorize, play through the this scale below:

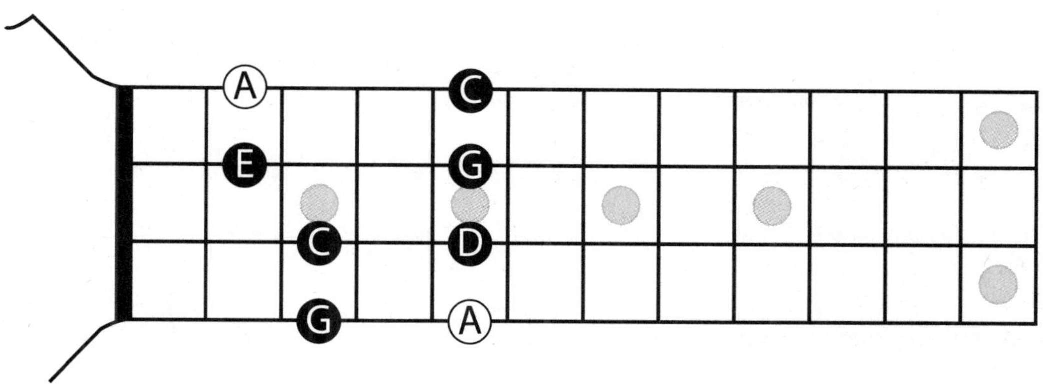

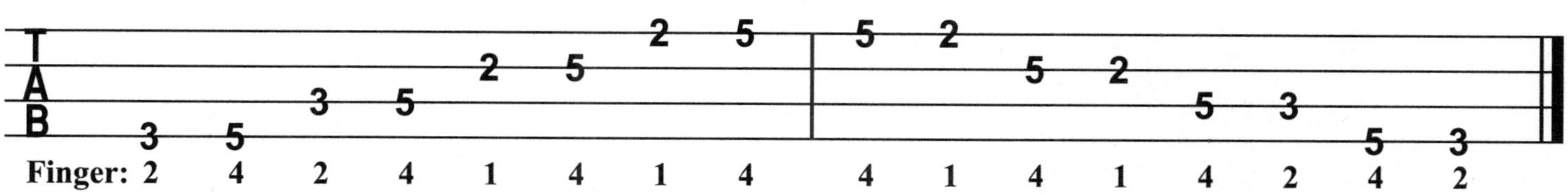

Make sure to use alternate plucking when playing these scales and memorize the finger patterns. Now you have all five minor pentatonic scale patterns in the key of "A." All of these patterns have the same notes, A – C – D – E and G played at different spots across the neck. Once you have these five patterns memorized you'll be able to change keys by just moving these scale patterns up or down the neck.

Minor Pentatonic Triplet Pattern

Positions 4 & 5

Below is the triplet pattern transposed to the 4th and 5th position minor pentatonic scale. Pay attention to your hand position and keep the bass neck up at a 30 degree angle.

4th Position

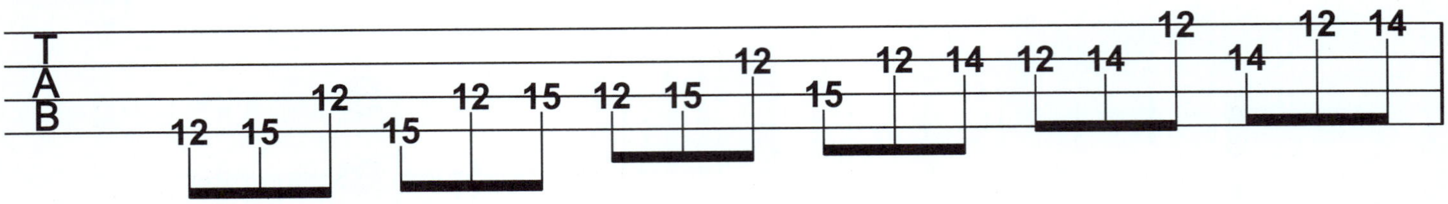

Finger: 1 4 1 4 1 4 1 4 1 4 1 3 1 3 1 3 1 3

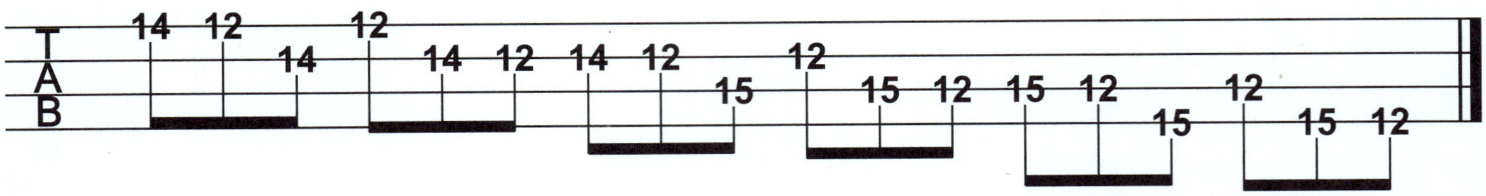

3 1 3 1 3 1 3 1 4 1 4 1 4 1 4 1 4 1

5th Position

Finger: 2 4 2 4 2 4 2 4 1 4 1 4 1 4 1 4 1 4

4 1 4 1 4 1 4 1 4 1 4 2 4 2 4 2 4 2

Music Assignment

Scales are meant to be used to create bass lines and melodies. After you play the scales forward and backward, try to mix the notes up and create your own patterns. This is how you begin creating your own style.

Black Pearl

Minor 6 - 2 - 5 - 3 Progression

This is a minor progression because it starts with the relative minor key note, which is A in the key of "C." You will learn more about relative minor theory as you progress through the course.

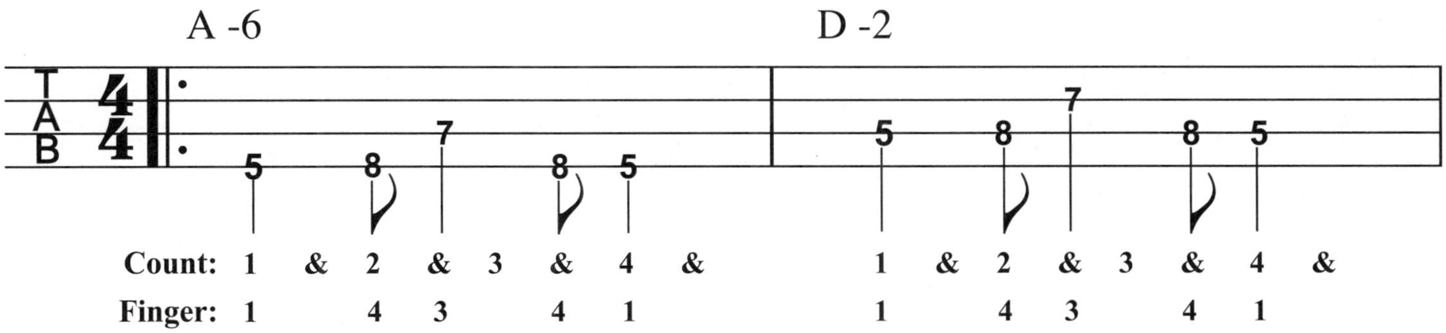

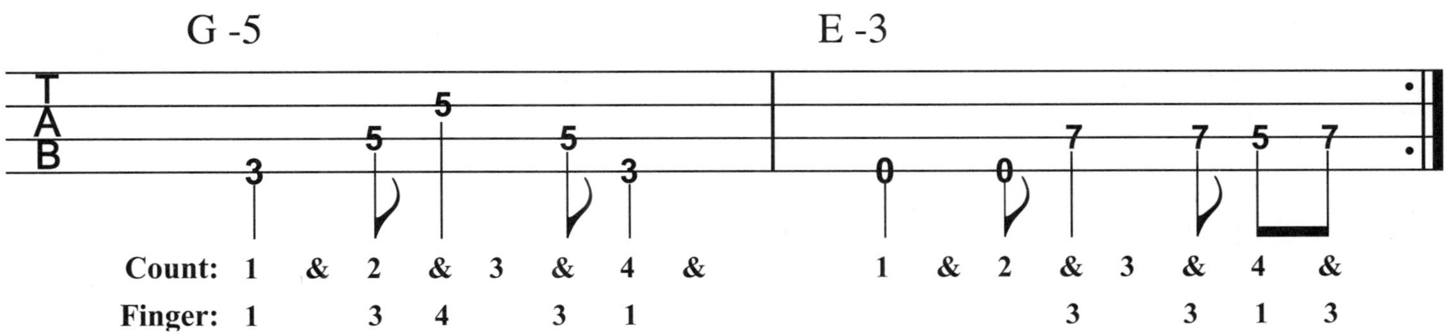

Finger Flexing #2

Here is another exercise that will help develop the coordination of both hands. In this exercise, there's a wide stretch to help open up your hand's reach to play harder passages.

The fret pattern that you are going to use is 1 – 4 – 3 – 4, using alternate plucking. Use the same finger as fret when you play this exercise and line your fingers up in a one finger per fret manner.

Hold your first finger down on each string, this will help to open up your hand and develop a reach while building coordination of both hands. Repeat each measure four times and use alternate plucking. Do the same pattern on all four strings.

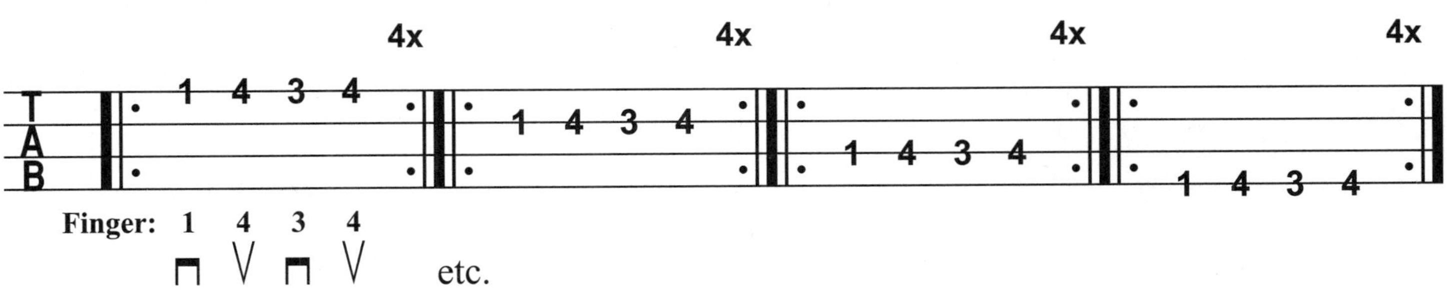

Build up speed gradually. This is a great time to use a metronome to help you gauge your progress. Increase the speed a notch every day to effectively improve your skill.

Music Assignment

Once you feel comfortable playing this pattern across all four strings, do the same pattern doubling each note. The pattern would look like this:

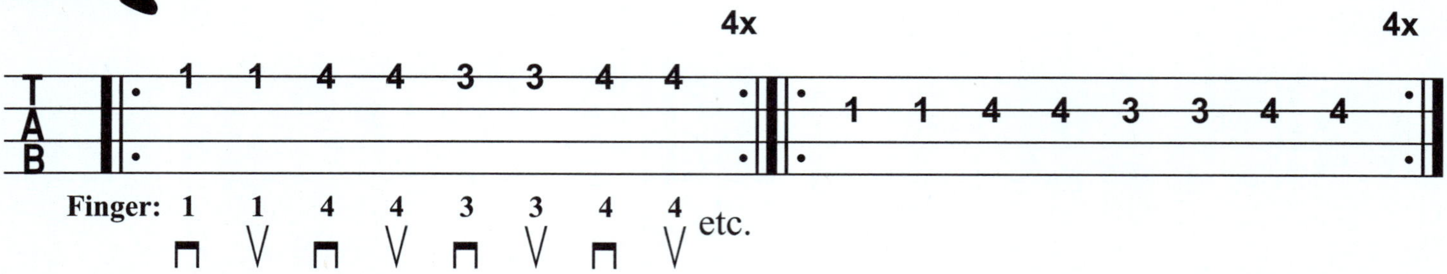

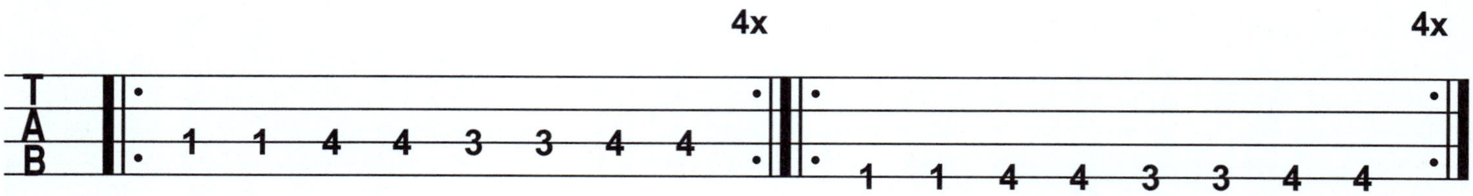

Epic Sun

1 - 5 - 6 - 4 Key of "G"

Here is another variation of the 1 – 5 – 6 – 4 progression in the key of "G". Make sure to pay close attention to the rhythm pattern and count along as you play the rhythm.

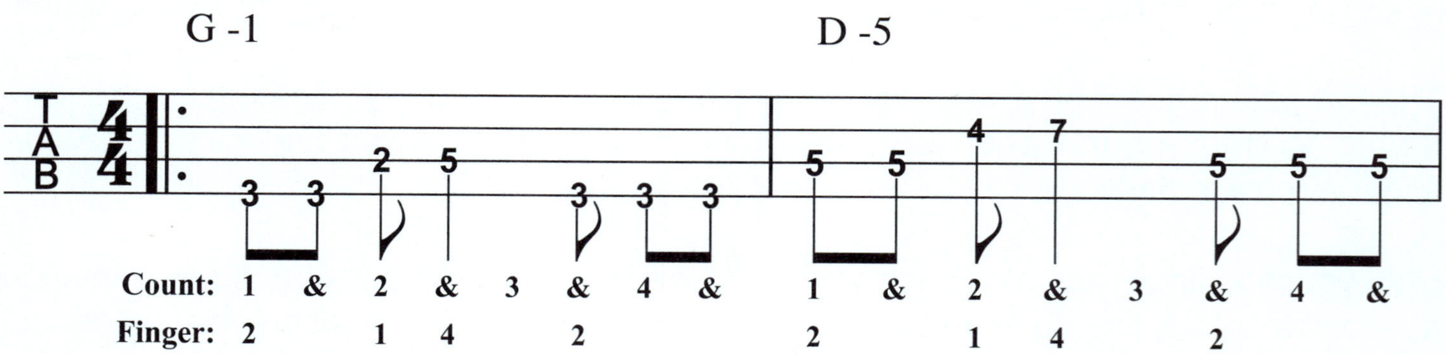

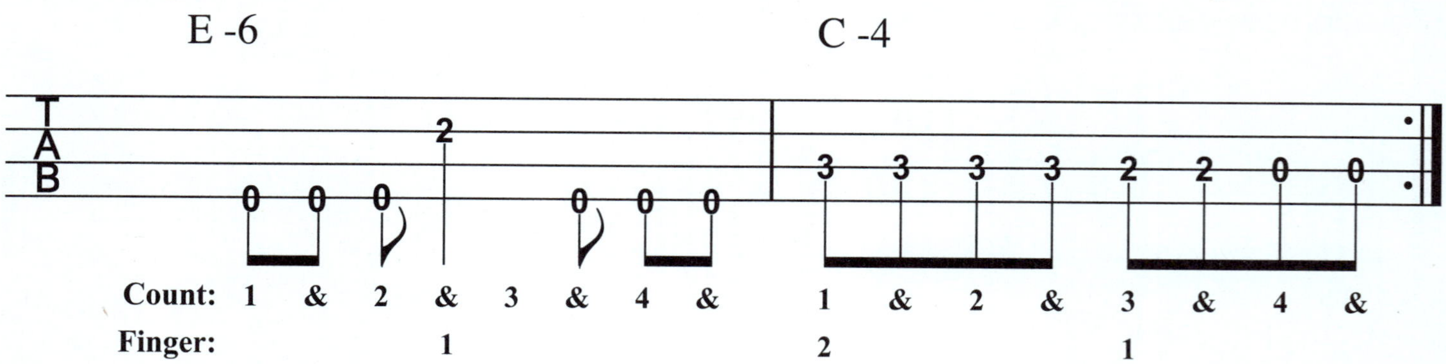

Using a Pick

Although using your fingers to pick the strings is the recommended technique there are times you may want to use a pick to get a different sound. You should hold the pick between your index finger and thumb with the point of the pick facing toward the strings.

Center the pick on the index finger of your right hand.

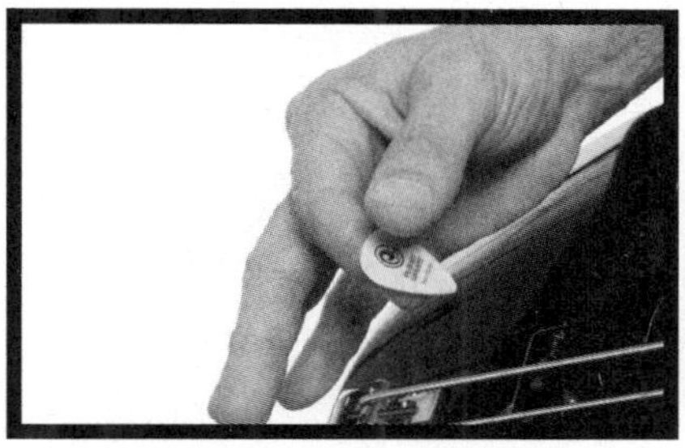

Bring your thumb down on top of the pick. Pinch your thumb and finger together and leave just the tip of the pick showing.

Leave your hand open and your other fingers relaxed (don't make a fist). Your thumb and finger should be placed in the center of the pick, grasping it firmly to give you good control.

Palm Muting

You learned how to use the mute technique to stop the sound completely. Another common way this technique is played is to lightly touch your picking hand against the strings just as they come off the bridge. Make sure not to go too far from the bridge because this will deaden the note completely. Make the notes come out slightly deadened but so you can still hear the pitch of each note. This is used in many genres of music and often in heavy rock music. Play the open 4th string on the next page using a pick to get familiar with this muting technique. Notice the "p.m." followed by a dotted line that indicates palm muting on the staff.

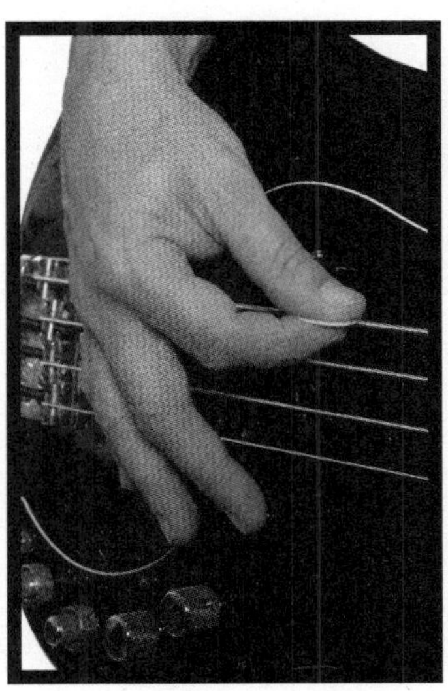

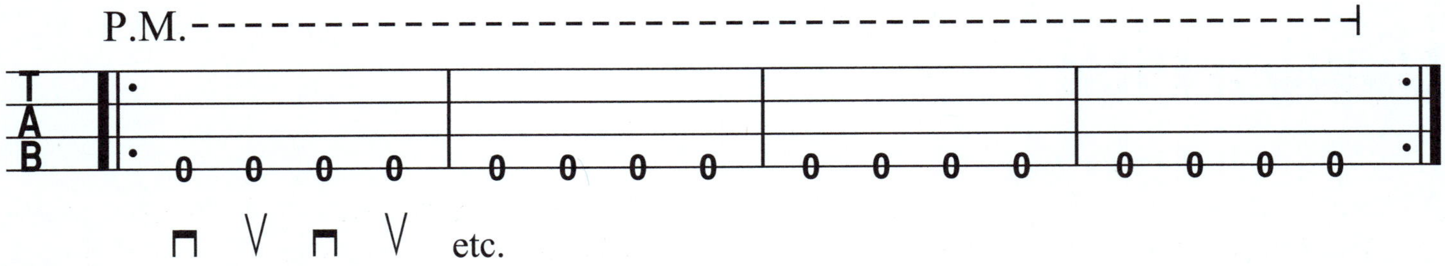

Rockit Center

Applying the Mute Technique

Here is a simple bass line to apply the muting technique. All the notes are on the E and A strings so you can keep a consistent mute on those strings for the entire progression. Use the band backing track to get the full band sensation.

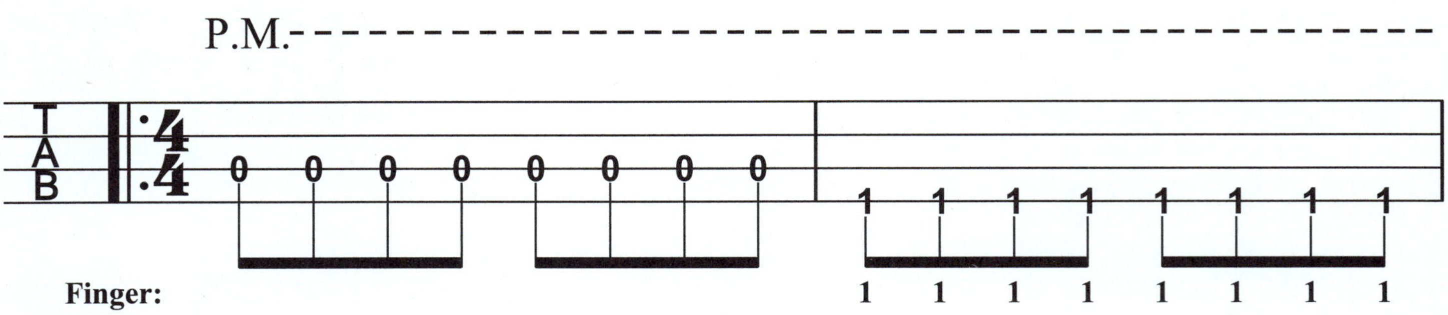

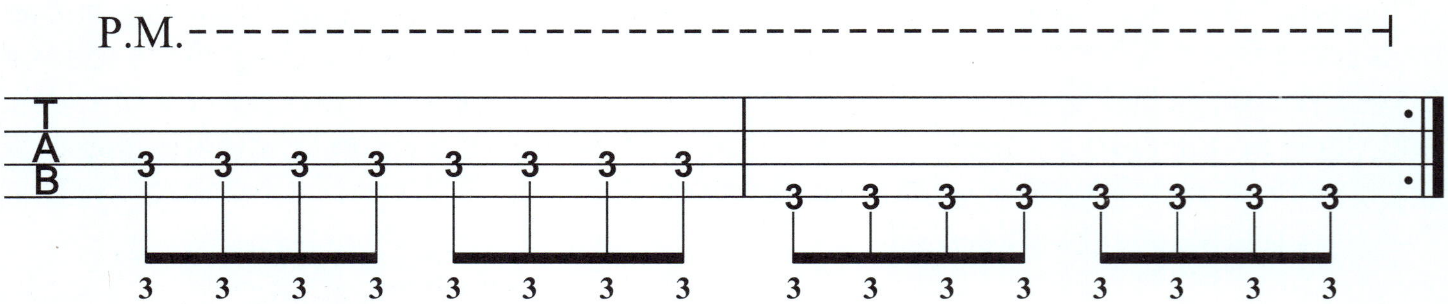

Music Assignment

Apply the muting technique used in this lesson to some of the bass lines you have learned earlier in the book. Adding the mute technique will give each progression a new dynamic sound.

Basic Slap & Pop Technique

Slap and pop is a popular bass plucking technique used in many genres of music. For the slap, make sure to use the side of your thumb slapping the bass string to sound a note. It is a very quick movement and the thumb should not stay on the string. The higher notes are snapped or popped to sound the note. Place your middle finger of the plucking hand under the string and snap it up to generate the sound. Both the slap and pop are very percussive techniques and should be hit and snapped quick and hard.

Slap

Let's start with the slap technique, with the side of your thumb slap your thumb against the 4th string right after the end of the neck as shown in the diagram. Make sure to bounce your thumb off the string right after it hits to allow the note to ring. Play a series of slaps on the 4th string to get familiar with the technique.

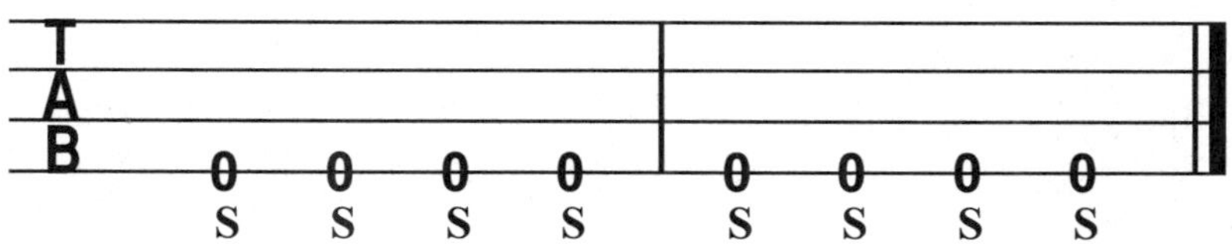

Pop

Now let's go through the pop technique. On your plucking hand, bend your index finger in a hook shape and place it under the 1st string. Pull your hand up keeping it in a locked position. Play a series of pops on the 1st string to get familiar with this technique.

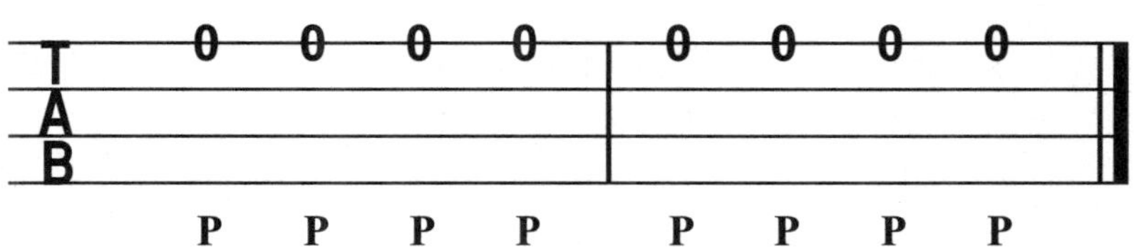

Slap & Pop Exercise

In this example you will slap the open E string and pop the open G string. Once you have the bass line so you can play it smoothly play it along with the backing track.

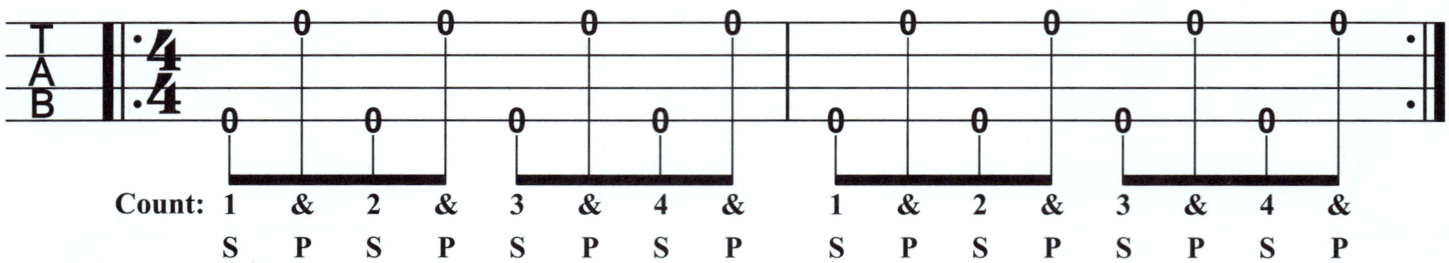

Applying the Slap & Pop Technique

Now let's apply the slap & pop technique into a song. Below is a simple song that will incorporate three octave shapes. Play each separately first then put them together with the backing track. This song is played with a swing or shuffle feel so pay close attention to the backing track for the rhythms timing.

Example 1

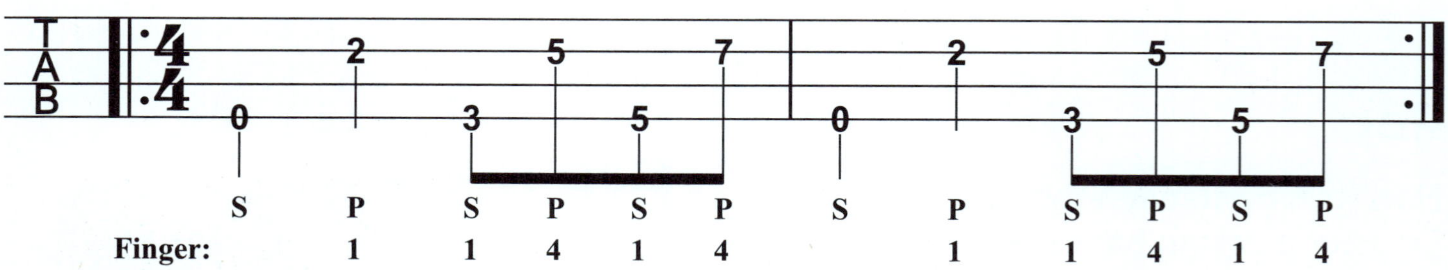

Example 2

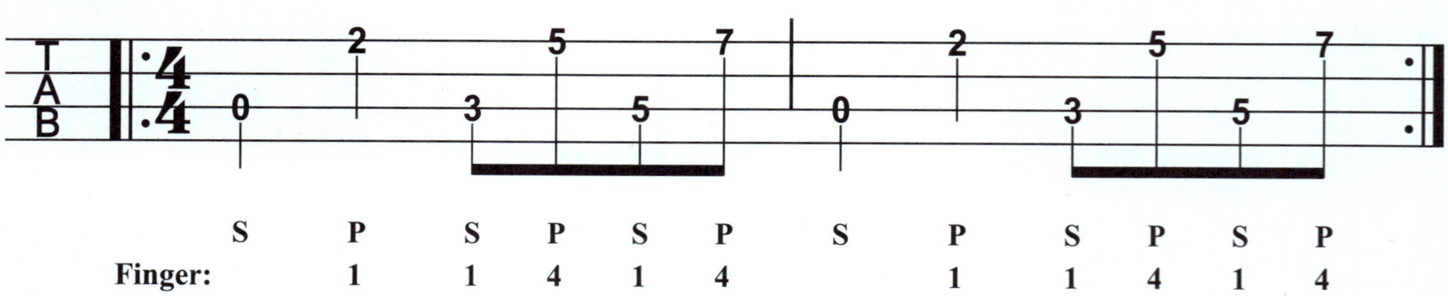

Warm Up Exercises

In this lesson you will learn a warm up routine, great to use when you first start your playing session. A good warm up routine is essential to becoming a good bass player. Once you learn each pattern, continue to play them all the way up the neck using alternate plucking.

Example 1

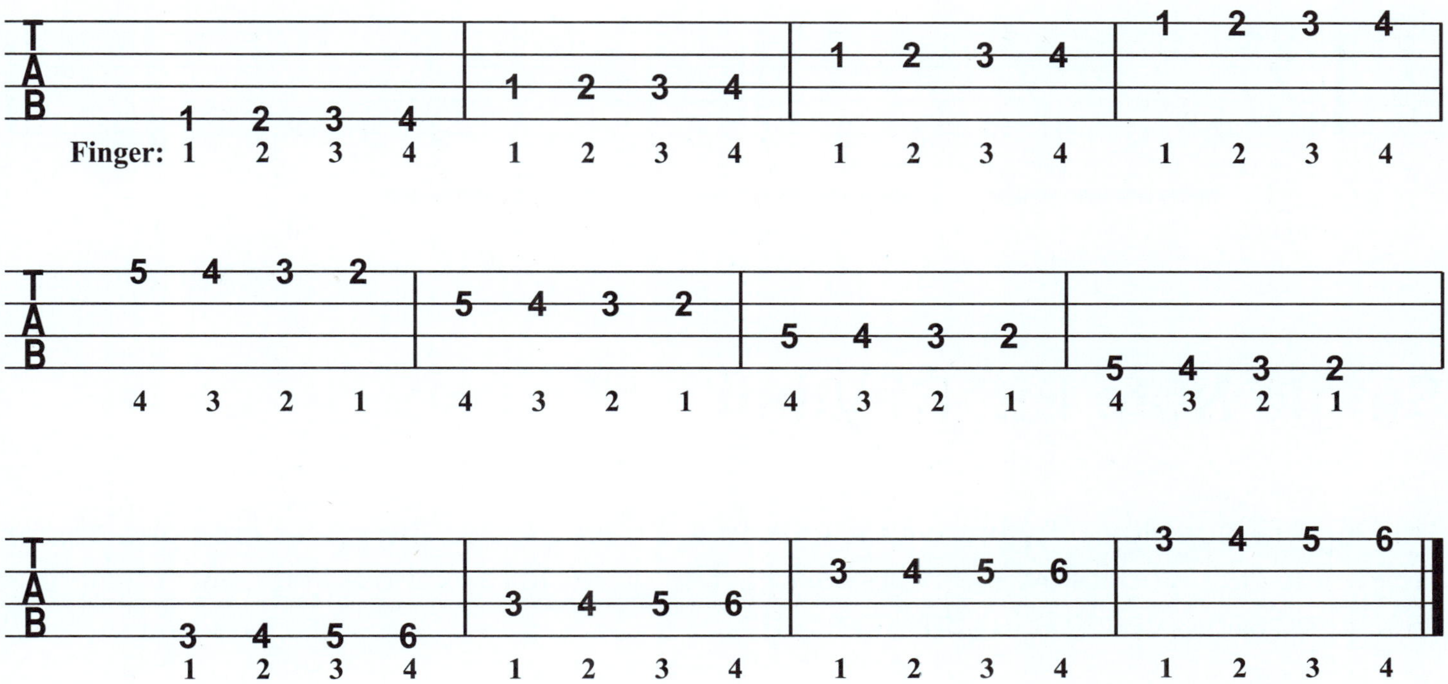

Example 2

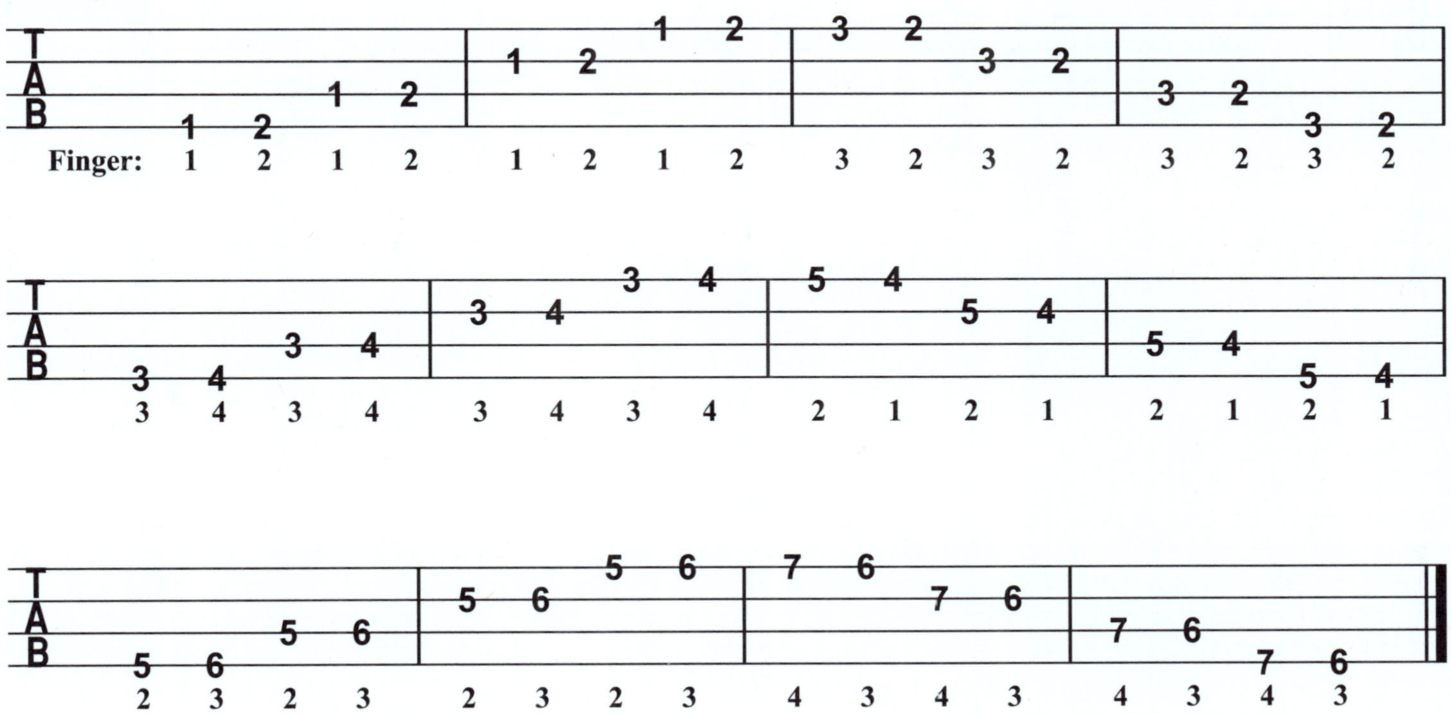

Heavy Bass Progression

This is a simple but effective bass line. The timing is eighth notes until the last two notes which are quarter notes. The last two notes are a half step apart and create a dark sound. This is common in heavy rock or metal music. Make sure to use alternate plucking and play along with the backing track to create a full band sound.

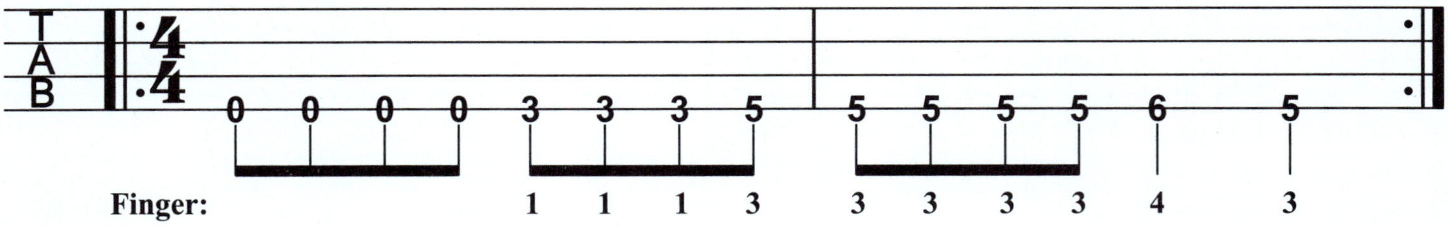

Single Note Riff Rhythm

This is a 12 bar blues rhythm with a rock feel. I have placed the chord changes above the staff to help you follow the progression. The guitar follows the same pattern with the bass in unison creating a full driving sound.

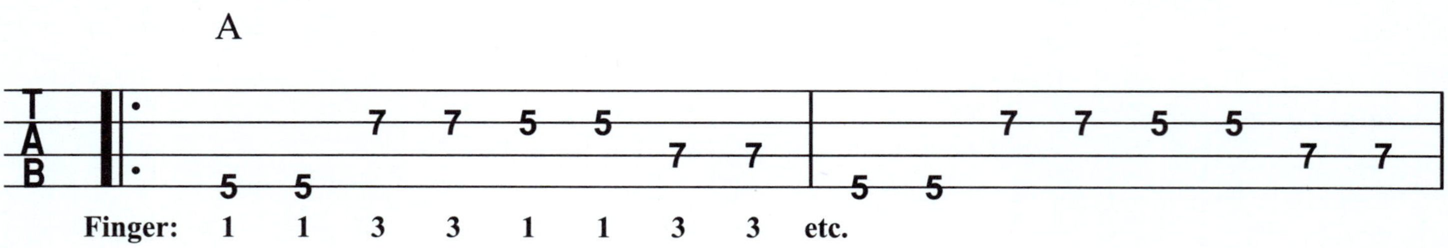

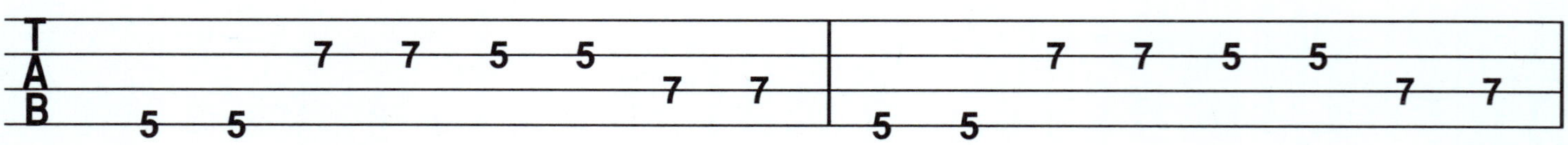

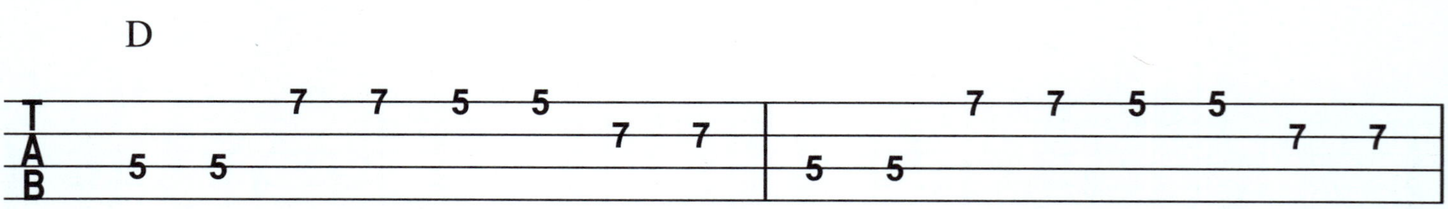

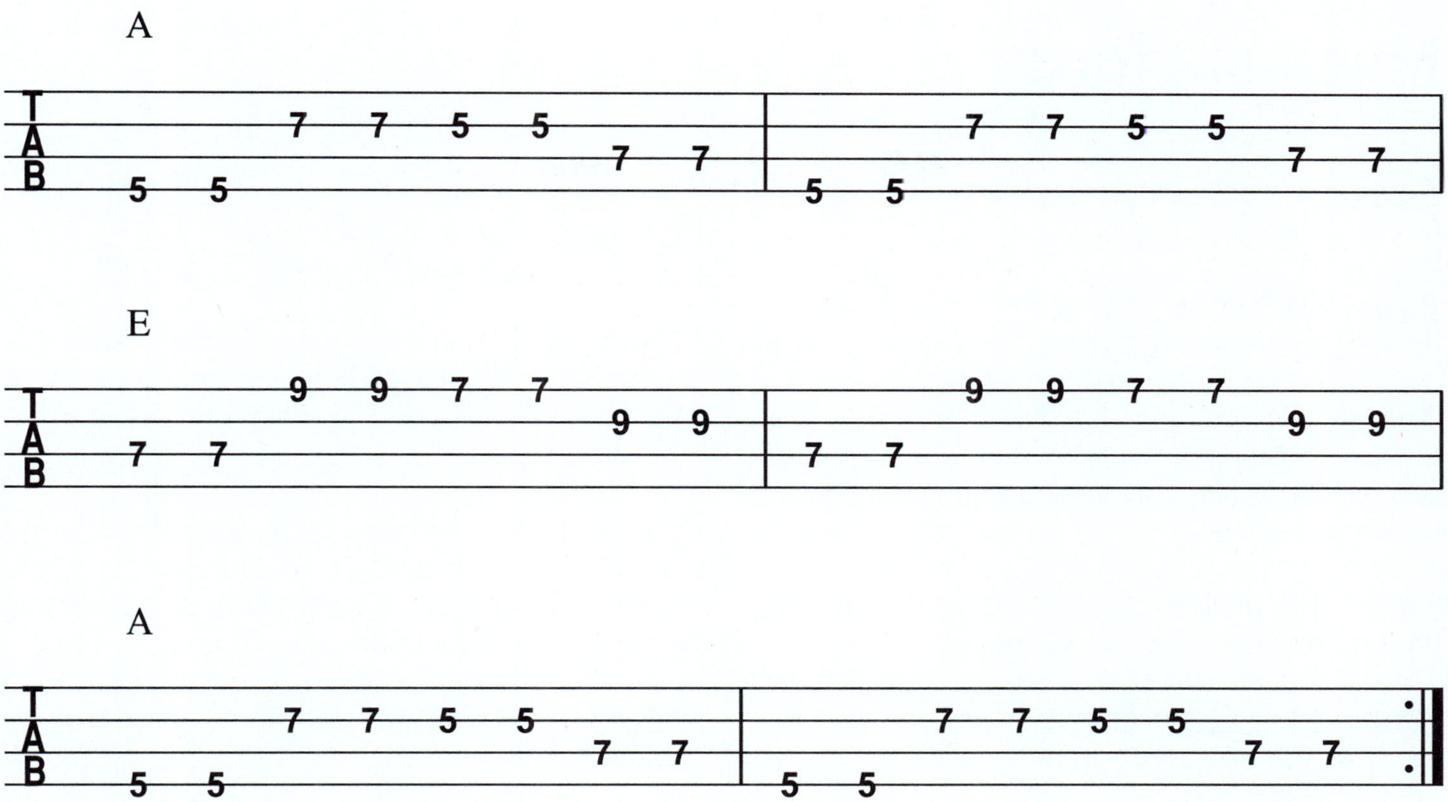

Bass 1 Quiz #4

You're ready to take your next quiz now! Please review all the lessons in the previous section then go to page 4 to see where to take your quiz.

Musical Words

Action – Height of the strings from the fret board to the string itself.

Beat – The regular pulse of music which may be dictated by a metronome, or by the accents in music.

Bridge – The bridge is located on the body of the bass and transfers sound from the strings to the body of the bass. This is held in place by screws or string tension.

Body – The main section of the instrument where the bridge and tailpiece are located.

Fretboard or Fingerboard – The area on top of the neck that you press the string upon to create a note or frequency.

Flat – An accidental symbol placed to the left of a note, indicating that its pitch should be lowered by a half step.

Fret – The metal bars along your fretboard that separate the notes on the neck.

Headstock – Top of the instrument where the tuners or machine heads are located.

Interval – The distance between two pitches.

Machine Head – A device to control the tension of the strings. With a slight turn of the machine head, the player can tighten or loosen the tension to raise or lower the pitch of the string until it is in tune.

Measure – A musical term signifying the smallest division of a song, containing a fixed number of beats, marked off by vertical lines on the staff. The distance between two bar lines on a staff.

Melody – A succession of single tones containing rhythm and pitches arranged as a musical shape.

Neck – The middle of the bass where the strings are stretched over the fretboard.

Nut – Piece of plastic or bone between the headstock and fretboard. Guides the strings from the fretboard to the tuners on the headstock.

Pickguard – Piece of material placed on the body of the bass to protect it from pick scratches.

Pickup – Device that takes the string vibration that you create and transform it into an electronic signal. This signal it then used in amplifiers to boost the sound.

Pop – A plucking technique where you put a finger under the string and pull or snap upward to sound the note. Usually played with the index or middle fingers on the higher strings.

Saddles – Piece on the bridge that holds the string in place.

Scale – A series of notes in ascending or descending order that presents the pitches of a key or mode, beginning and ending on the tonic of that key or mode.

Sharp – An accidental symbol placed to the left of a note, indicating that its pitch should be raised by a half step.

Slap – The technique in which the string is being struck with the side of the thumb to sound a note. Very much like hammers on a piano strike the strings.

Tempo – The speed of the rhythm of a composition. Tempo is measured according to beats per minute.

Timing – The beat of musical rhythm. The controlled movement of music in time.

Triplet – Three notes of equal length that are to be performed in the duration of two notes of equal length.

Truss Rod – A long rod inside your bass neck used for stabilizing a wooden neck to its proper angle.

Changing a String

Old bass strings may break or lose their tone and become harder to keep in tune. You might feel comfortable at first having a teacher or someone at a music store change your strings for you, but eventually you will need to know how to do it yourself. Changing the strings on a bass is not as difficult as it may seem and the best way to learn how to do this is by practicing. Bass strings are fairly expensive so it's important to get it right the first time you try to restring your bass. How often you change your strings depends entirely on how much you play your bass, but if the same strings have been on it for months, it's probably time for a new set.

Before removing the old strings from the bass, examine the way it is attached to and try to duplicate that with the new string. On some electric basses, the string may need to be threaded through a hole in the back of the body.

Follow the series of photos below for a basic description of how to change a string. Before trying it yourself, read through the quick tips for beginners on the following page.

Loosen the string.

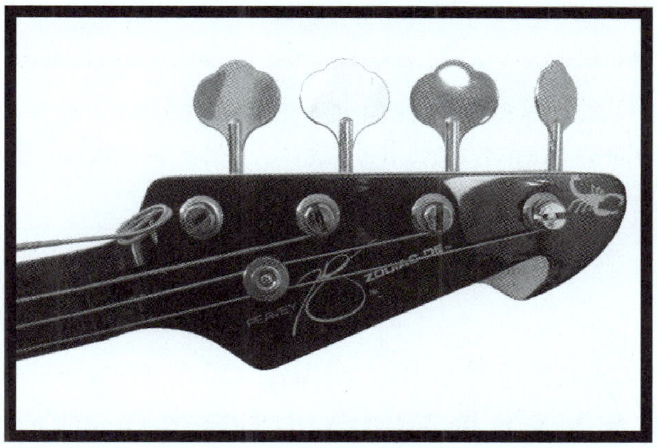

Remove the old string from the post.

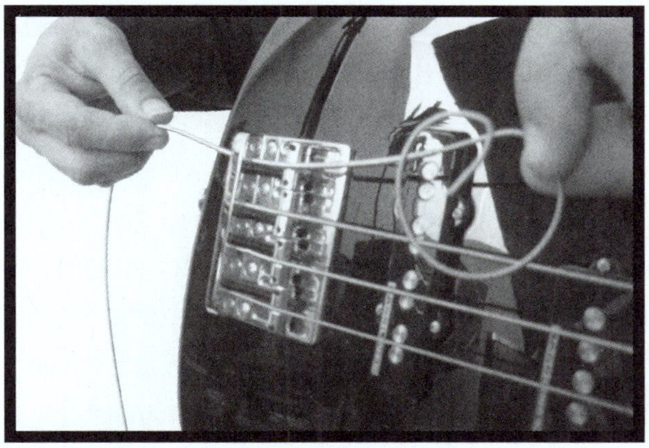

Pull the string through the bridge and discard it.

Remove the new string from the packaging and uncoil it.

Thread the end of the new string through the bridge.

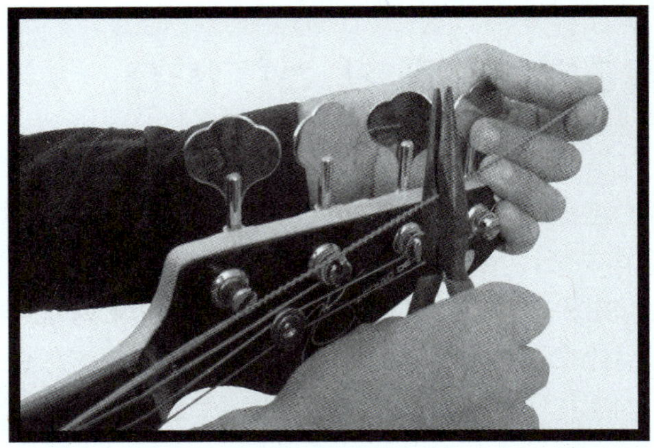

Cut the excess length from the string.

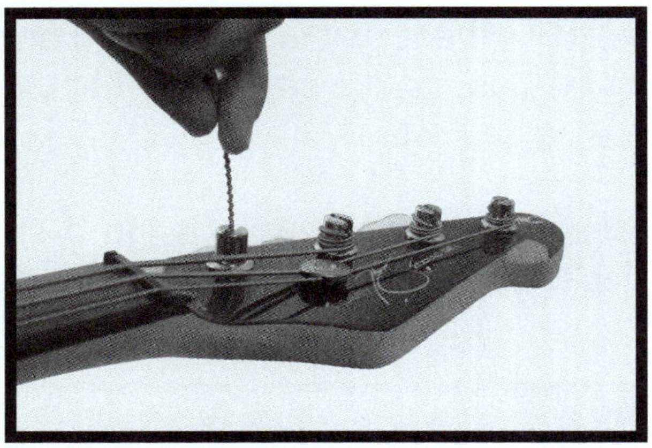

Hold the string in place just after the nut with your finger and tighten up the slack in the string with the machine head.

Carefully tighten the string and tune it to the proper pitch.

You can cut the old string off the bass but you may want to unwind it instead and save it as a spare in case you break a string later. Check to make sure you have the correct string in your hand before putting it on the bass. The strings may be color coded at the end to help you identify them.

Thread the new string through the bridge and cut the end of the string approximately three inches past the tuner you are anchoring the string to. Insert the cut end into the top of the machine head and bend the string around it. Be sure to wind the string around the tuning post in the proper direction (see photos). The string should wind around the post underneath itself to form a neat coil. Once the extra slack is taken up and the string is taught, tune it very gradually to pitch, being careful not to over tighten and accidentally break the new string. Check the ends of the string to make sure it is sitting correctly on the proper bridge saddle and space on the nut. New strings will go out of tune very quickly until they are broken in. You can gently massage the new string with your thumbs and fingers once it's on the bass, slightly stretching the string out and helping to break it in. Then retune the string and repeat this process a few times for each string.

Bass Triads

A Major

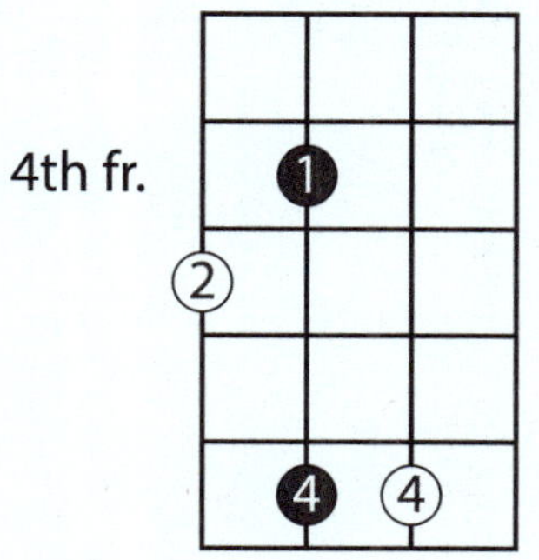

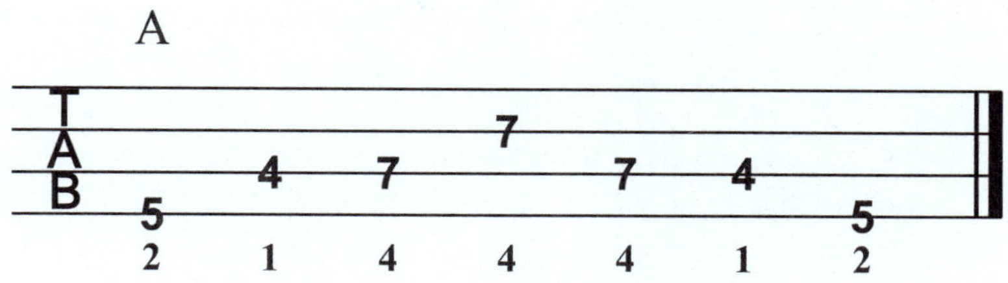

A Major

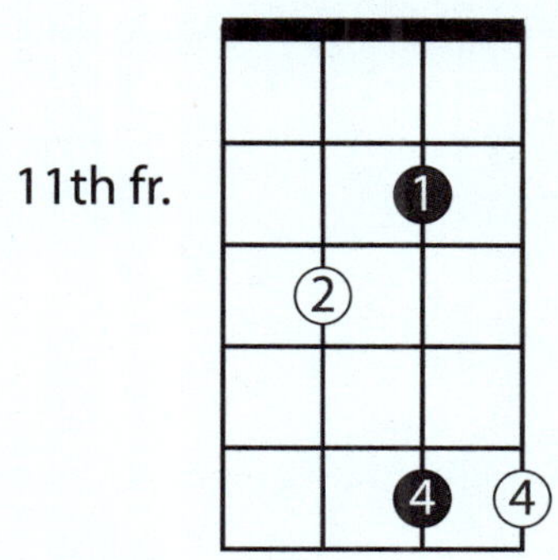

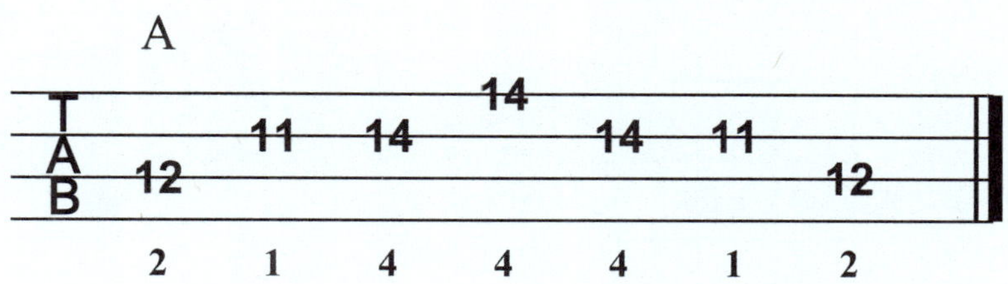

A Minor

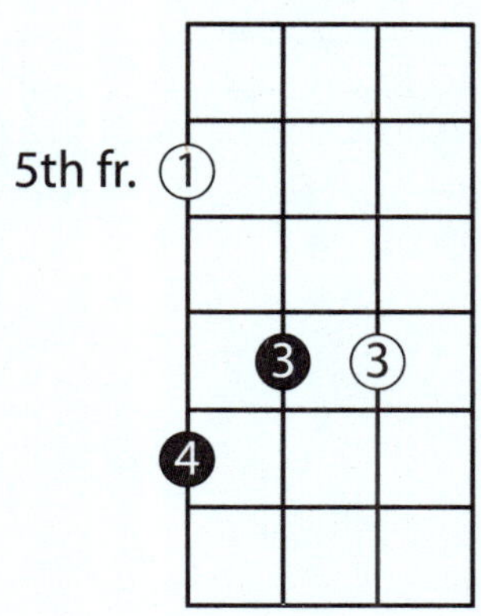

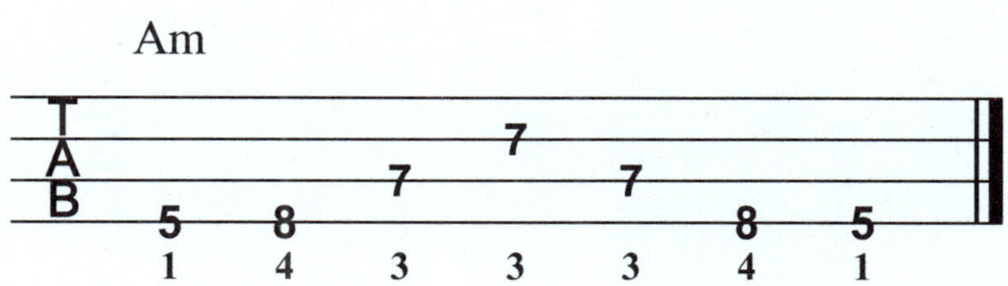

A Minor

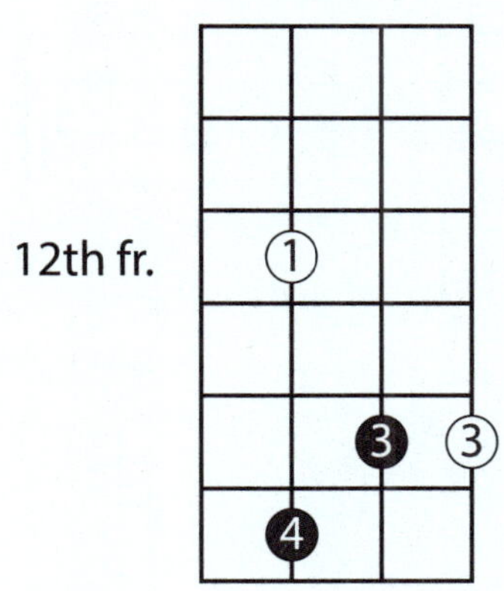

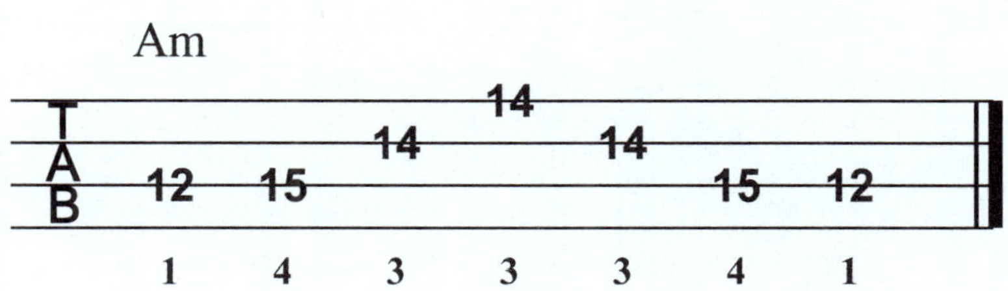

B Major

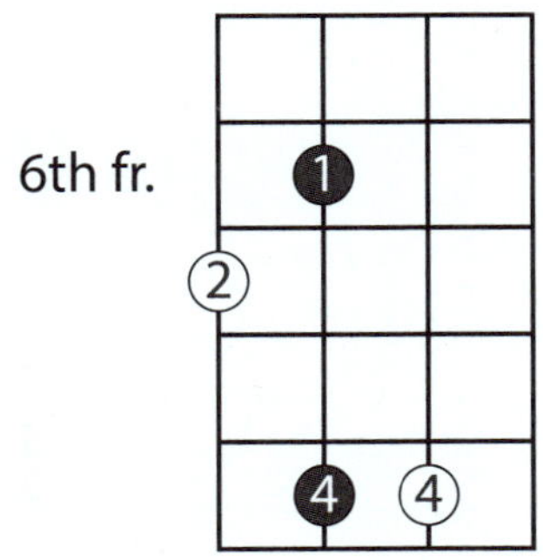

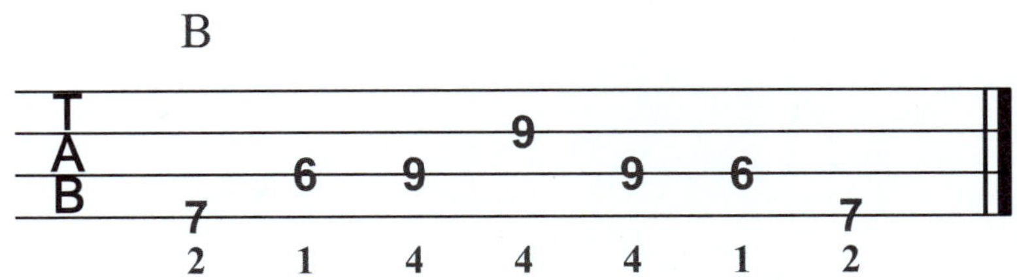

B Major

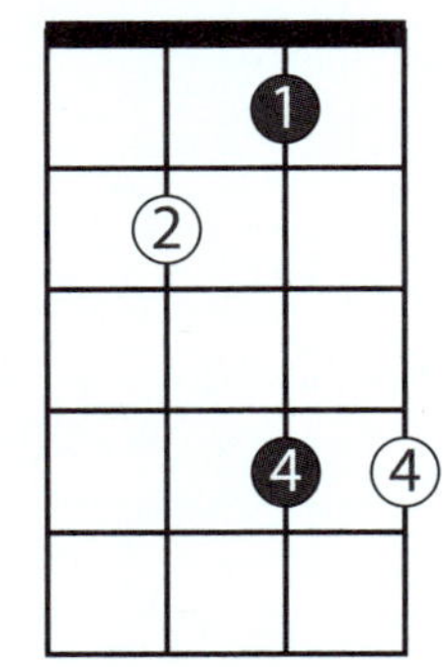

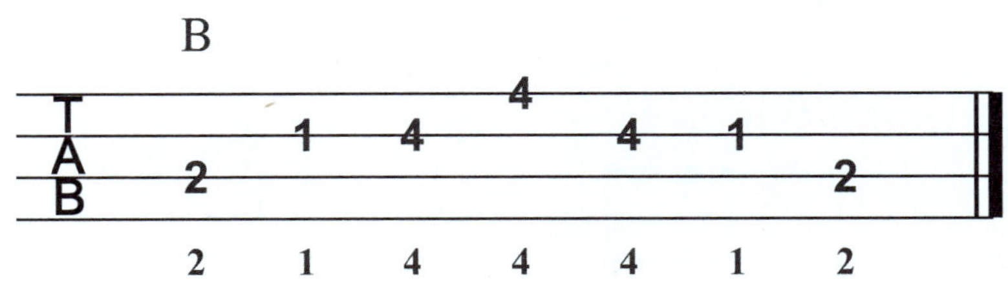

B Minor

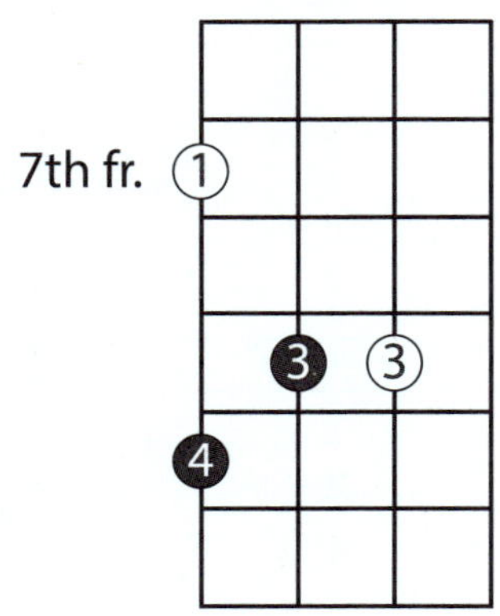

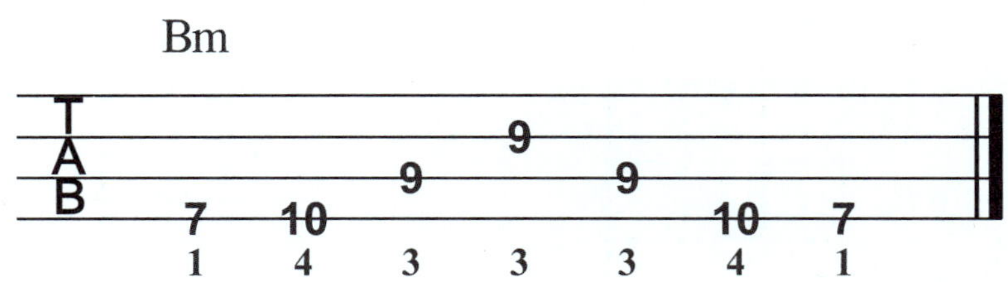

B Minor

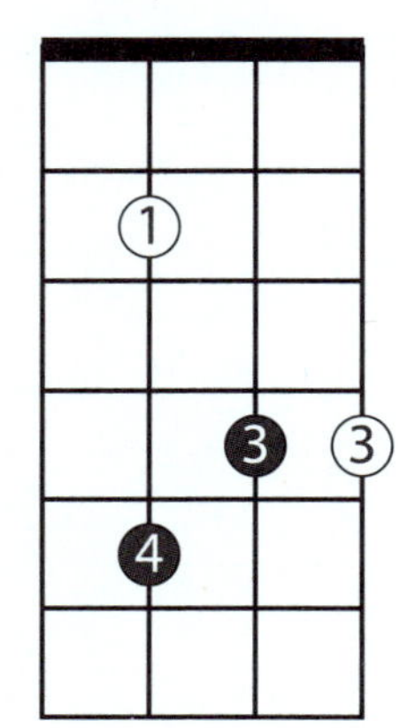

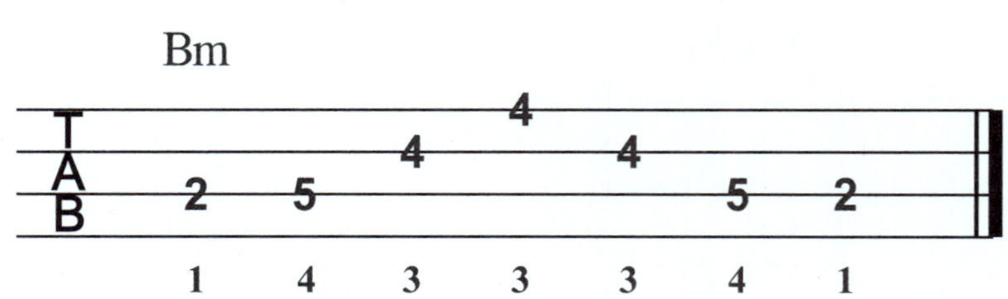

C Major

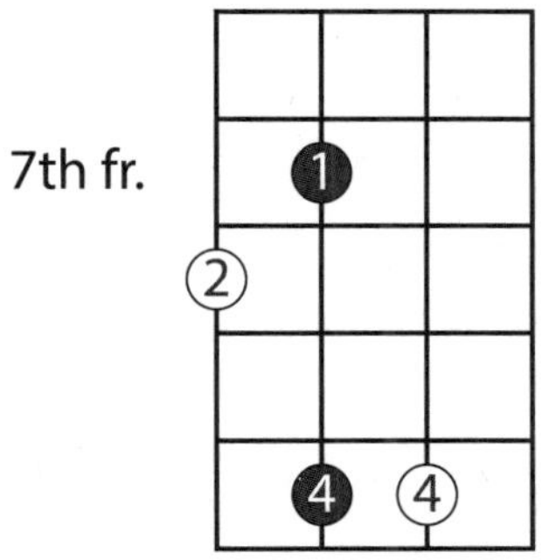

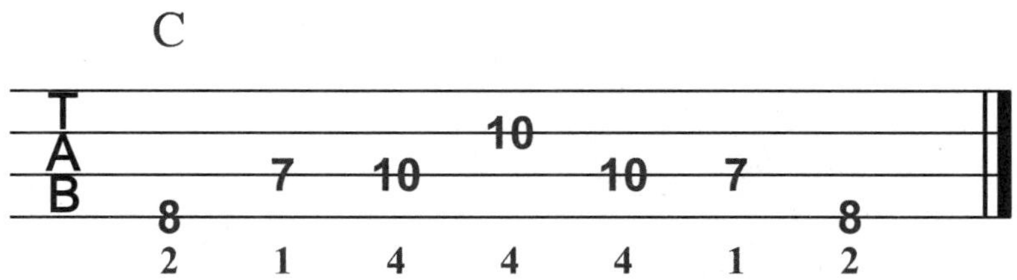

C Major

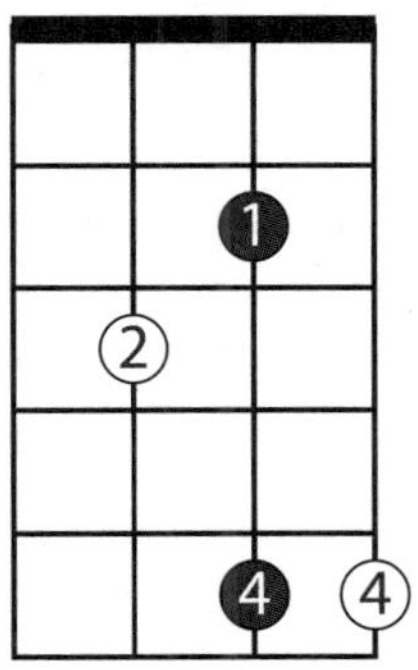

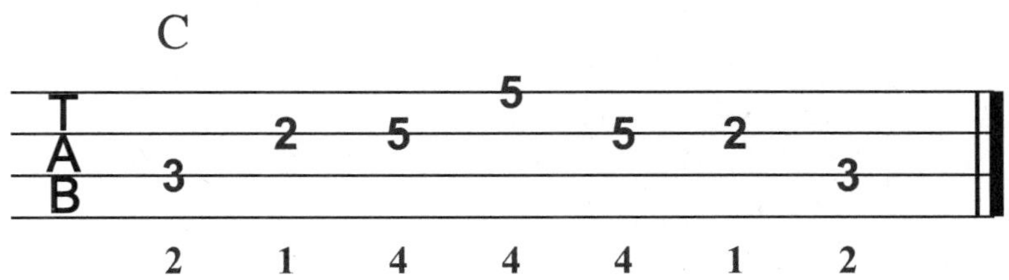

C Minor

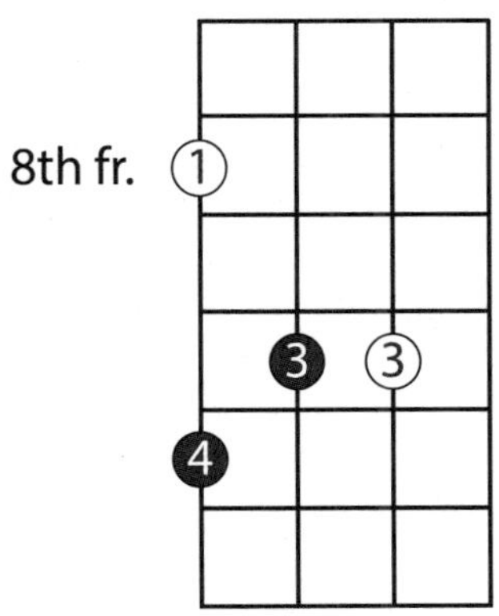

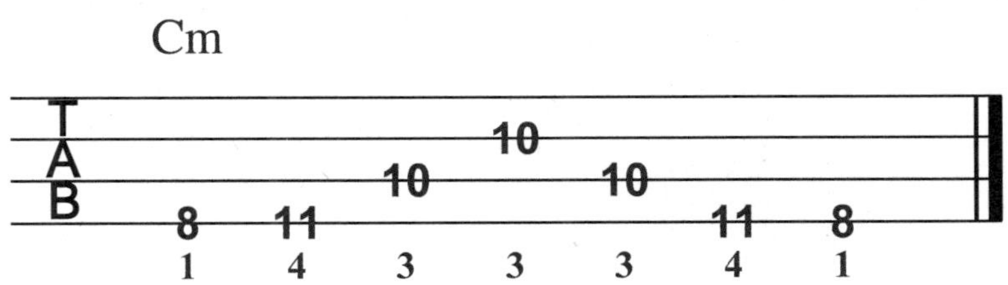

C Minor

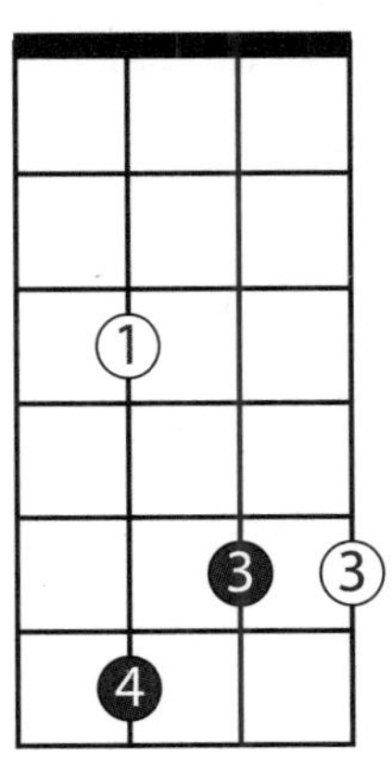

D Major

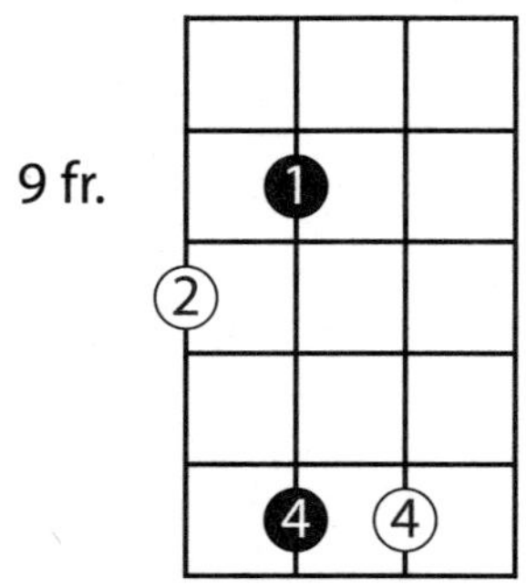

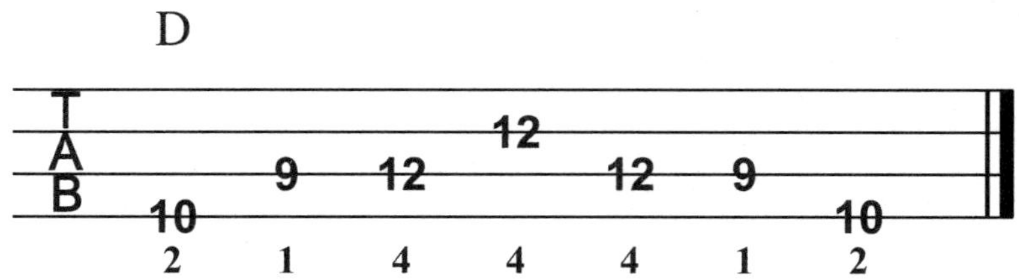

D Major

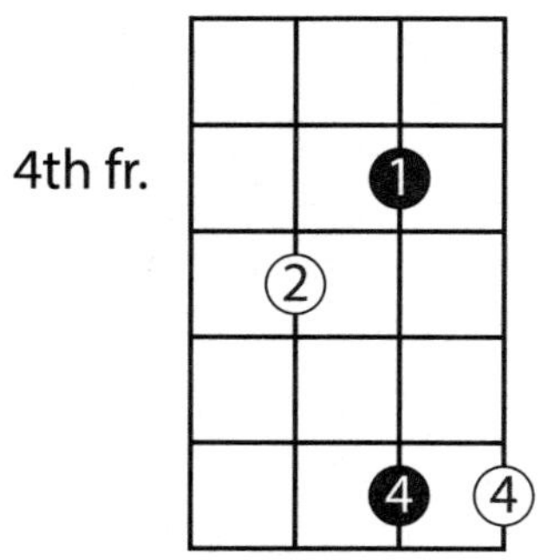

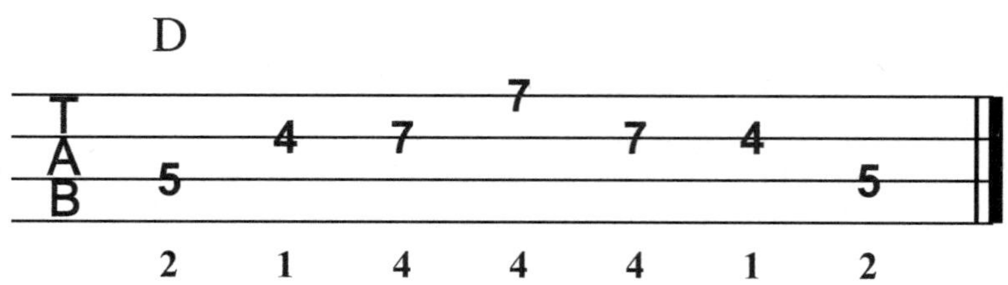

D Minor

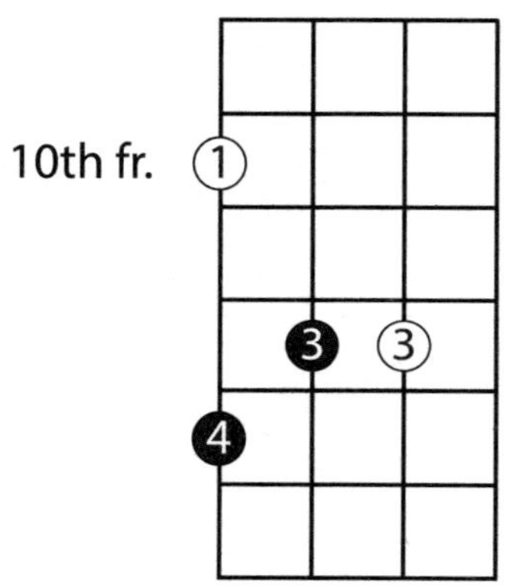

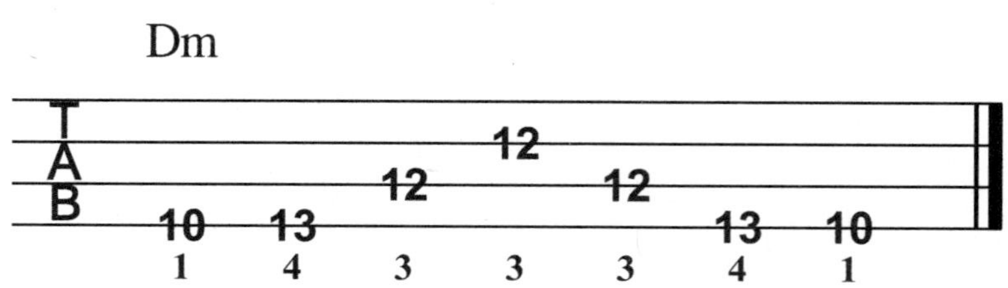

D Minor

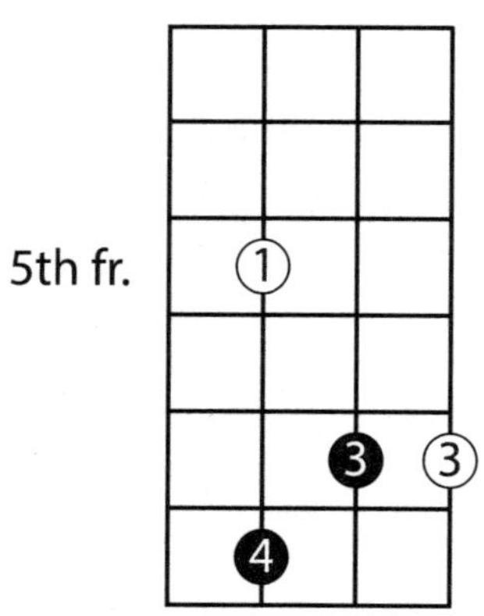

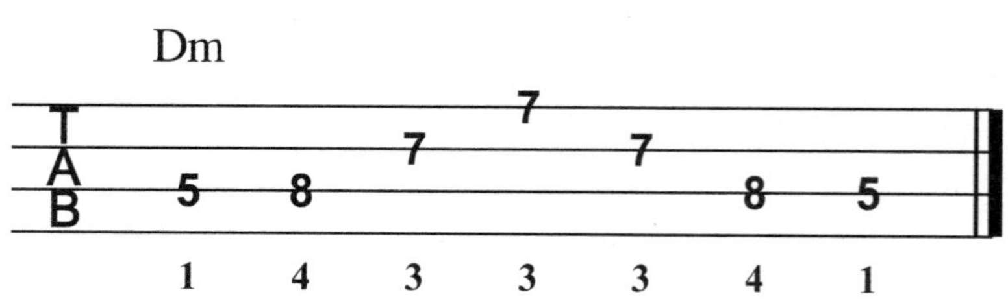

E Major

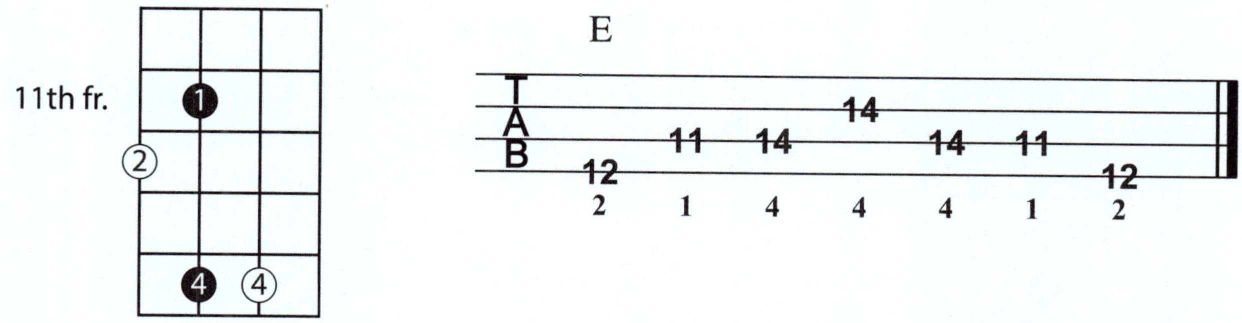

E Major

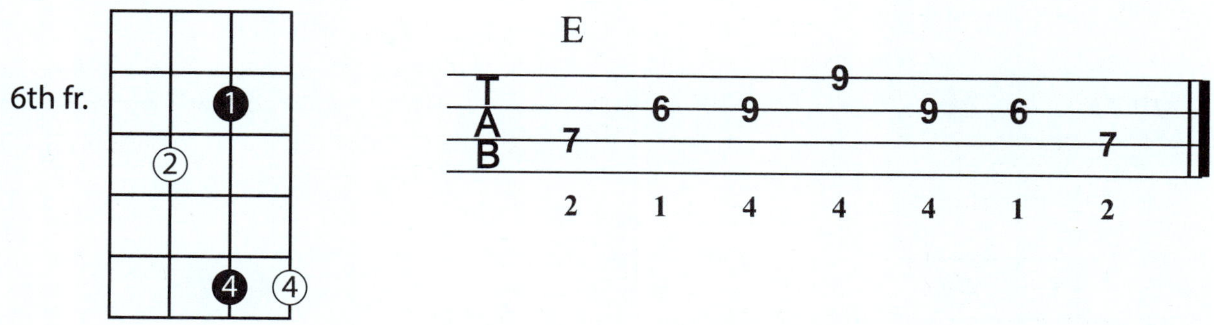

E Minor

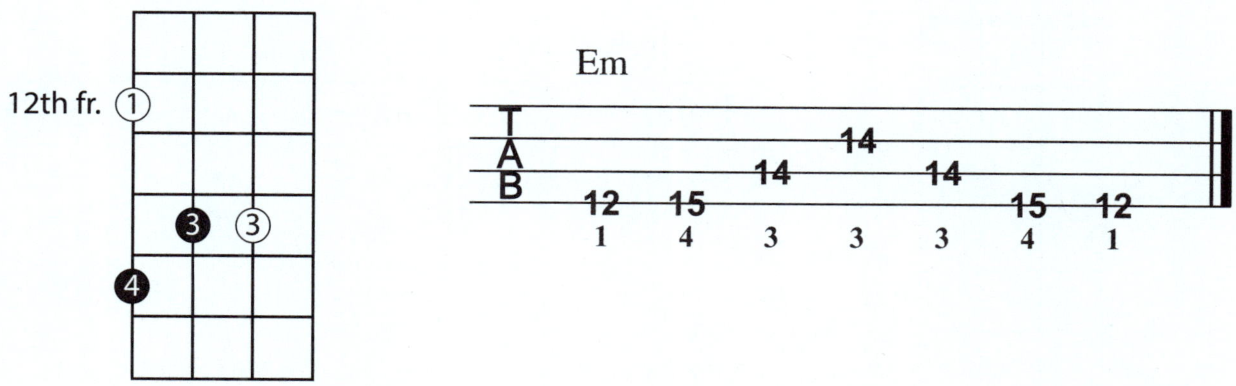

E Minor

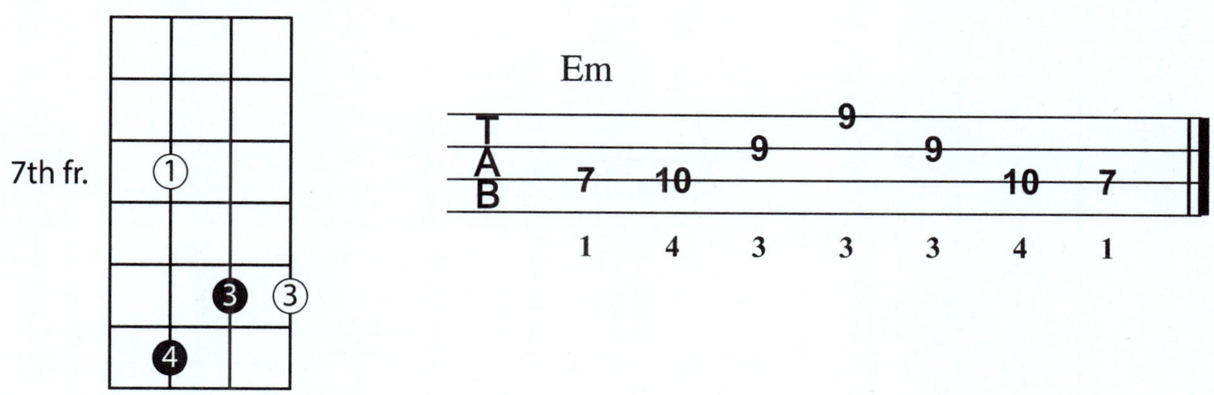

F Major

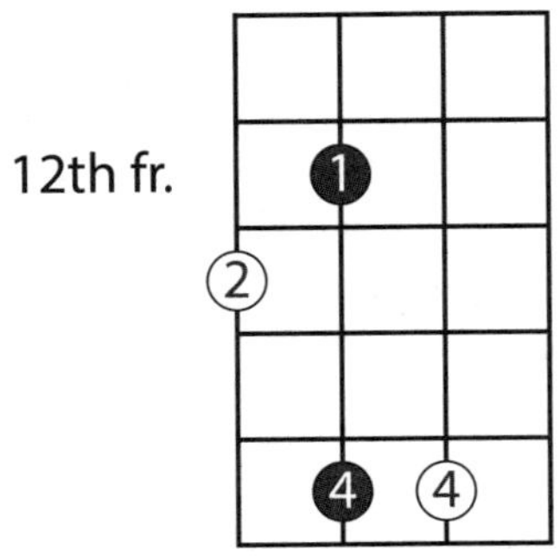

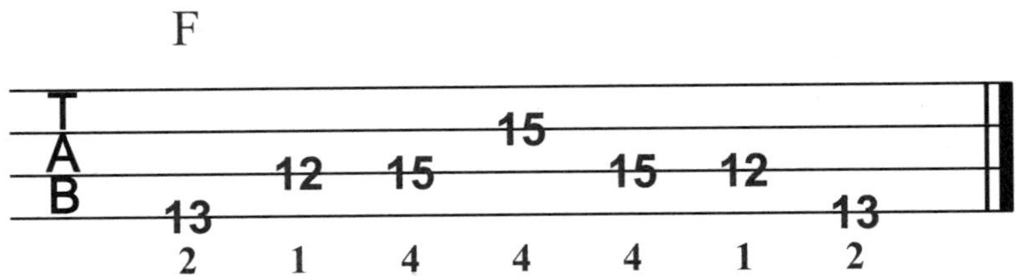

F Major

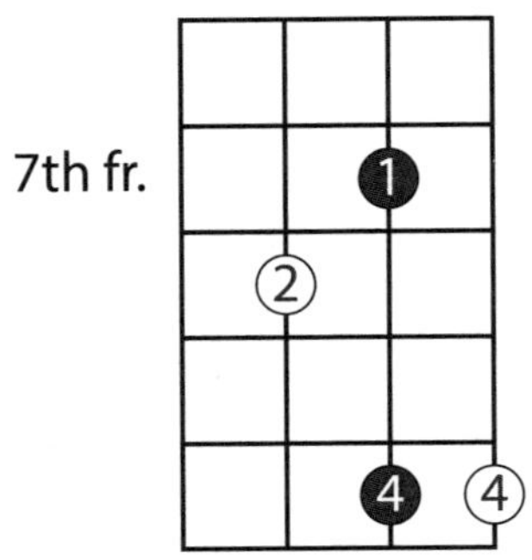

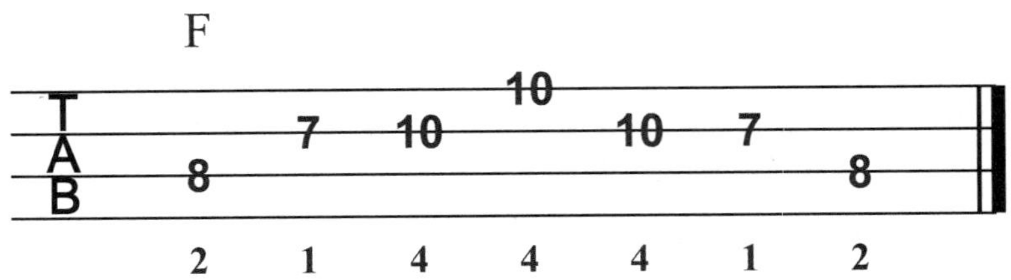

F Minor

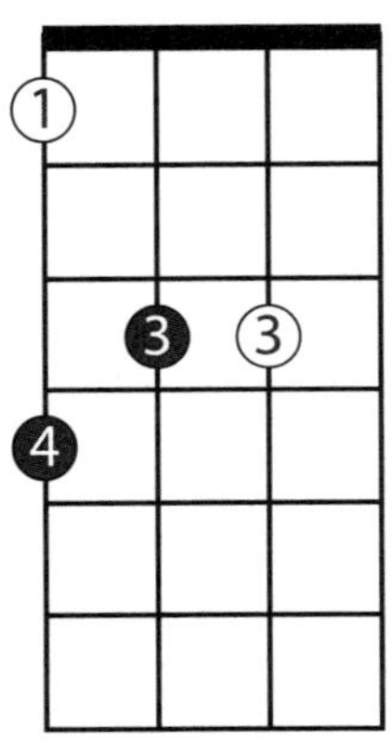

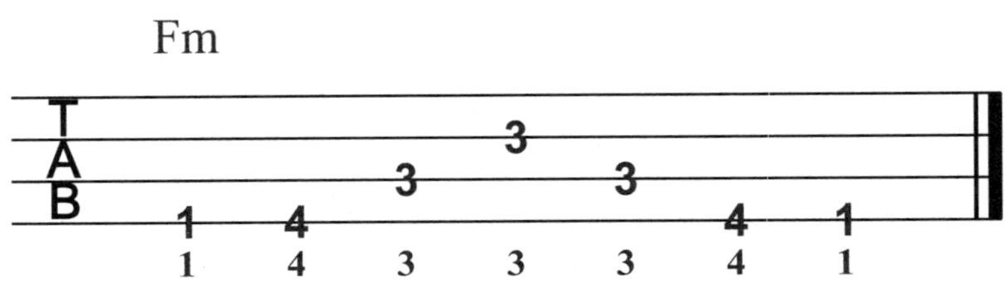

F Minor

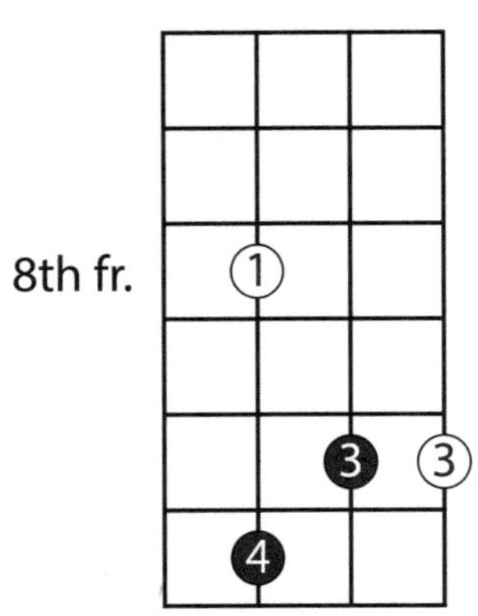

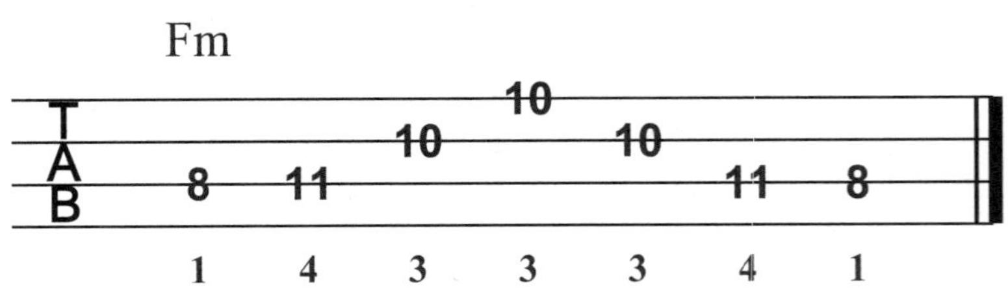

G Major

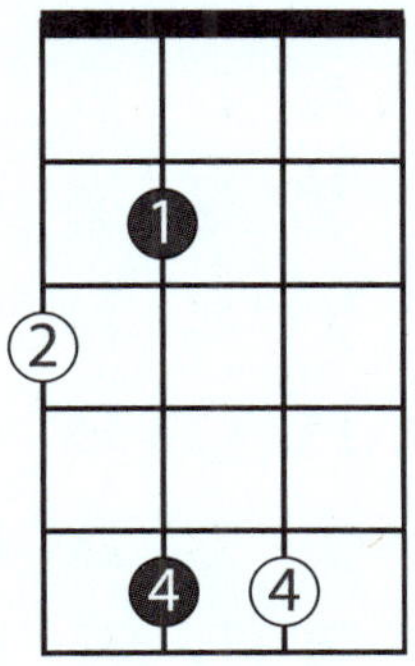

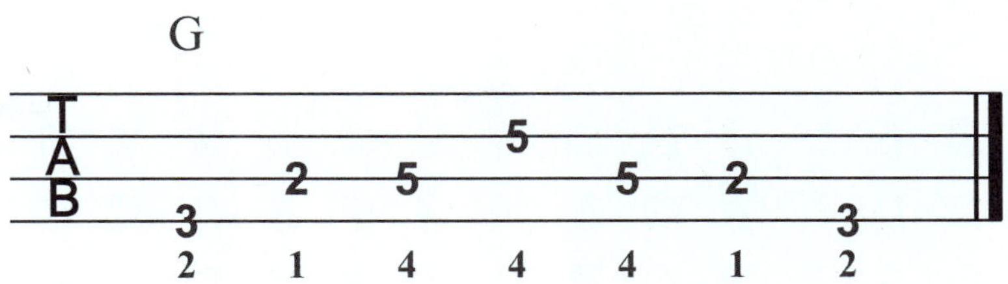

G Major

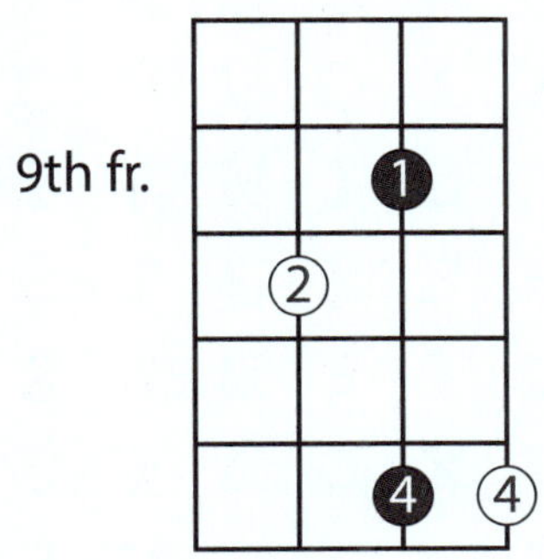

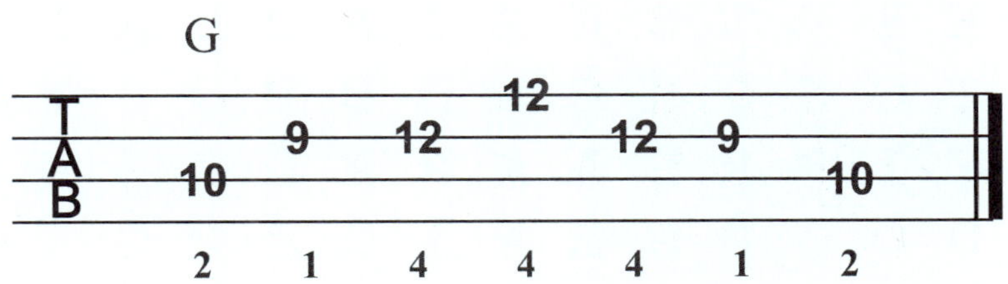

G Minor

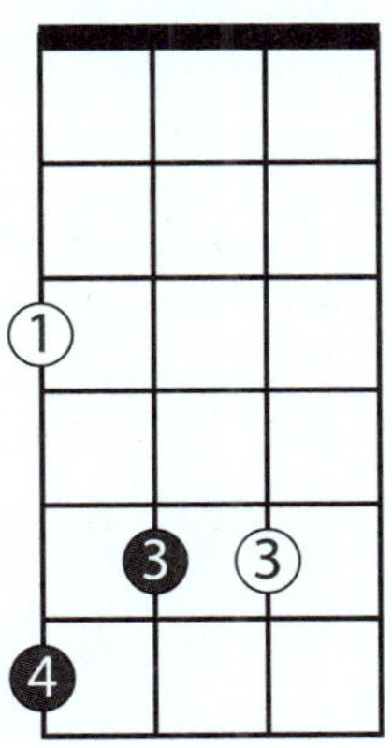

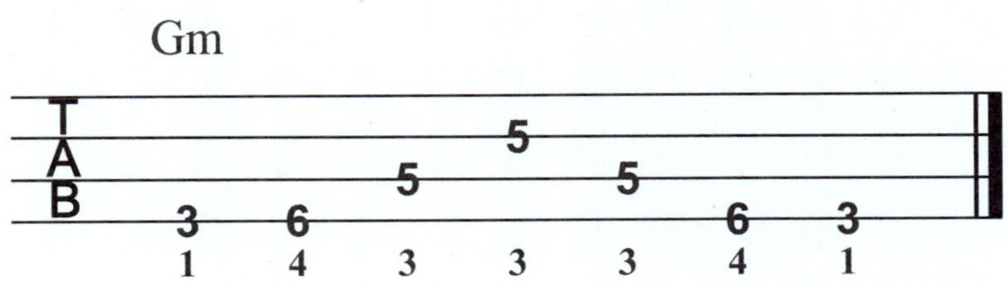

G Minor

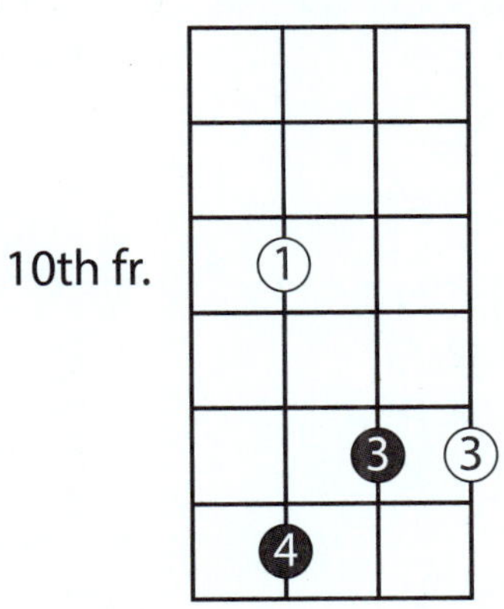

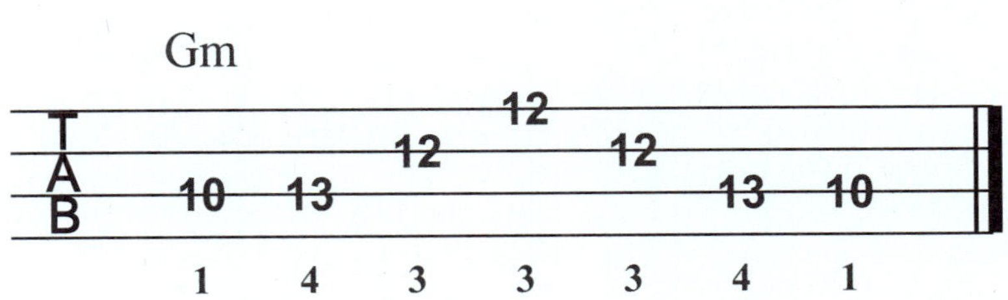

Word Search

T M E U Y J R D L S C L M V H M P U N D R I H T S

O L A D A W G A Z G F J O X G N J O X G Y F C Q Z

T X O J I T C E D Y F Y D K L P I I T E N O F L A

I N C U O D R H Q J Z R F I N S B B M O B B D F R

U W T R L R G E J S C I J F S A I J I L A M Z K N

P P A W M C P N V A K D B E I X K B E D S M A M X

K A V I Y V N I A Q P O R X H R C B D N S L R R G

M C E E V T S H S J A G H A R S O S N B J N T O K

B S T C S S K C N D O F O J Y I R X I G V H Q G N

L O Y I P R D A K R F L Z Z W J B L C I W S I W X

N W D O Q P N M P I C E P G H W U R E X J T S I N

J I Y Q H X J J F P S C L O C A C J I F B Z E R H

W Q T J D M N T O L J S T A P T A J X D B W U U G

Q S Q T D F H I G D E T E Y C J B E M H G V L N U

P M A H L X Y U E L R G H T W S G R P Q L E B A D

K F P Z J W B J A V V L T R I P L E T Y B L Y X A

F C H M H U N X V Y A Y K C D G U I Q K U L E E N

J F C Y R D Y H T O O R K O U H Q A Y O D E B T G

X M Q I A W O B H J D H B M U T E B L K W K E C D

O V V I H R G U Y A L V M X R U Q I W X N J B T U

H I R A C L V A W Y B A C B P D S H U F Z H V J D

O T E Z J S D C E V O Z P A A P S Y M D X Z M E D

W U T Z R K B U E I E G U T M L W Q L S H E M X H

V X S P W E C G S M I N O R A G A D K N P Q F J M

V P S G N O Z M A V B Q R P W B K B Q L N C T N F

Search Words:

- BASS
- BLUES
- BRIDGE
- FIFTH
- MACHINE HEAD
- MAJOR
- MINOR
- MUTE
- NOTE
- OCTAVE
- POP
- PROGRESSION
- RIFF
- ROCK
- SCALE
- SLAP
- THIRD
- TRIAD
- TRIPLET

Crossword Puzzle

Across

2. Lowers a notes pitch one half step
4. Raises a notes pitch one half step
5. Eight scale degrees above the root
7. Sounding a note by striking it with the side of your thumb
9. A device that clicks at an adjustable rate to help with timing
10. The 12 notes that make up all music
11. Type of note receiving 4 beats

Down

1. Short and detached
3. Three notes played in one beats time
6. Type of note receiving 1 beat
7. A group of notes that are in the same key
8. A symbol that tells you there will be a period of silence

Answer Keys

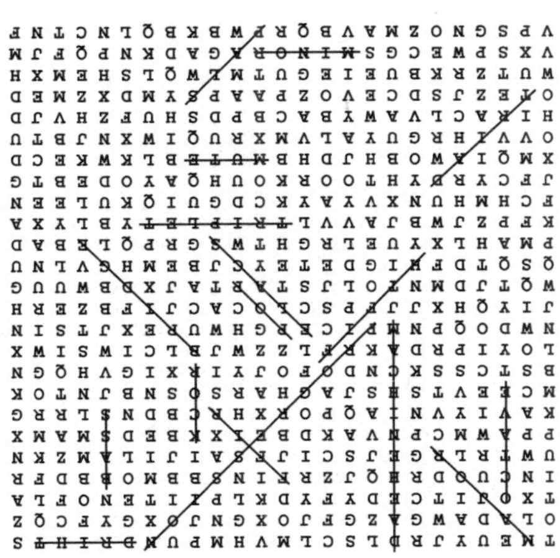

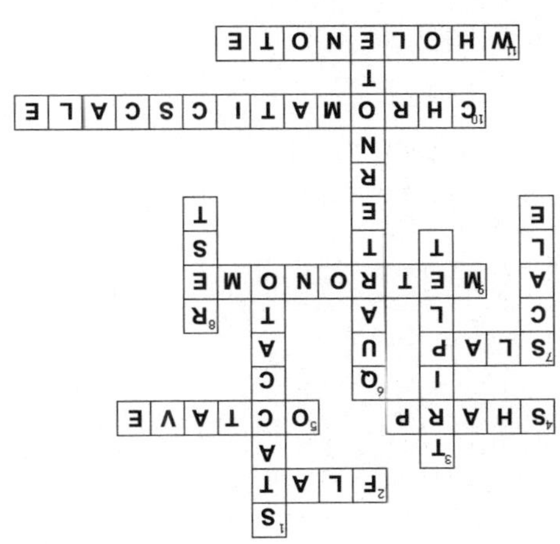

Rock House

LEARN BASS 2

The Method For a New Generation

Book 2 Videos	Book 2 Audio	Book 2 Worksheets
bit.ly/41HJbyK	bit.ly/4hEFMa4	https://bit.ly/41MmnOu

The Rock House Method

Presents

Learn BASS 2

Written & Method By: John McCarthy

Adapted By: Jimmy Rutkowski
Supervising Editor: John McCarthy
Music Transcribing & Engraving: Jimmy Rutkowski
Production Manager: John McCarthy
Layout, Graphics & Design: Jimmy Rutkowski
Photography: Jimmy Rutkowski, Rodney Dabney
Copy Editors:
Cathy McCarthy & John McCarthy

Cover Art Direction & Design:
Jimmy Rutkowski

HL00156775
ISBN 978-1-4950-5943-8
Produced by McCarthy Publishing®

Table of Contents

My Mojo Is Back

Shuffle Blues 1 - 4 - 5

Here is a blues shuffle rhythm in the key of "A." This rhythm is a common 1 – 4 – 5 progression. I've included the chord change on top of the staff so you can see the progression clearly. Make sure to use the backing track to create a full band sensation.

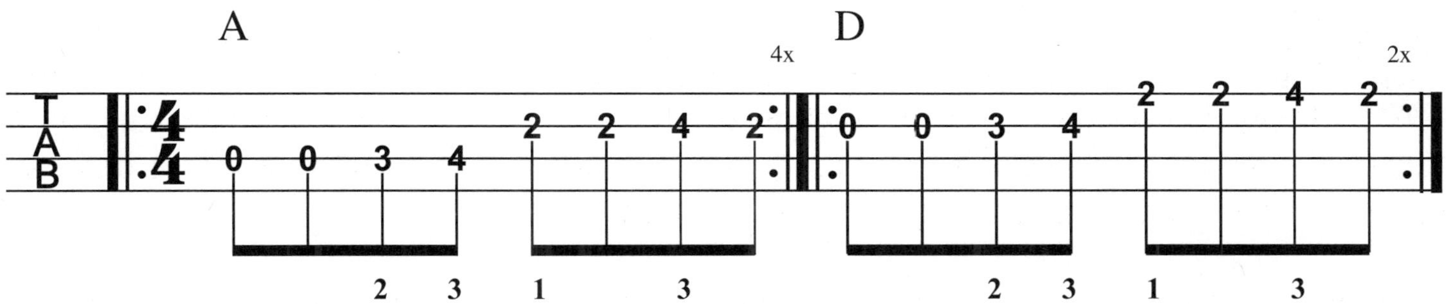

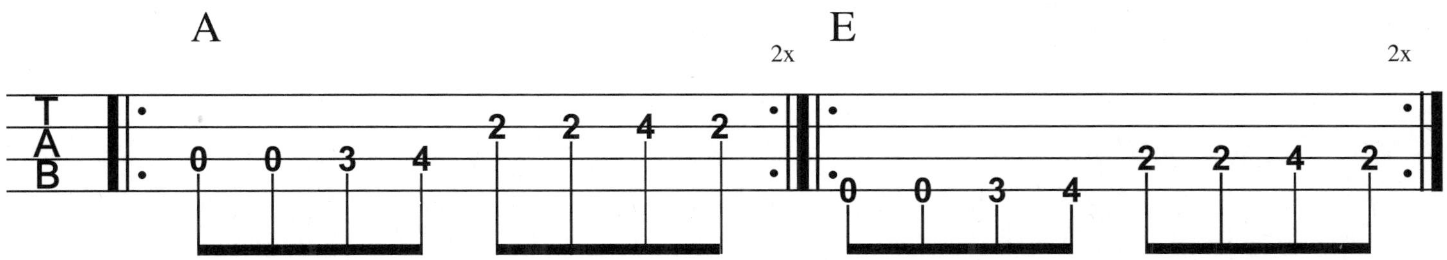

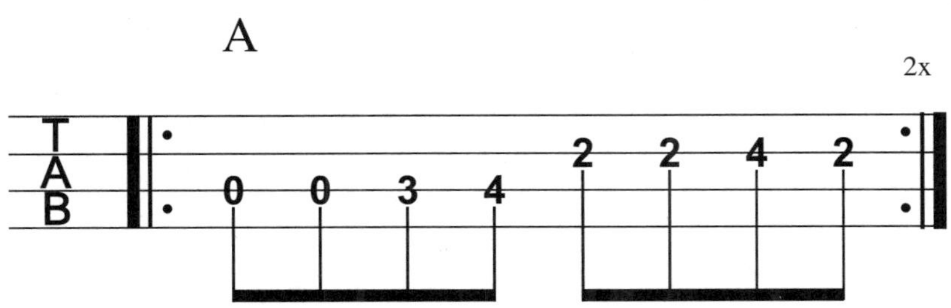

The Shuffle Feel

The shuffle feel is a common rhythm that has been used by many great blues artists. This uneven rhythm, also called the swing feel, has a bouncy feel that makes your body sway to the music. Play the example below of the shuffle feel. The way the notes are spaced depicts the timing.

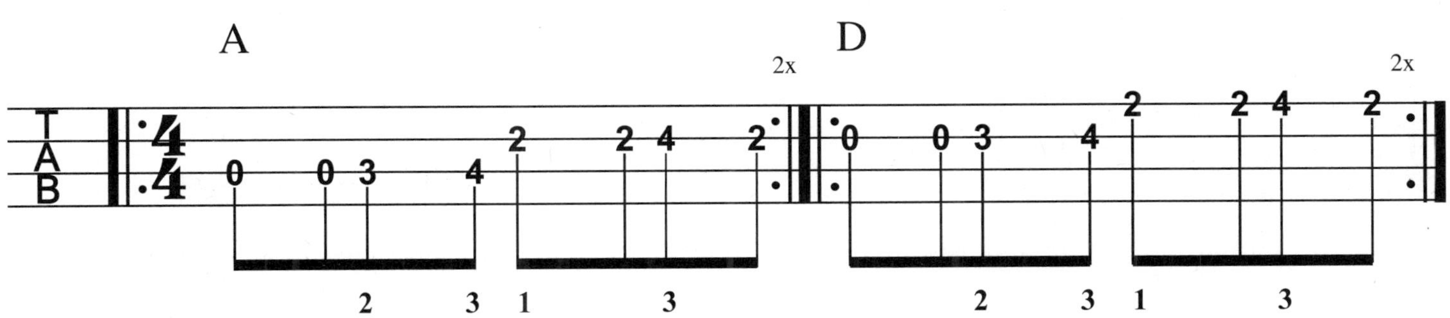

Minor Pentatonic Scales Key of "E"

Scale Professor

The two most popular keys in rock and blues music are A and E. In Book 1 you learned all five pentatonic scales in the key of "A." In this lesson you will learn these five scale patterns in the key of "E." It's easy to change keys with these scales; just move the scale patterns you already know to different frets.

The 1st scale position always starts on the root note or the key. In the key of "A," the 1st scale position starts on the 5th fret which is an A note. In the key of "E" the 1st scale will start with the open 4th string which is an E note. This position can also be played an octave higher at the 12th fret.

Look at the following scale diagrams and see where all five positions are played in the key of "E." Pay close attention to where all the E notes (root notes) fall within each position.

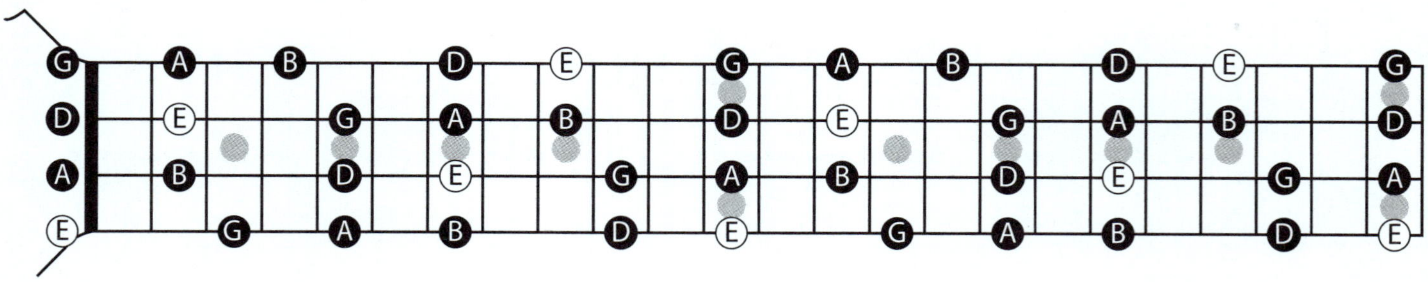

1st Position (open)

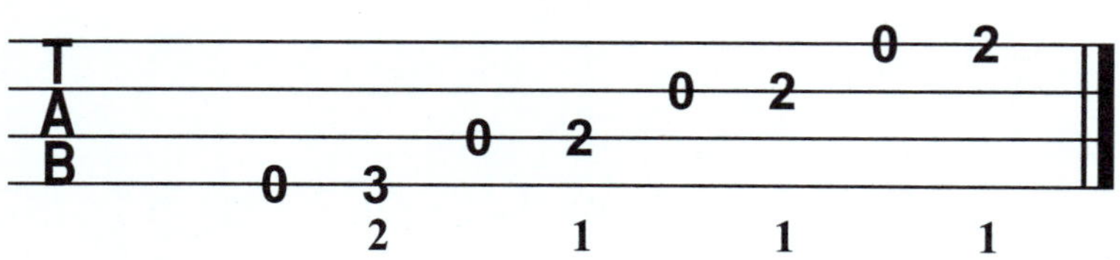

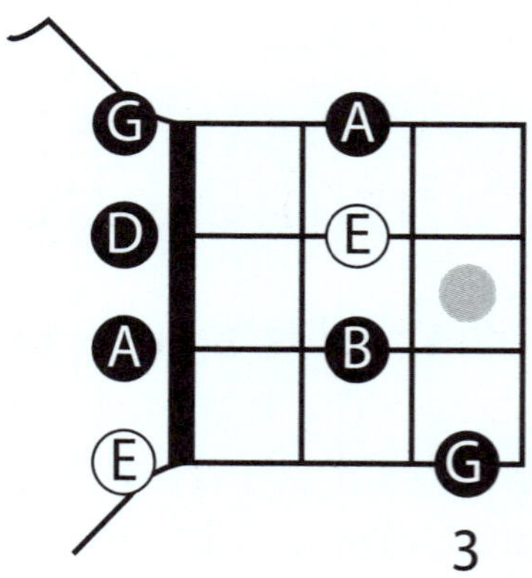

2nd Position

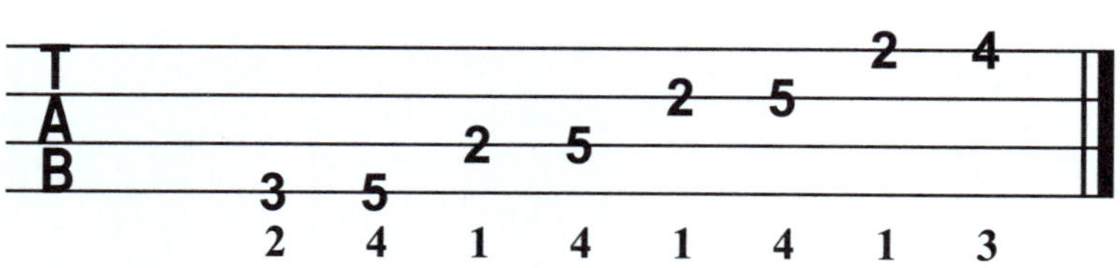

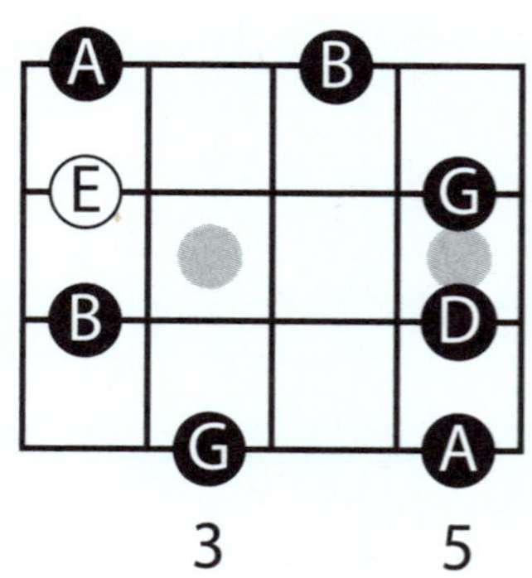

3rd Position

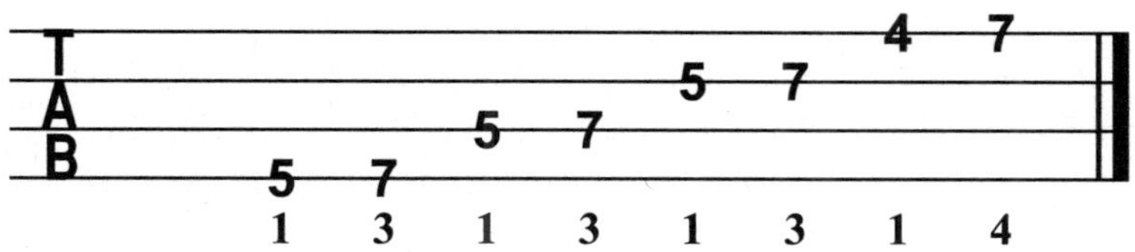

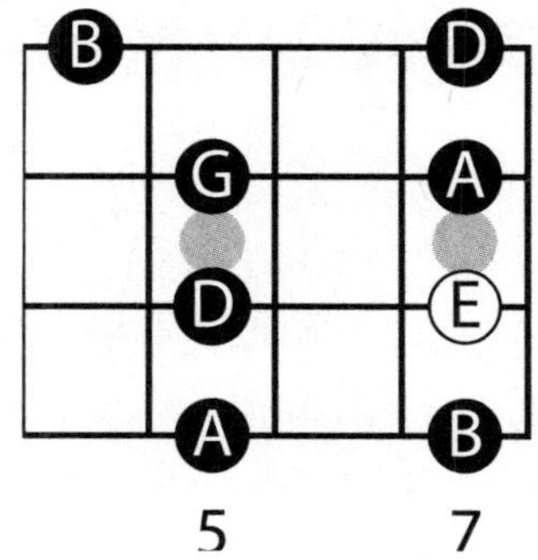

4th Position

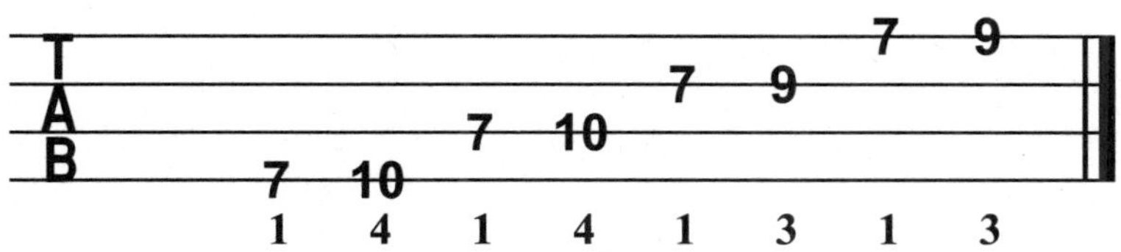

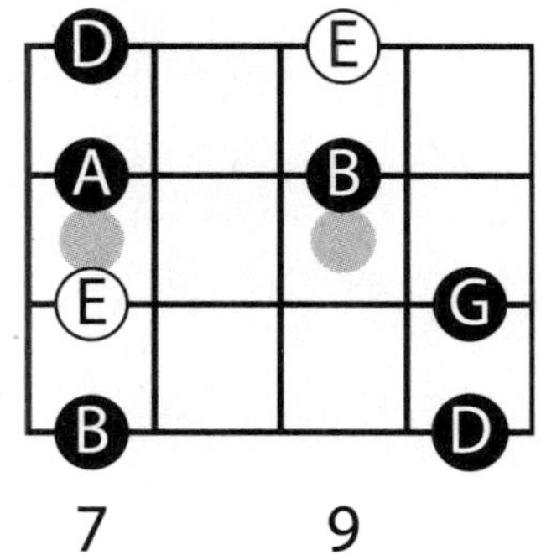

5th Position

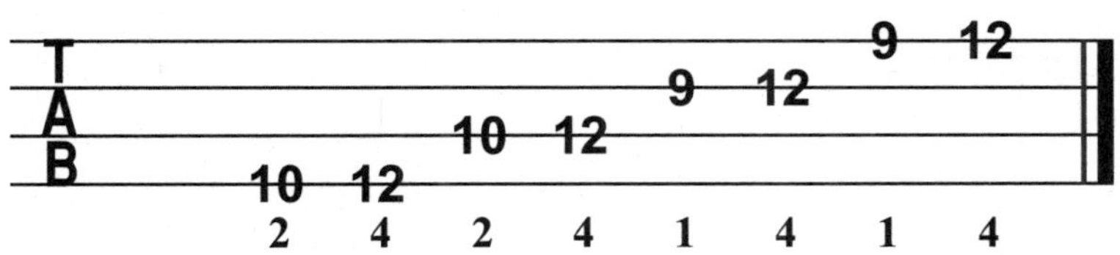

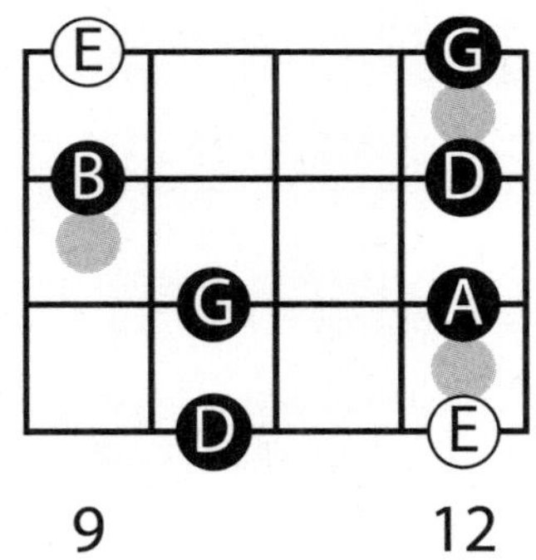

1st Position (octave)

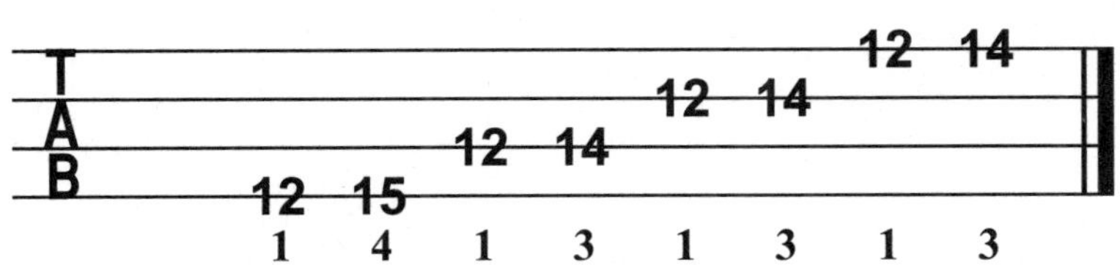

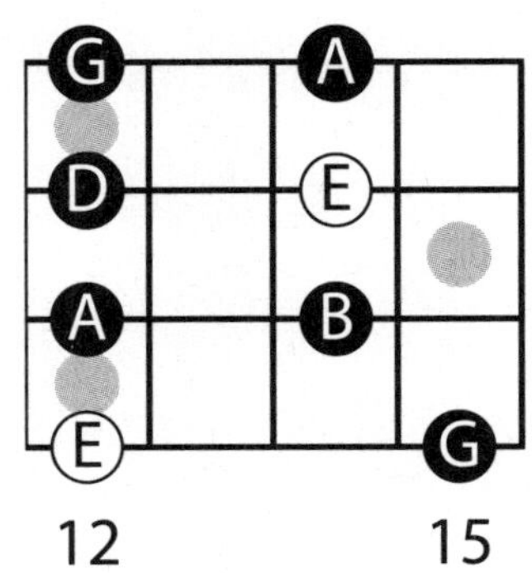

Single Note Patterns Key of "E"

Follow the tablature below to play the double and triplet patterns in the key of "E" with the 1st and 2nd scale positions. The double pattern is written with no timing on purpose. First play this pattern in eighth note timing then move to sixteenth notes to make it more challenging. Remember to use alternate plucking and build your speed up gradually. Make sure every note is plucked clearly before increasing your speed. I recommend that you use a metronome to gauge your progress.

Double Pattern – 1st Position

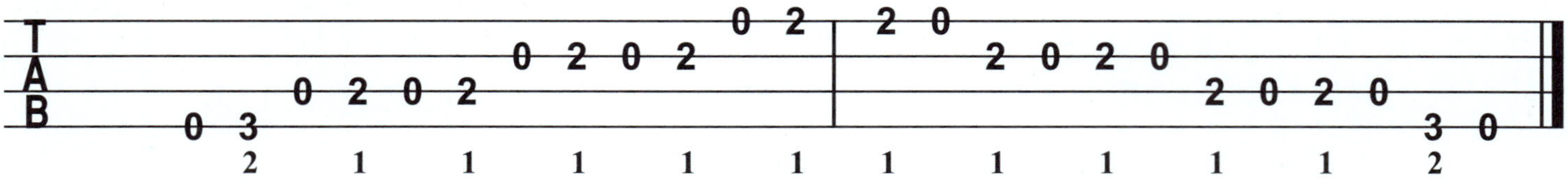

Double Pattern - 1st Position (Octave)

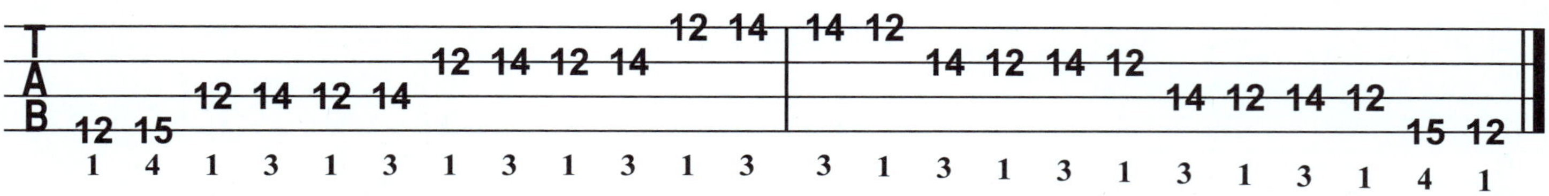

Double Pattern - 2nd Position

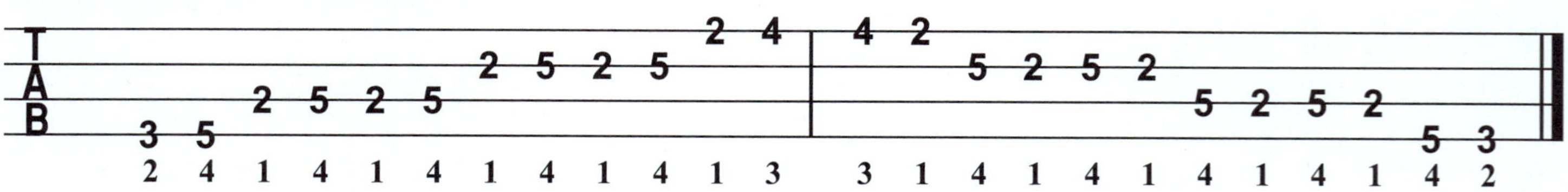

Triplet Pattern – 1st Position

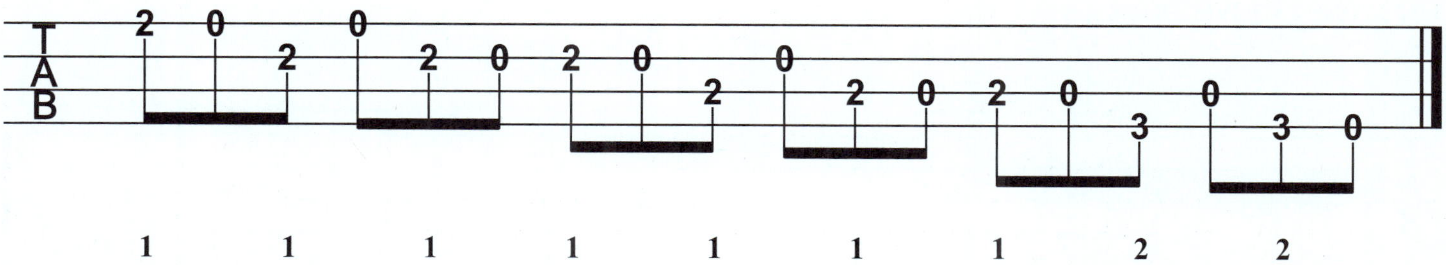

Triplet Pattern - 1st Position (Octave)

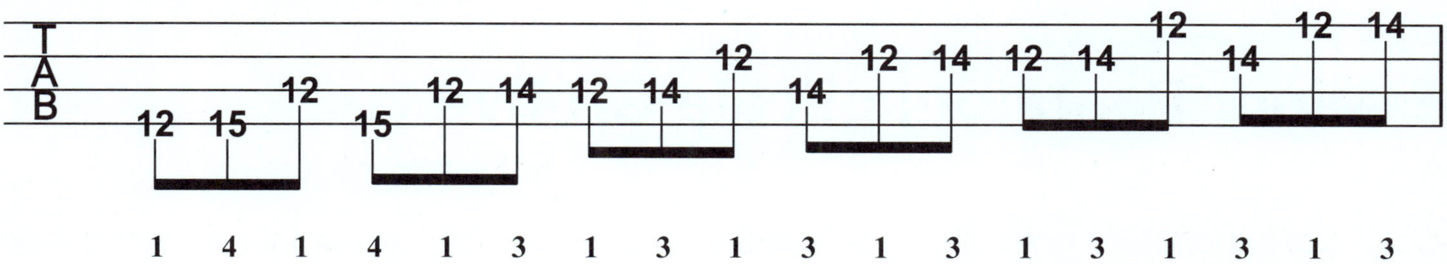

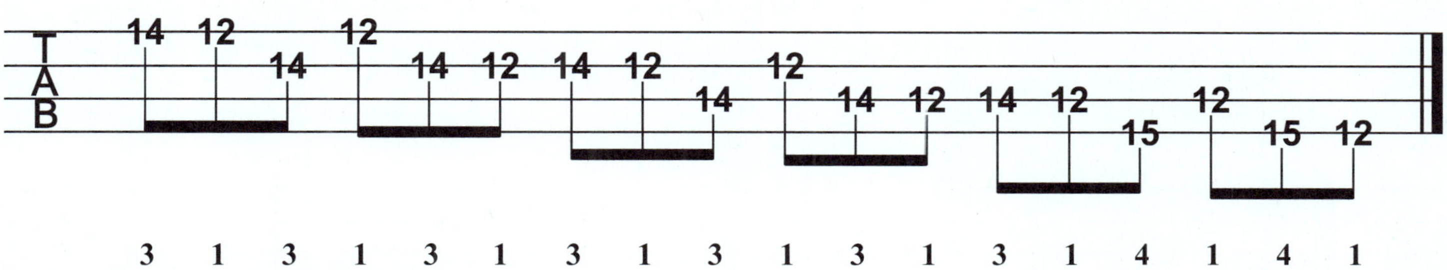

Triplet Pattern - 2nd Position

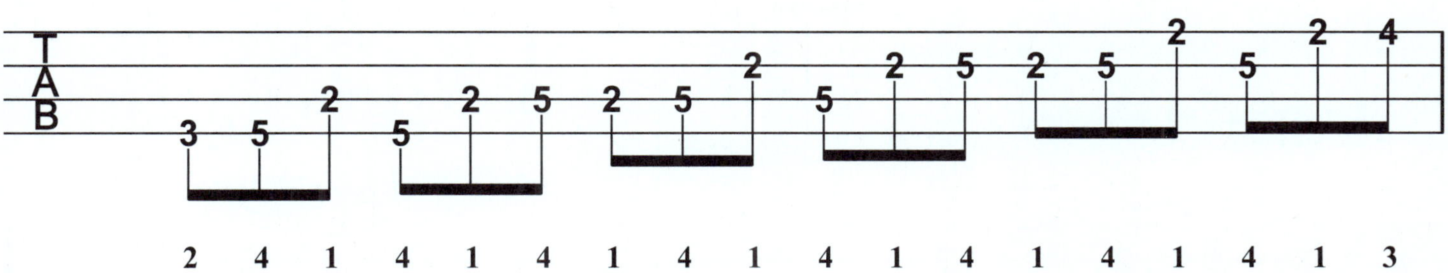

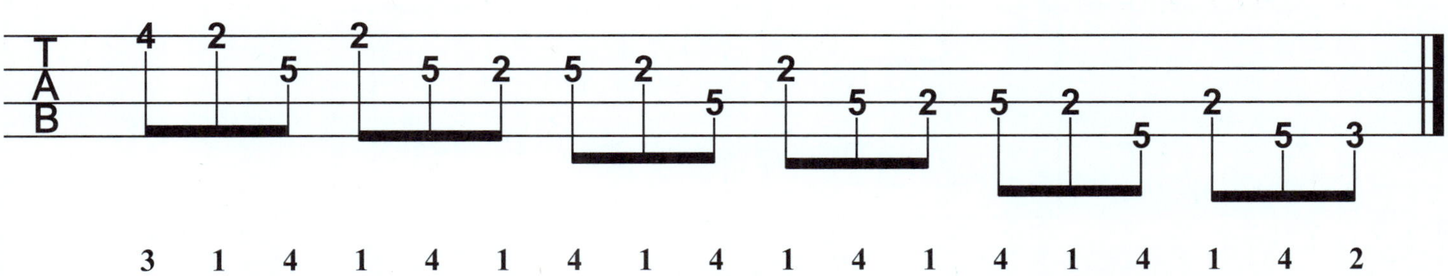

The Finger Drag

Often when playing bass lines you will need to play two adjacent strings with one finger. The most effective way to pluck these is to drag your finger from one string down to the next. In this exercise you will drag with your index and middle fingers. Don't pick the finger up and pluck the next string just let the finger drag off one onto the next string with one swift movement.

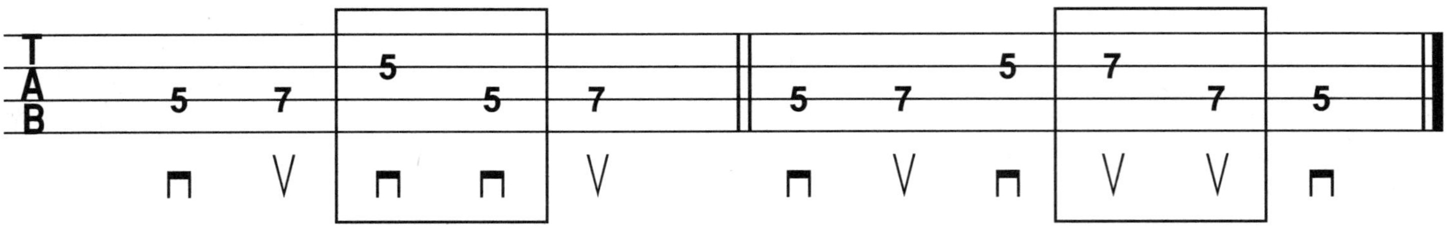

E Minor Pentatonic Scale Groove

Scales are groups of notes that you will use to create bass lines within a certain key. Here is a great example of a bass line created directly from the E minor pentatonic scale first position. I've outlined where the finger drag technique is used in this bass line.

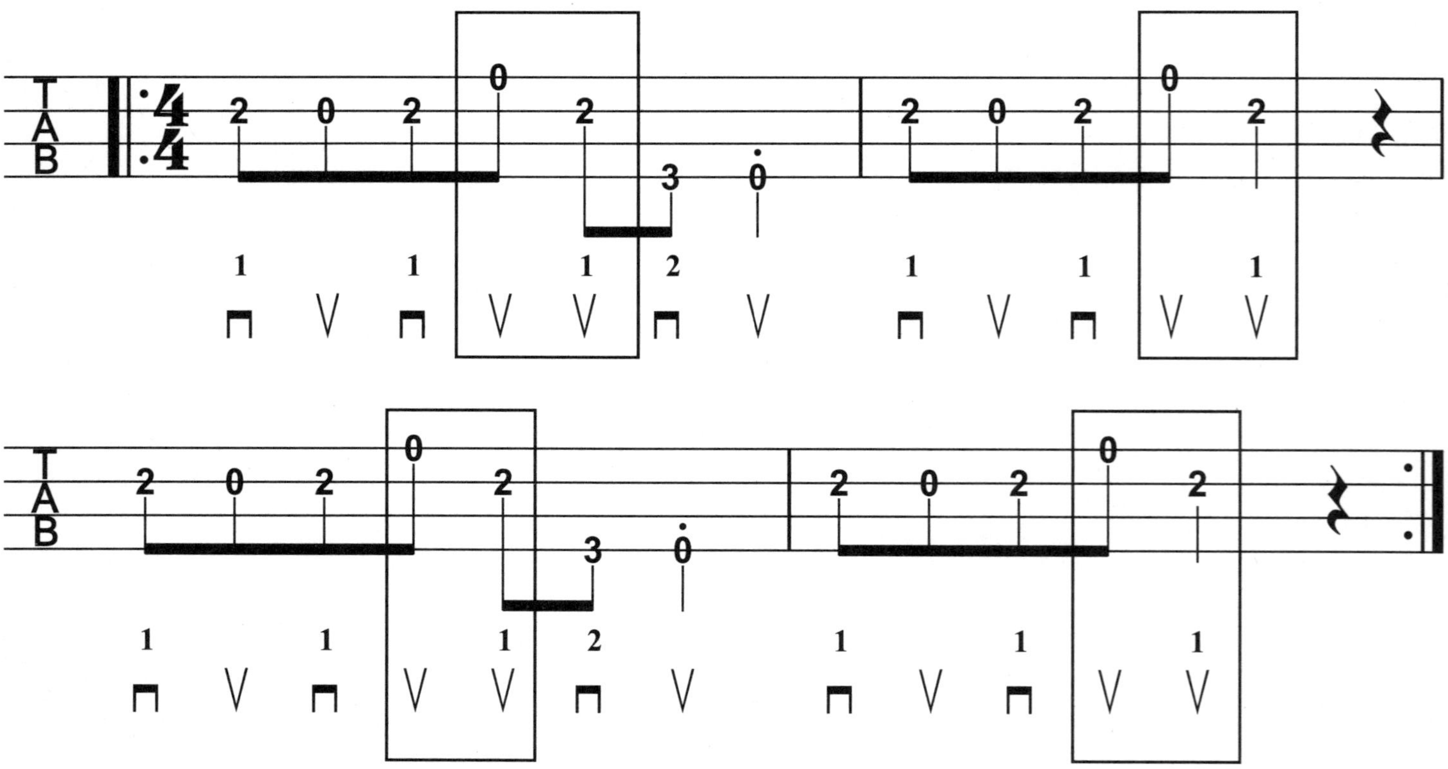

Connecting the Scale Patterns - Pentatonic

If you look closer, the five minor pentatonic scale patterns connect like a puzzle. These five scale positions fit together perfectly like Legos™. The second half of the 1st position is the first half of the 2nd position; and so on, through all five scales.

Look below to see how this works with the scales in the key of "E". I've used a full neck diagram so you can see all the scales across the neck and how they connect.

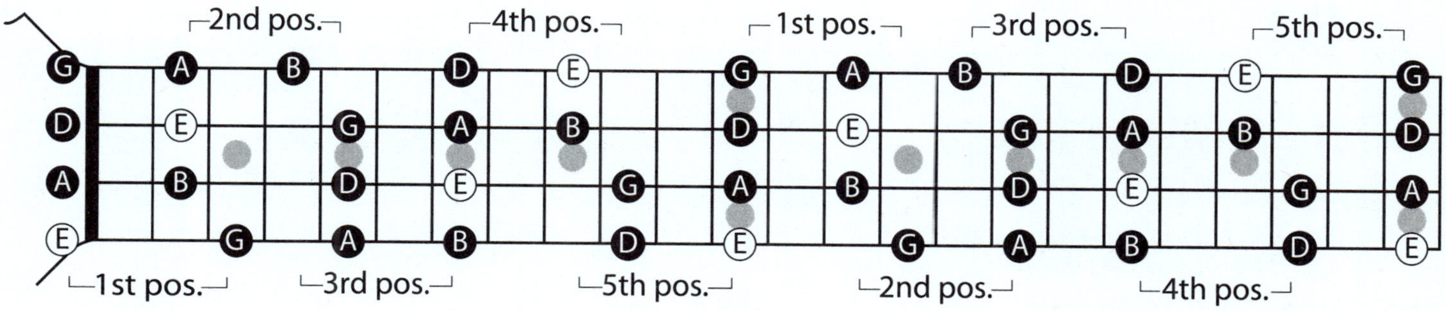

There is a commonality; the fret distance between each position is always the same. For example, in any key the 2nd position scale will always start 3 frets higher then the 1st position. Refer to the chart below to see the relationship of each position to the next. This will help you easily play these scales in all keys.

- **1st to 2nd position - 3 frets up**
- **2nd to 3rd position - 2 frets up**
- **3rd to 4th position - 2 frets up**
- **4th to 5th position - 3 frets up**
- **5th to 1st position - 2 frets up**

Below are all five minor pentatonic scales in the key of "E" so you can see the fret distance relationship between each:

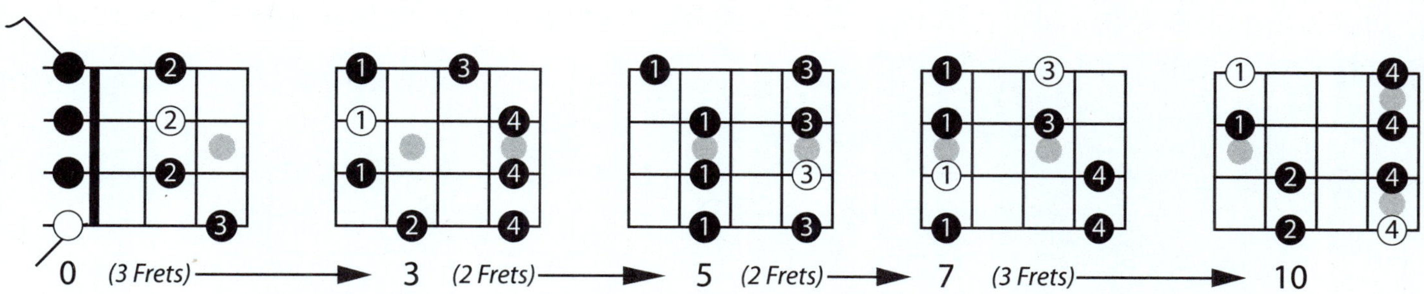

Remember the Day

6 - 4 - 1 - 5 Progression Applying Octaves

Now you will apply the octaves using the slap and pop technique. Take note that you are slapping on the bass drum hits when you play this with the backing track.

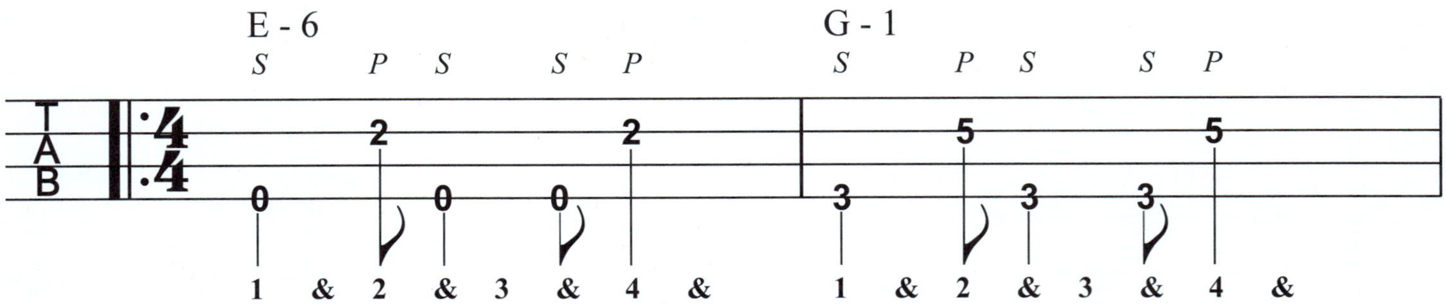

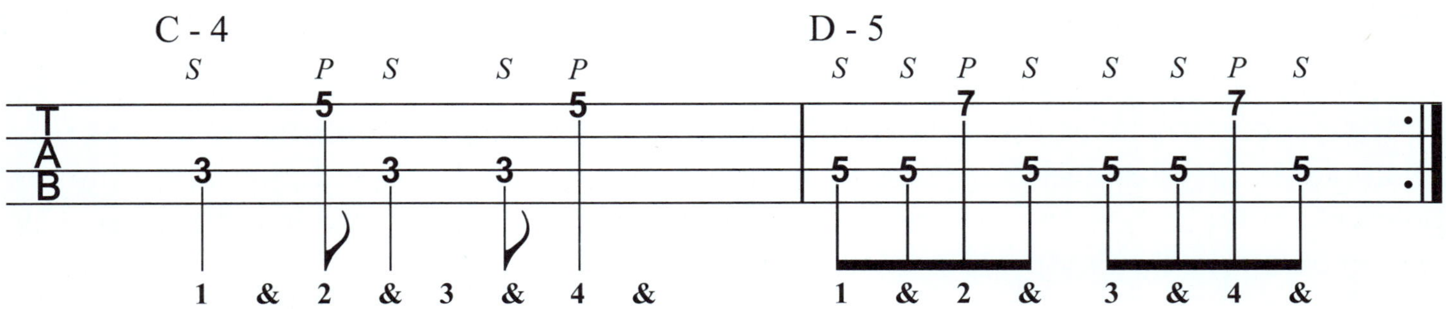

Hammer Ons

Hammer ons are a widely used bass technique. On the staffs below, you'll see curved lines (or slurs) connecting tab notes. This indicates that you'll be plucking the first note, but not plucking the second note. The second note will be sounded by pushing your finger down in a hammer like fashion to make the sound resonate. The "H" on top of that note represents the hammer on note. Play through the following exercise and remember to pluck the first note (which is your first finger), and hammer on the second note (which is either your third or fourth finger).

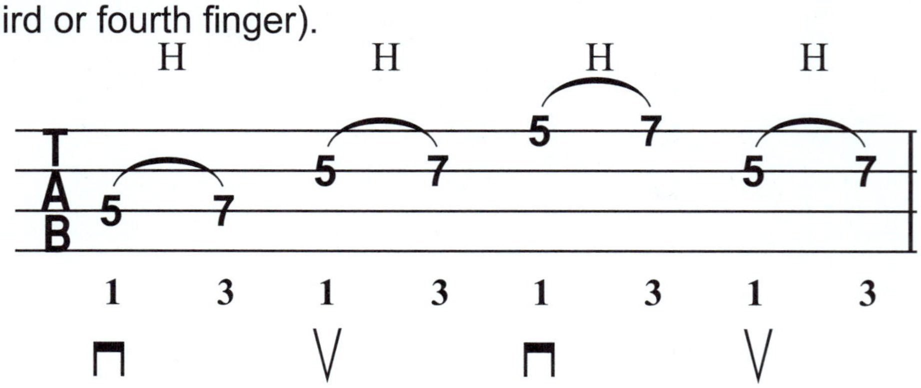

The second exercise is applied to the minor pentatonic scale. These patterns start on the 4th string and go down in three string intervals. Read the tablature, take your time, and master the hammer on technique because it is widely used in bass guitar.

1st Position

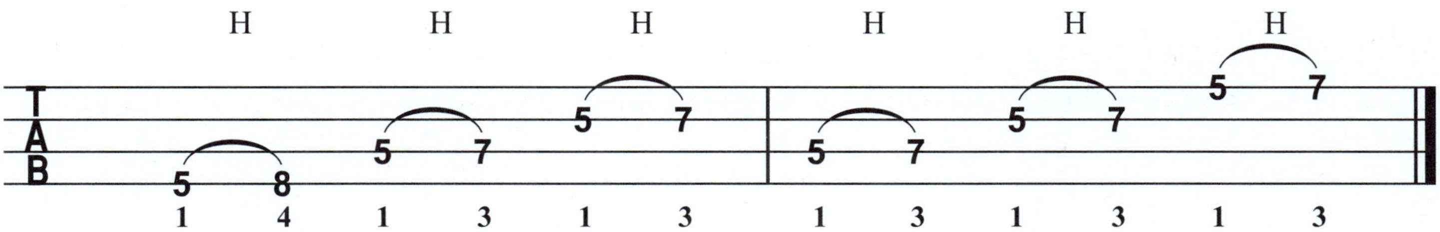

2nd Position

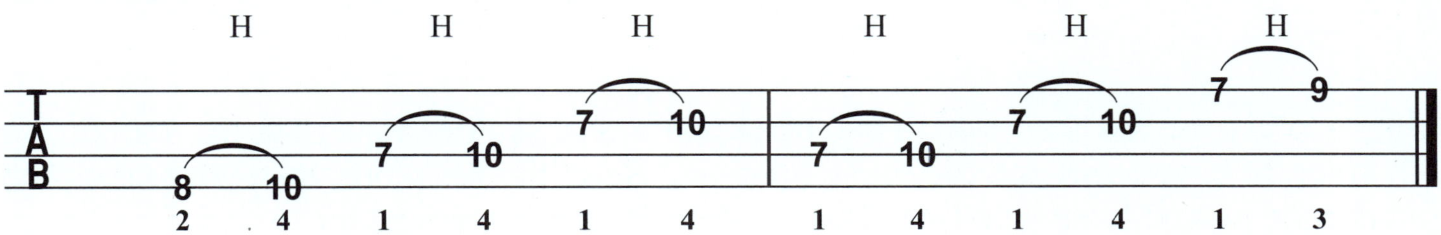

Music Assignment

After you feel comfortable doing the hammer ons take all the minor pentatonic scales you've learned so far and apply the hammer on technique. This will help you memorize the scales and also master this technique.

Inspirational Quote

"Music is a higher revelation
than all wisdom and philosophy.
Music is the electrical soil
in which the spirit lives, thinks and invents."

Ludwig van Beethoven

Pull Offs

Pull offs are basically the opposite of hammer ons. Instead of pushing your finger down to sound a note, you're going to pull off (or snap off) your finger to sound a note. You'll need to hold a finger down to pull off and one pluck will sound two notes.

Notice on the staff below there are two tab notes with a curved line (or slur) connecting them. The "P" on top of the second note represents the pull off. Play your first pull off now.

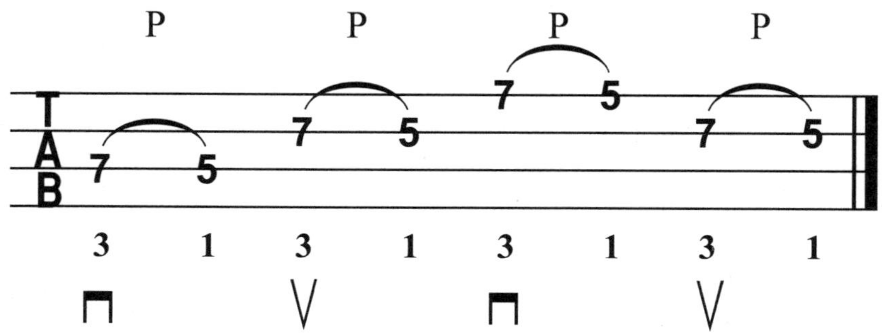

The second exercise is applied to the minor pentatonic scale. These patterns start on the 4th string and go down in three string intervals. Read the tablature, take your time, and master the pull off technique because it is widely used in bass guitar.

1st Position

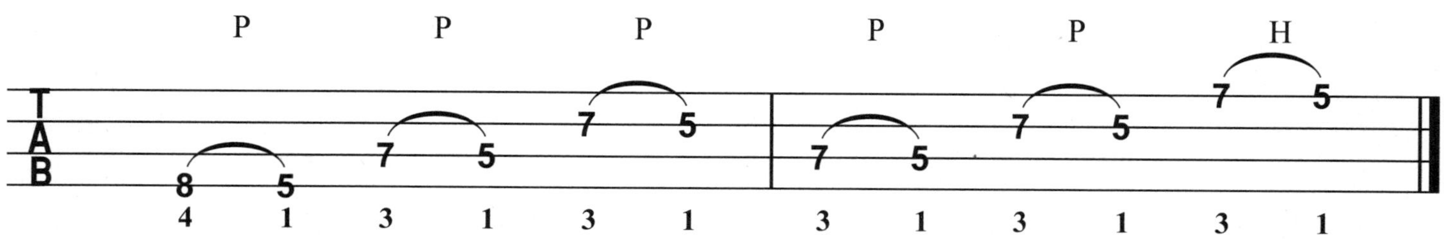

2nd Position

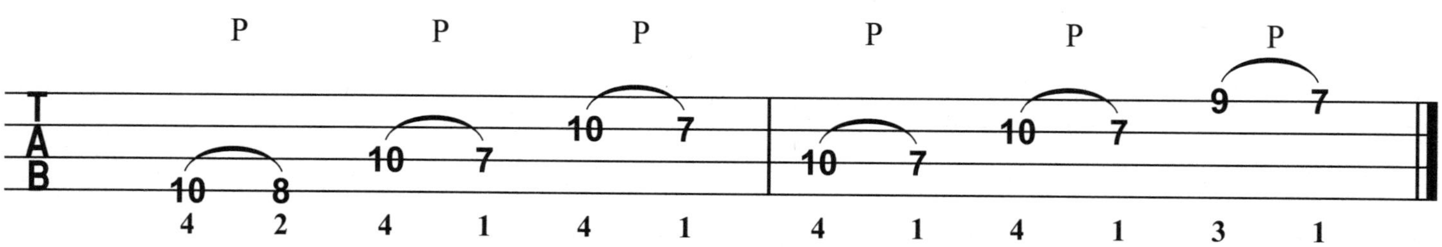

Music Assignment

After getting familiar with playing the pull off, and playing it through the first two minor pentatonic scales, apply this to all five minor pentatonic scales in the key of "A."

Hammer Ons in a Bass Line

Here is a bass line that incorporates the hammer on technique. It is important that you apply new techniques so you can start to use them to create your own bass grooves.

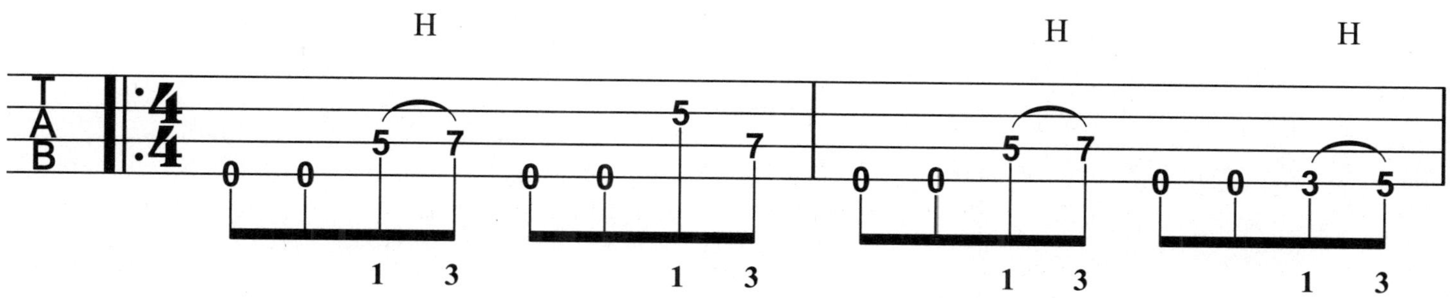

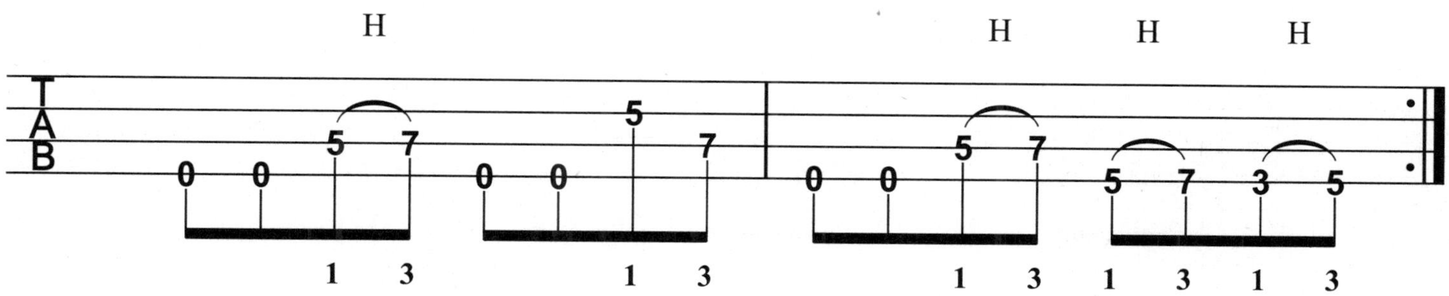

Pull Offs in a Bass Line

Here is a bass line that incorporates the pull off technique. Make sure to snap your finger off to sound the second note.

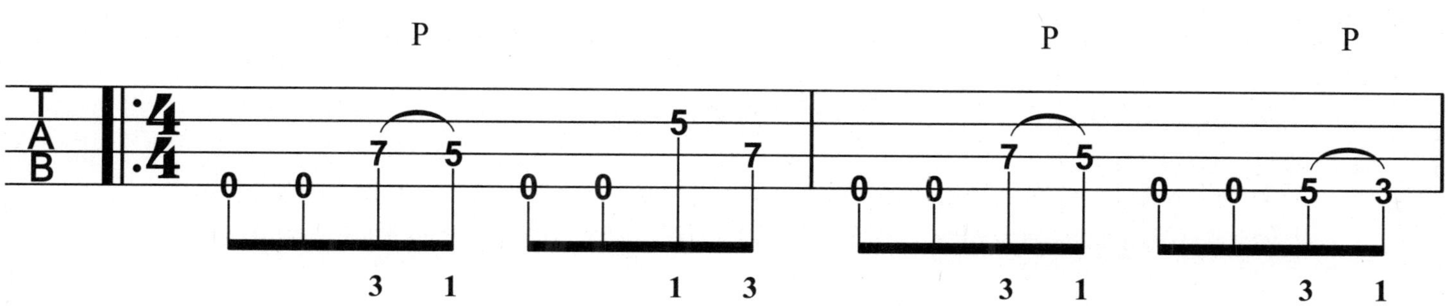

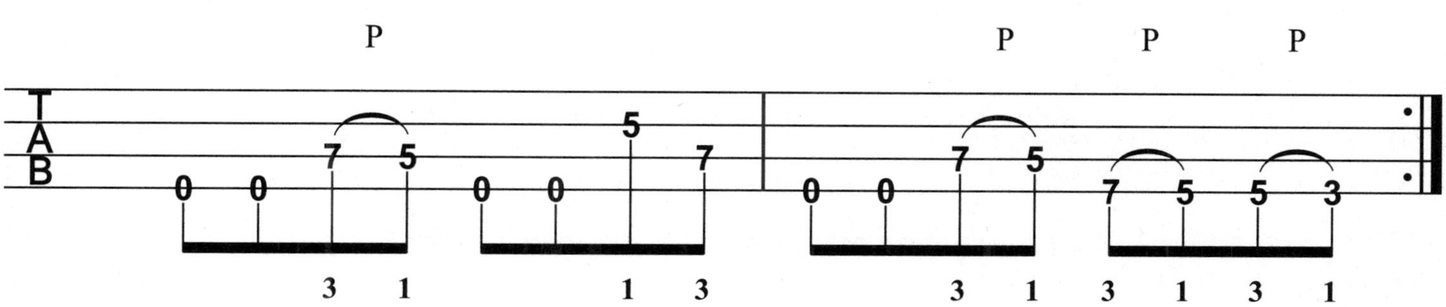

Minor Blues Progression

Here is a popular minor blues progression in the key of "B." This is a 12 bar blues progression so it will repeat every 12 measures. Make sure to use the backing track once you can play the entire progression with ease.

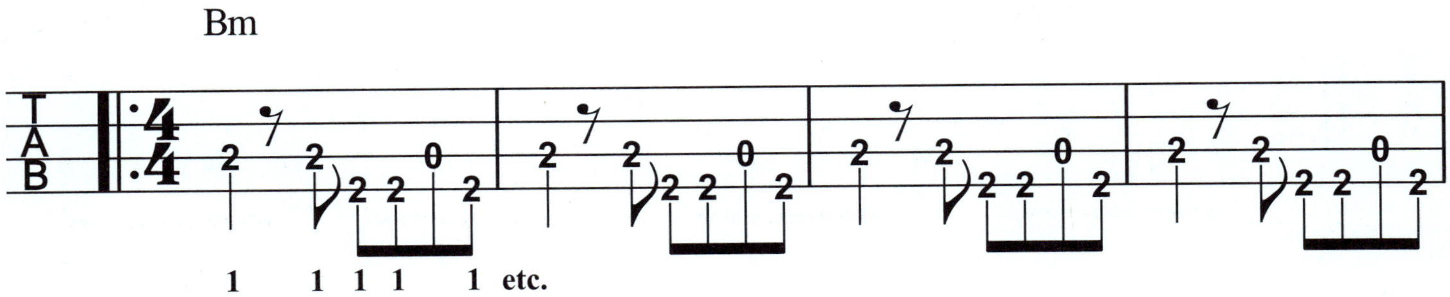

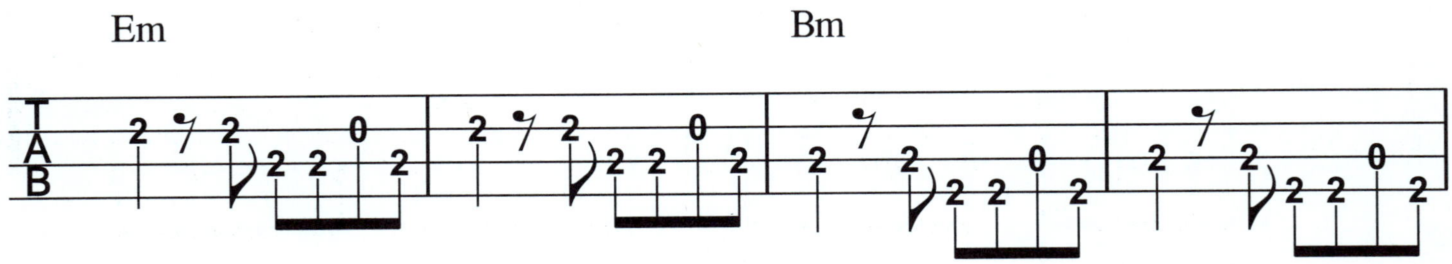

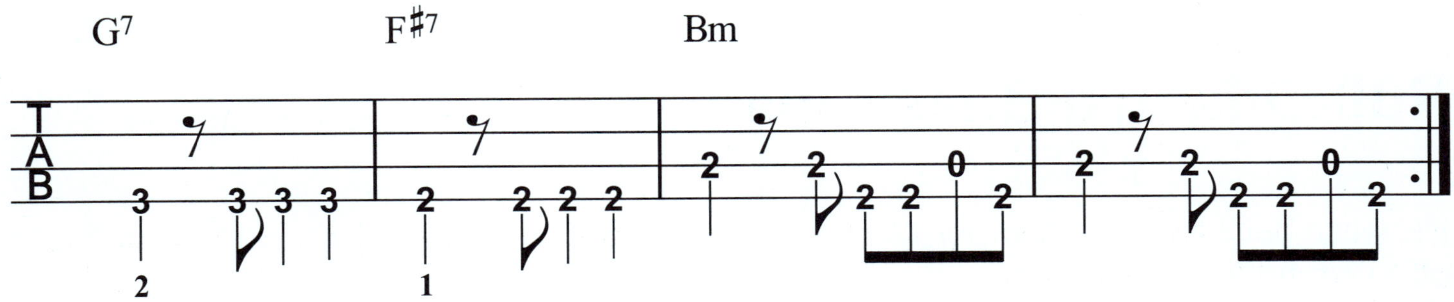

Turnaround

A turnaround is a riff at the end of a progression that brings you back to the beginning smoothly. Substitute the following for the last measure of the song above as a turnaround.

Root Notes

The root note is the most important note of a scale; it is also the name of the scale and at times referred to as the "Tonic" or "Tonal Center."

In an A minor pentatonic scale, the A note would be the root note. In this lesson take all five minor pentatonic scales and locate every root note within each pattern. Look at the diagrams below and you'll see the root notes depicted.

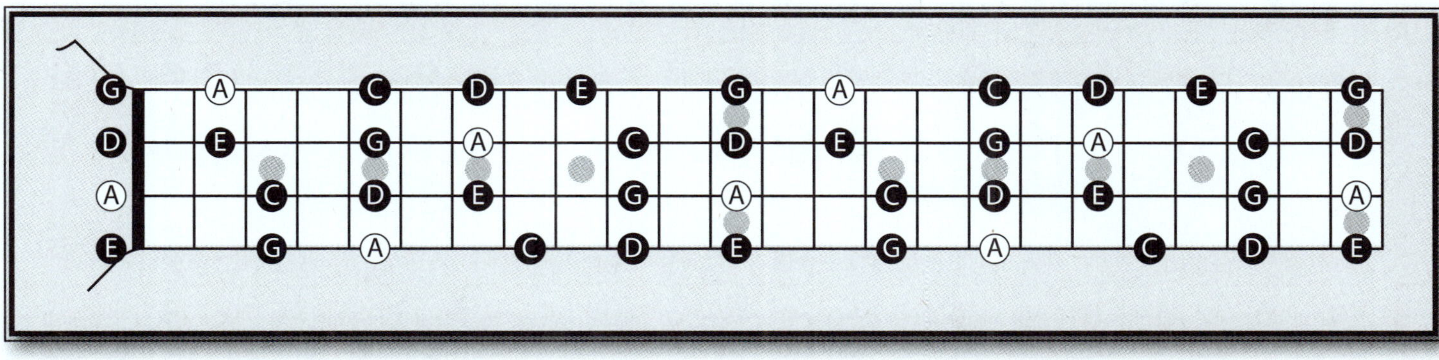

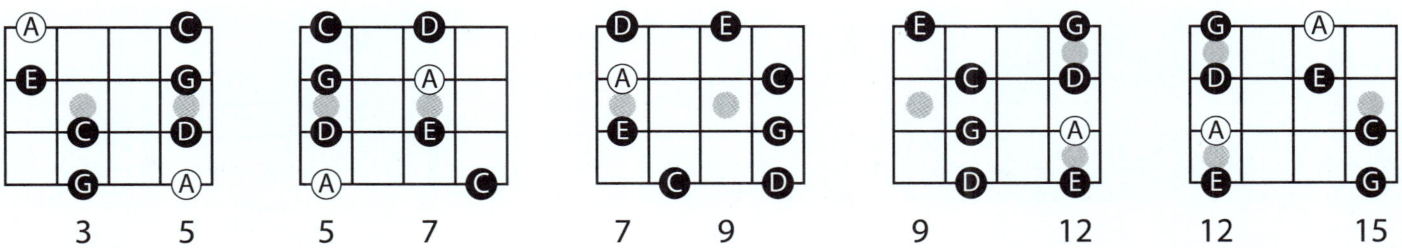

Try playing only the root notes for each scale pattern up the neck. This is a great exercise for you to memorize where the root notes are in each scale pattern. As you're creating bass lines, these are great notes to start or stop on. Look at the staff on the below and see all the root notes only in tab:

House of the Rising Sun

In this progression you will play notes in a triplet feel. Pay close attention to the fingering to help you get the rhythm feel. The timing is the same for each measure so once you have the timing for the first measure apply the same for the rest.

The Major Scale Formula

The major scale is the mother of all music. I call it this because most music starts from the major scale, and we make other scales or chords by altering the notes of the major scale.

Let's learn the formula used to create a major scale. A major scale is constructed using a series of whole steps and half steps. The pattern is: whole step, whole step, half step, whole step, whole step, whole step, half step, or commonly written W – W – H – W – W – W – H. If you start on any note and use this formula you will create a major scale. The starting note will also be the root note (or key). Here's an example: start with a root note C on the 3rd string, 3rd fret and create a C major scale up this string.

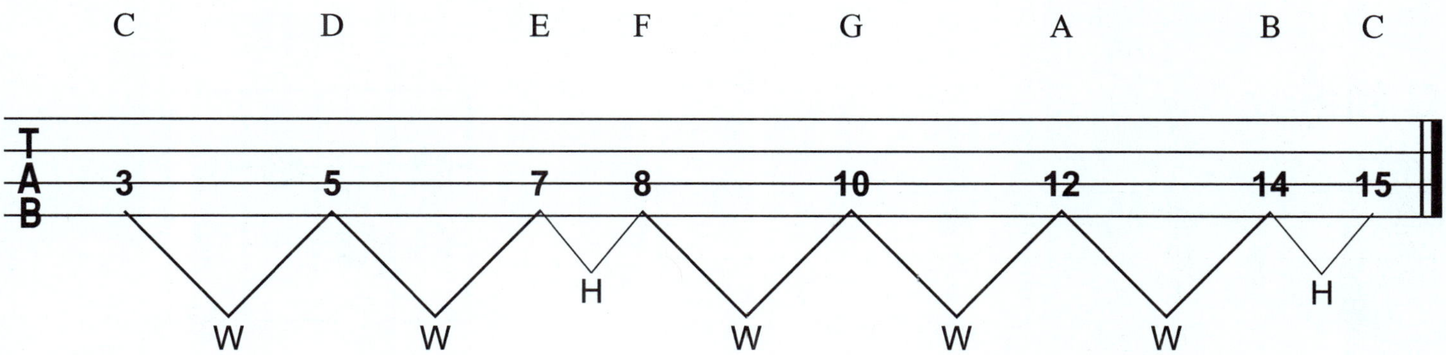

W - C to D
W - D to E
H - E to F
W - F to G
W - G to A
W - A to B
H - B to C

The C major scale is C – D – E – F – G – A – B – C. This will be the only natural scale, meaning the only scale that won't need any sharps or flats to make the formula work. Every other scale will have at least one flat or one sharp.

You just learned a C major scale up one string by using the major scale formula. You wouldn't usually play a scale up one string like this. In the next lesson you'll learn how to play those same exact notes in one position patterns.

Major Scale One Octave Patterns

SCALE PROFESSOR

Here are two one octave major scale patterns in the key of "C". The C note (root note) is shown inside of a white dot. The first root note is on the 4th string the second is on the 3rd string. These are movable patterns so you can play these starting on any fret of the bass.

C Major

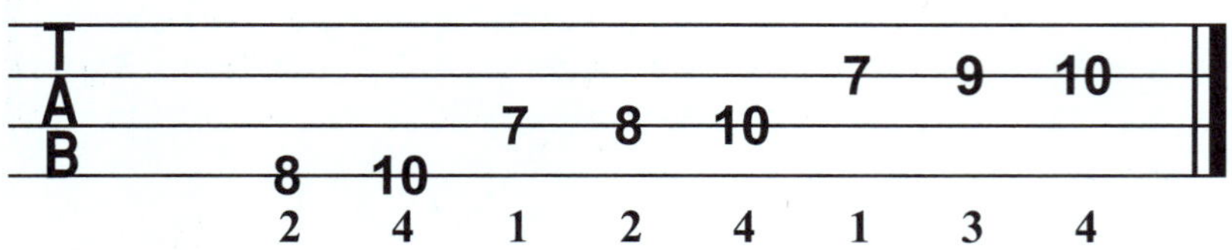

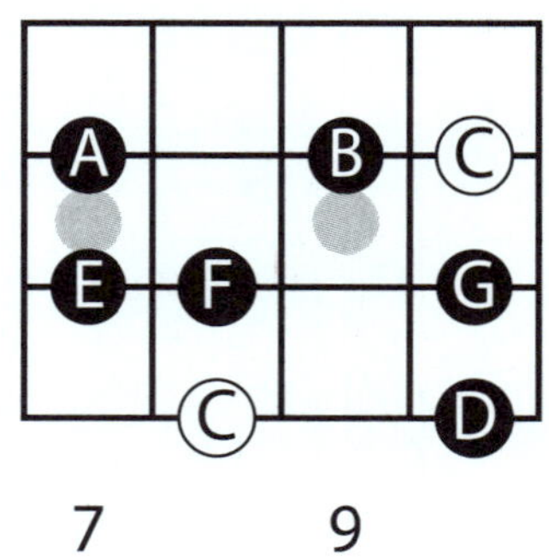

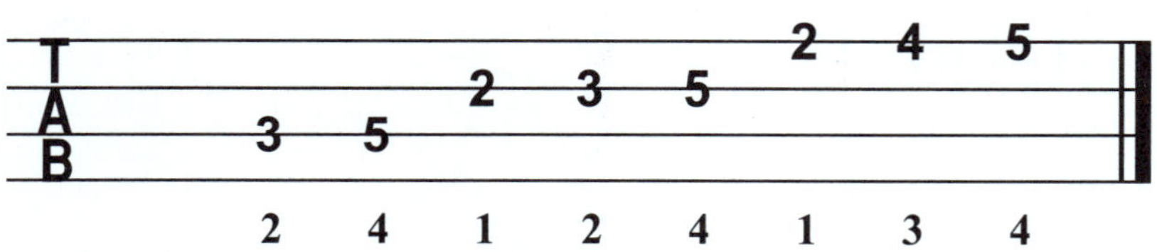

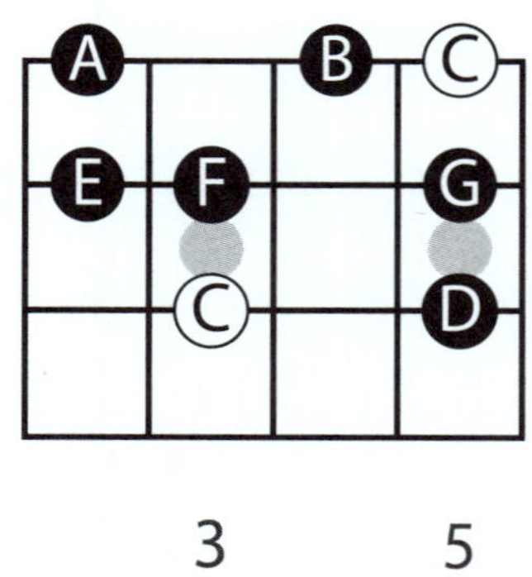

As you play these two scale patterns say the name of each note out loud as you pluck them. This will help you to train your ear connecting each note with a pitch. Also memorize the finger pattern which is the finger numbers used on each string. In this case it will be:

1 - 3 - 4

1 - 2 - 4

2 - 4

Music Assignment

After you have these patterns memorized move them to different frets and get familiar playing them in other keys. Remember the first note of each pattern is the key or root note. I've outlined them in the key of "G" and "B" below, after you play them in these keys transpose them to the keys of A and D. You will see these patterns as you play bass lines.

G Major

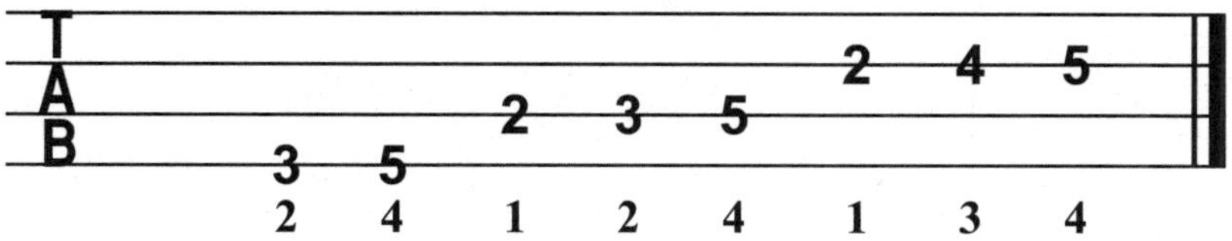

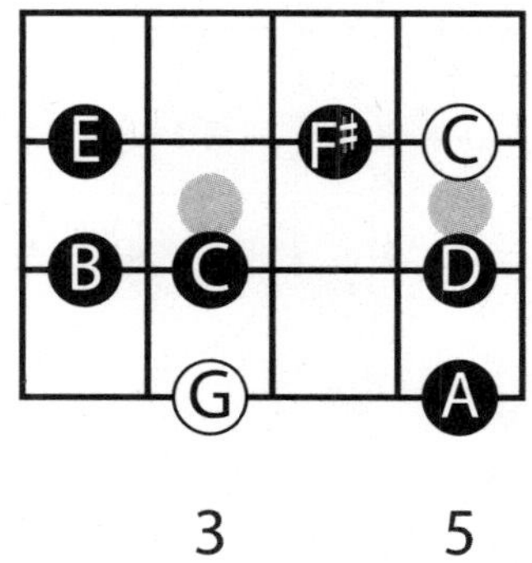

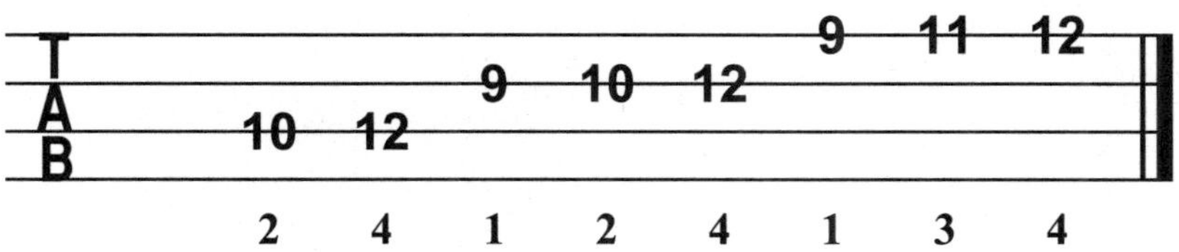

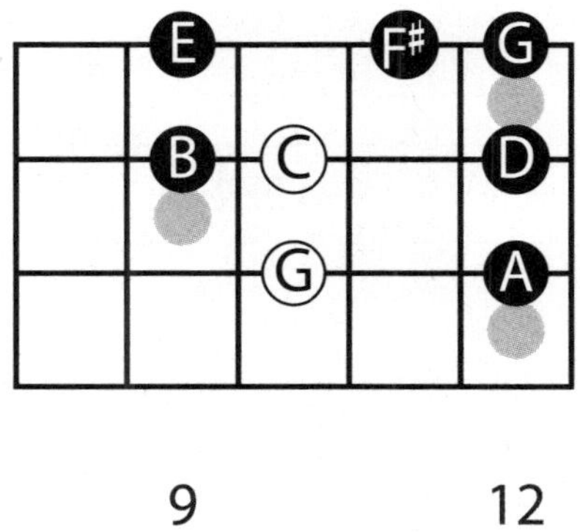

B Major

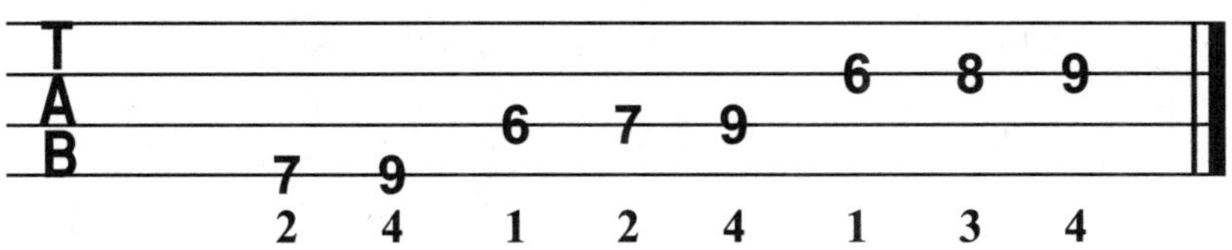

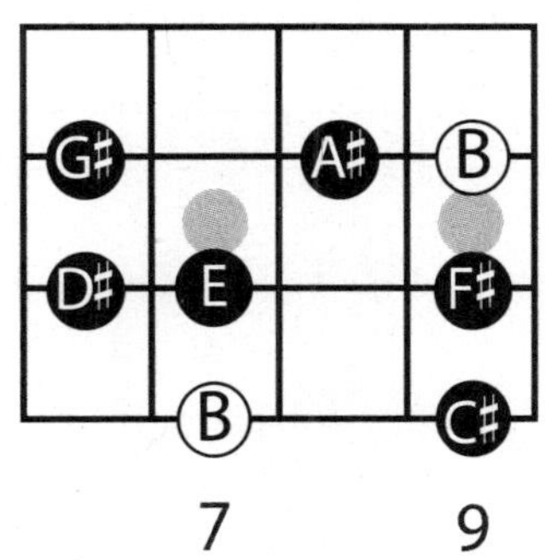

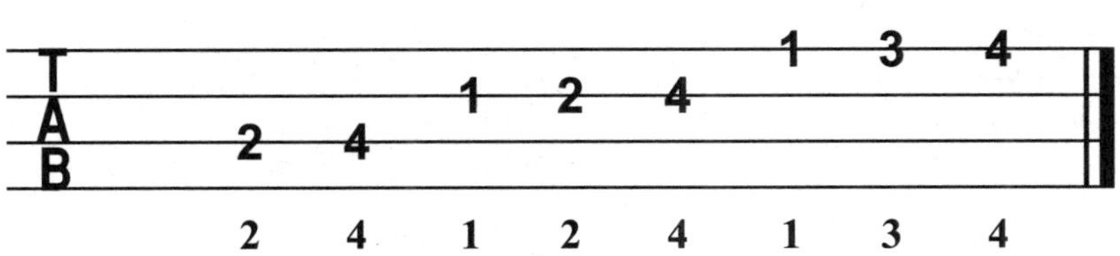

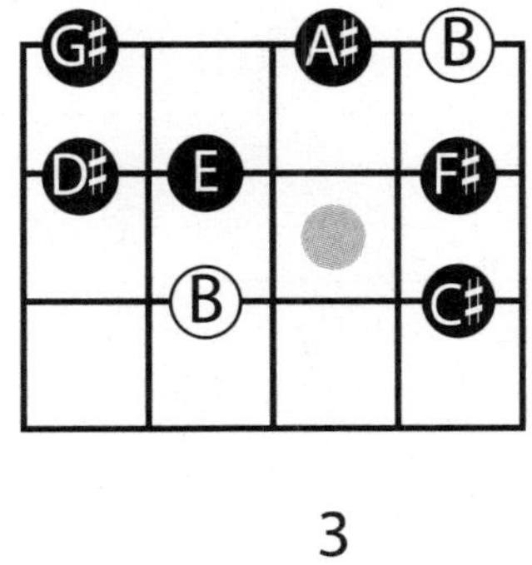

Major Scale Four String Patterns

These five scale patterns contain all the notes in the C major scale spanning your whole bass neck. The root notes are depicted with white dots. I've also included a full neck diagram of where all the C major notes fall across the neck.

1st Position

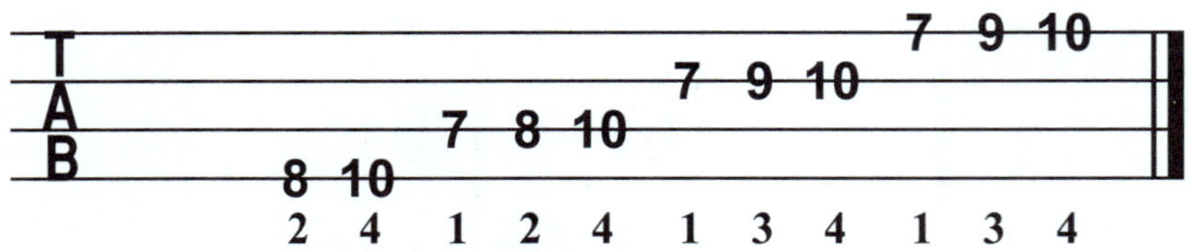

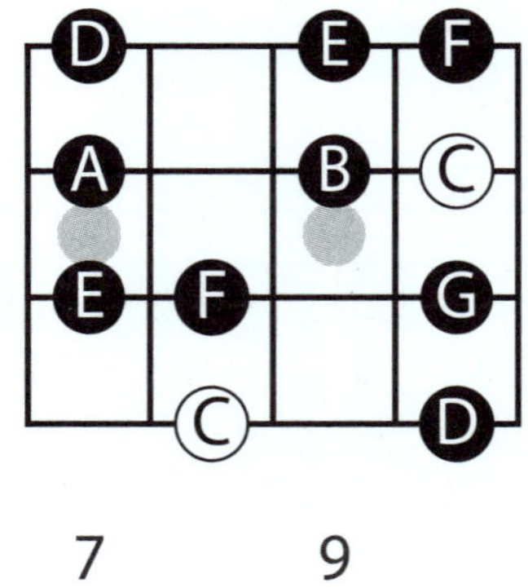

2nd Position

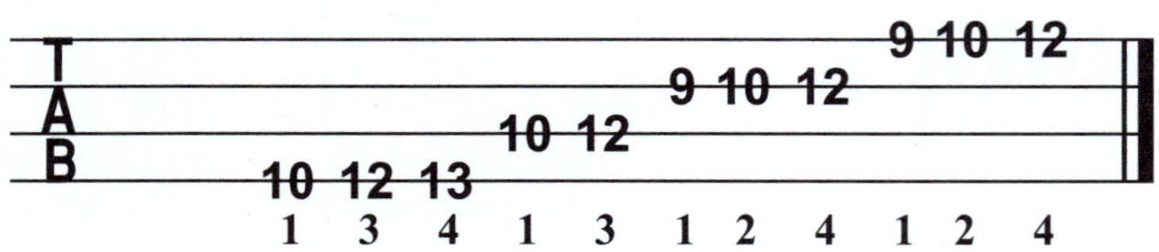

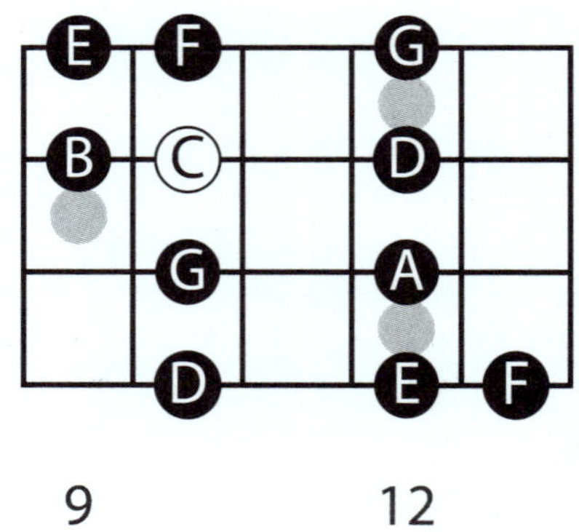

3rd Position (Octave)

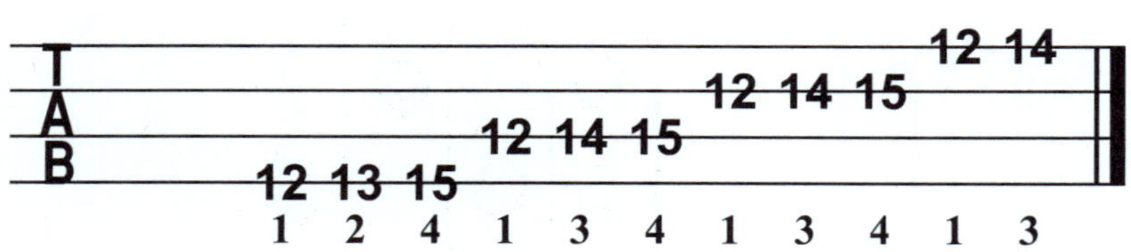

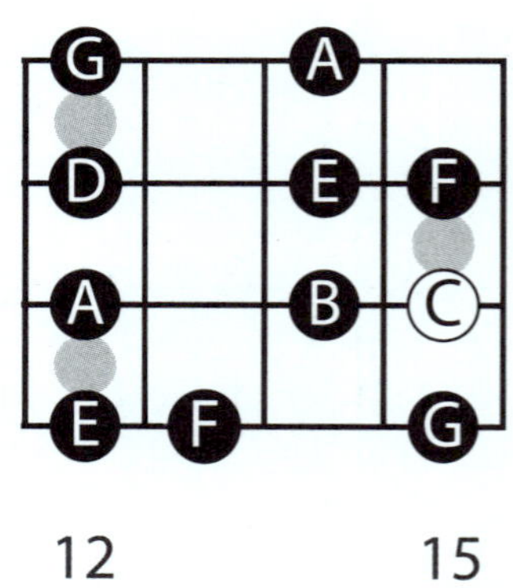

3rd Position (Octave Lower)

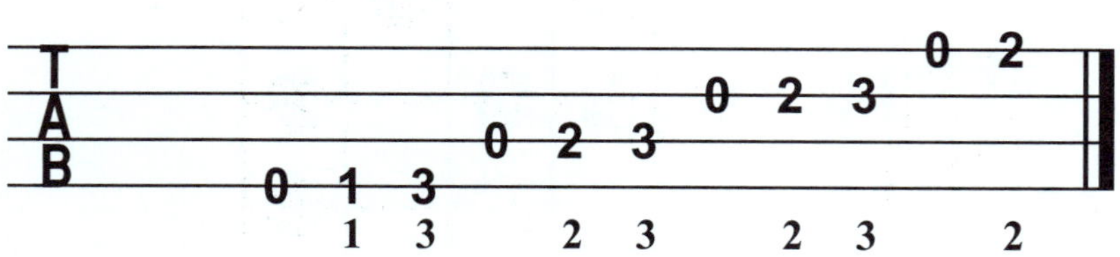

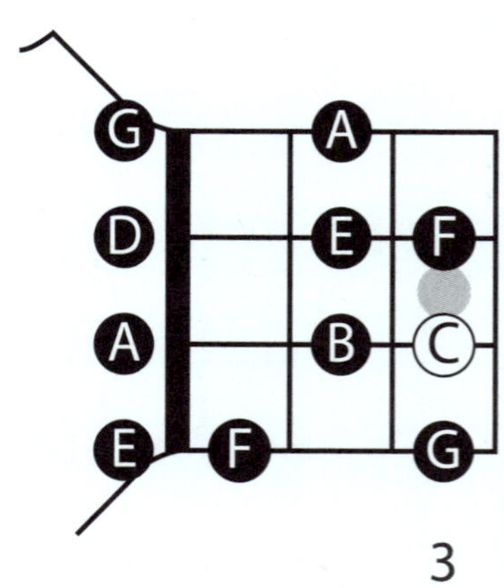

4th Position

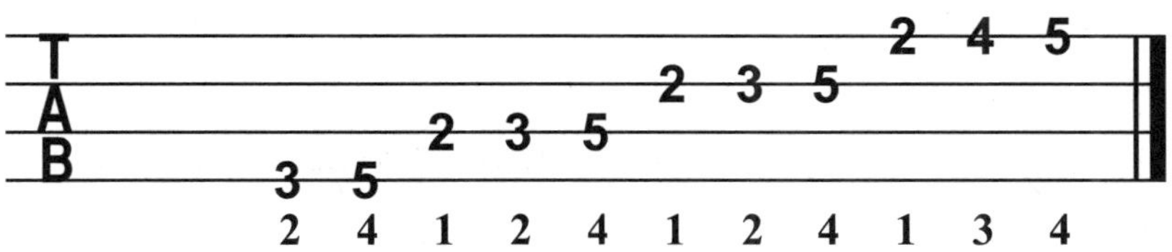

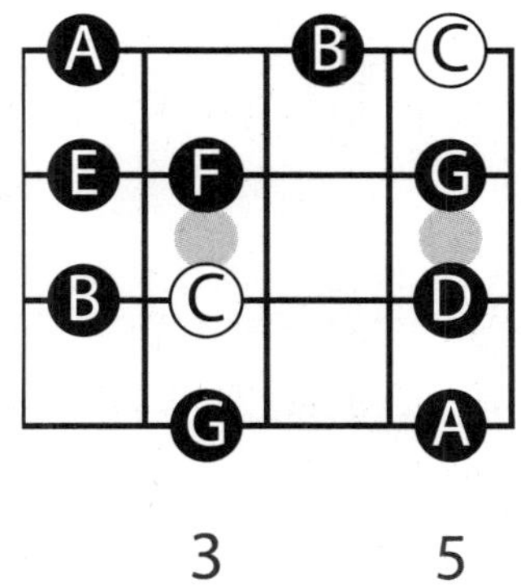

5th Position

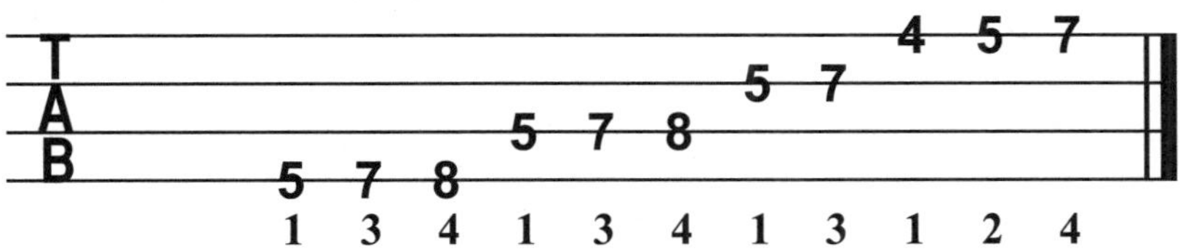

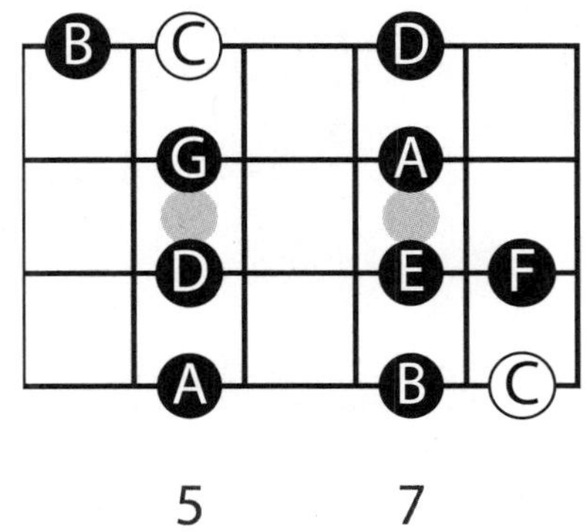

Music Assignment

This is a full neck diagram that shows every note in the C major scale across the bass neck. Find all the four note patterns you learned in this lesson in this diagram. It's important to start seeing the scales across the neck together as a whole and not just small scale patterns.

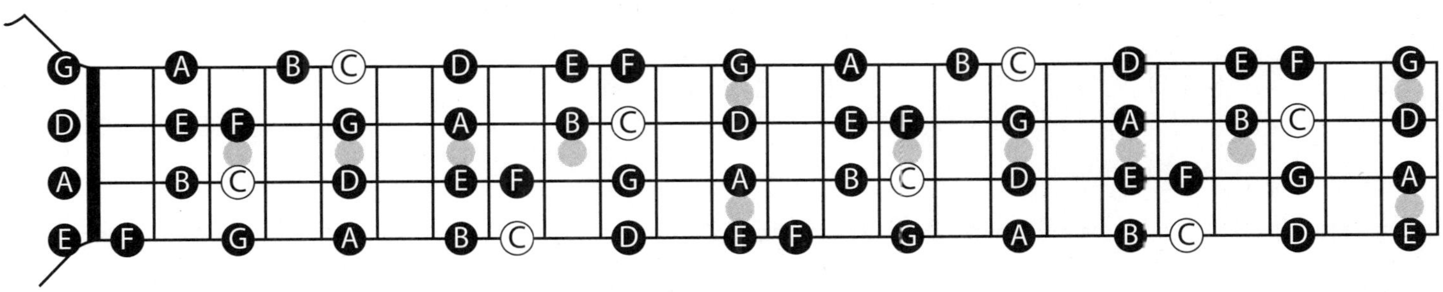

Bass 2 Quiz #1

You're ready to take your next quiz now! Please review all the lessons in the previous section then go to page 4 to see where to take your quiz.

Walking Bass Lines

Walking bass lines are one of the most melodic sounding bass parts. Those of you who are fans of swing jazz or blues are probably already familiar with the walking bass sound. In this lesson you will learn standard blues influenced walking bass lines. Blues walking bass lines have a more structured repetitive pattern. Jazz walking bass lines tend to be more improvisational in nature, almost like playing a bass solo.

Example 1

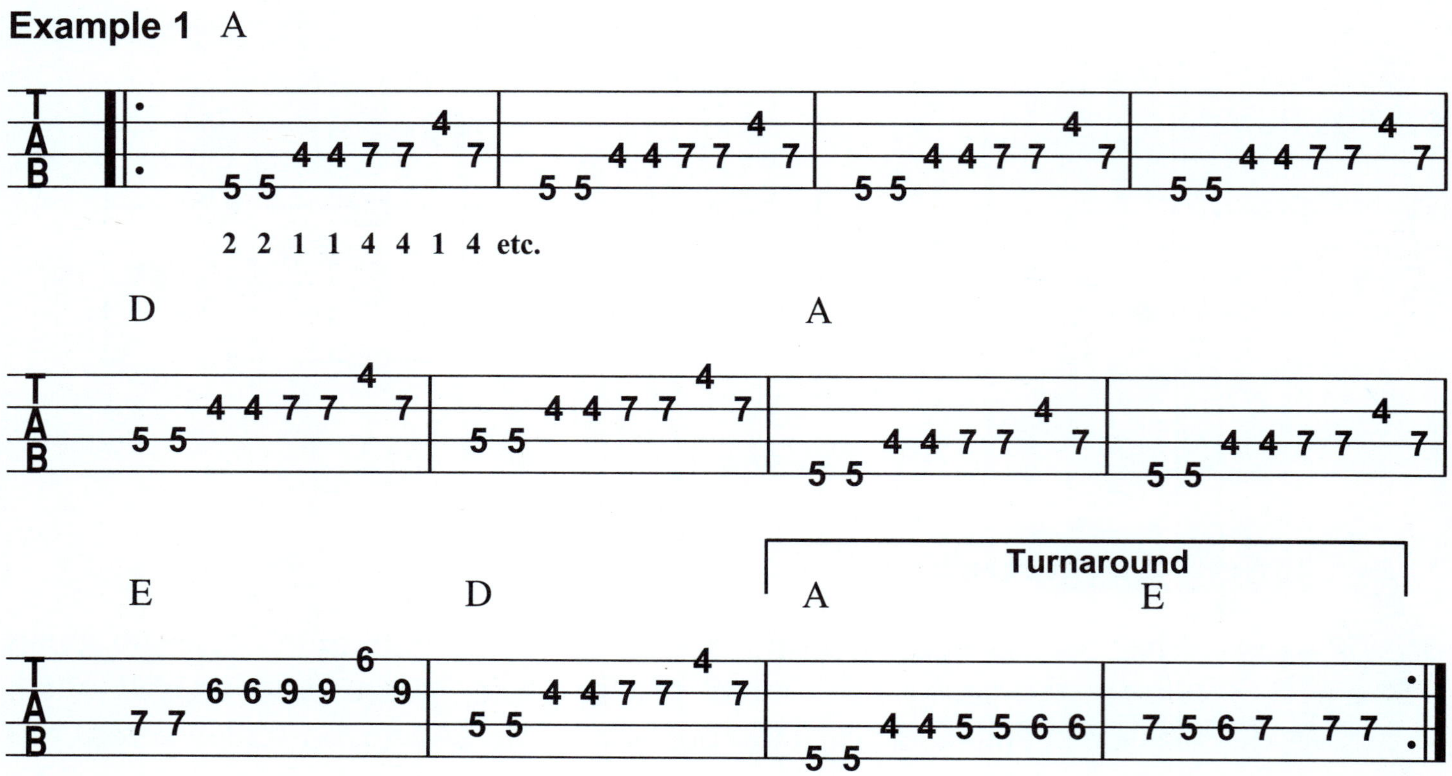

Example 2

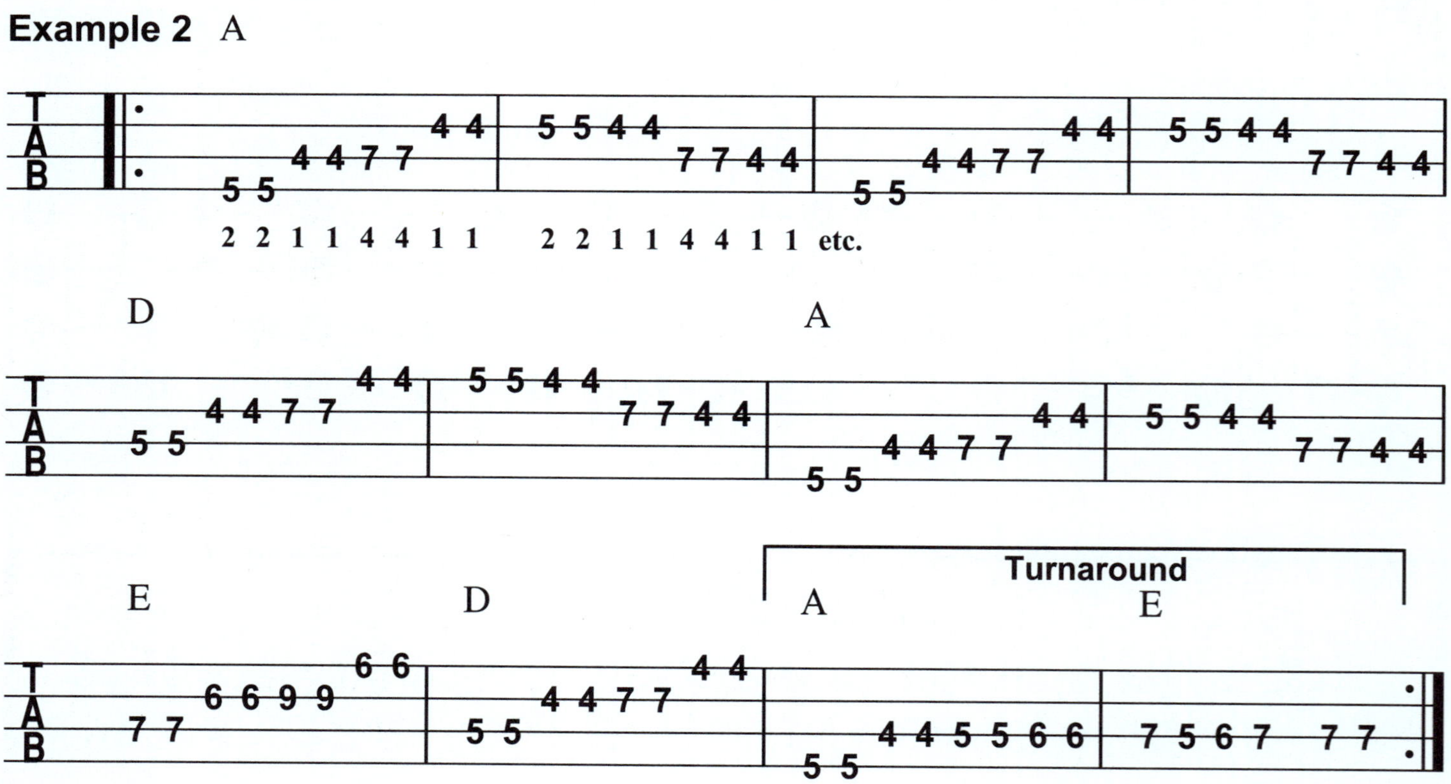

Ramone

This is a heavier rhythm feel. Notice the there are consistent eighth notes using alternate plucking for each measure to achieve a heavier rhythm sound. Make sure to play this along with the backing tracks.

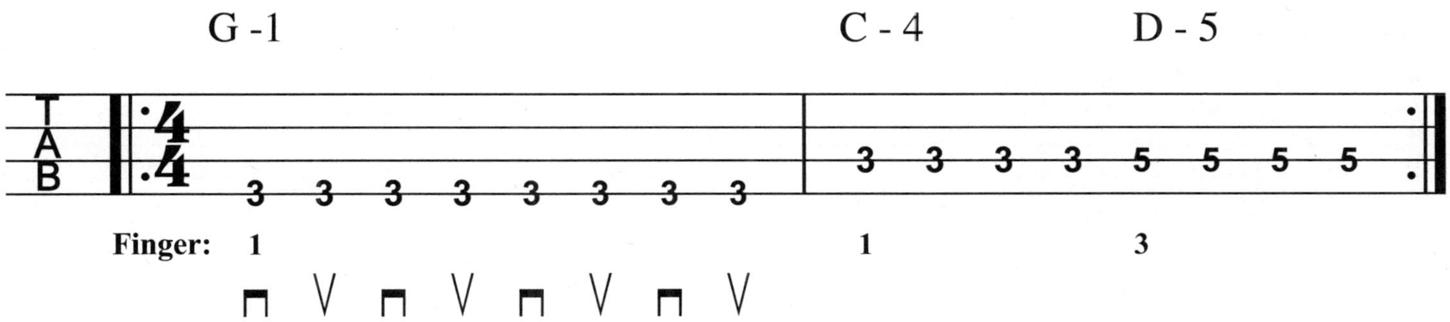

Voodoo Girl

6 - 2 - 1 - 5 Progression

For this progression you will use minor triads for the first two measures under the A and D minor chords. For the C and G chords you play notes from the major scale of each. Make sure to play this with the backing tracks.

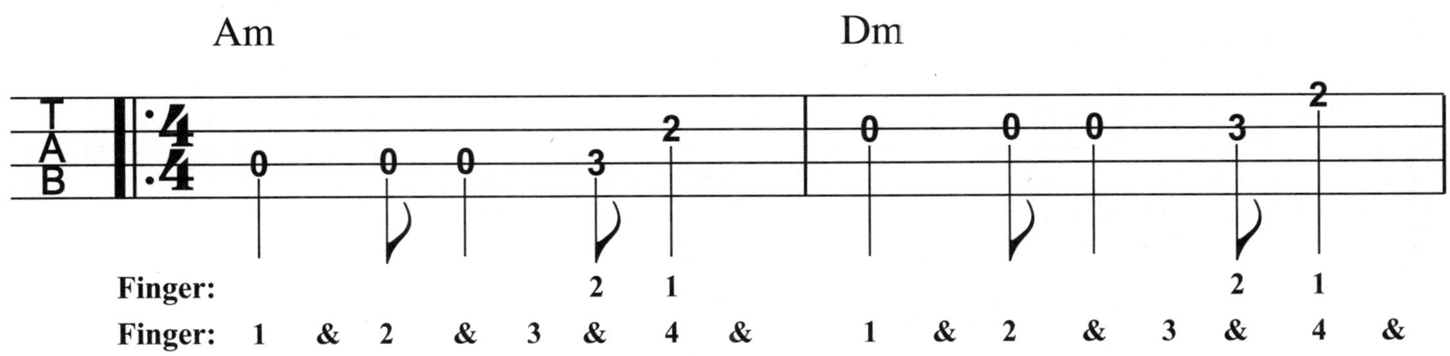

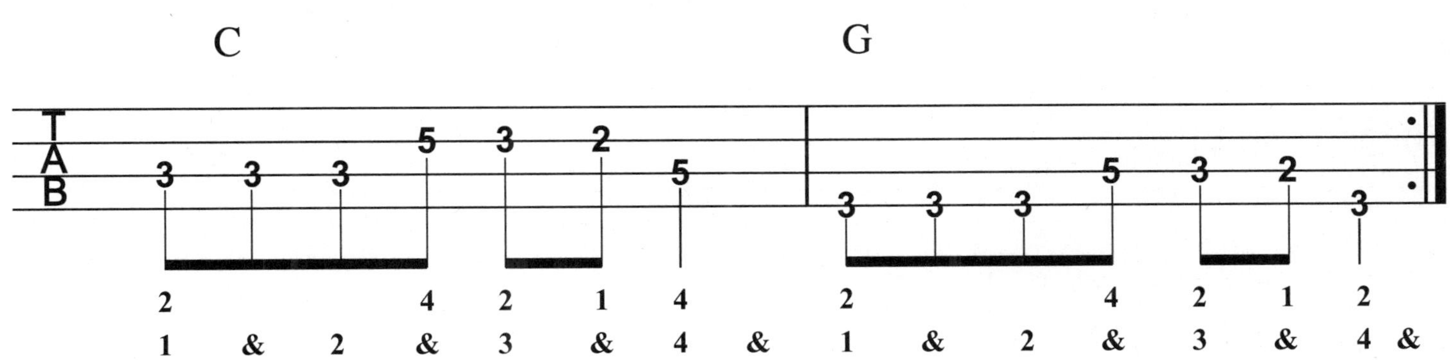

Exercise Routine

Here is a series of exercises to help develop coordination of both hands together. It's important to have a series of exercises that you practice daily to improve your technique. This will enable you to play more challenging bass lines.

The Killer

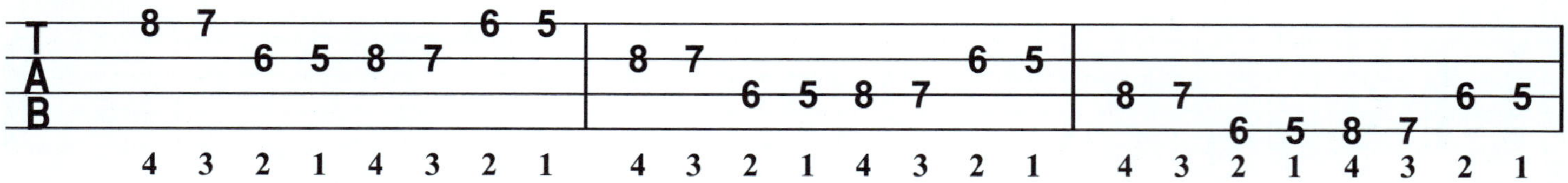

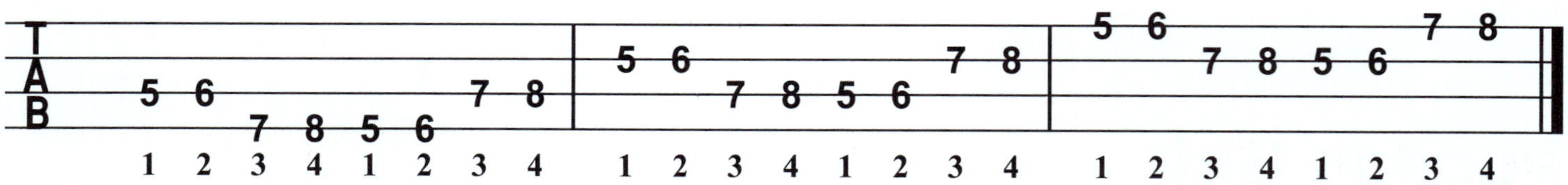

Finger Twister

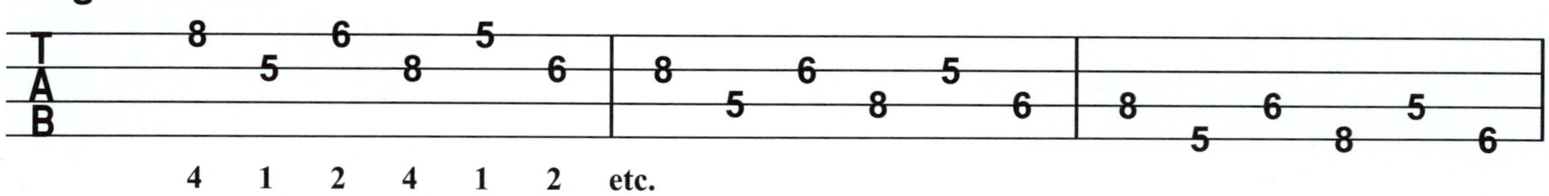

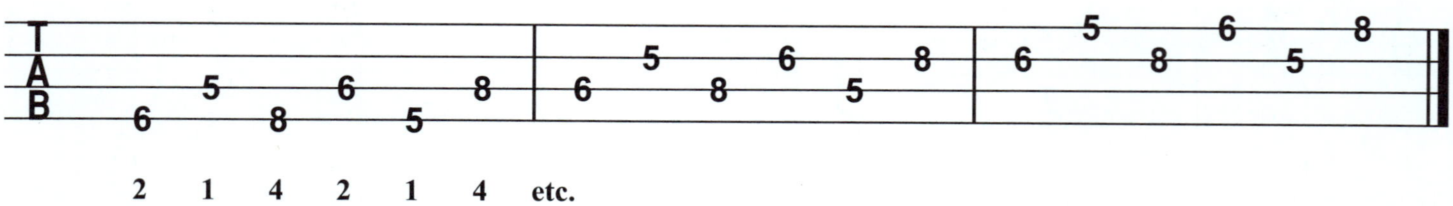

Finger Drag Exercise

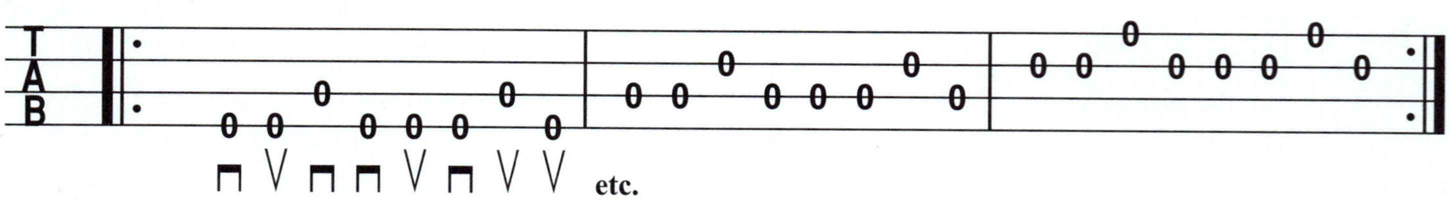

Lateral Pivot Exercise

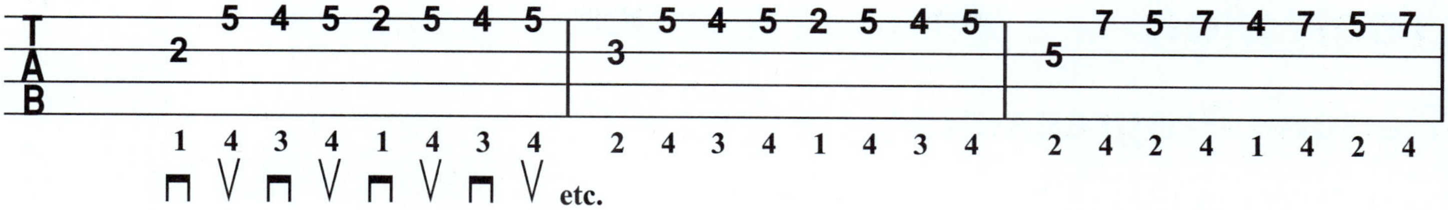

Following the Root Notes

Many times when you are creating bass lines you will follow the root note for each chord in the progression. A trick you can use when playing with a guitarist is to watch what fret they play the chord and play the note on that same fret on your 3rd or 4th strings.

Below is a progression that I wrote out so you can see how the bass can follow the chord changes.

Guitar Chord Progression

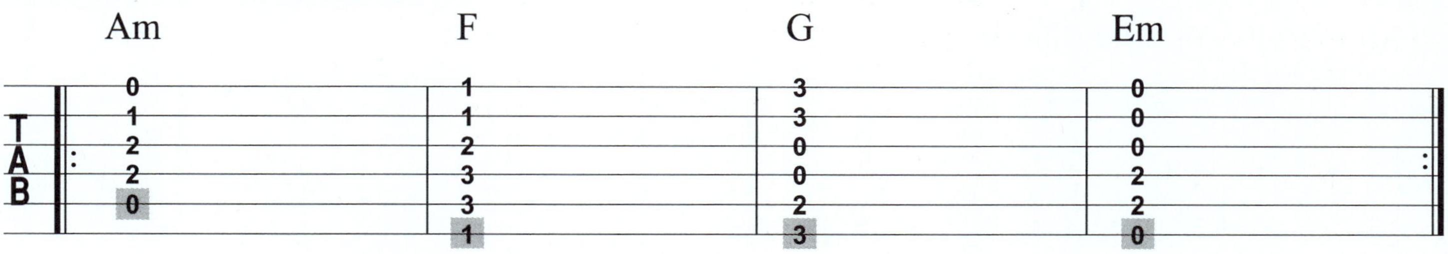

Bass Line

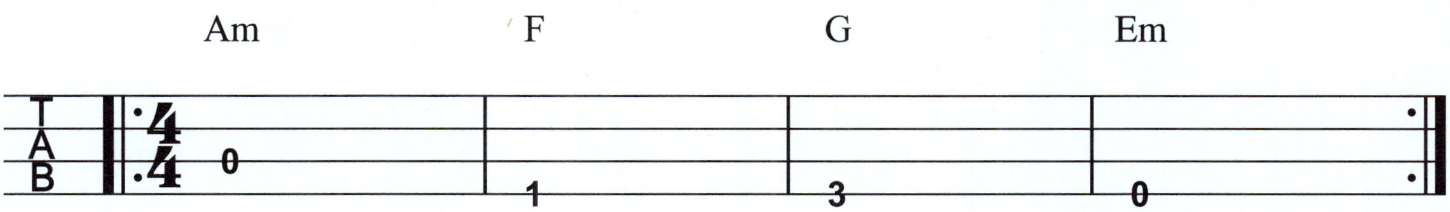

Yeah Mon

Reggae Progression

This is a reggae rhythm progression using major triads. Use the backing track to help understand the timing for this rhythm.

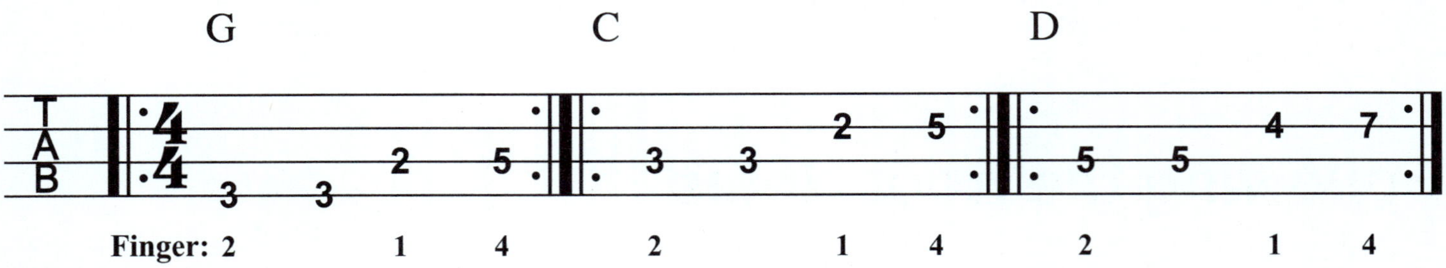

Notes in the 5th Position

You have previously learned the notes in the first position witch spanned the first four frets. Now let's go through the notes starting in the 5th position using the chromatic scale. Play the notes below and call out the name of each as you do so, this will help you memorize the names effectively.

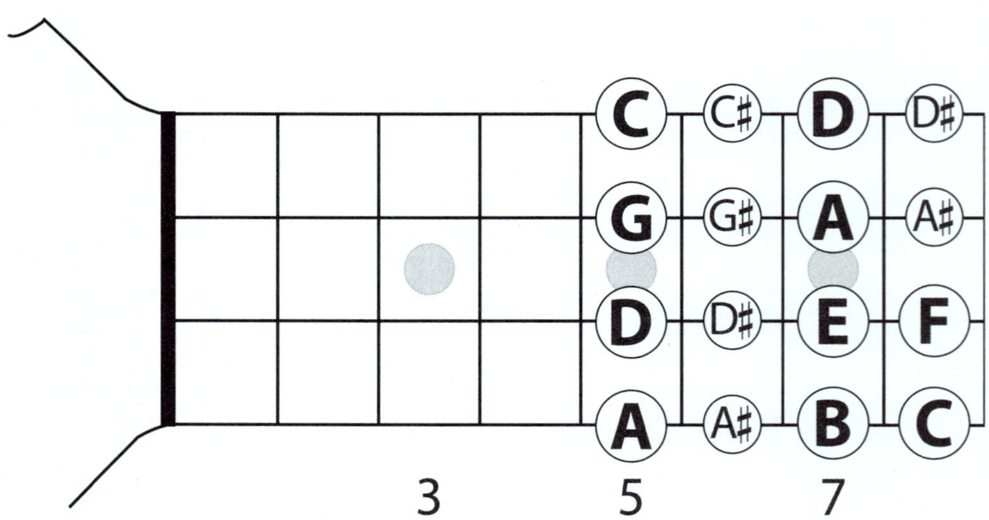

Find Any Note on the Bass

Using the chromatic scale and the names of the open strings you can learn the name of any note on the bass. It's very important to memorize the note names to help as you study how triads and scales are formed.

Below is a complete neck diagram showing the names of every note on the bass. Start with each string open and move one fret at a time up the neck to the 12th fret. Say out loud the name of each note. Once you have done each string several times you are ready to move on to the next part of this lesson the music assignment.

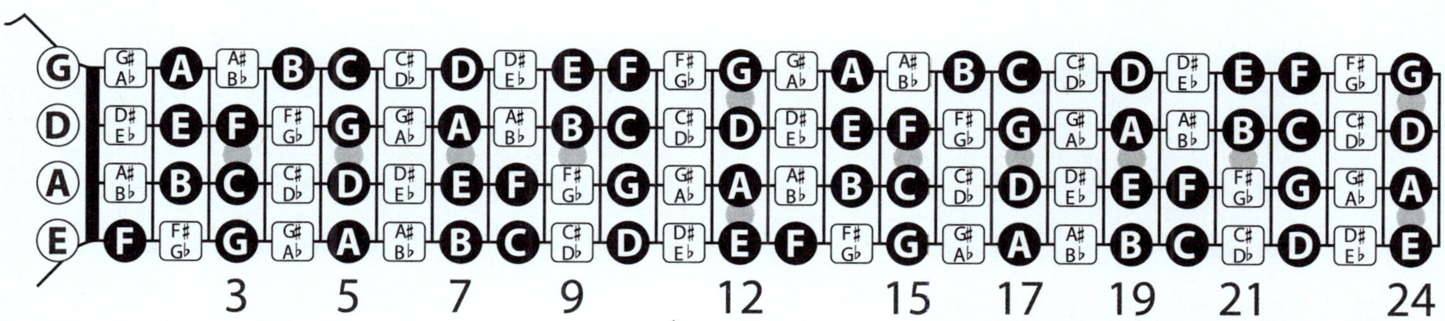

One thing to note, the bass repeats its notes after the 12th fret. This is why most basses have two dots at the 12th fret. For example the open 4th string is an E note when you get up to the 12th fret it is an E note again. The 4th string 1st fret is an F note and 12 frets higher on the 13th fret is another F note.

Music Assignment

Below is a series of string and fret numbers. Your assignment is to find the name of each note without using the chart above. You need to be able to find the name of any note just using the open strings and the chromatic scale. I've given you the first answer as an example.

1. 1st string 7th fret – **answer D note**
2. 4th string 3rd fret –
3. 2nd string 8th fret –
4. 4th string 7th fret –
5. 3rd string 10th fret –
6. 1st string 5th fret –
7. 2nd string 3rd fret –
8. 4th string 9th fret –
9. 3rd string 4th fret –
10. 1st string 3rd fret –

Slap & Pop Groove

In this example you will slap the open E string and pop the open G string. On the fourth beat of each measure there is a two note riff to add a little melody into the riff. Once you have the bass line so you can play it smoothly play it along with the backing track.

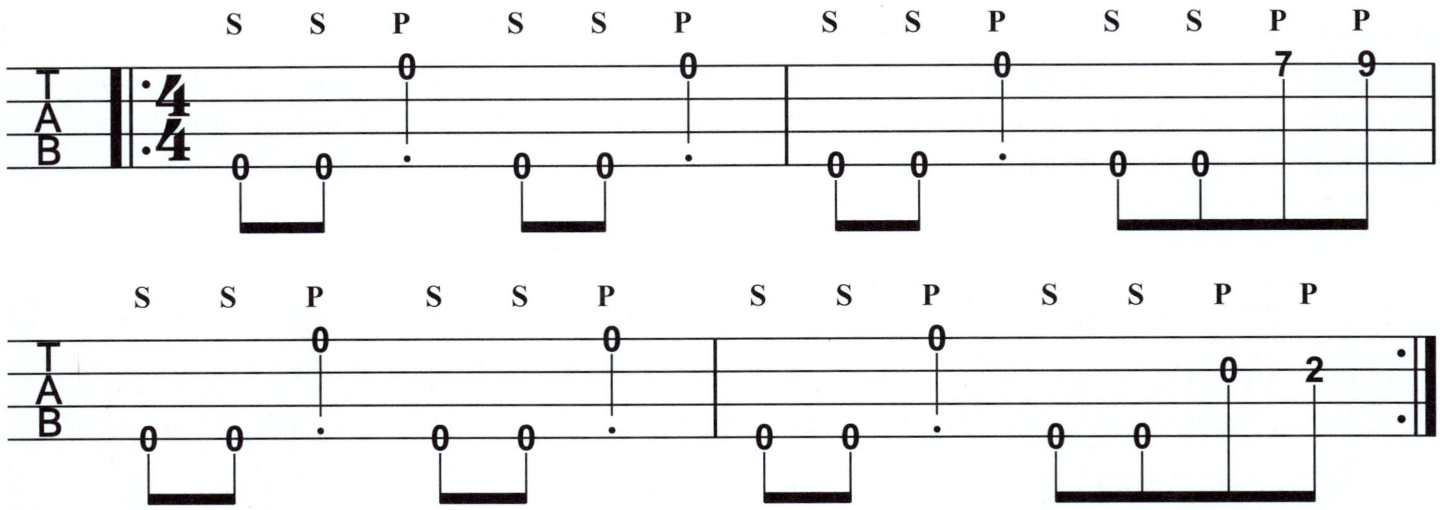

Music Assignment

A great way to practice the slap technique is to play the C major scale 1st position forwards and backwards using the slap technique to sound each note. Here are a few things that will help you slap more effectively. Make sure to strike the thumb hard and move it away from the string quickly, this will help make a solid tone. Also make sure to mute the strings around the note you are slapping, because you are striking the strings hard the other strings will have a tendency to ring out.

Legato

In Book 1 you learned staccato, legato is the opposite of staccato. The definition of legato is smooth and connected. To play notes with a legato technique you will use hammer ons, pull offs and slides. To play a slide you pluck the first note and while holding the pressure down on the note you slide the finger up or down the neck to another note. When notes are to be played using legato there will be a curved line also known as a slur placed over these notes.

Example 1 Slides **Example 2 Hammer Pull Offs & Slides**

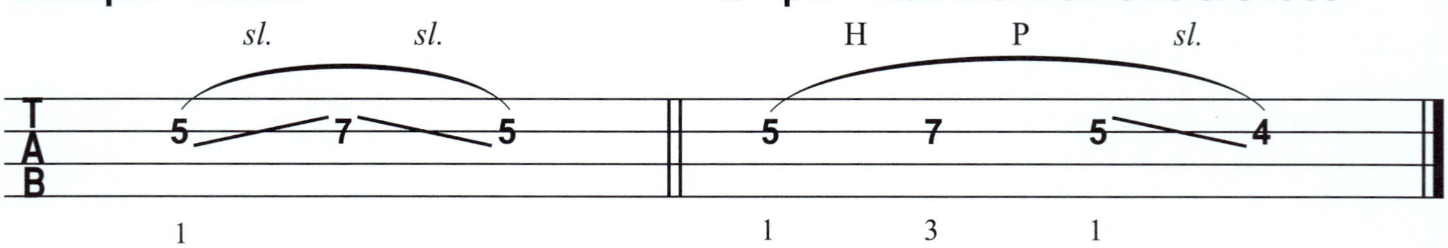

Hammer Pull Off Single Note Pattern

Here is a pattern that combines the hammer on and pull off together to form a great sounding technique. There will be three notes sounded with only one pluck. Pluck the first note and with one swift motion hammer and pull of the next two notes.

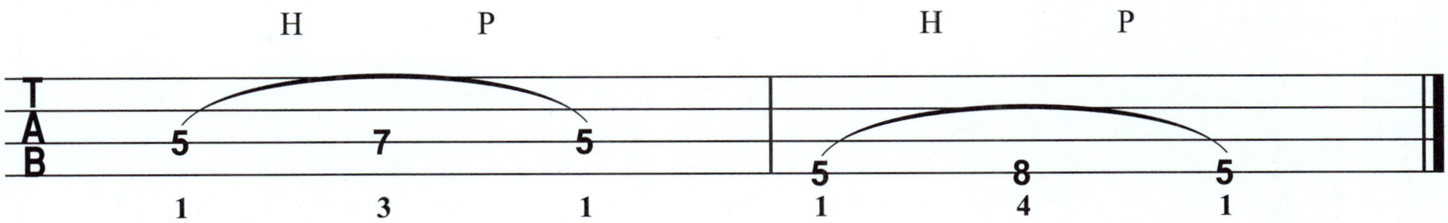

1st Position

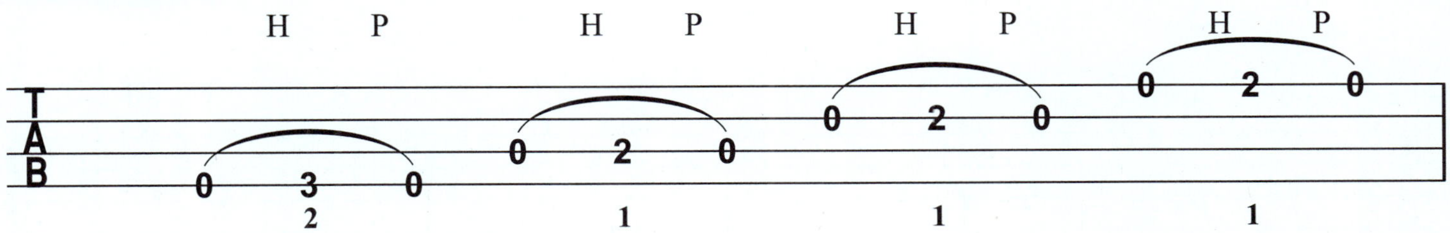

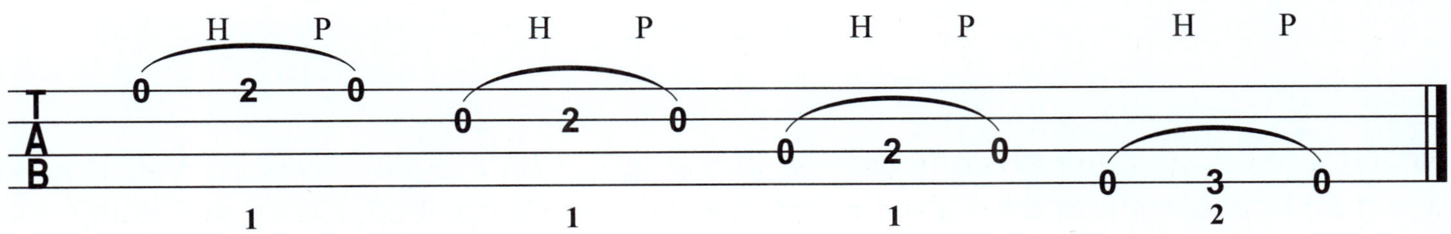

1st Position (Octave)

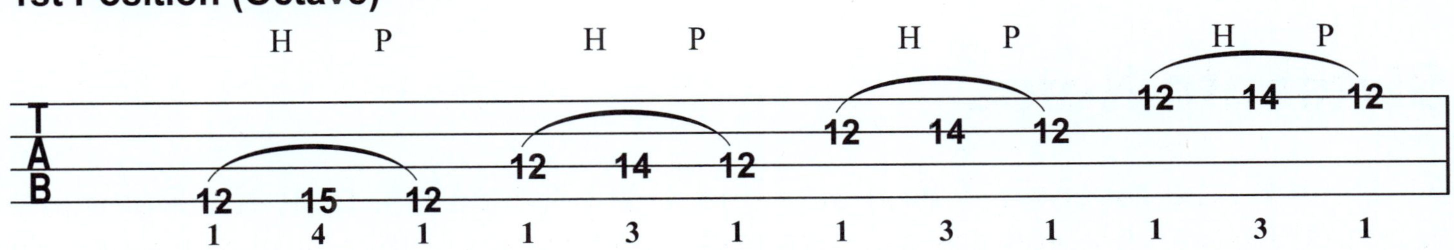

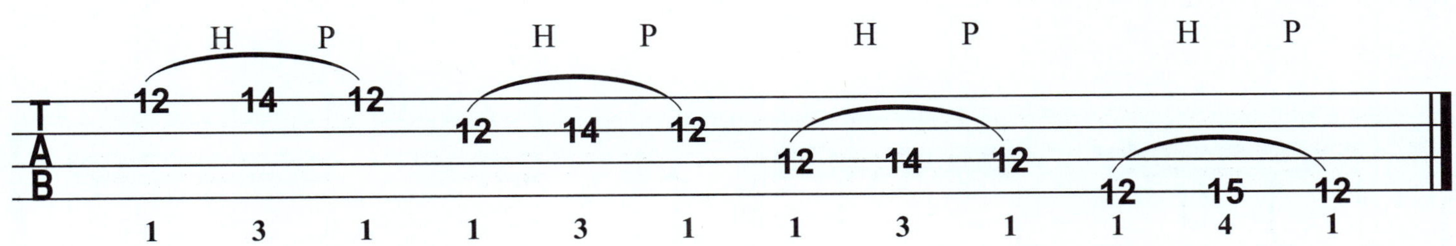

Sunday Groove

Hammer & Pull Offs in a Bass Line

Here is a bass line that incorporates the hammer on pull off technique. After you feel comfortable playing this bass line play it along with the backing track and apply it in a band setting.

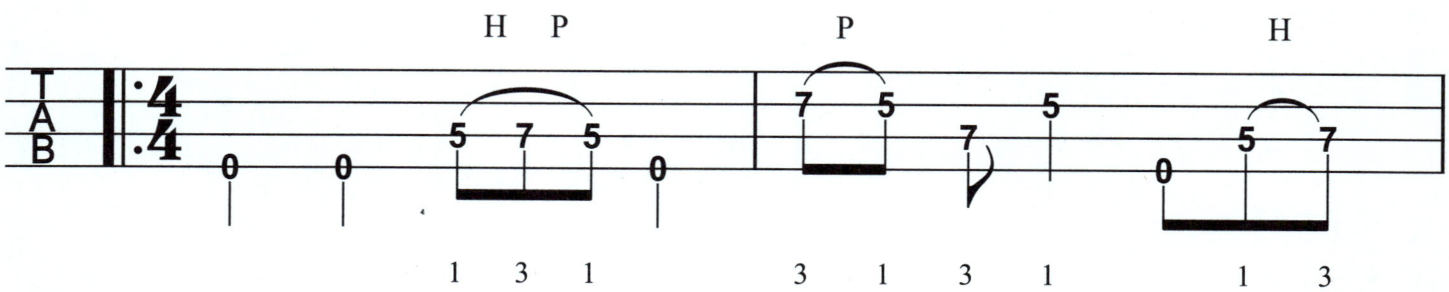

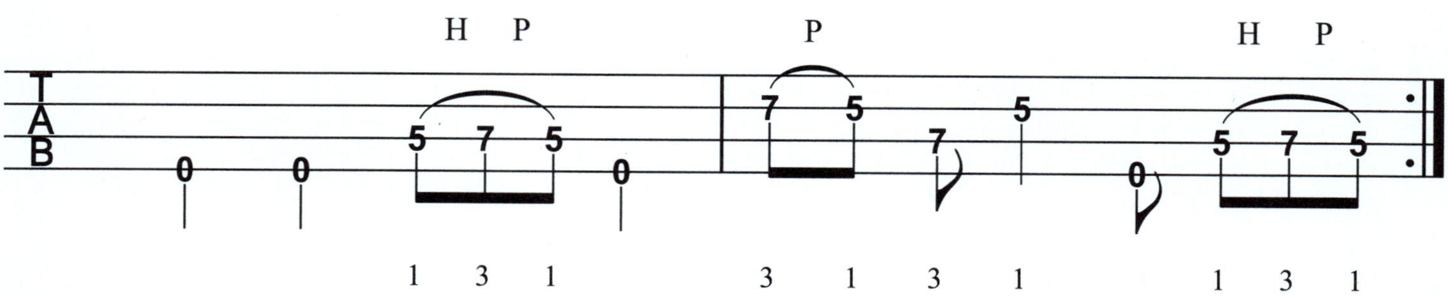

Notice that the hammer pull offs used in this progression are played as triplets. This is common because there bare three notes in each hammer pull off. Count the timing out loud before you play the progression. There is quarter notes, eighth notes and triplets here and it may take a little practice to get the feel of the timing.

Sixteenth Notes

A sixteenth note receives ¼ beat of sound. It subdivides one beat into four equal sections. Sixteenth notes are twice as fast as an eighth note. Count out sixteenth notes now as follows:

There are four subdivisions for every one beat. Tap your foot down on each beat or number. Now play sixteenth notes on the 4th and 3rd strings using alternate plucking.

Example 1

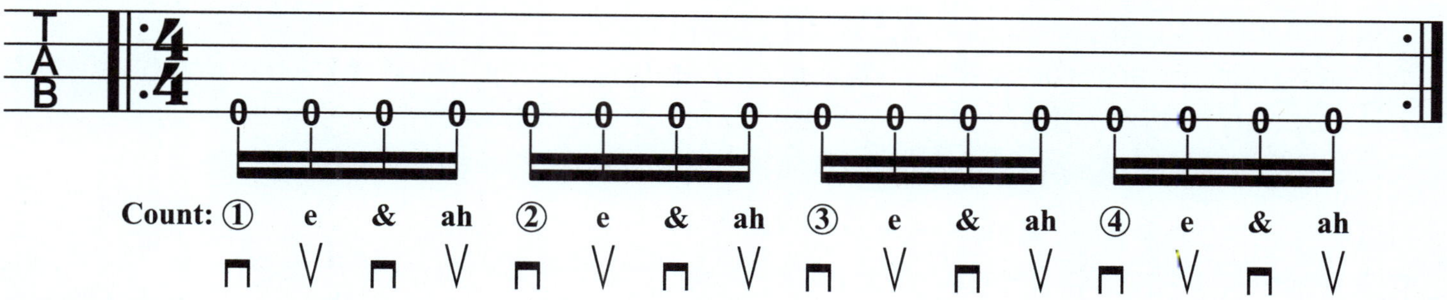

Example 2

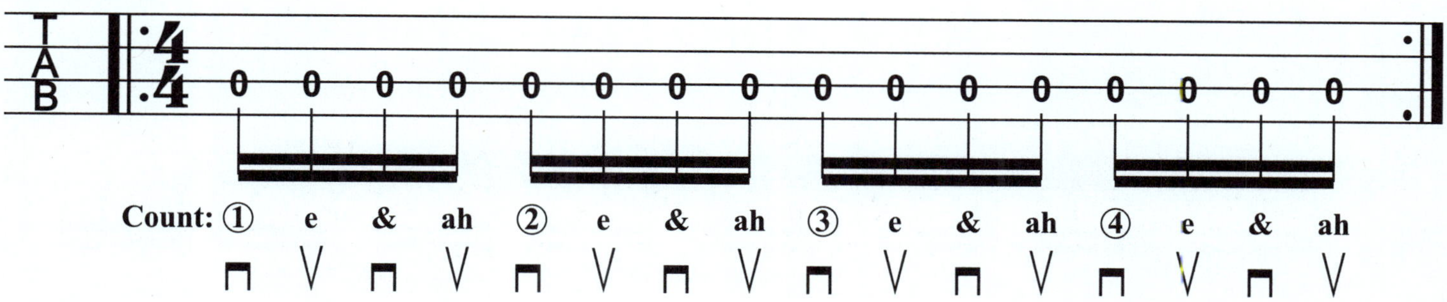

Accent (pluck harder) on the down beat to get a true sixteenth note feel.

Music Assignment

Count eighth and sixteenth notes along with your favorite music. As a song is playing, tap your foot and count along using eighth and sixteenth note timing. Get familiar counting these note values because they are very common in every genre of music.

Inspirational Quote

"When people hear good music,
it makes them homesick for something they never had,
and never will have."

Edgar Watson

Hit it Hard

Sixteenth Notes in a Bass Line

This bass line incorporates the sixteenth notes you just learned. Make sure to use the new counting method, 1 – e – & – ah, as you play the following bass line.

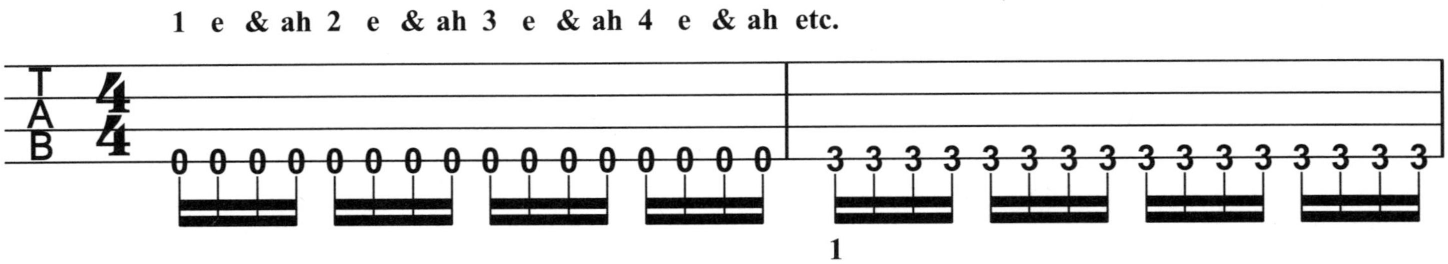

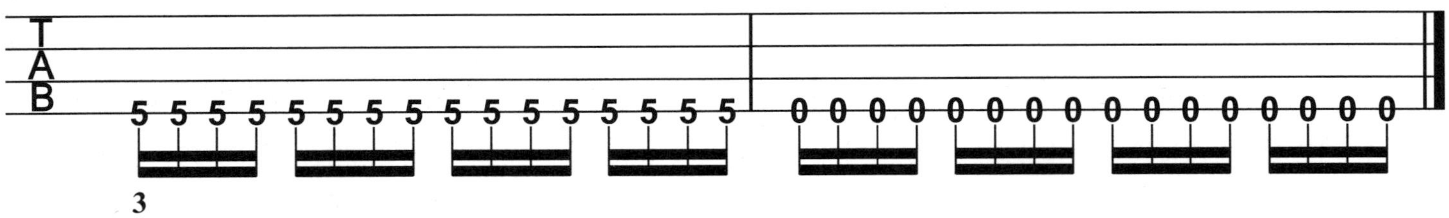

Canon Progression

Canon is a very popular classical piece and many rock and pop songs have borrowed its structure. I've outlined the chord changes above the staff, The bass plays the root notes for each chord.

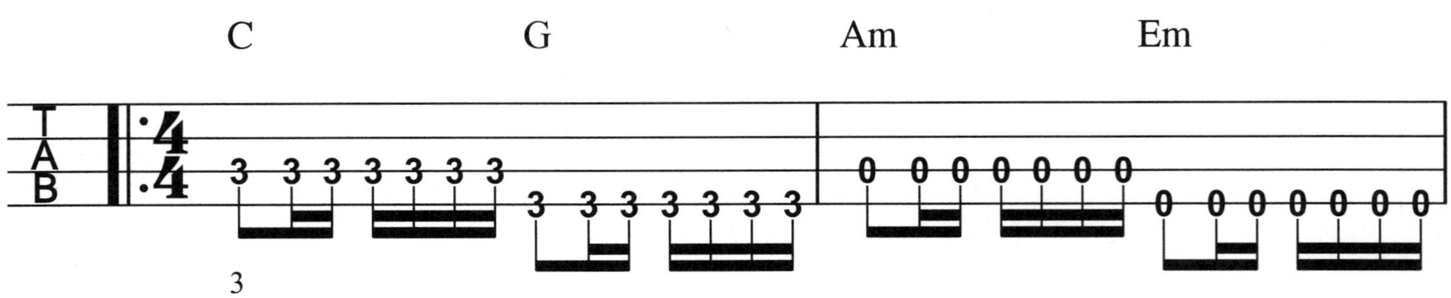

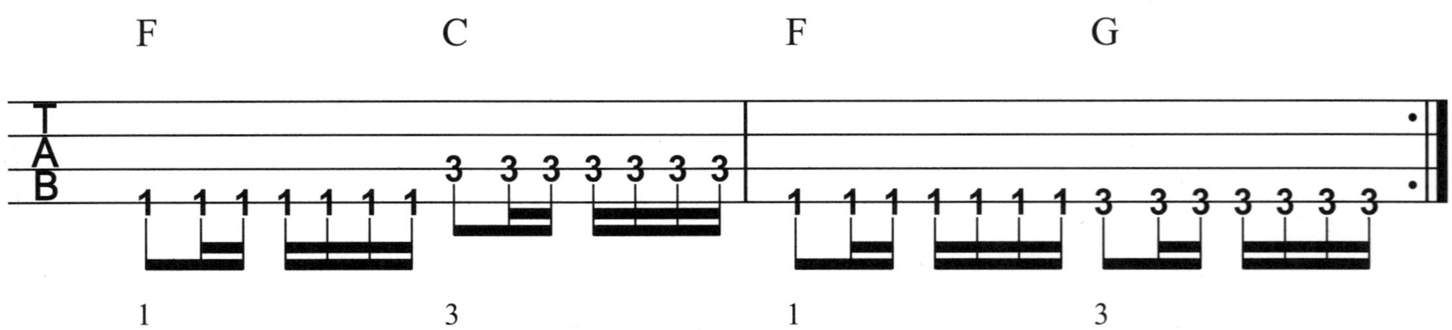

Syncopated Bass Lines

A syncopated rhythm has accents that are not in the common places as a straight rhythm. I like to think of a syncopated rhythm as a rhythm that moves and makes your body move with it. In this rhythm you will find syncopated accents. Pay close attention to the staccato markings below the staffs.

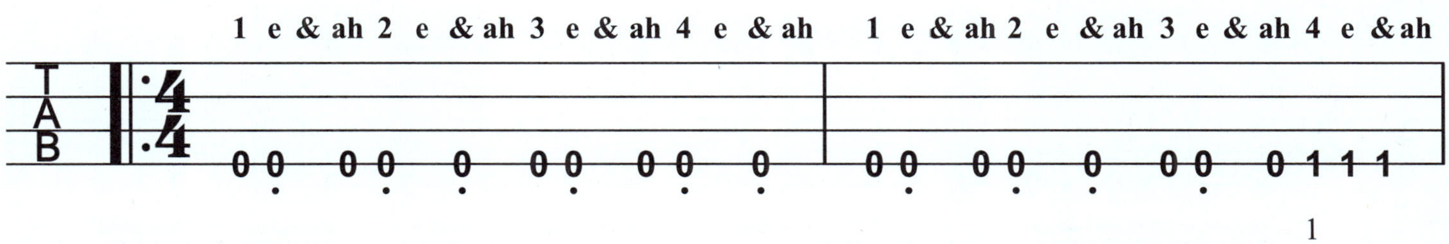

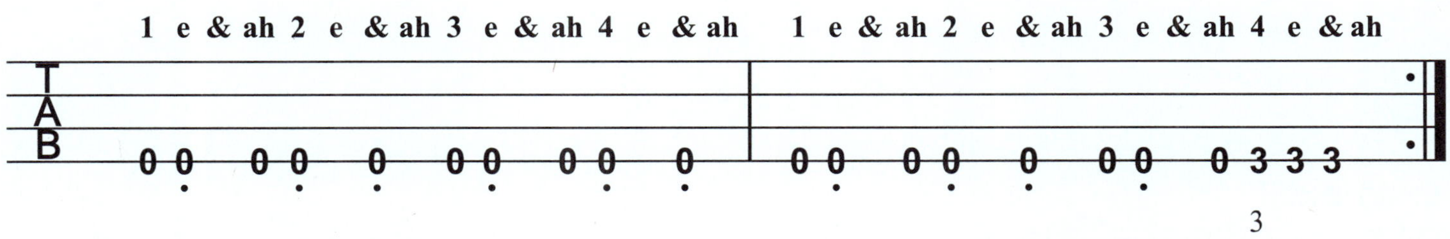

Syncopated Bass Line with 5ths & Octaves

Now you will add fifths and octaves into the syncopated rhythm. This is more challenging so take your time starting off slow and building your speed gradually.

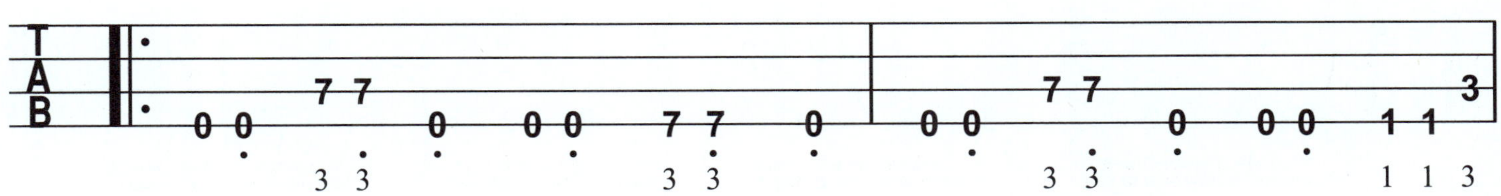

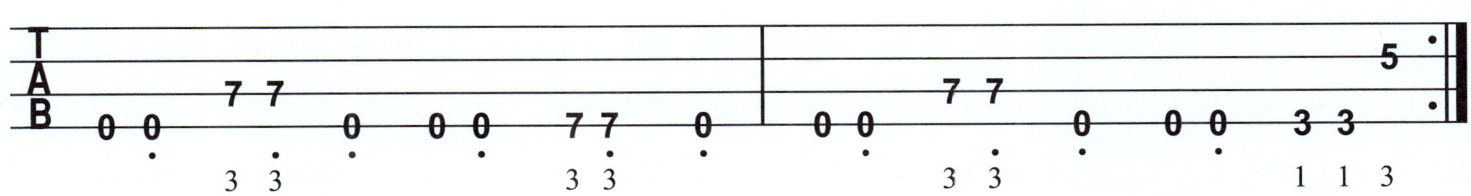

Slap & Pop Sixteenth Note Grooves

Here are three slap and pop grooves that accent different sixteenth note timings. Pay close attention to where each pop comes within each groove. This will give it a syncopated feel.

Example 1

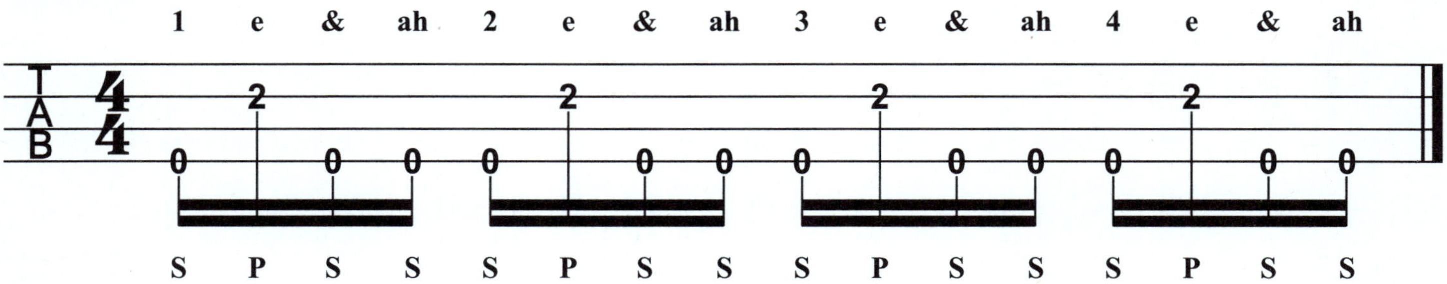

Example 2

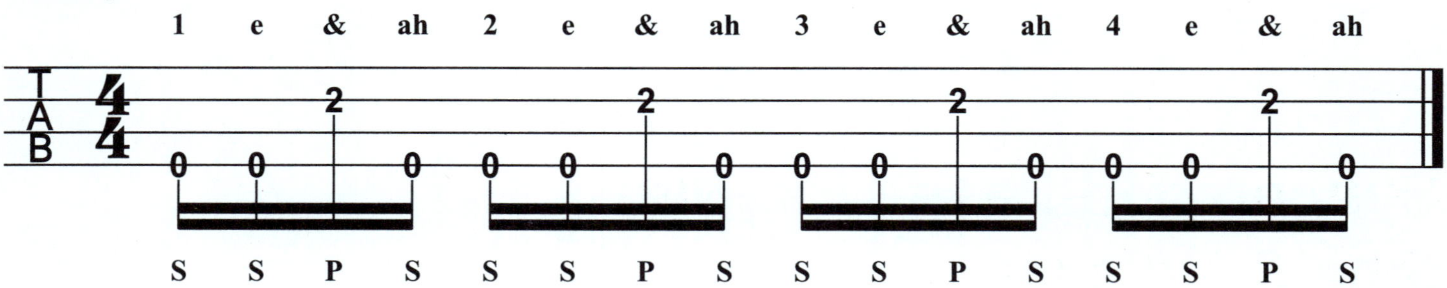

Example 3

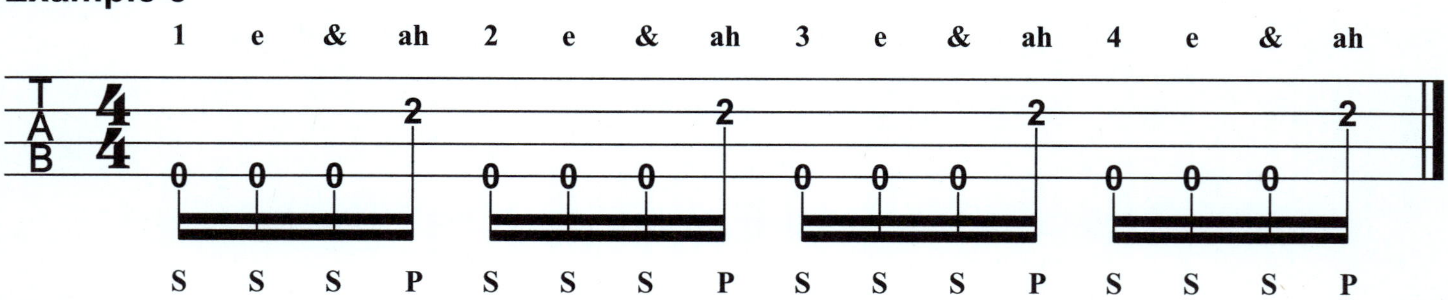

Bass 2 Quiz #2

You're ready to take your next quiz now! Please review all the lessons in the previous section then go to page 4 to see where to take your quiz.

Intervals

An interval is the distance between two notes. Each interval has a distinct sound. As you play the following intervals make sure to listen closely to the sound of each. These intervals are used in chord construction and harmony. It is very important that you work hard to memorize their sound.

Minor 2nd

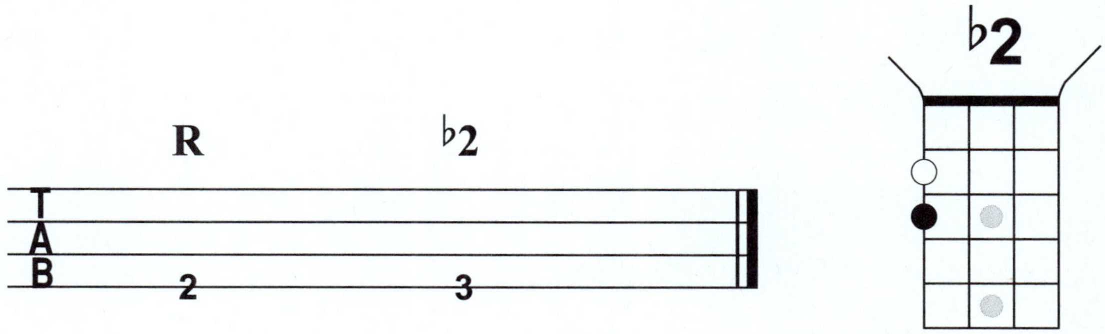

Major 2nd

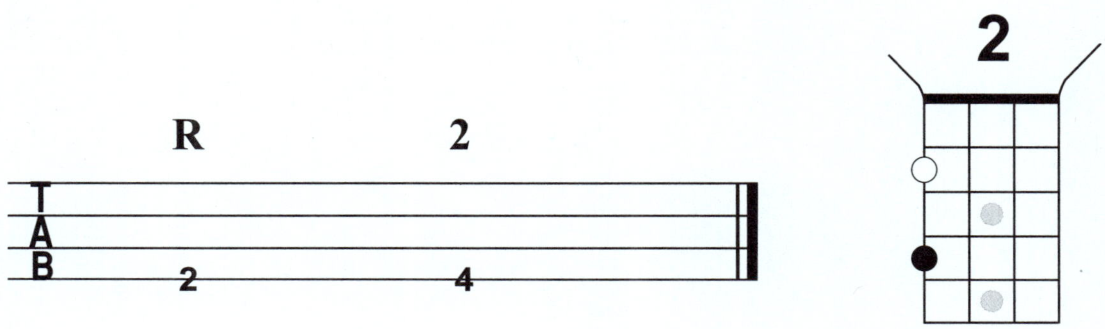

Minor 3rd

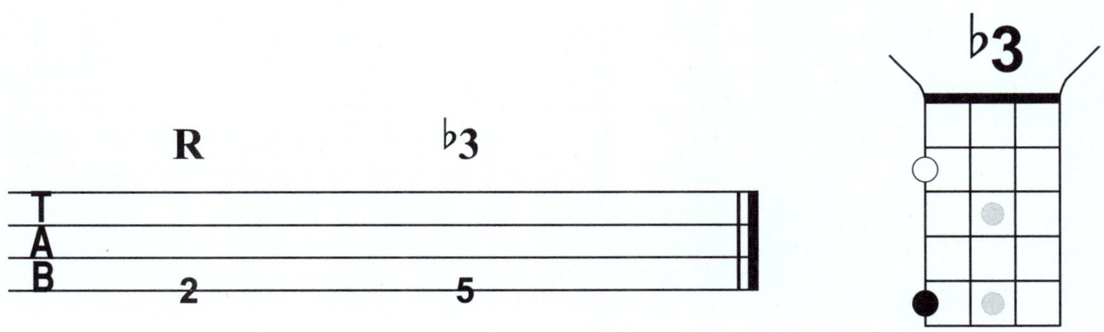

Major 3rd

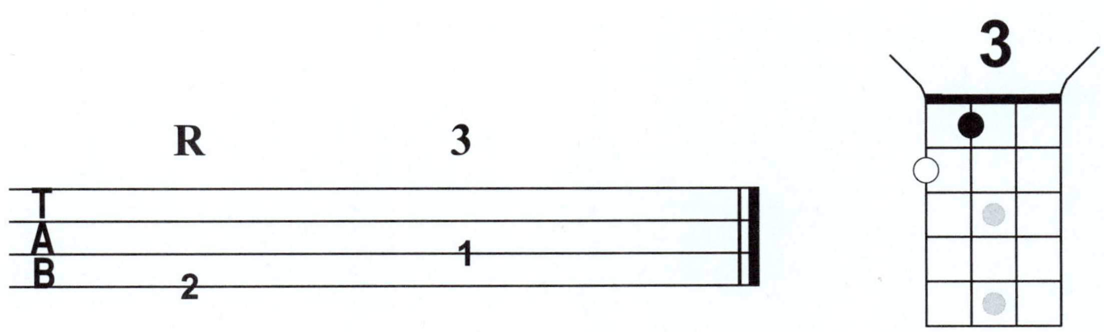

Perfect 4th

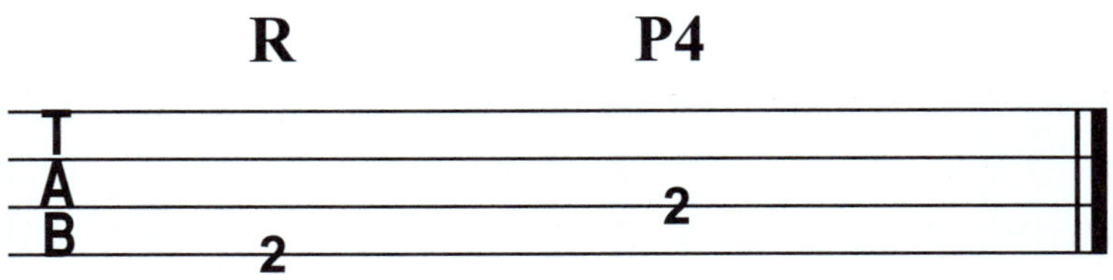

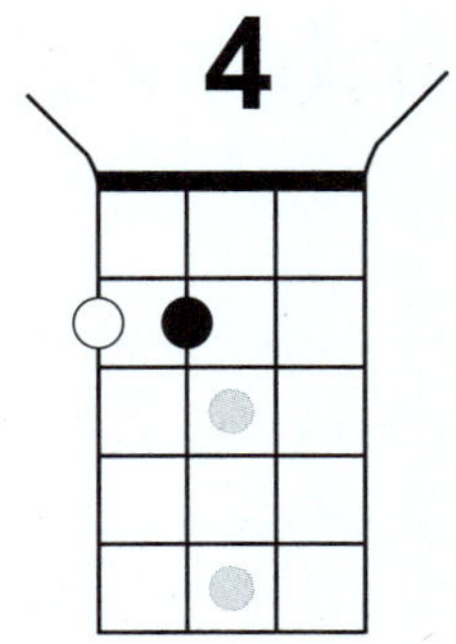

Augmented 4th/Diminished 5th

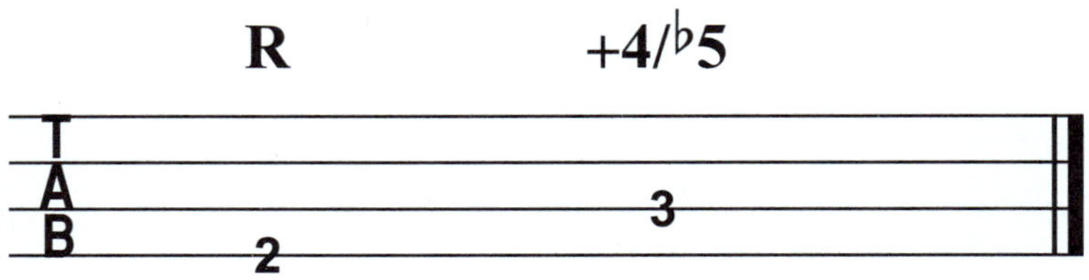

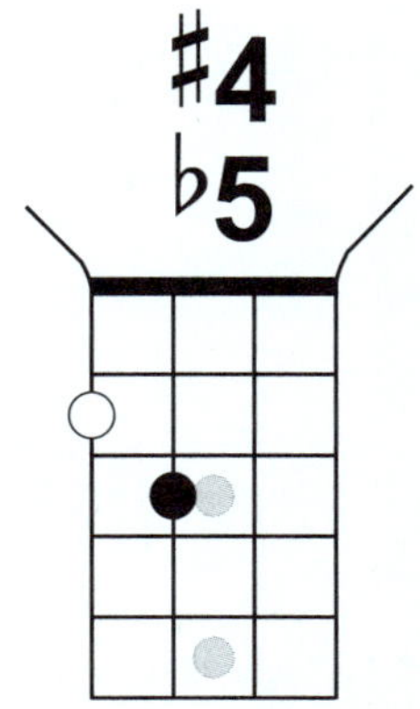

Perfect 5th

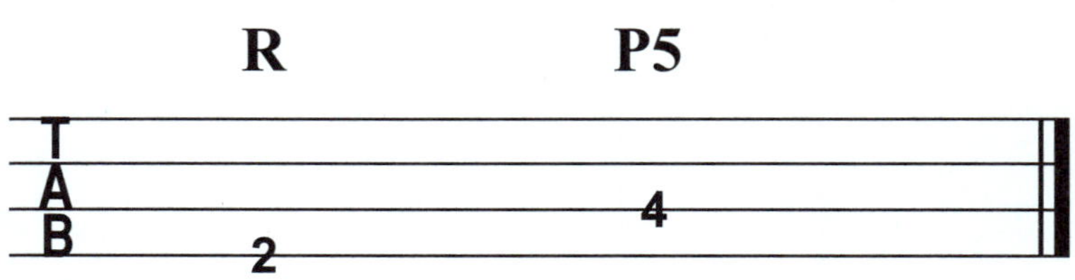

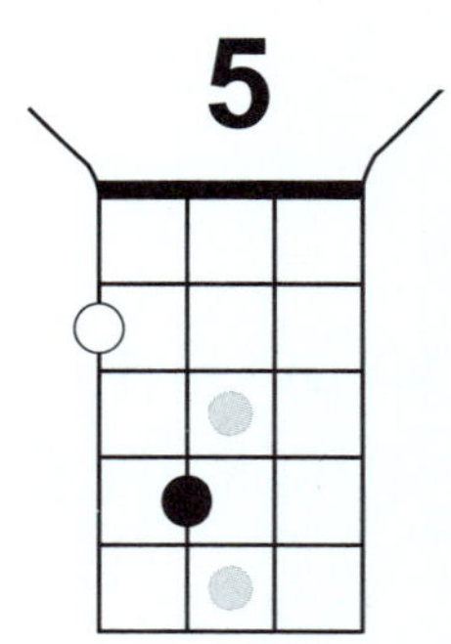

Minor 6th

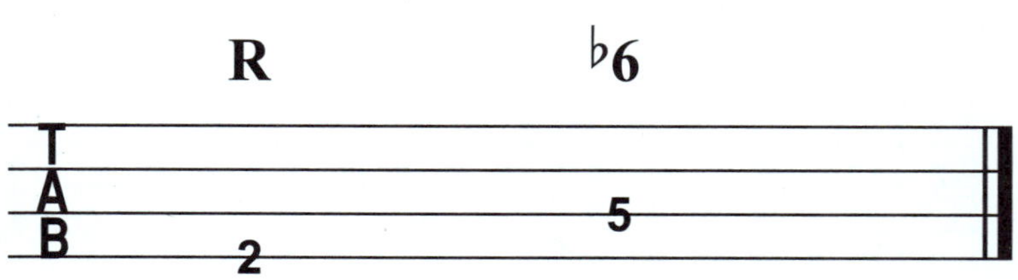

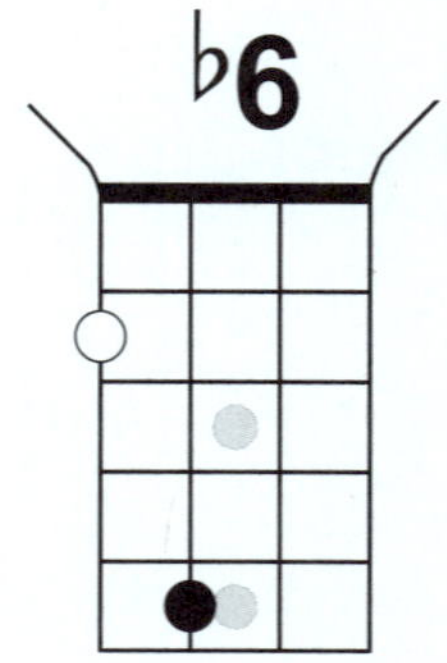

Major 6th

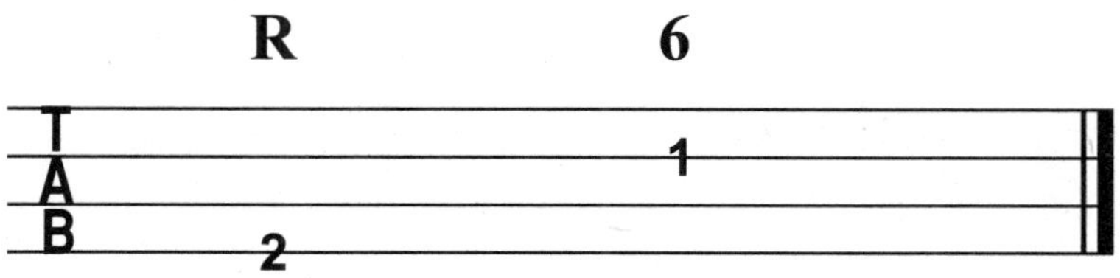

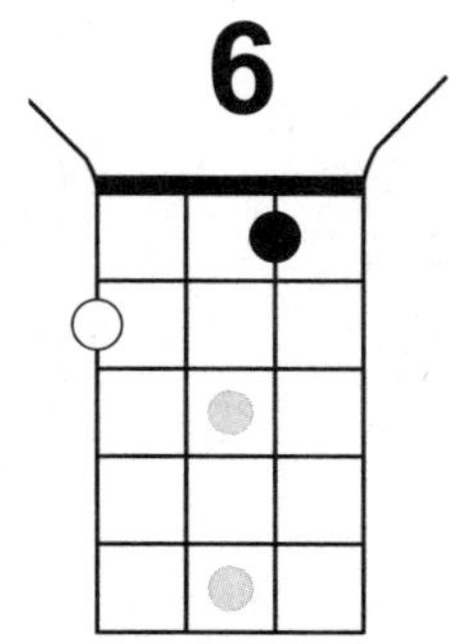

Minor 7th

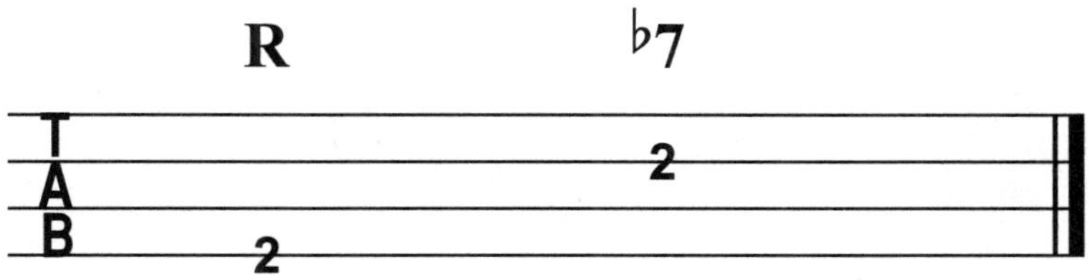

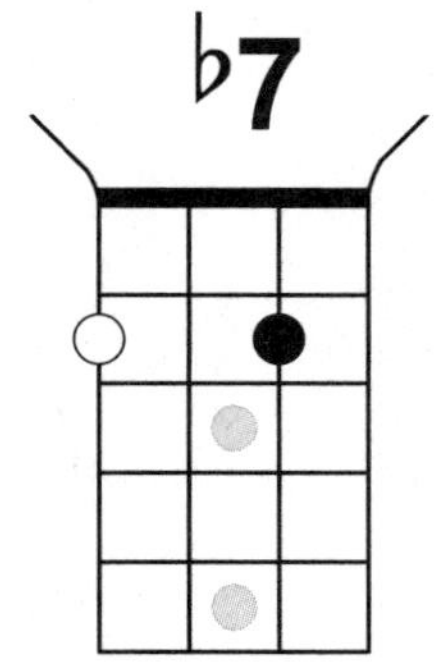

Major 7th

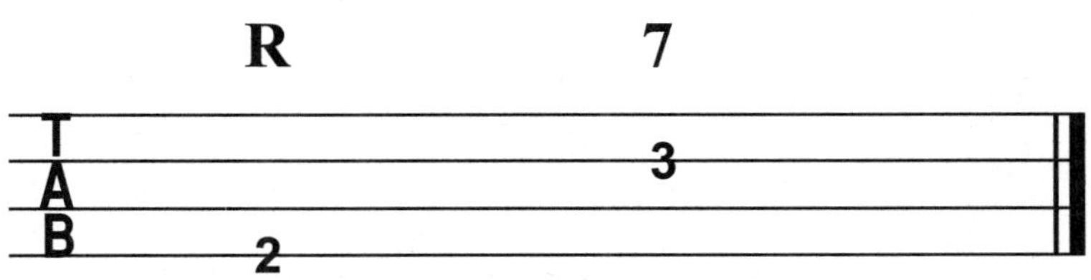

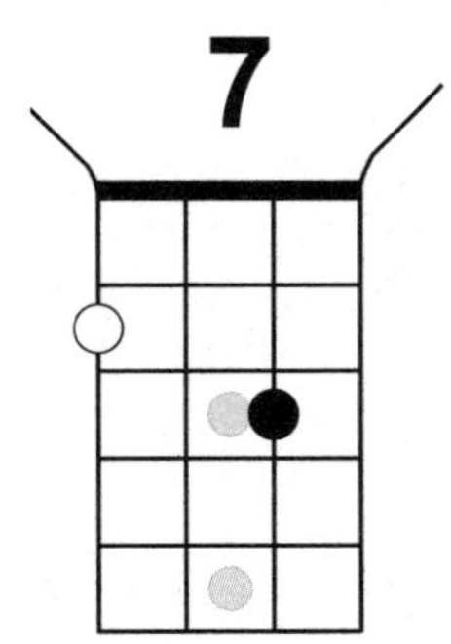

Perfect Octave

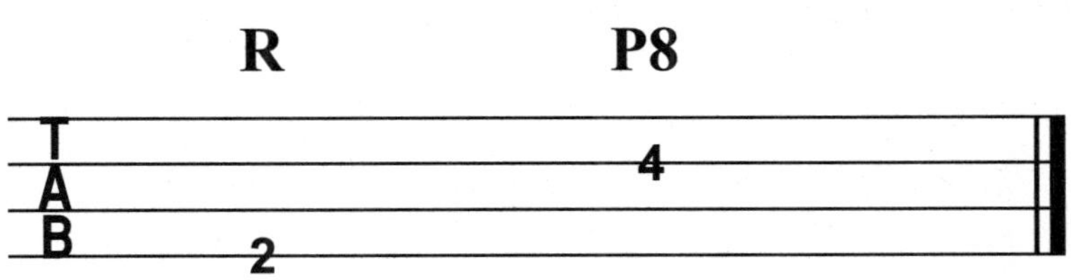

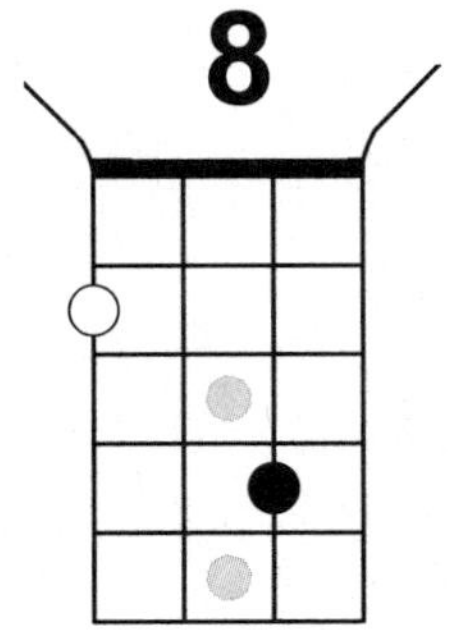

Turn Things Around

This is another blues shuffle rhythm with a turnaround in the last measure. The turnaround brings the progression back to the beginning in a seamless circle fashion.

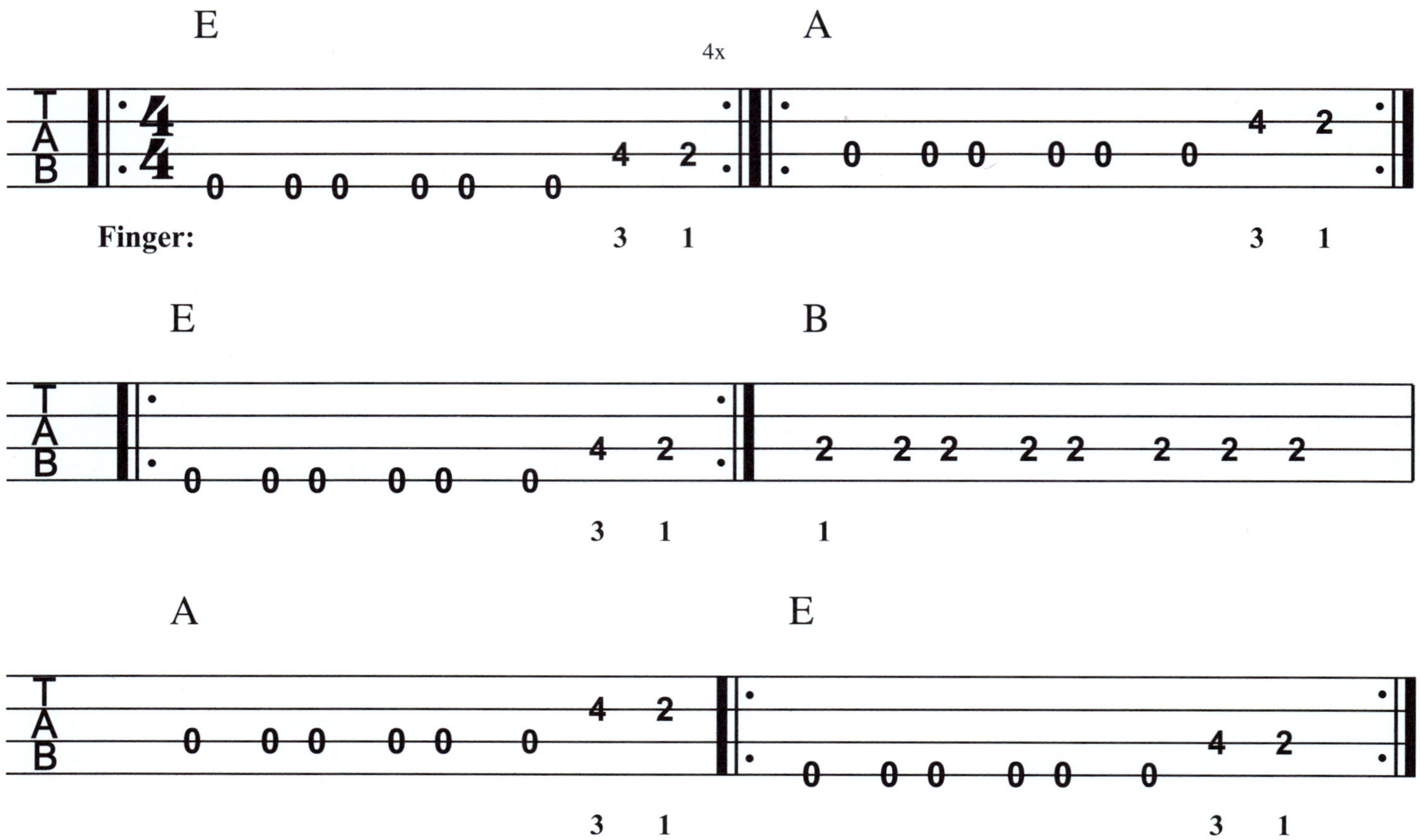

Drop D Tuning

Drop D tuning lowers the 4th string E down one whole step while all the other three strings stay at standard pitch. From high to low the strings would be:

(Thinnest) 1st String	2nd String	3rd String	(Thickest) 4th String
G	**D**	**A**	**D**

Now put your bass into drop D tuning. Here is an easy way to do it: if starting from standard tuning you already have a D open string the 2nd string, pluck this string open and let it ring out, then pluck your 4th string open and tune it down slowly until you hear the pitches come together. Remember all the other three strings stay standard tuning.

Altered Tunings

Although they are not used in this book there are other versions of altered tunings where strings are lowered anywhere from a ½ to 2 whole steps. Let's look at a few popular altered and drop tunings: D tuning has all four strings lowered one whole step, drop C tuning is the same as D tuning except the low E string is lowered another whole step to C.

D Tuning

(Thinnest) 1st String	2nd String	3rd String	(Thickest) 4th String
F	**C**	**G**	**D**

Drop C Tuning

(Thinnest) 1st String	2nd String	3rd String	(Thickest) 4th String
F	**C**	**G**	**C**

B tuning simulates the bottom 4 strings of a 5 string bass. For this tuning every string is dropped 2 whole steps. This tuning loosens the tension on the neck drastically; you may need to adjust the bass truss rod to tune in this fashion.

B Tuning

(Thinnest) 1st String	2nd String	3rd String	(Thickest) 4th String
D	**A**	**E**	**B**

Drop D I-IV-V Progression

The I-IV-V progression is the most popular chord progression. This chord progression is constructed by building chords off the 1st – 4th and 5th degrees of a major scale. Many songs in all genres of music have been written using this chord structure so it should sound familiar.

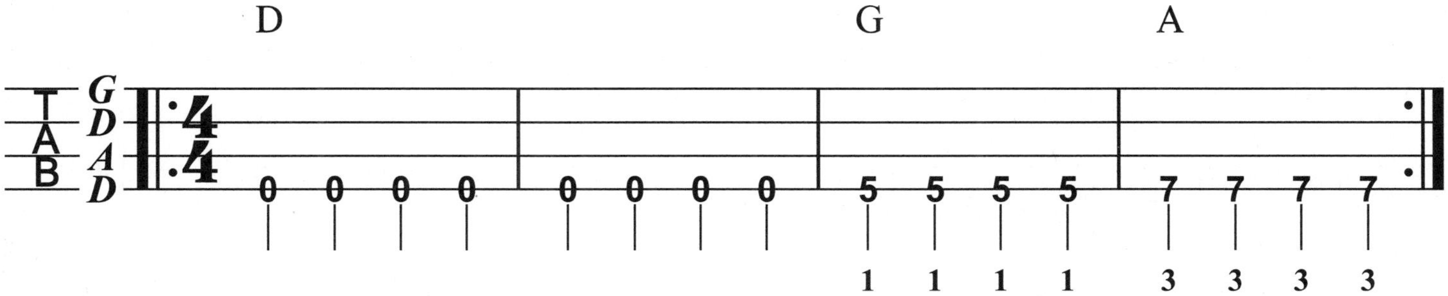

Mean Street

Drop D Bass Line

Here is a bass line that incorporates the drop D tuning. Once you feel comfortable playing the bass line play it over the backing track and hear the full heavy sound this tuning creates.

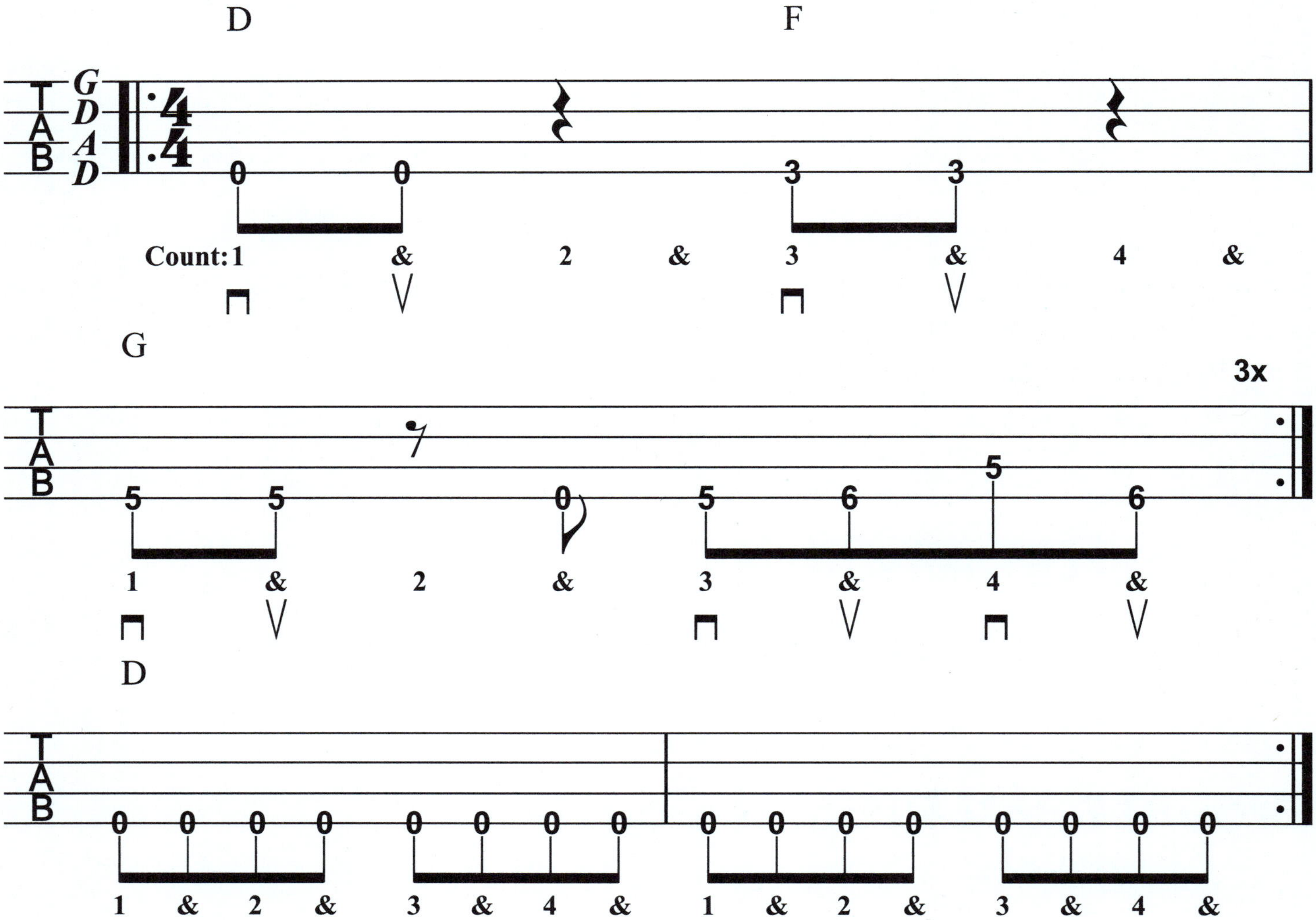

Practice Tips

To ensure constant progress and high motivation you have to develop practice habits that will keep you interested and challenged. Here are a few tips:

Practice Consistently - You need to give your fingers a chance to gain muscle memory. Practice every day even if it is for a short amount of time, be consistent.

Practice Area - Have a practice spot set up so you can have privacy to focus on your playing. It is a great idea to have a music stand to help position your music so you can sit comfortably.

Practice Schedule - Set a scheduled practice time each day and make this a routine. Other times in the day you can play for fun and jam a little.

Big Bottom

Bass Chords

Chord Professor

Here are a few examples of using chords in a bass line. These pieces use single notes and chords separately and combined to form great bass lines. Below are the chords that are used in these bass lines.

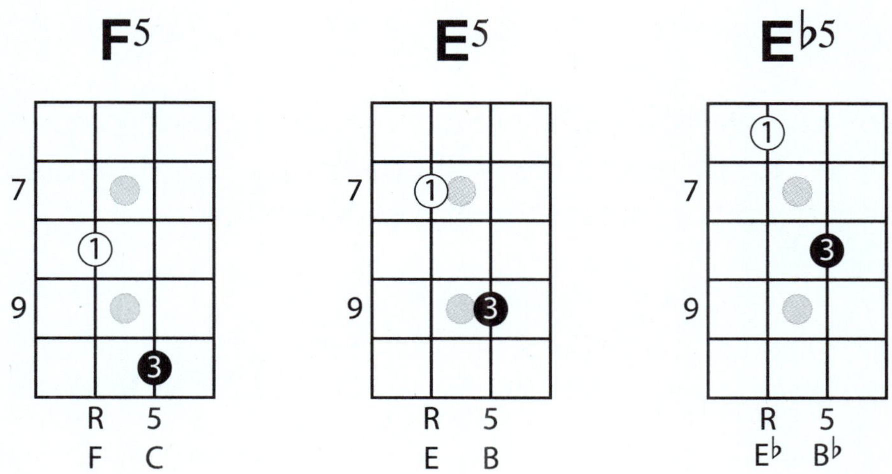

Example 1

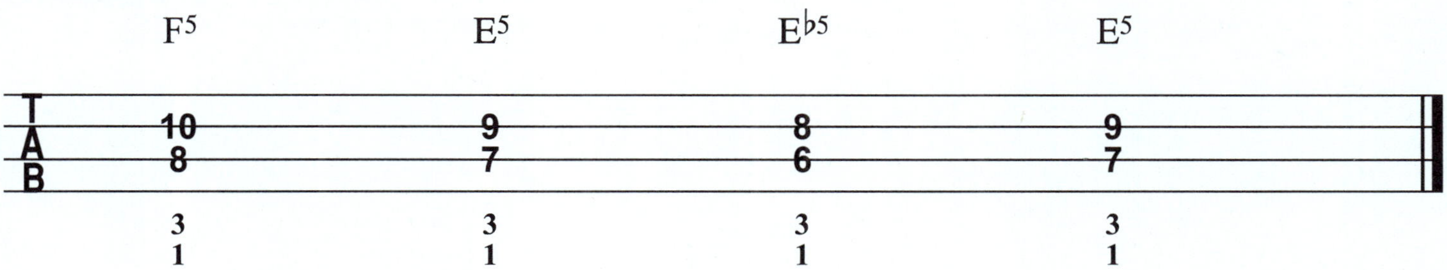

Example 2

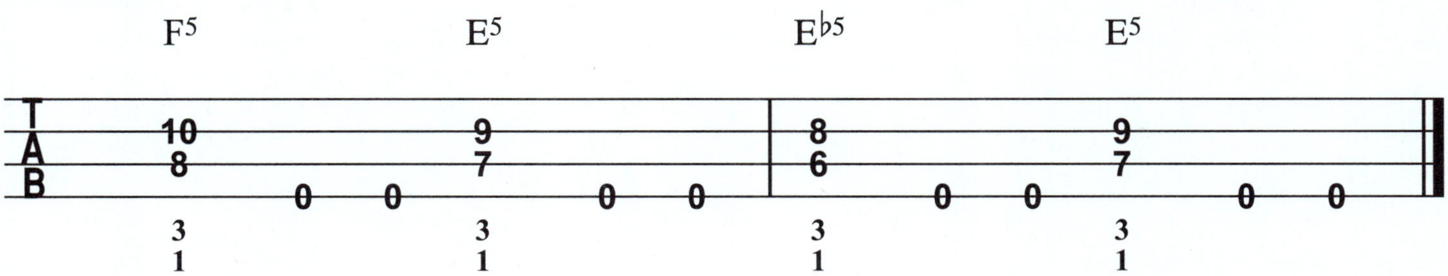

Example 3

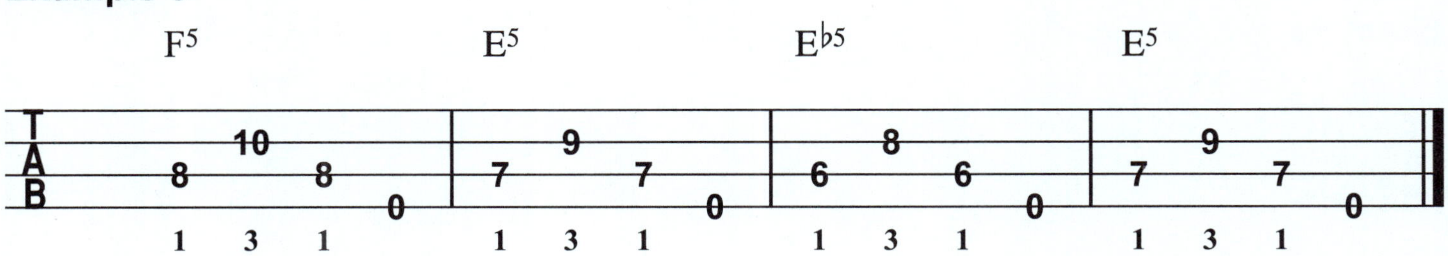

Music Assignment

After you have played these chords in these three examples it's time to make your own bass line with chords. Using basic power chords like in these examples create your own bass line. Combine strumming, and plucking to the notes. You should write your creations out in tablature to build a collection of your own ideas. This will help you to develop your own style and sound.

Vibrato

Vibrato is a technique where you slightly shake a note to give it a wider sound spectrum. This can be compared to a singer's wavy sound created as they hold out a note. You want to make the notes on your bass sing in a similar fashion.

Example 1

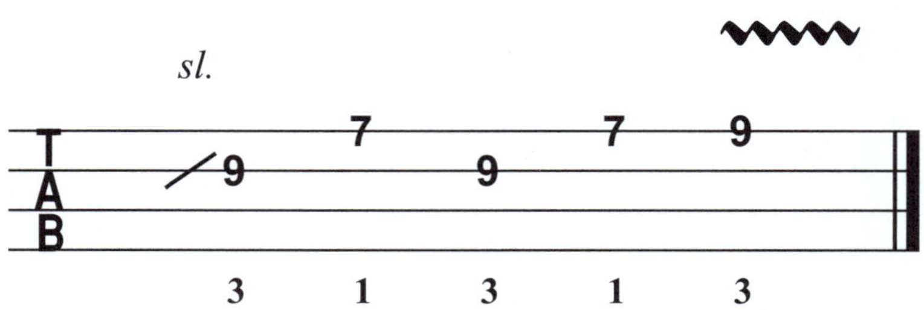

Example 2

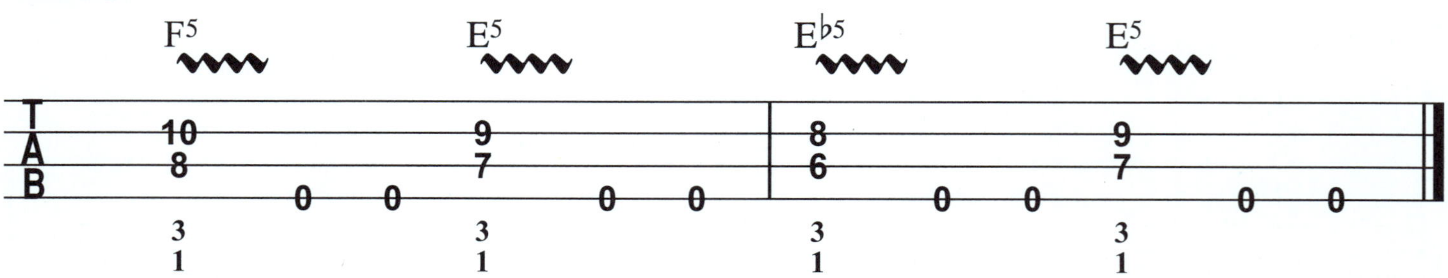

Example 3

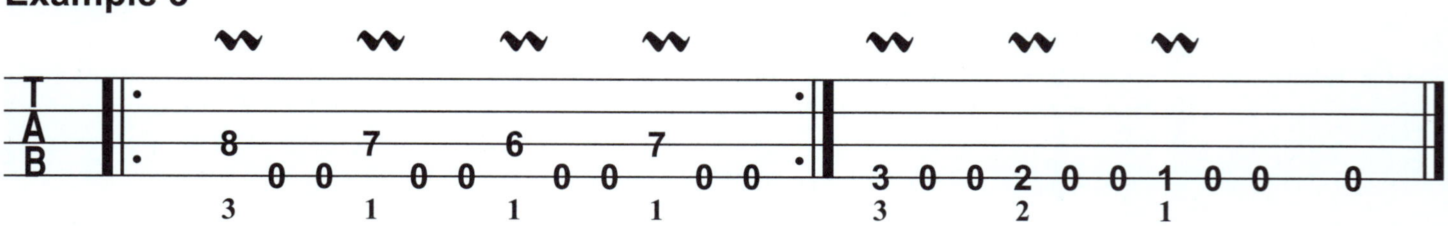

Hammer Ons and Pedal Tones

Now you will play a bass line using hammer ons while pedaling the open A string. Pedaling is going back to a note or group of notes within a phrase. Make sure to use the backing track to apply this bass line in a full band fashion.

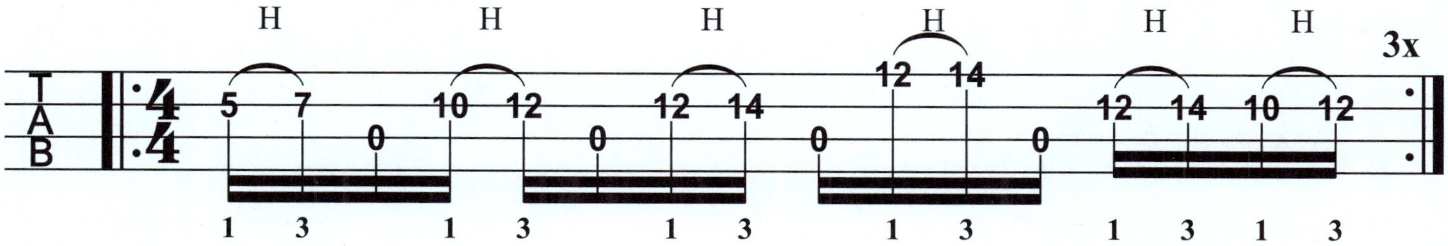

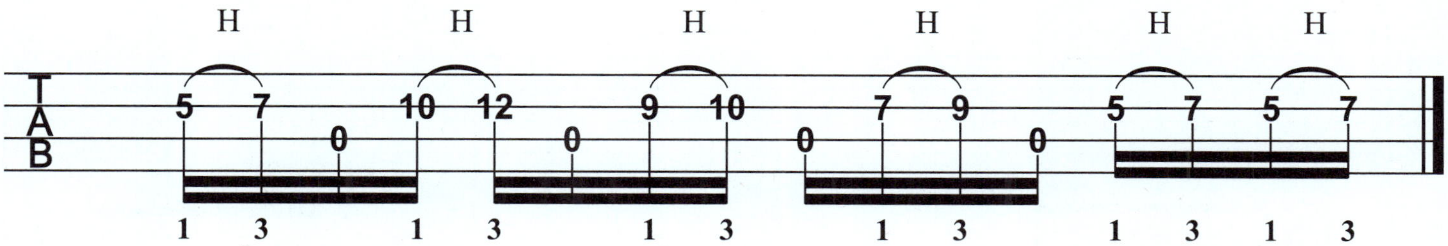

The Mexican Snake Song

This song is a I – IV – V – IV progression in the key of "C." Make sure to play this over the backing track to apply it in a full band fashion.

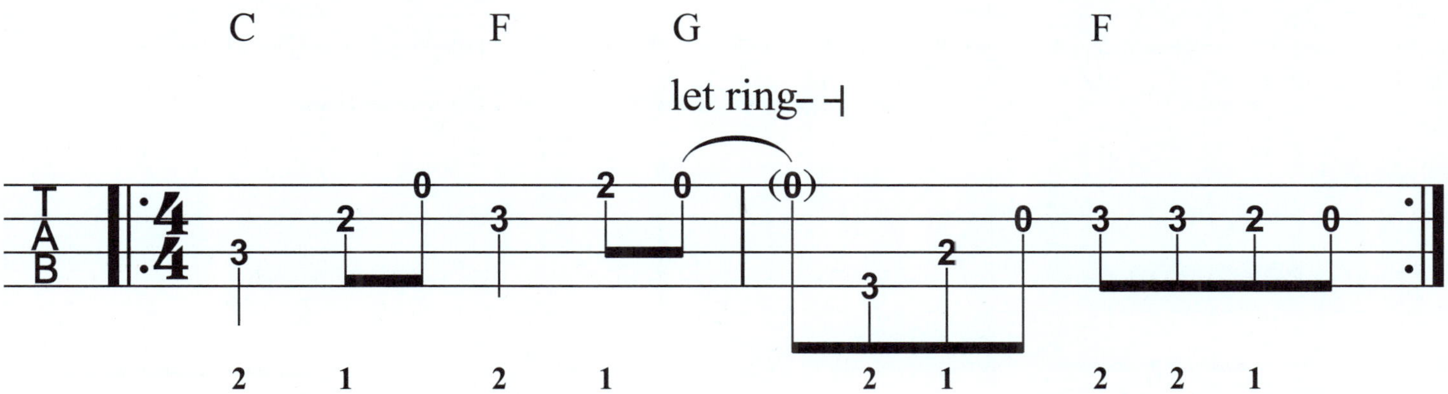

Riff Oriented Bass Lines

Often bass lines are formed by playing in unison with the guitar or keyboard player adding more focus to a riff. This bass line has a few sections that I've outlined for you. Play each section then put them all together with the backing track. This bass line is in drop D tuning.

Main Riff

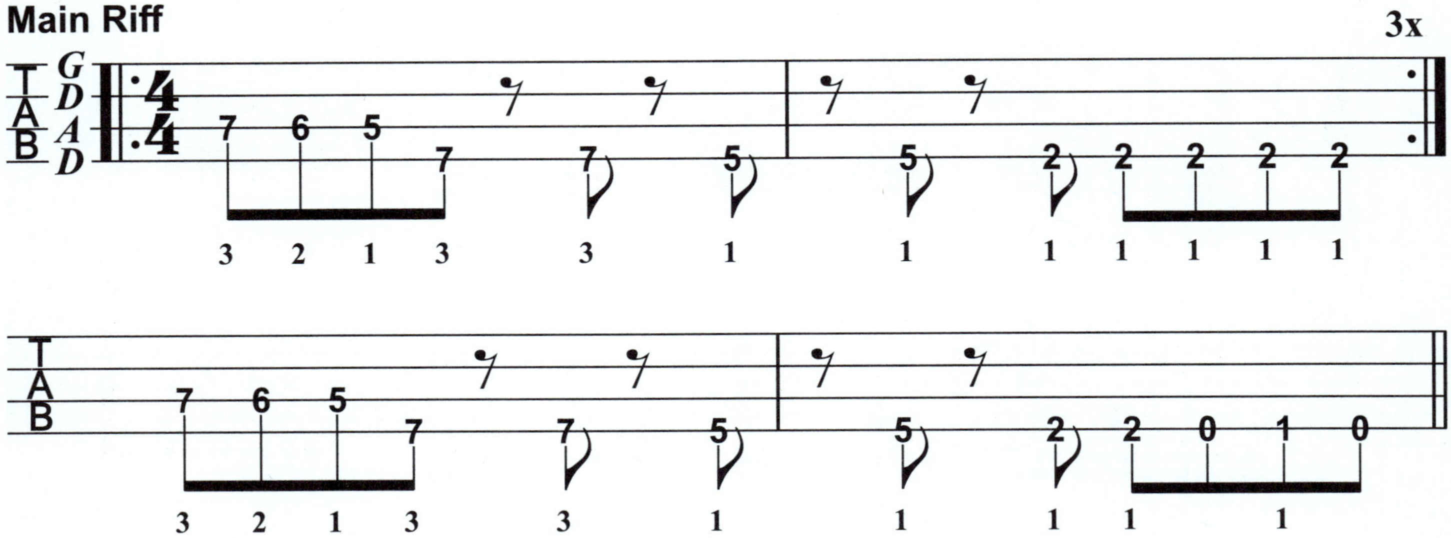

B Section

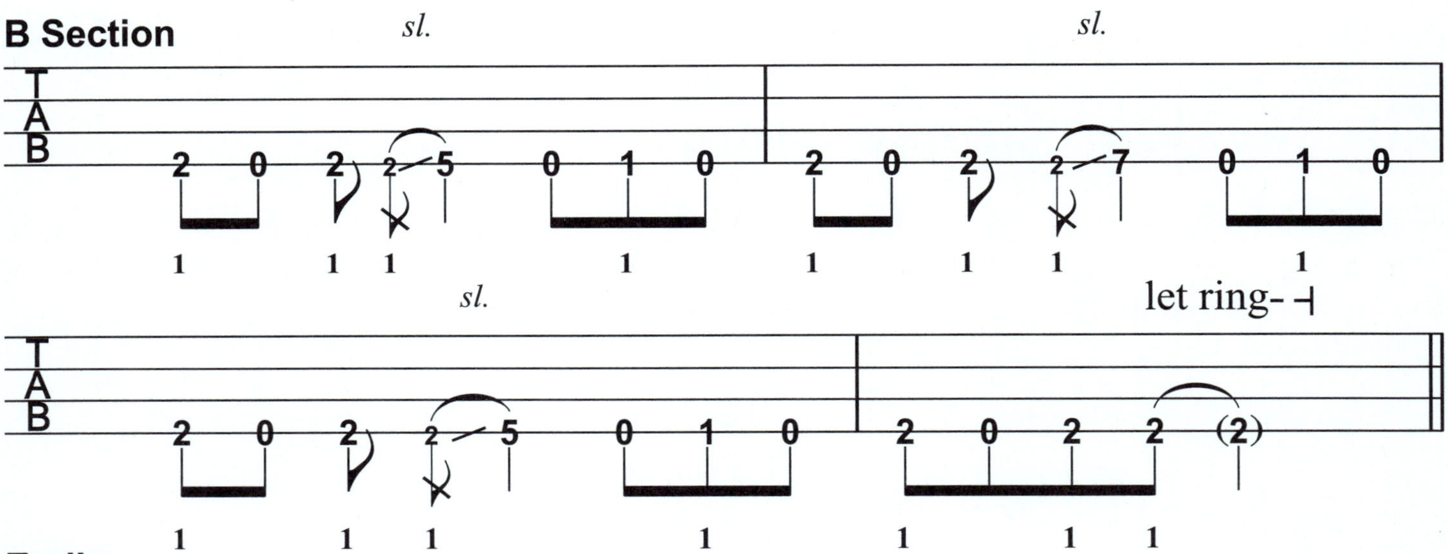

Ending

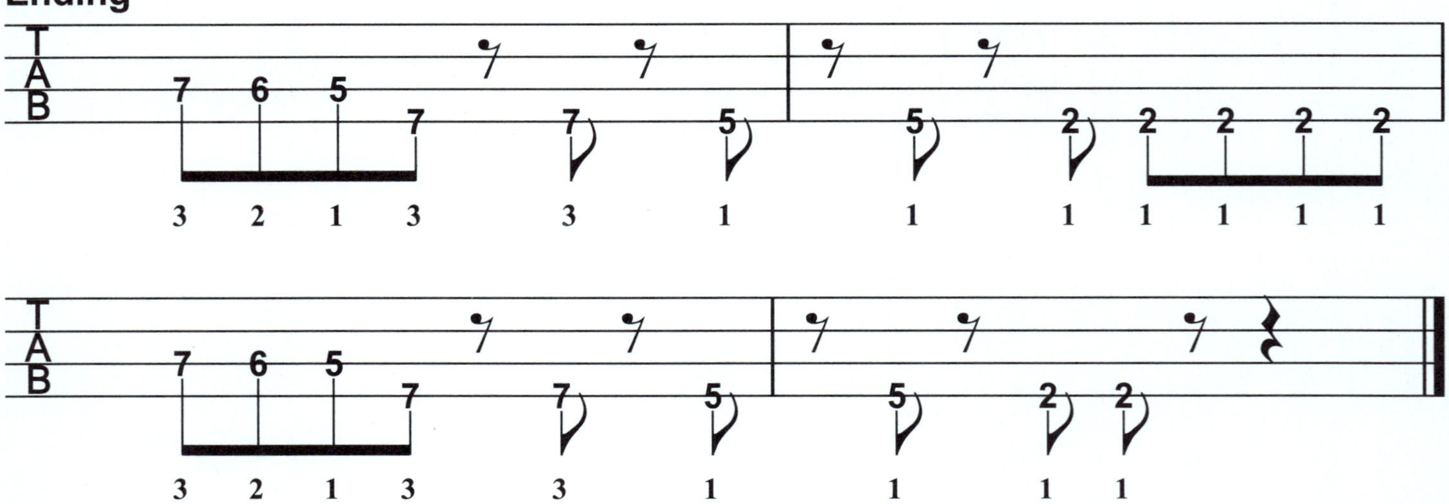

Playing with the Guitar

Many bass lines are formed by playing riffs that are also playing with the guitar. Here is a great example of a bass line where the guitar plays the riff along with the bass line. This is in drop D tuning so make sure to tune your 4th string down to D.

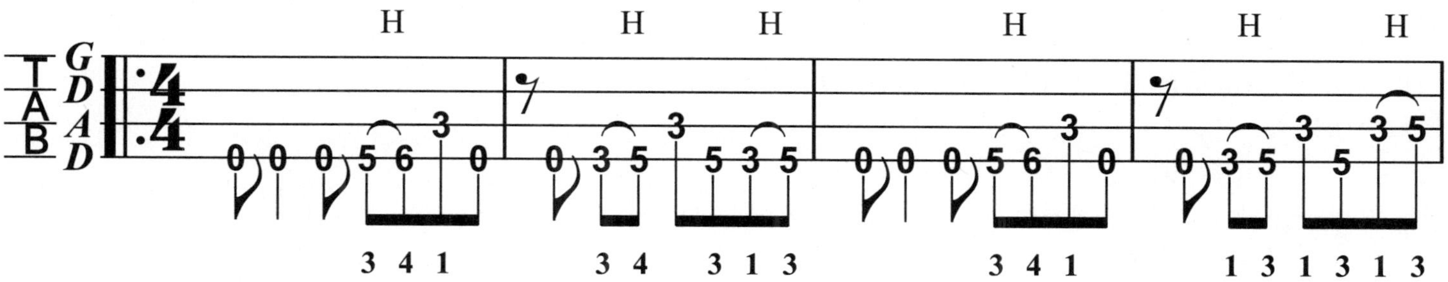

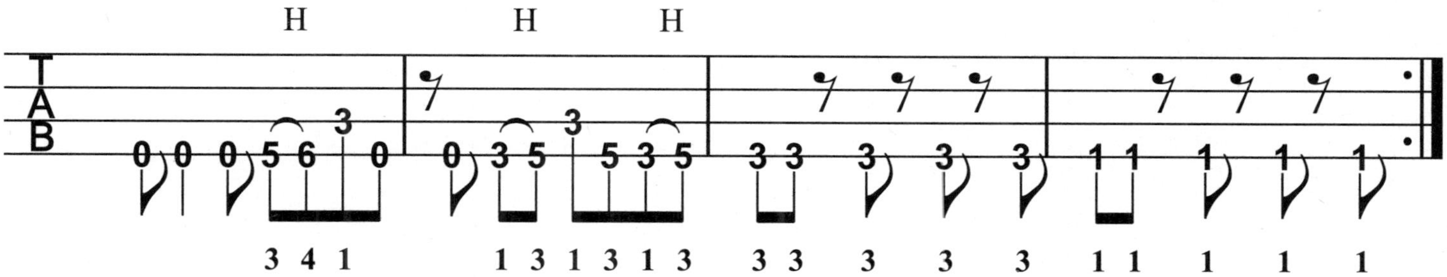

Syncopated Sixteenths

Sixteenth notes can be played many ways. In this bass line they are played in a syncopated fashion creating a lively rhythm. Notice when you play this with the backing track that the bass drum hits along with the five sixteenth notes in the beginning. This creates a very powerful heavy sound.

Example 1

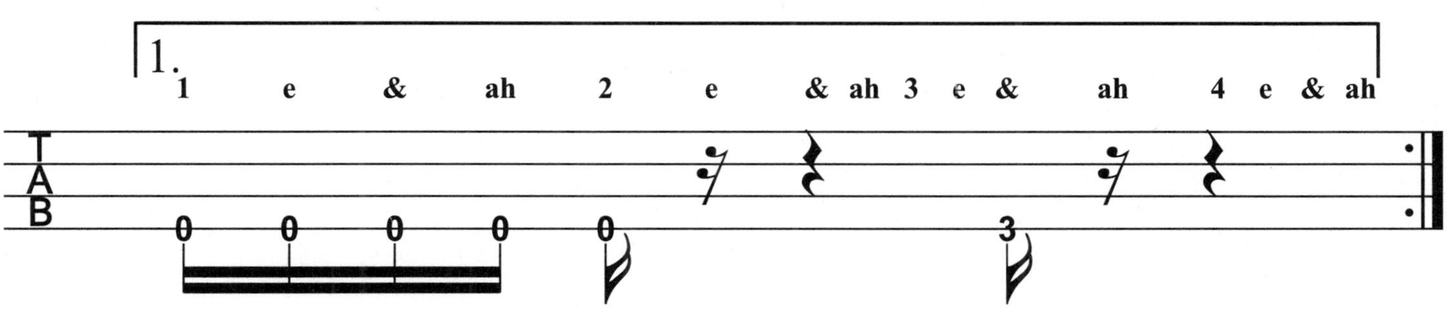

Here is a version of this bass line using eighth notes. You can play this along with the same backing track as the sixteenth note example.

Example 2

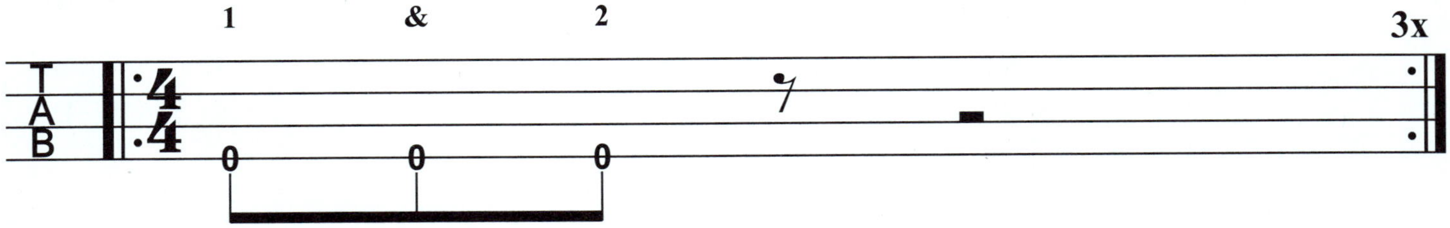

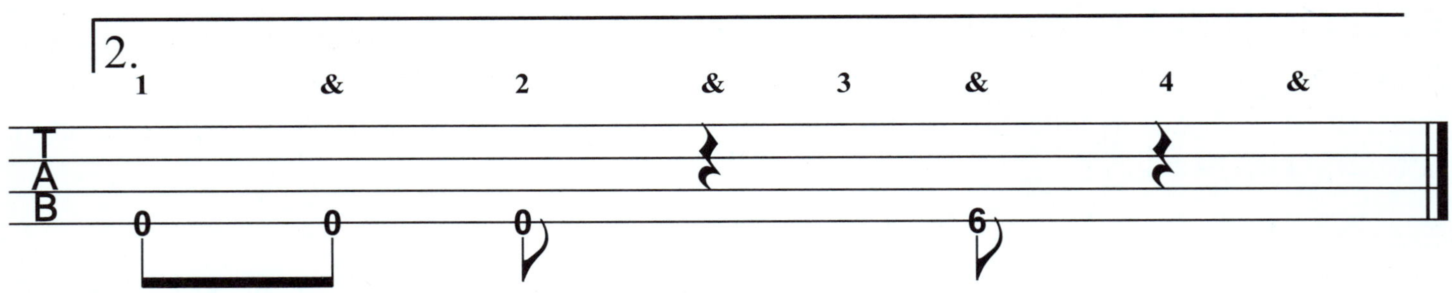

Dotted Notes

The dot after a note increases the duration of the note by half of its original value. If the basic note is a half note (2 beats), the dotted note is 3 beats or counts. A dotted quarter note would receive 1 ½ beats or counts. The ii-V-I Progression on the next page will use the dotted quarter notes.

Dotted Quarter Note — Dotted Half Note

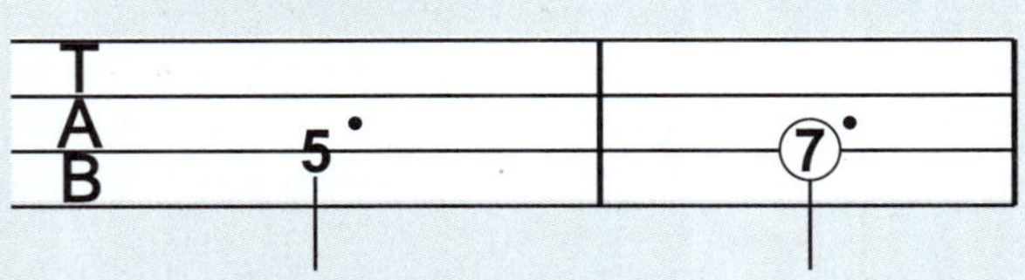

Dotted Quarter Note

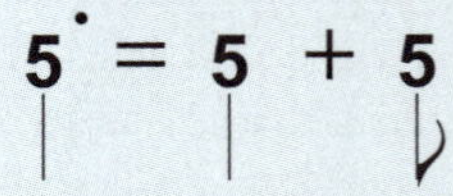

1 1/2 Beats

Dotted Half Note

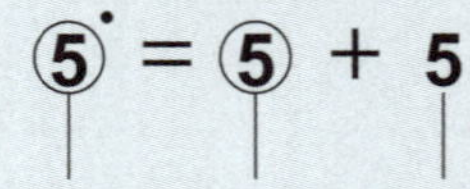

3 Beats

The ii-V-I Progression

Another common chord progression is the 2 – 5 – 1 progression (also written ii – V – I). In this progression chords are built from the 2nd, 5th and 1st degrees of a major scale. You will use triads to outline the chord changes. This progression is most popular in jazz music but can be found in many other genres. The progression in the lesson is in the key of "C."

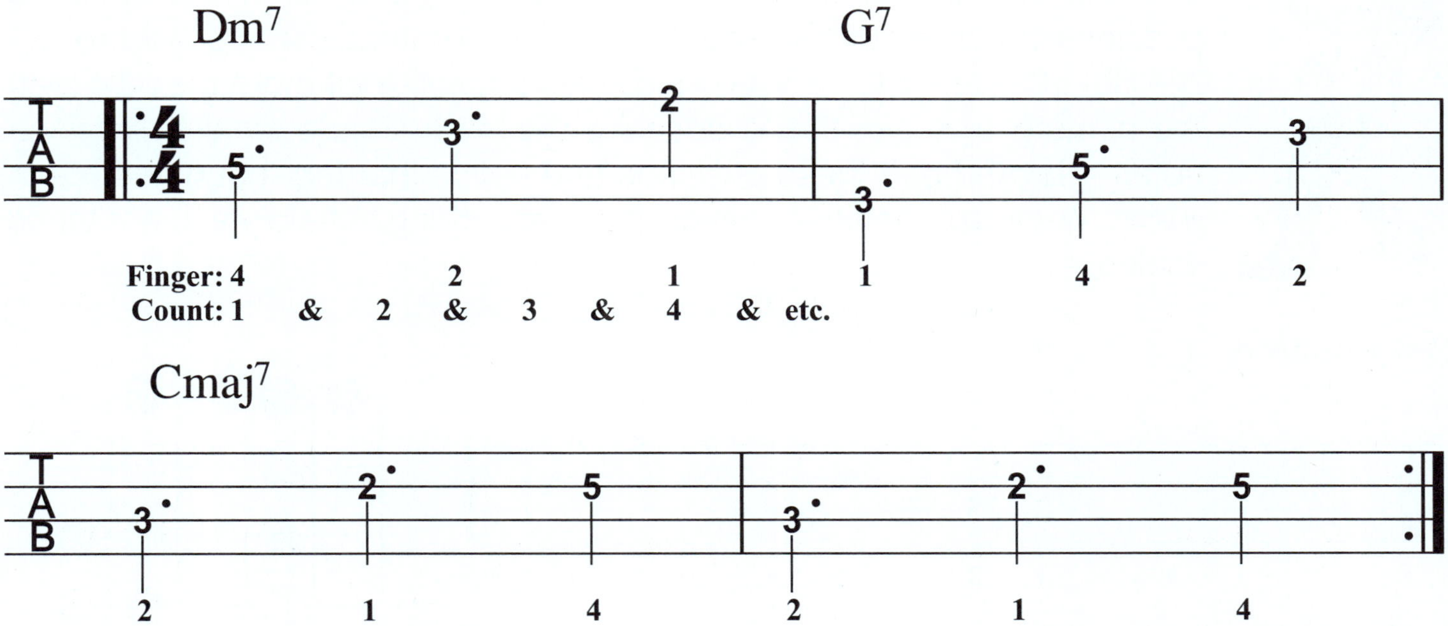

Combining Major and Minor Triads

Here is a great example of applying your triads together to create a complete bass line. Make sure to use the triad shapes you learned to make the transitions easier.

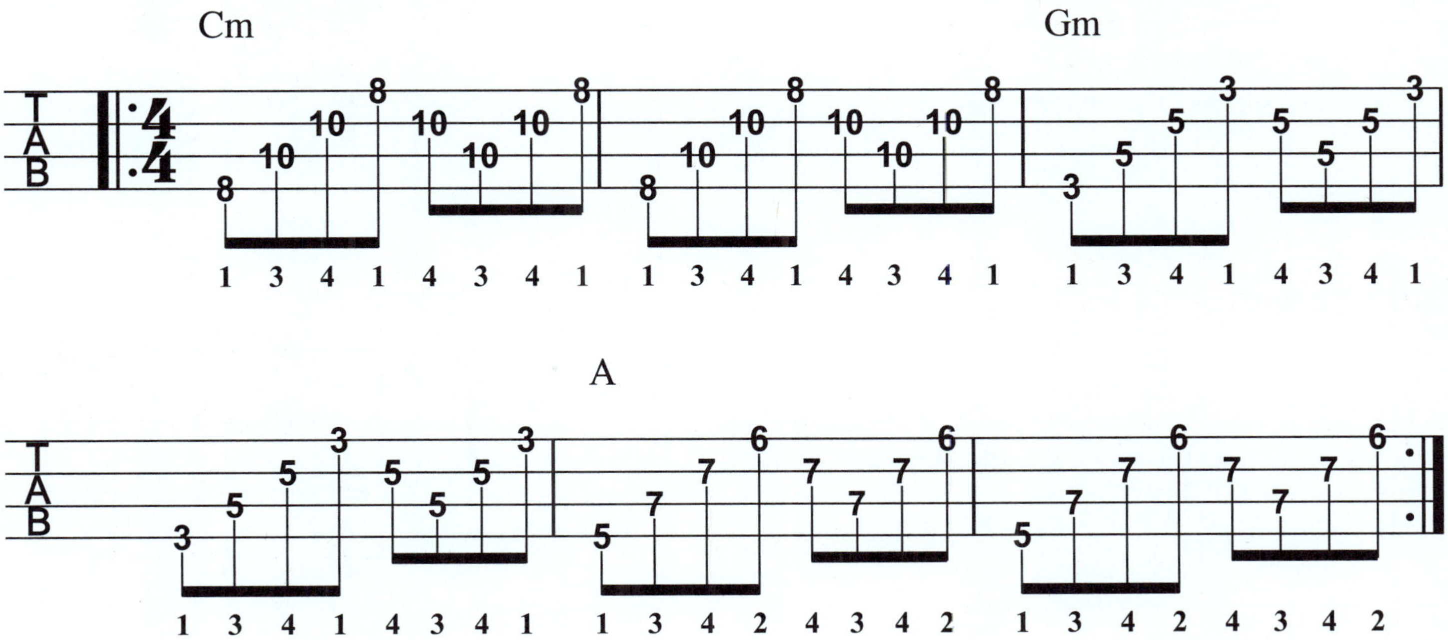

Natural Minor Scales

Key of "G" positions 1, 2 & 3

SCALE PROFESSOR

The natural minor scale is a seven note scale. It is the pure minor scale also known as the Aeolian mode. In this lesson you will learn the first three positions in the key of "G". The notes of the G natural minor scale are G – A – Bb – C – D – Eb – F – G. This scale sounds a bit more melodic then the pentatonic scale, this is because the intervals are smaller between notes. Play through these positions and notice that the root notes are in white. Memorize the finger patterns on each string to help you learn these scales.

1st Position

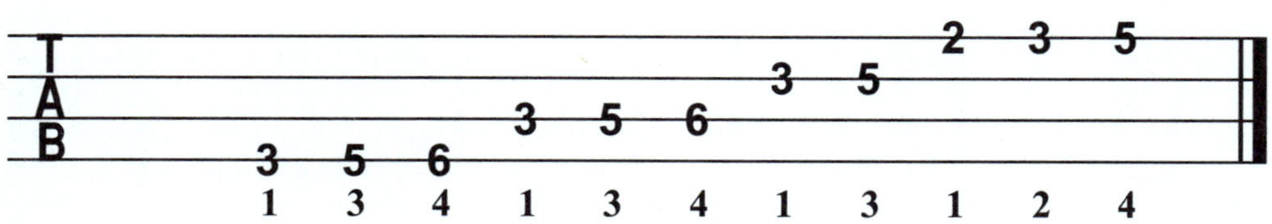

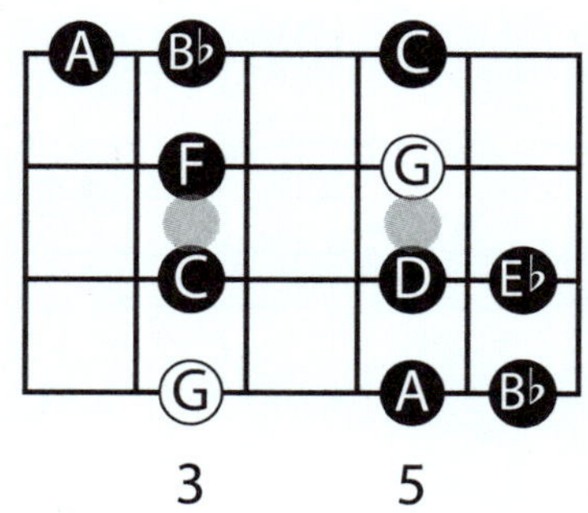

2nd Position

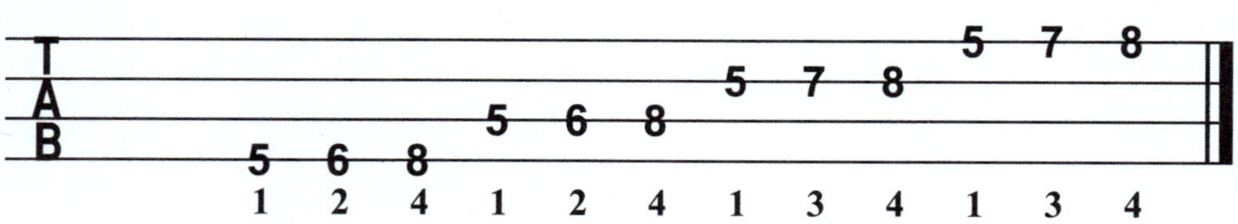

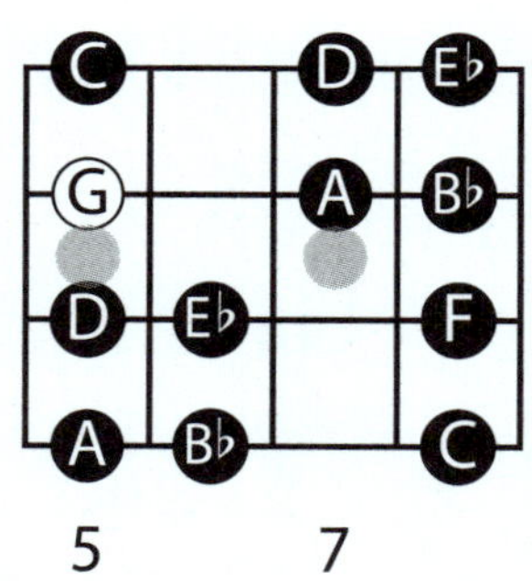

3rd Position

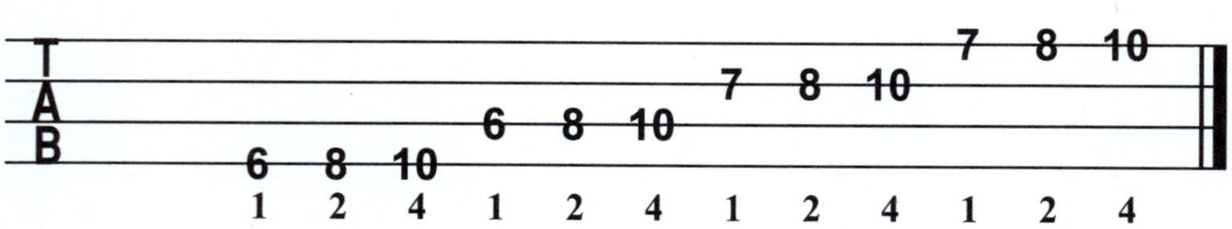

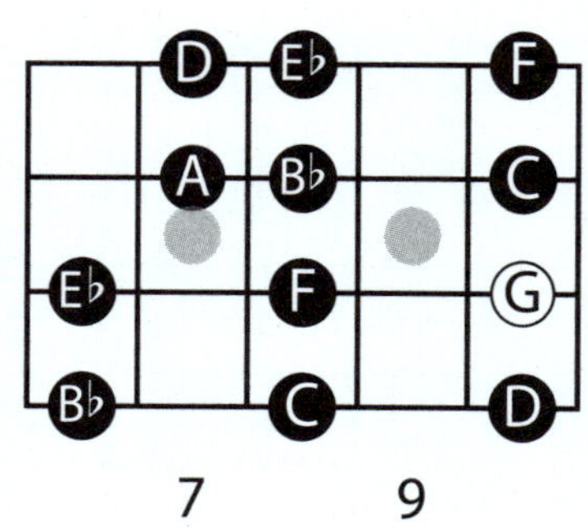

Natural Minor Triplet Pattern

Now that you have learned a few natural minor scale positions, lets put them into an interesting pattern. By varying the notes into patterns you can see how they can be transformed into bass lines.

1st Position

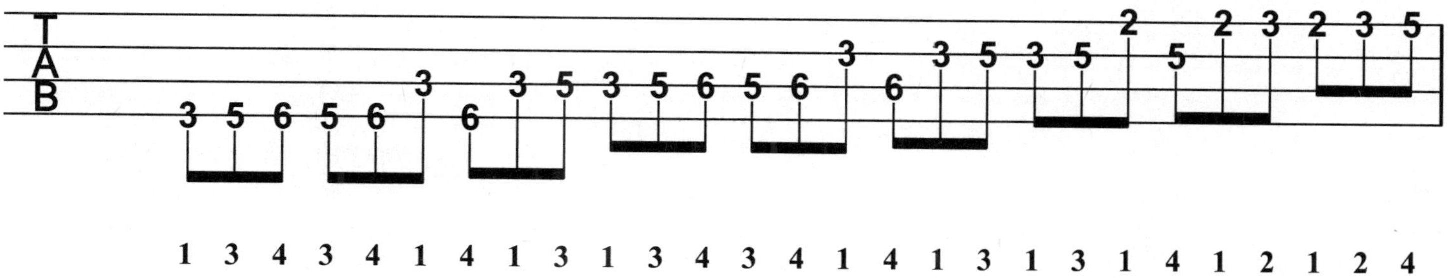

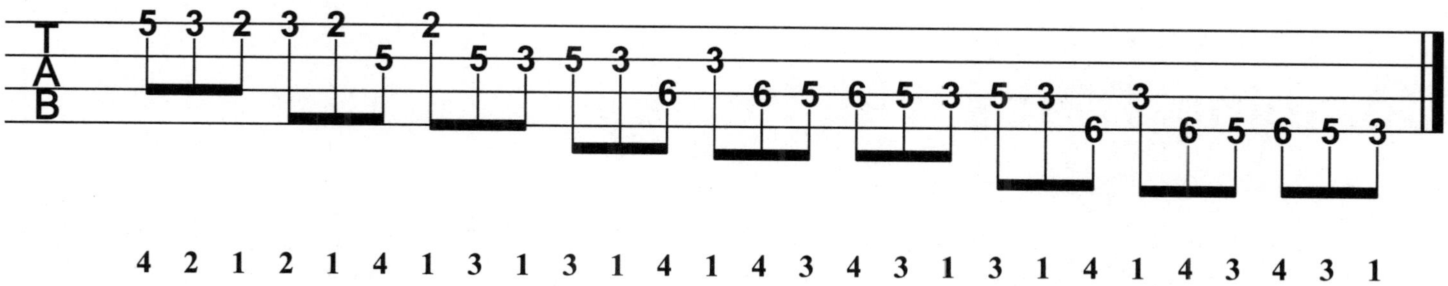

2nd Position

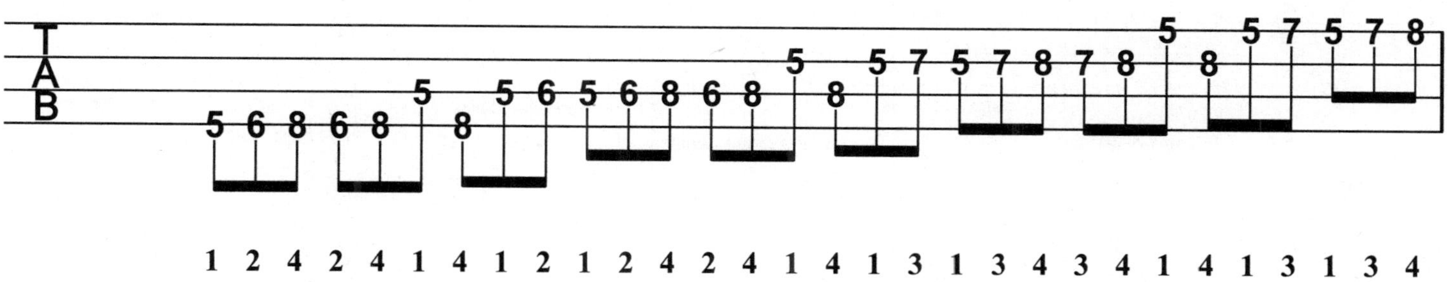

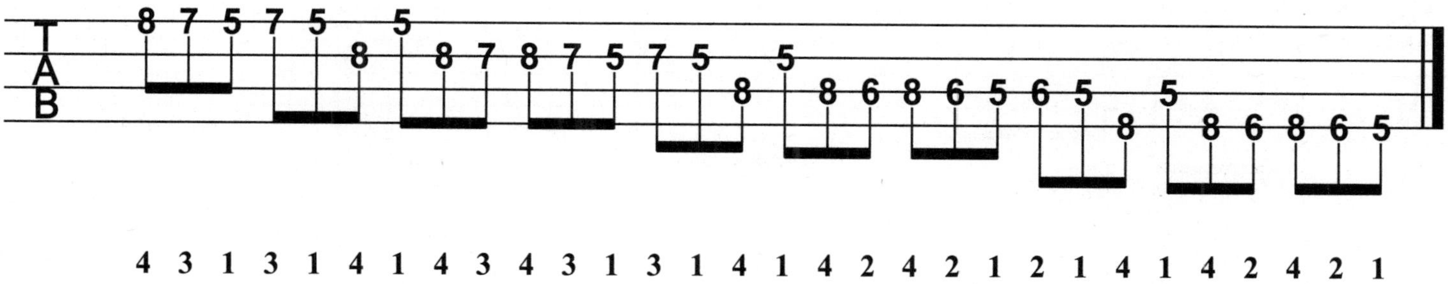

3rd Position

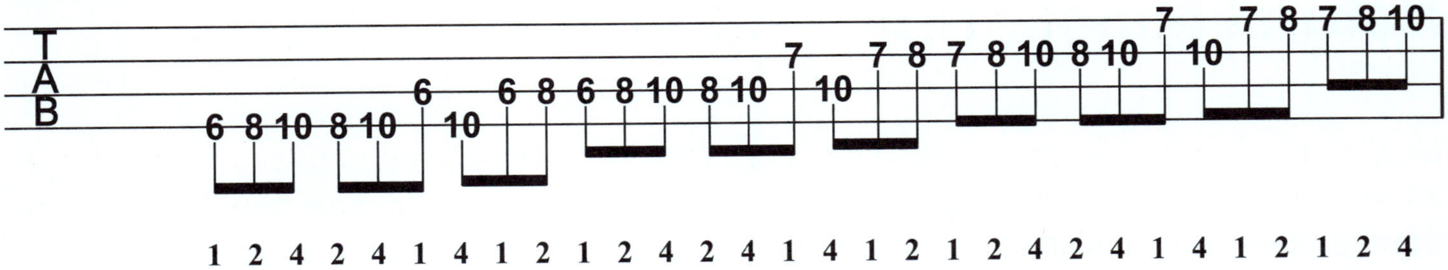

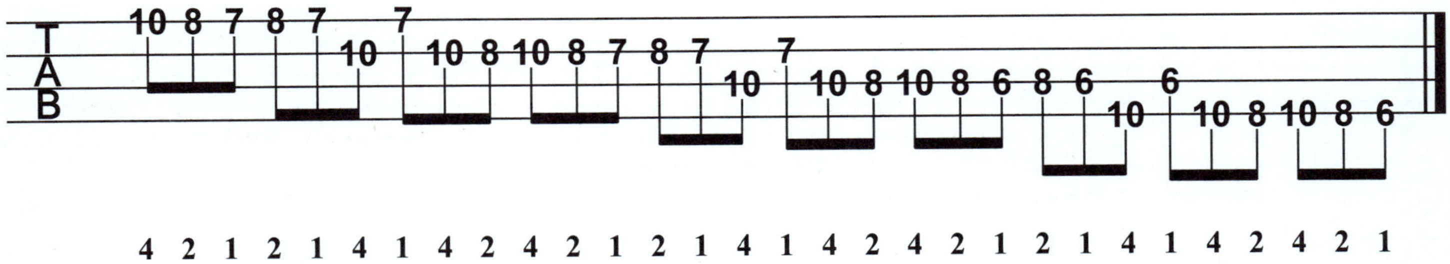

Combing Triads with Scales

When you combine triads and scales you have all the tools to create interesting and complex bass lines. Here is a bass line that combines these techniques:

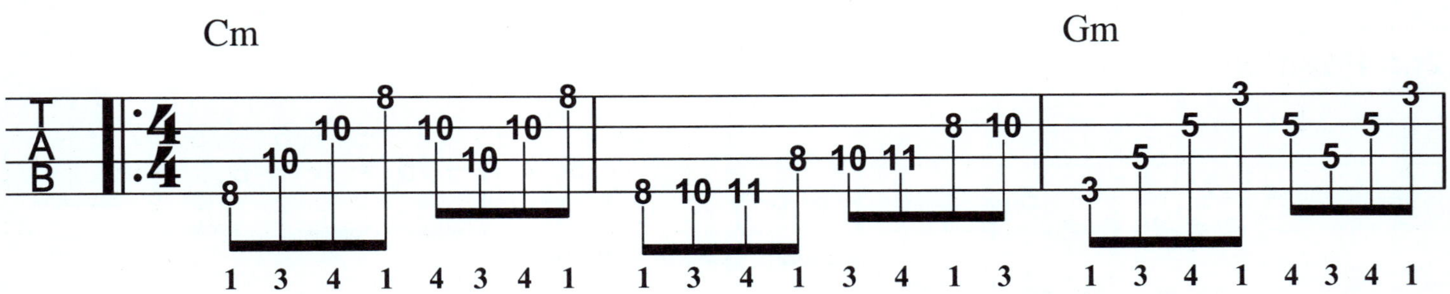

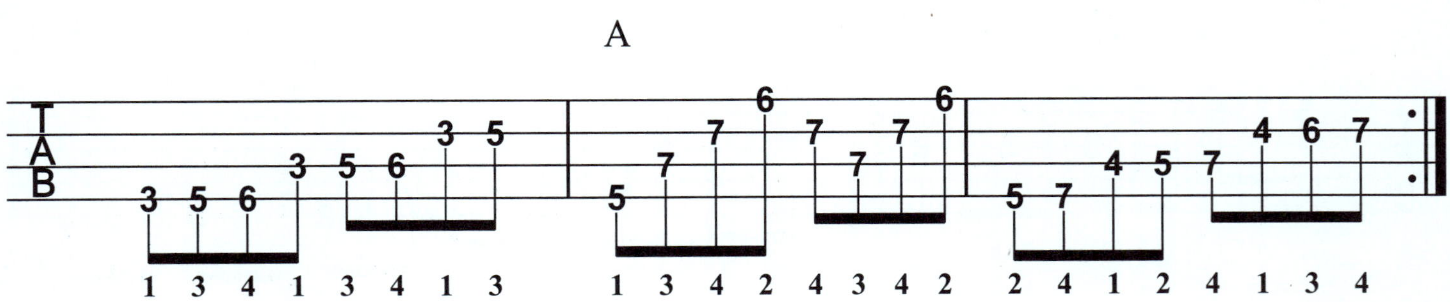

Natural Harmonics

Natural Harmonics are “chime-like” notes that are sounded by lightly touching the string above a point in the string length which divides the string into equal parts. Using Harmonics will help you obtain very high pitch notes difficult or impossible to reach by fretting. When playing harmonics at the 12th fret, we are dividing the string into two halves, which oscillate to produce the bell like chime called a harmonic. The harmonics at the fifth fret divide the string into quarters, the 7th fret into thirds. Other natural harmonics do occur, but these are the most common.

Notice in the diagram below that the locations of the Harmonics are actually over the fret and not in the fret. To play the Harmonic, gently touch the string over the fret without pressing down, then pluck the string. In this book harmonics will be depicted by a star over the tab note with the word “Harm.” over it.

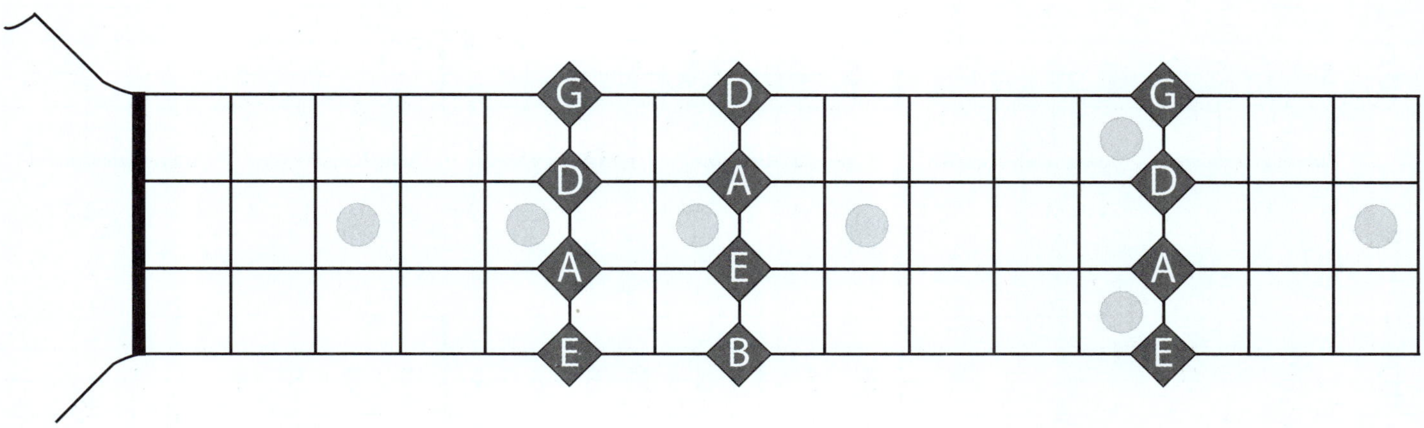

Example 1

Example 2

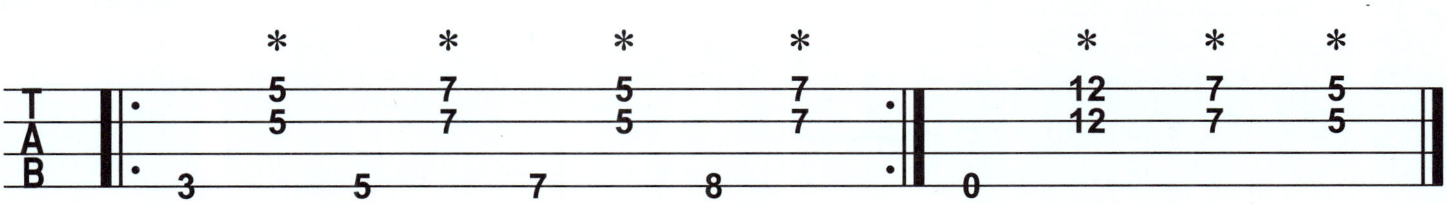

Blues Town

This is a common eighth note shuffle blues rhythm. Make sure to play this over the backing tracks and jam with the band!

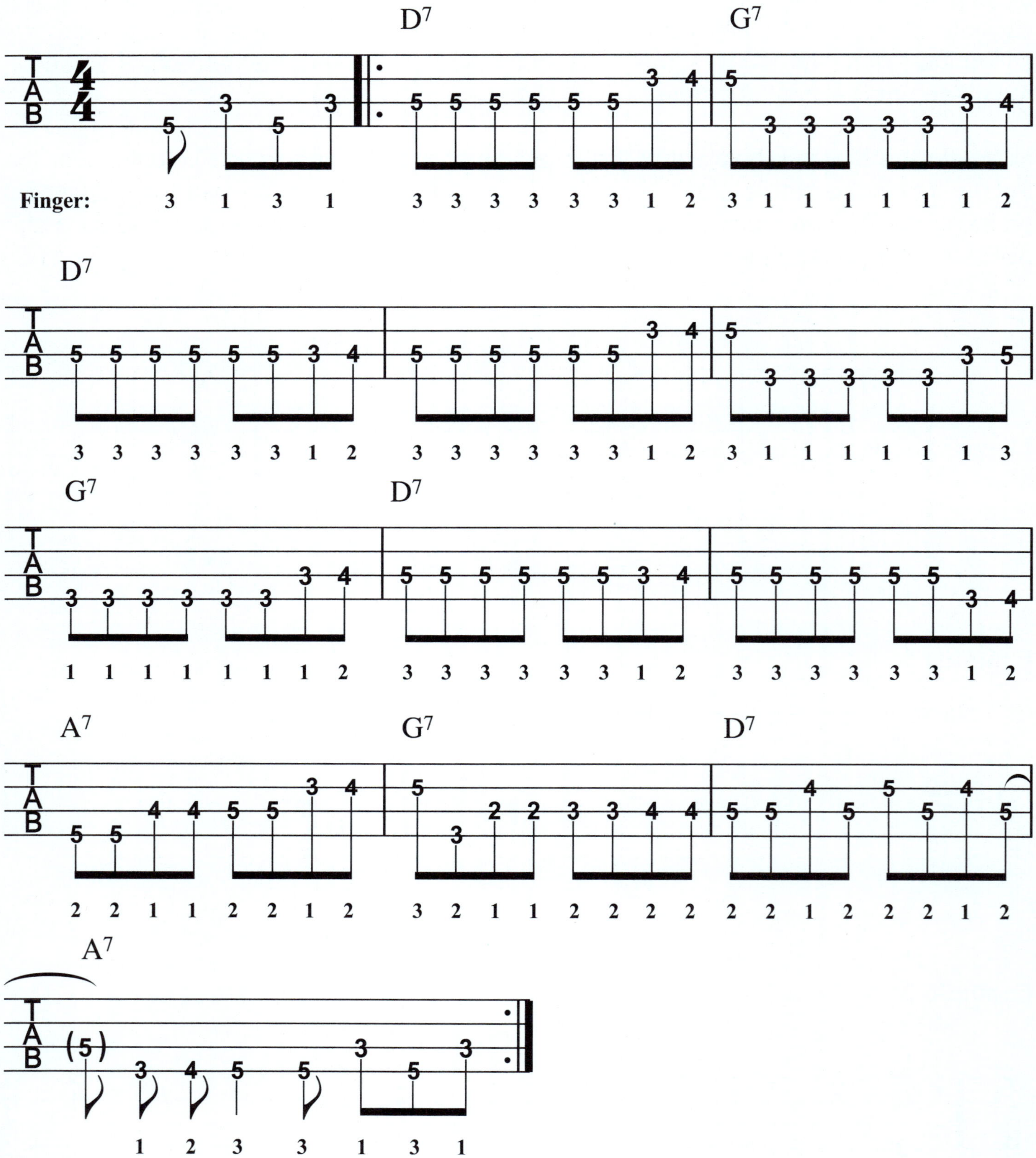

First & Second Endings

Sometimes the composer wants to repeat a section in a song and add a different ending. These are called first and second endings. First and second endings are notated by numbered brackets over each ending. The endings can be any number of measures in length. In the example below each ending is one measure in length. Note the repeat sign between the endings. This means that you play through ending one, go back to the beginning play up to the first ending, skip the first ending and play the second ending. Play through the example below. In the next lesson you will use first and second endings within a song.

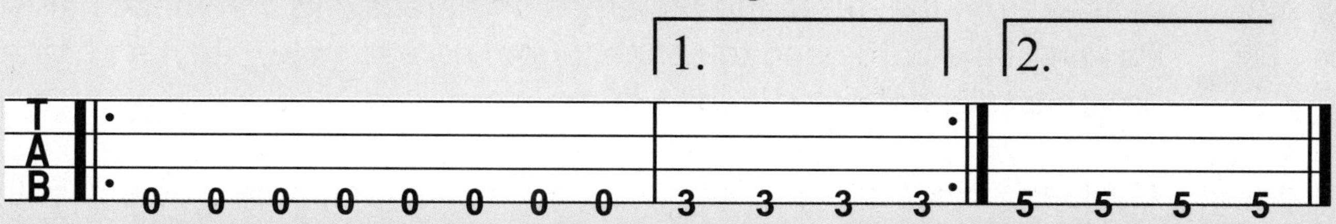

Complete Bass Progression

Now that you have learned hammer ons, pull offs and alternate plucking lets put these techniques all together in a complete bass progression.

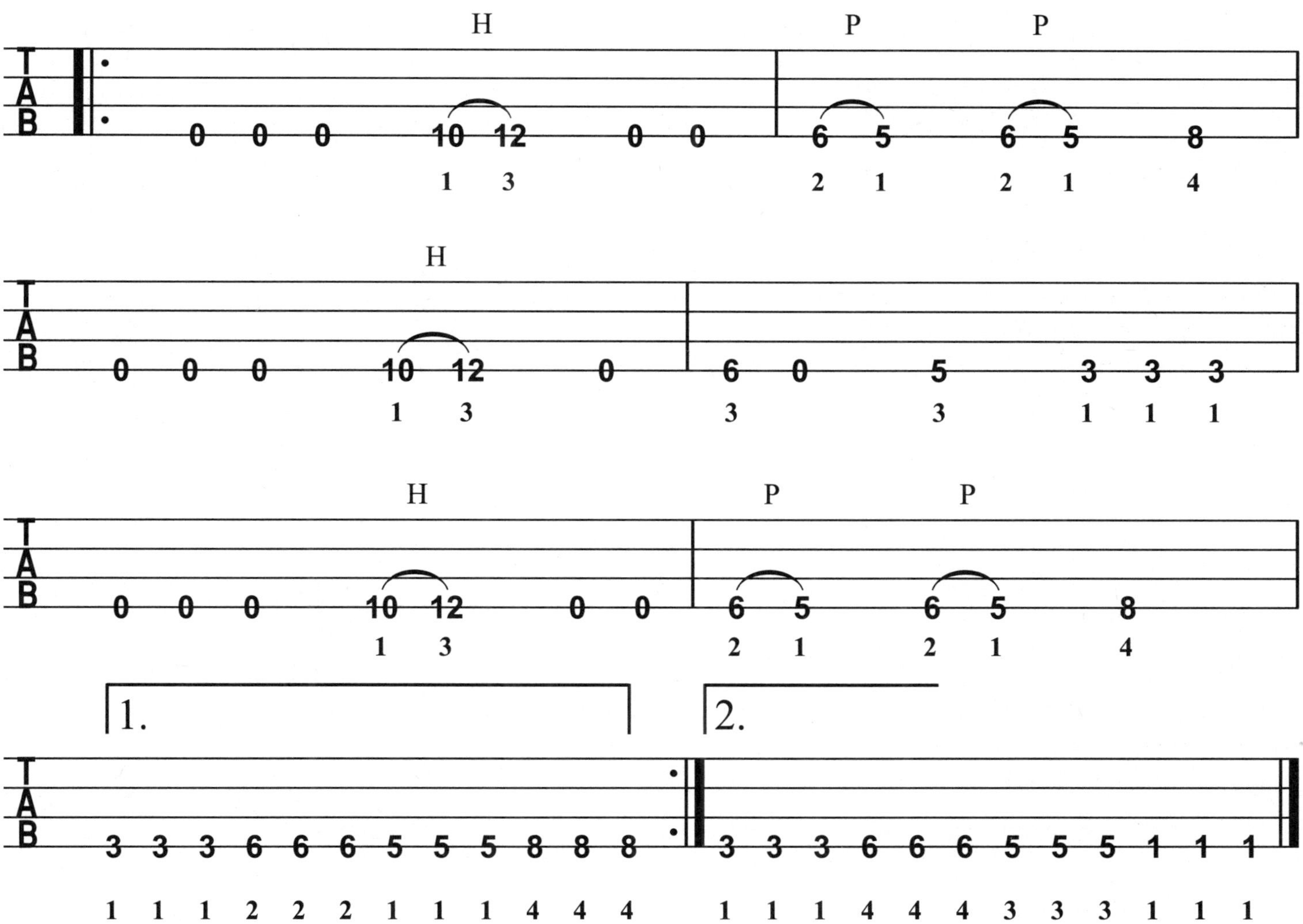

G Blues Scales

SCALE PROFESSOR

The blues scale is a slight variation of the minor pentatonic scale. They contain one extra note between the 4th and 5th steps of the scale, called a passing tone. This particular passing tone is the flatted 5th of the scale, also known as the blues tri-tone. Using the blues tri-tone adds color and character to bass lines. This note is a chromatic passing tone because it passes from the 4th to the 5th steps of the scale in chromatic half steps. Passing tones are used to connect from note to note within a phrase and are generally not held for long durations.

The following G blues scales are the same as the minor pentatonic scales with the addition of the blues tri-tone. The squares in the scale diagrams indicate where the blues tri-tones are played. Practice and memorize the G blues scale positions.

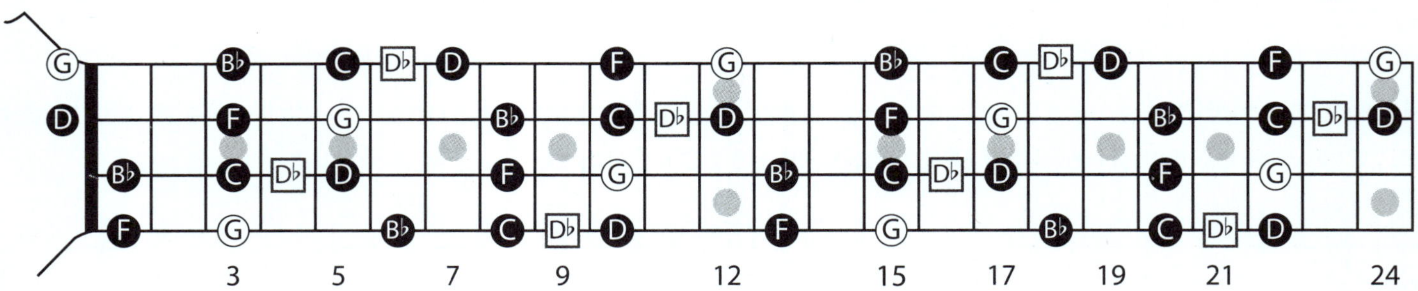

1st Position

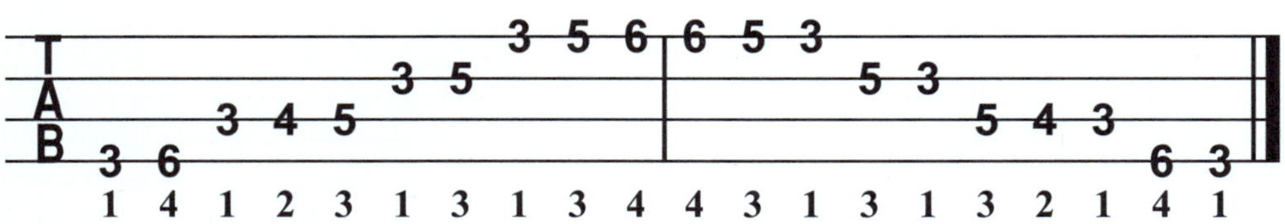

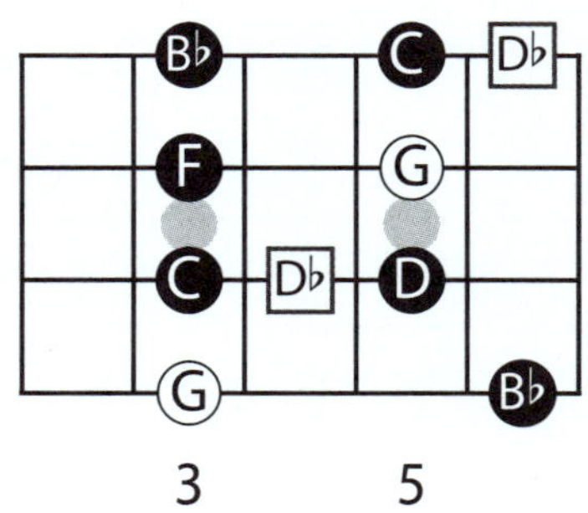

2nd Position

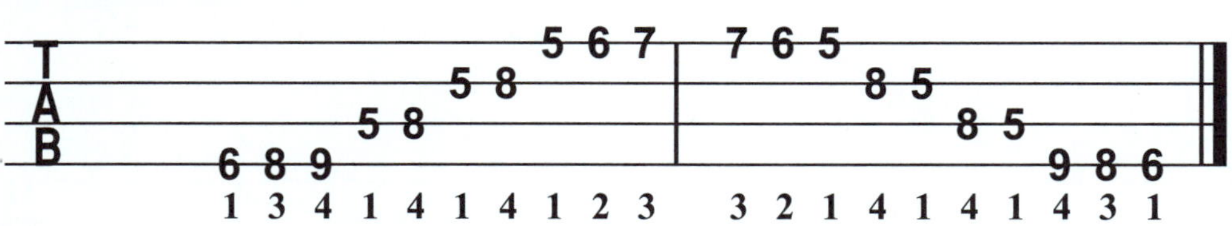

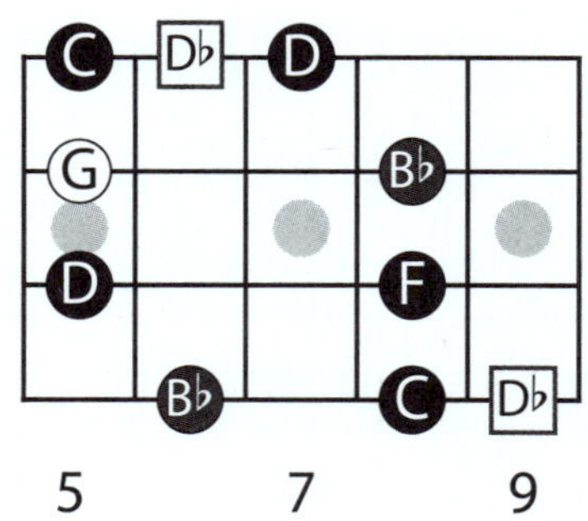

3rd Position

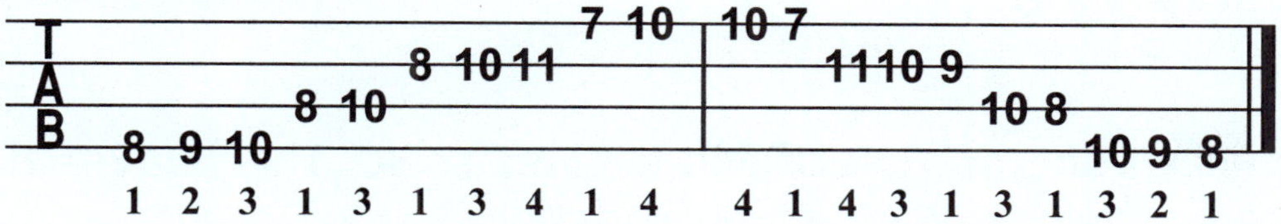

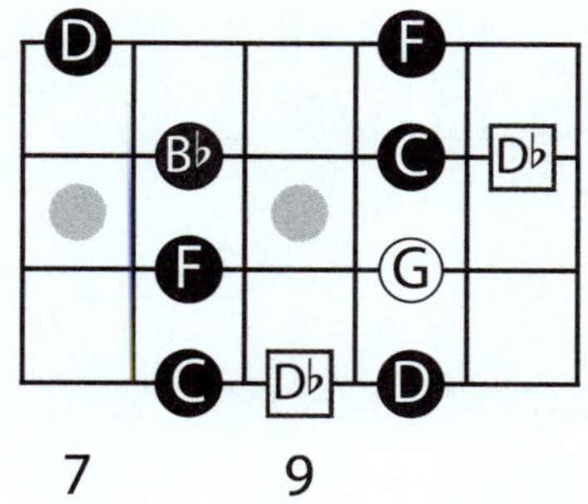

4th Position

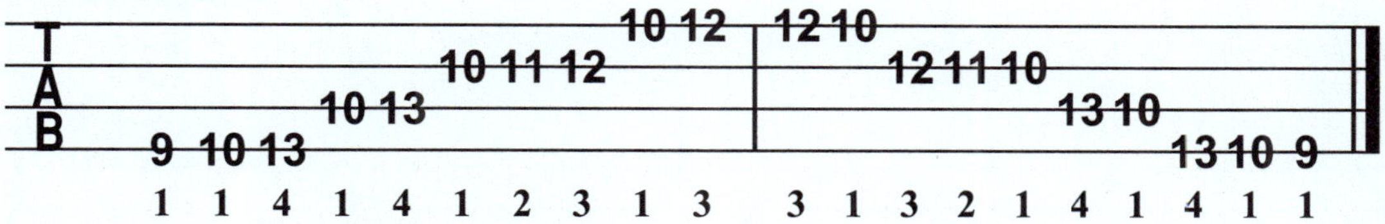

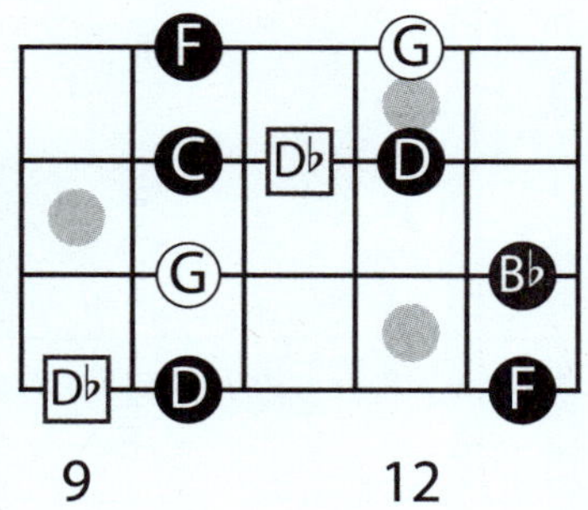

5th Position

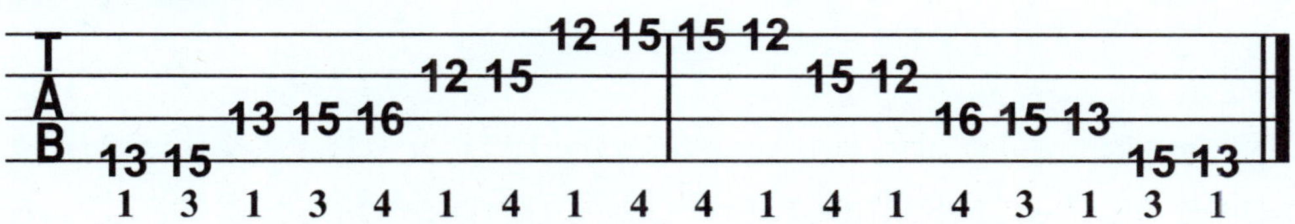

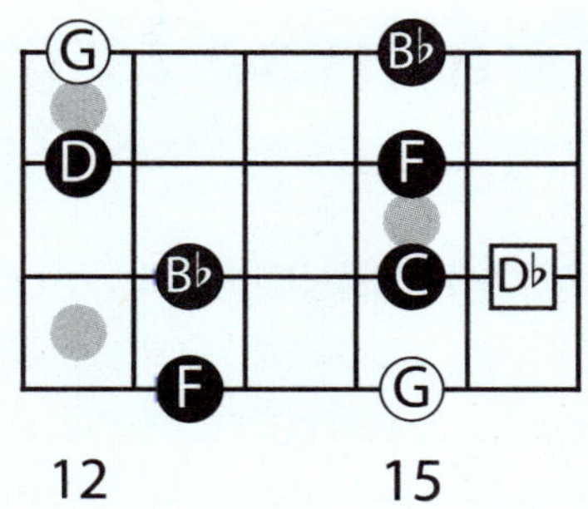

1st Position (Octave)

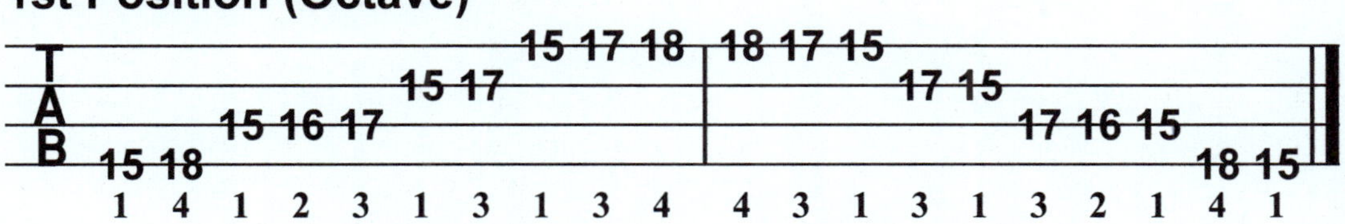

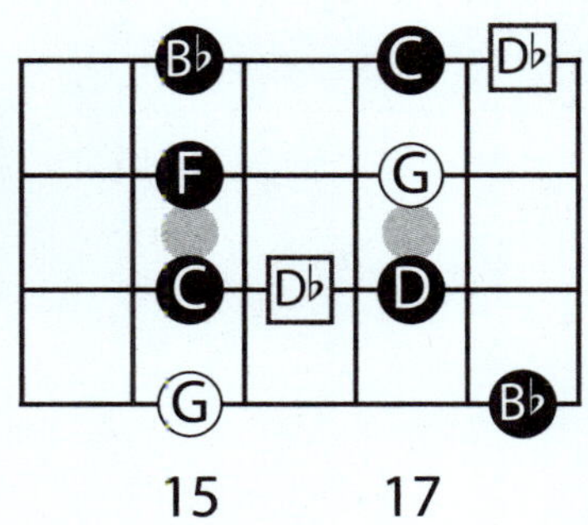

G Blues Scale Groove

This bass groove comes directly from the 1st position G blues scale. This is a great example of how to use the blues scales to create bass lines.

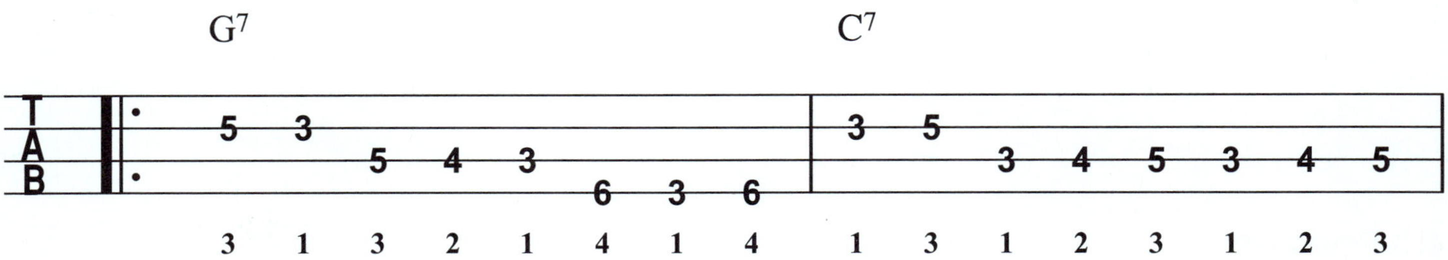

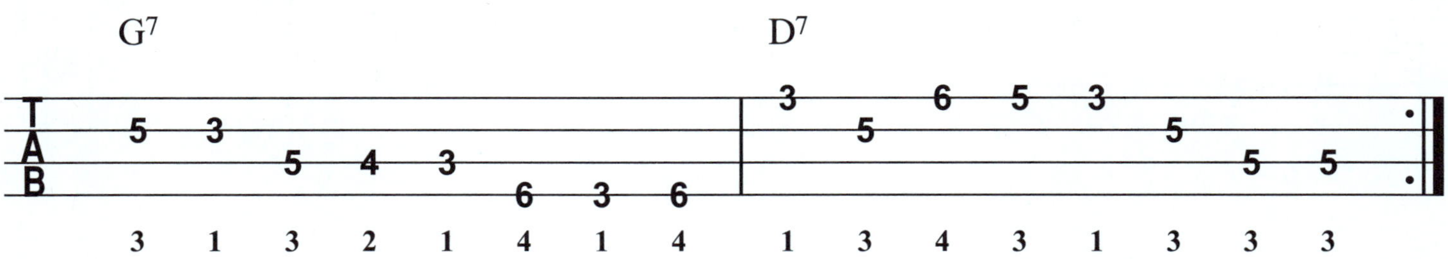

G Minor Hammer On Groove

In this lesson you will combine the slap, pop and hammer on techniques to create a great bass groove. Notice the “x” notes on the staff, these are dead or muted notes that have a percussive non musical sound. You will apply the slap and pop techniques to muted or deadened notes in this bass line.

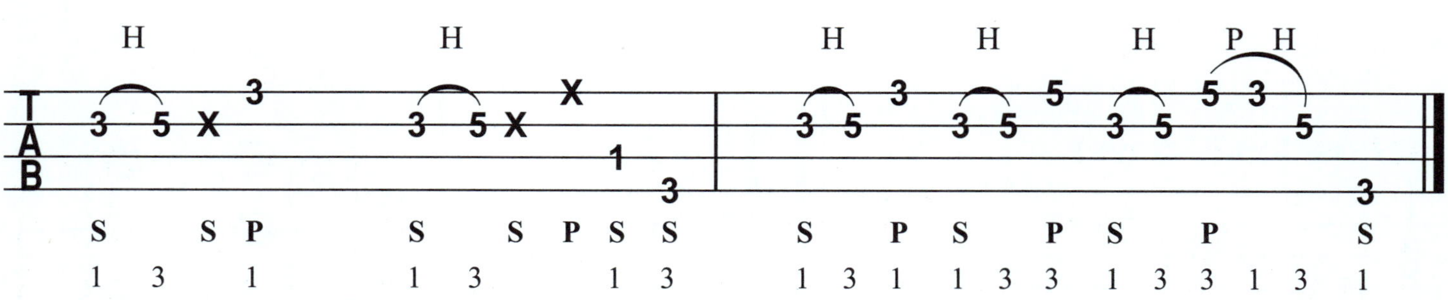

S = Slap **P = Pop**

5 String Pentatonic Minor Scales Key of “A”

1st Position

E G A C D E G A C D

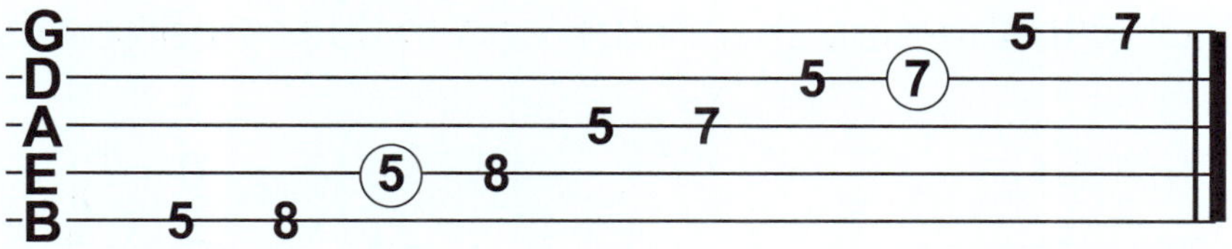

Finger: 1 4 1 4 1 3 1 3 1 3

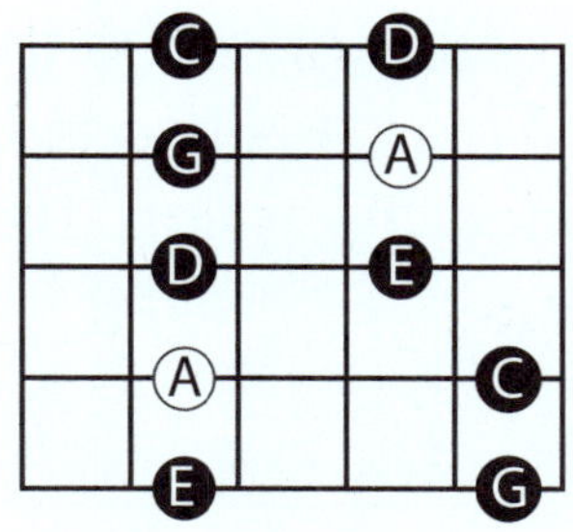

5 7

2nd Position

G A C D E G A C D E

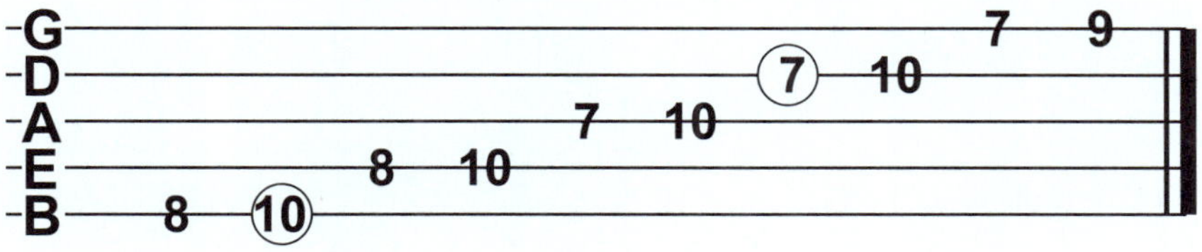

Finger: 2 4 2 4 1 4 1 4 1 3

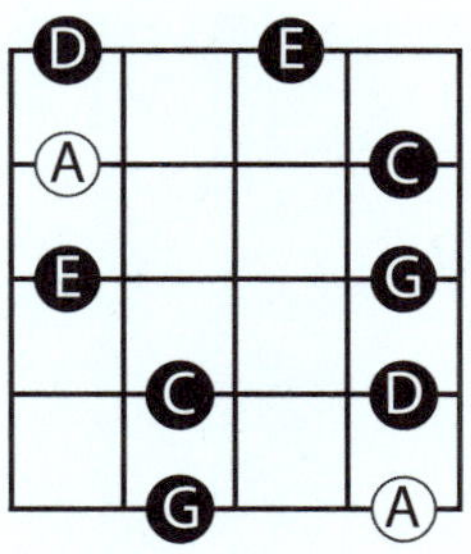

7 9

3rd Position

A C D E G A C D E G

Finger: 1 4 1 3 1 3 1 4 1 4

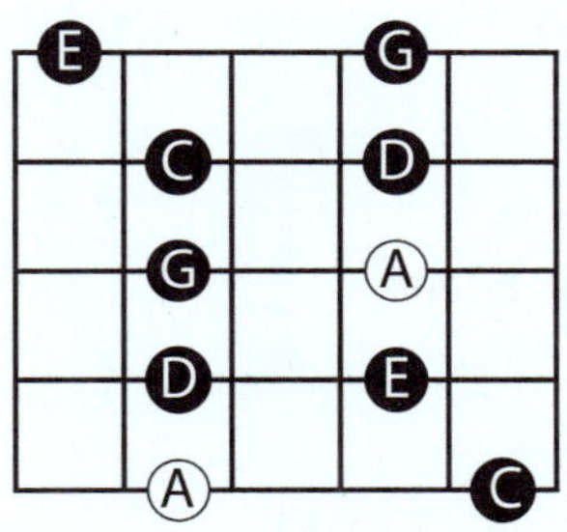

9 12

4th Position

C D E G A C D E G A

Finger: 2 4 1 4 1 4 1 3 1 4

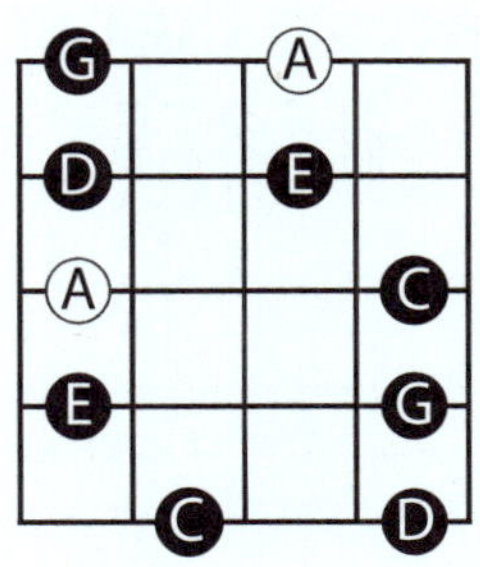

12 15

5th Position

D E G A C D E G A C

Finger: 1 3 1 3 1 3 1 4 1 4

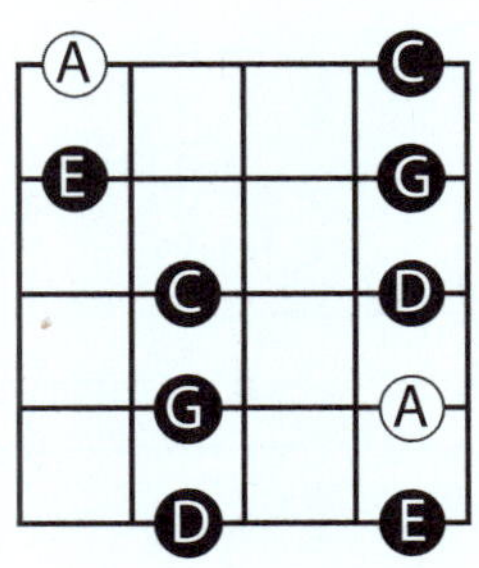

3 5

Riding Low

A bass line can often be the main hook of a song. This is a classic example of such a bass line. This bass line is in G minor and comes from the G minor pentatonic scale. I've also included a version that is played with the slap technique and includes percussive muted slaps.

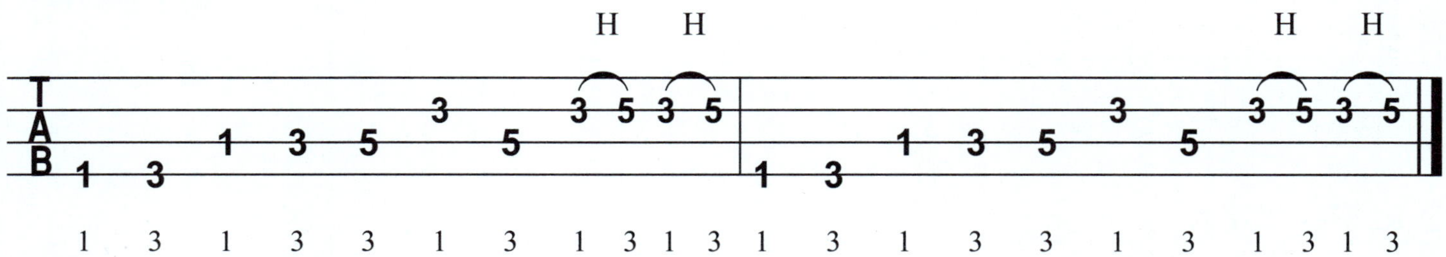

Slap Version

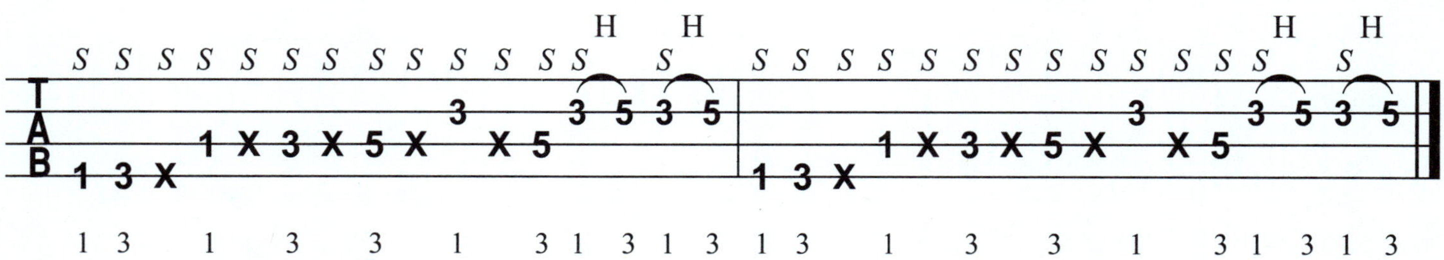

X = Mute Slap

Dyno-mite

There are staccato rhythm sections that happen twice within this rhythm. The timing is complicated in this progression so take you time and practice this slowly at first.

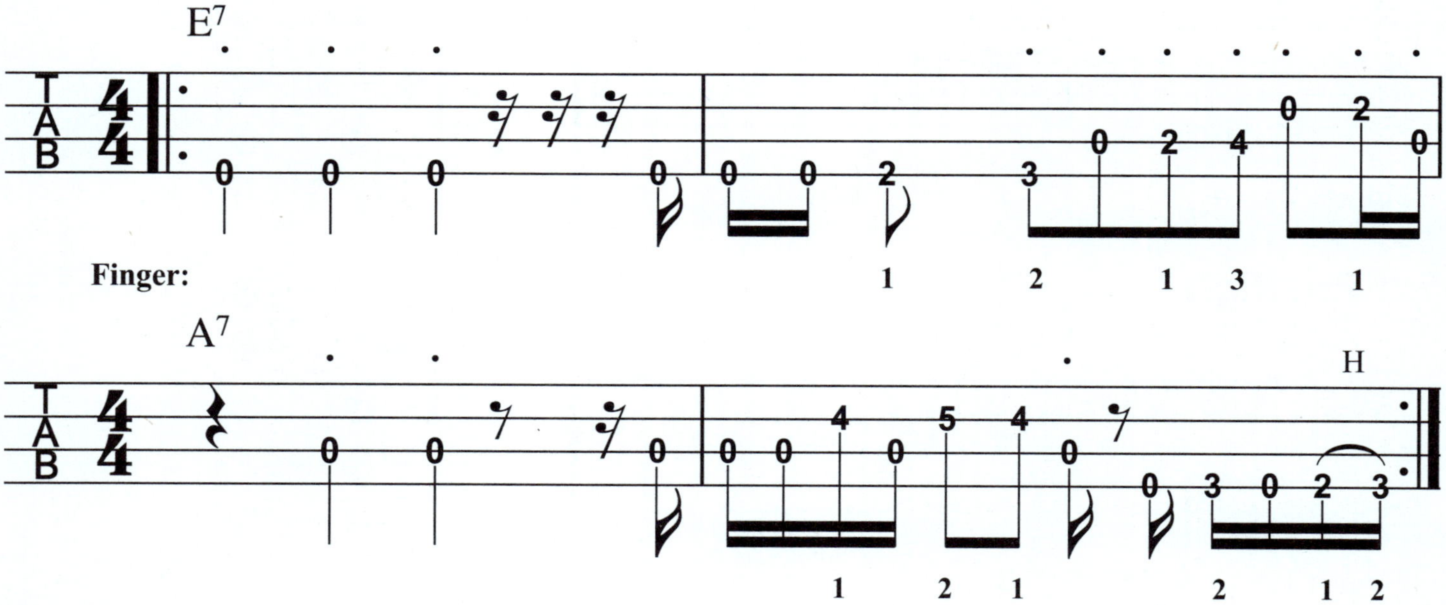

Stormy Tuesday

This progression is a jazz influenced blues progression. Follow the changes above the staff to understand the changes better. Play this with the accompanying backing tracks to hear the full band sound.

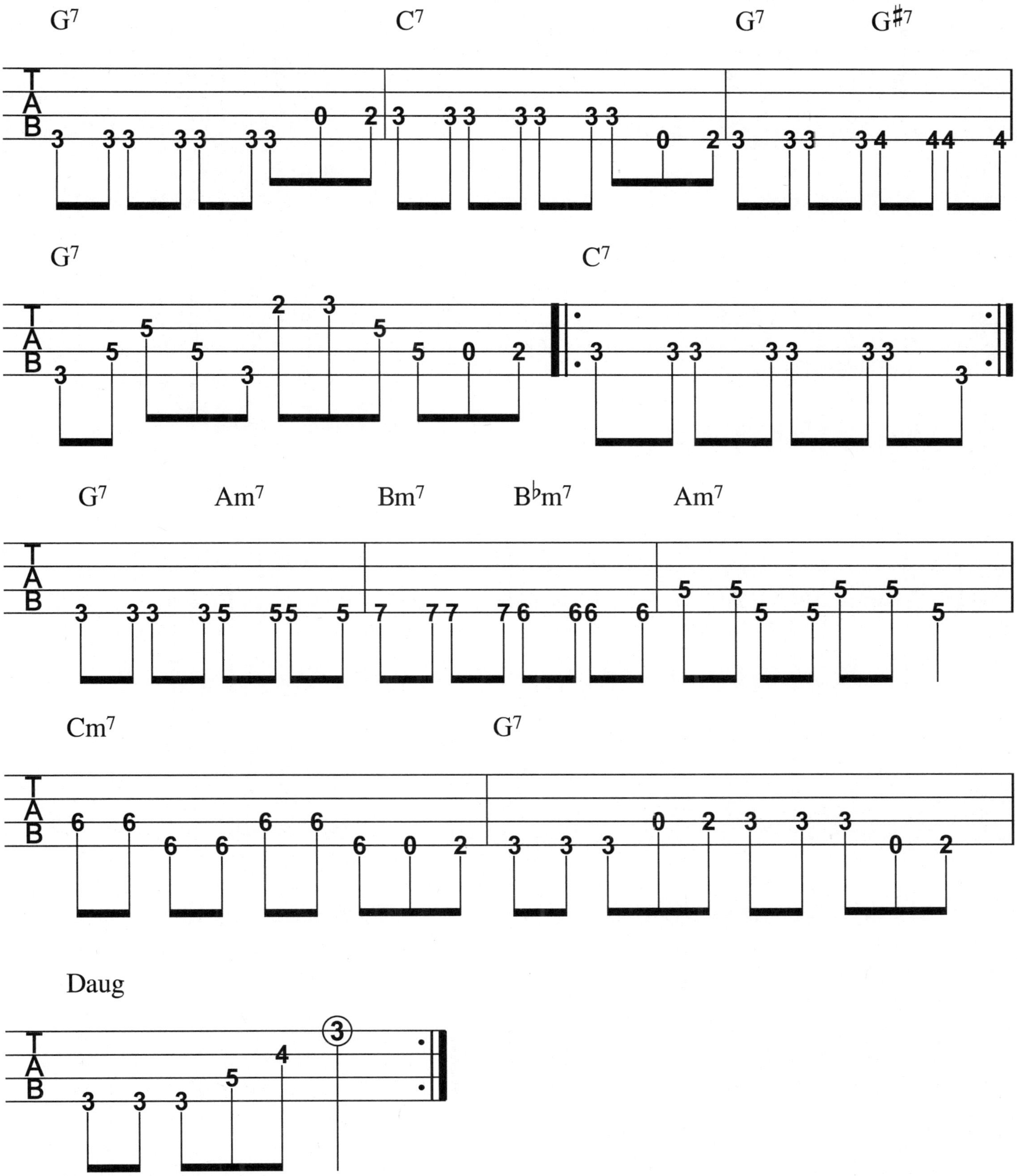

Shuffle and Swing

This is an E minor walking blues progression. Pay attention to the chord progression on top of the staff, I've included this to help you follow the progression and understand it more effectively. Play this with the accompanying backing tracks.

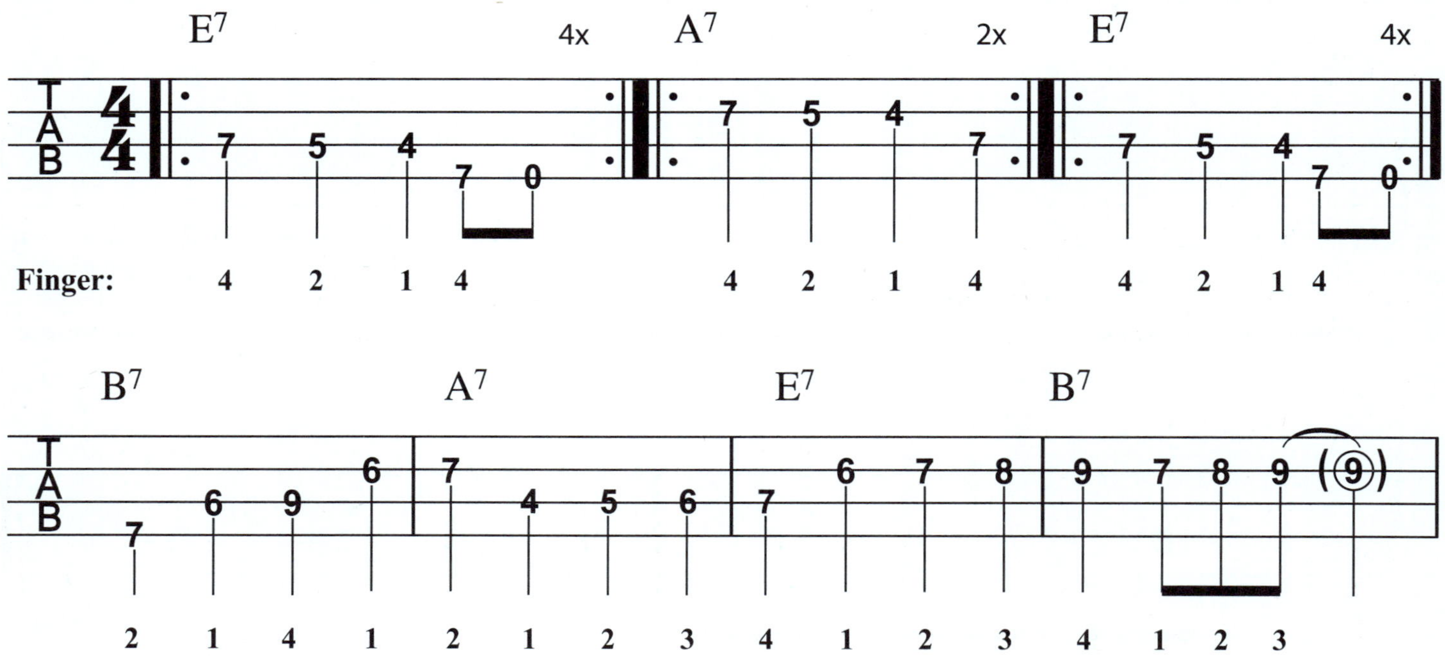

Verse & Chorus

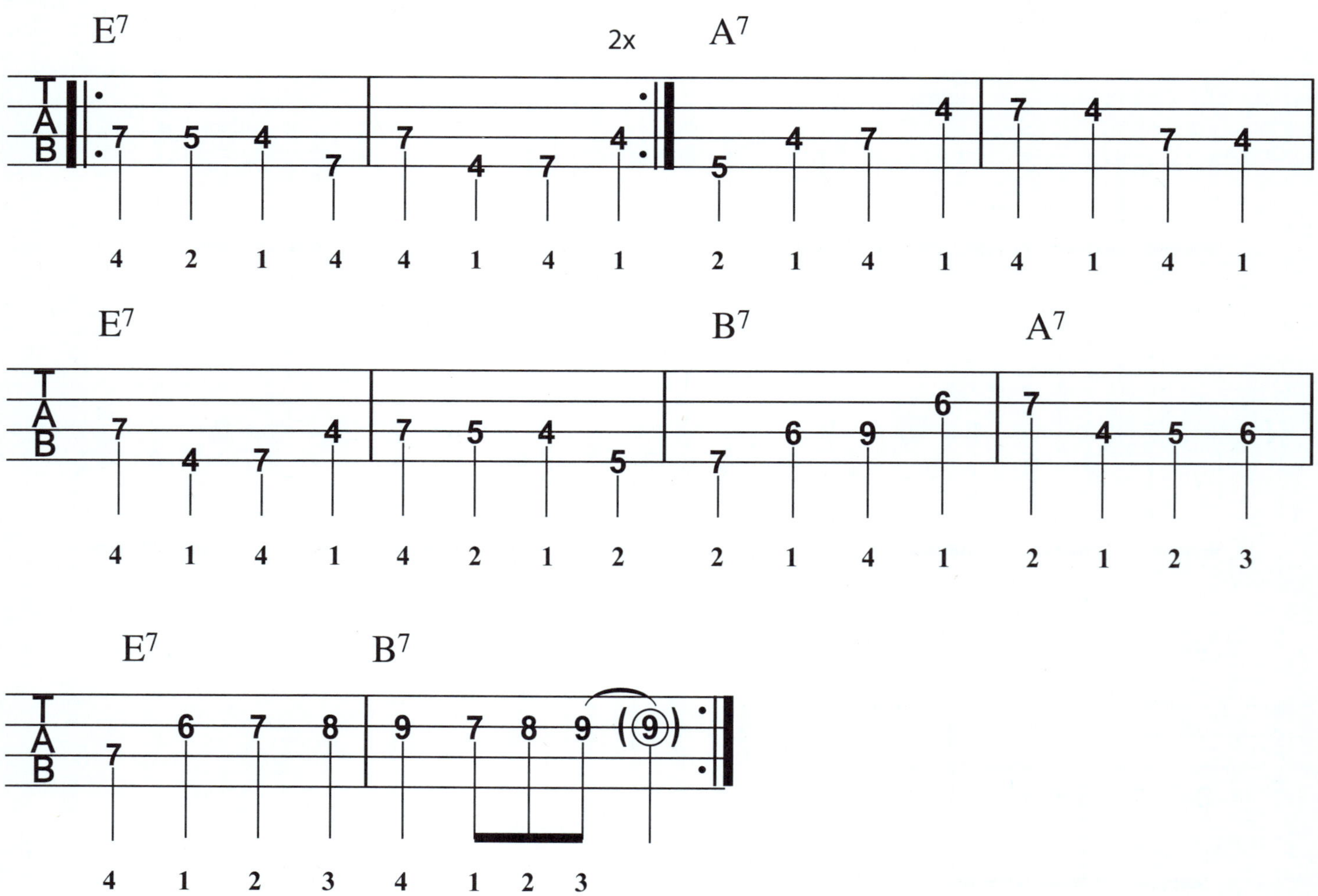

Verse & Chorus (Variation 2)

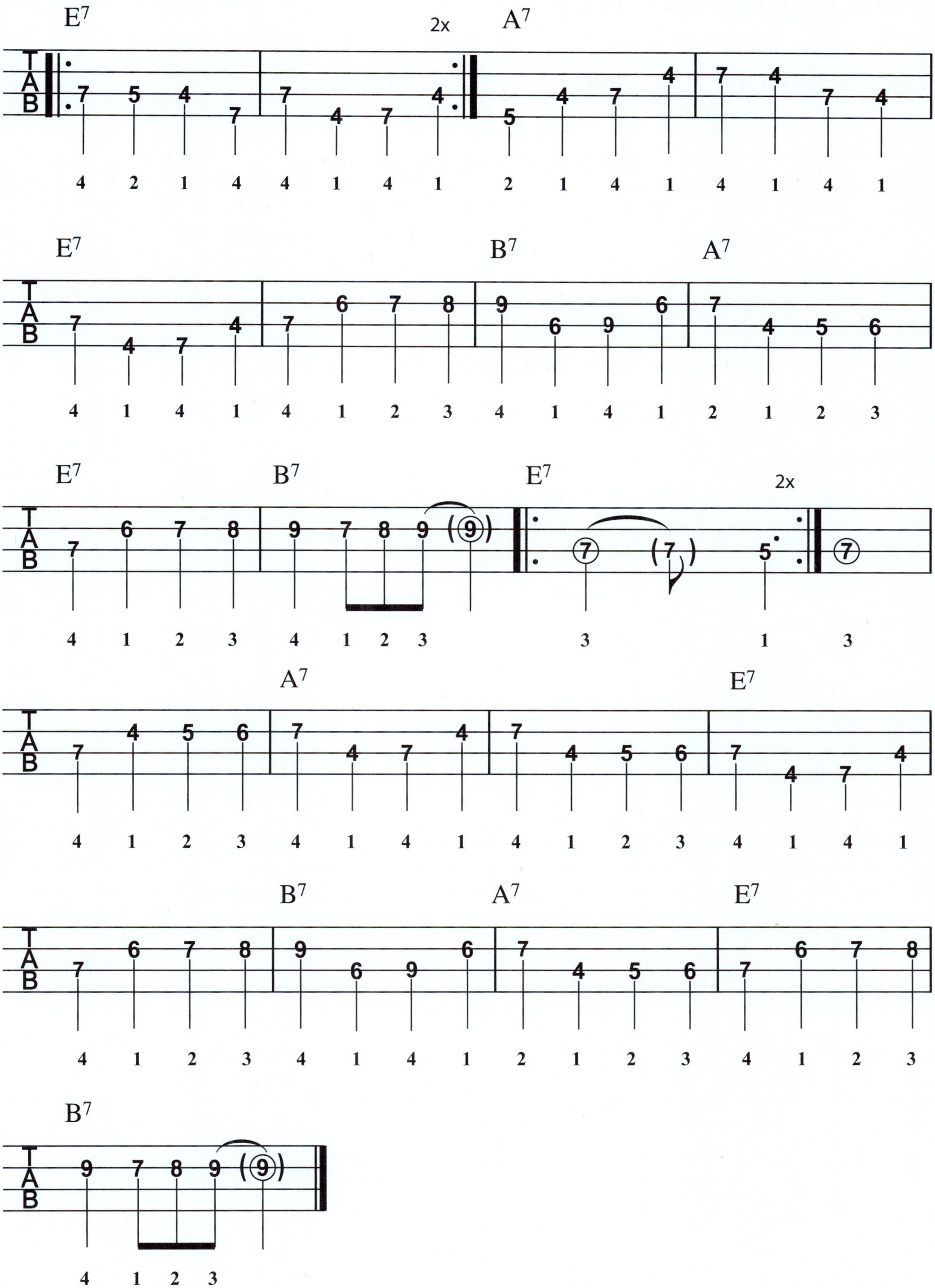

5 String Modes Key of "C"

1st Position

1st Position C Major Scale

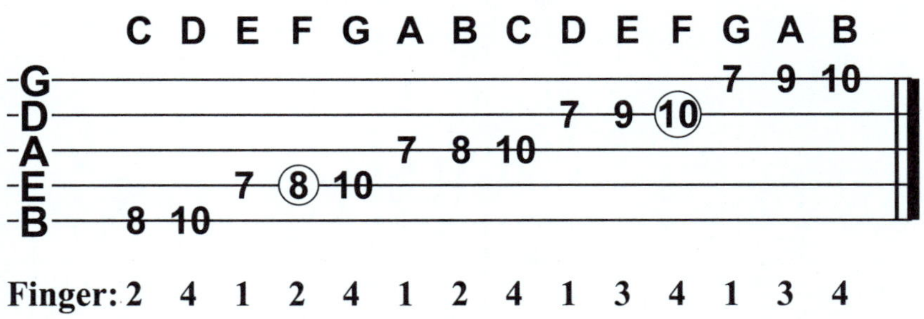

C Ionian

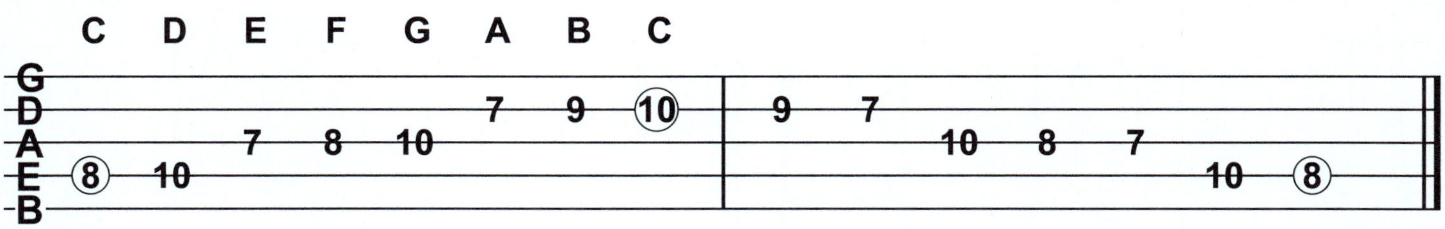

D Dorian

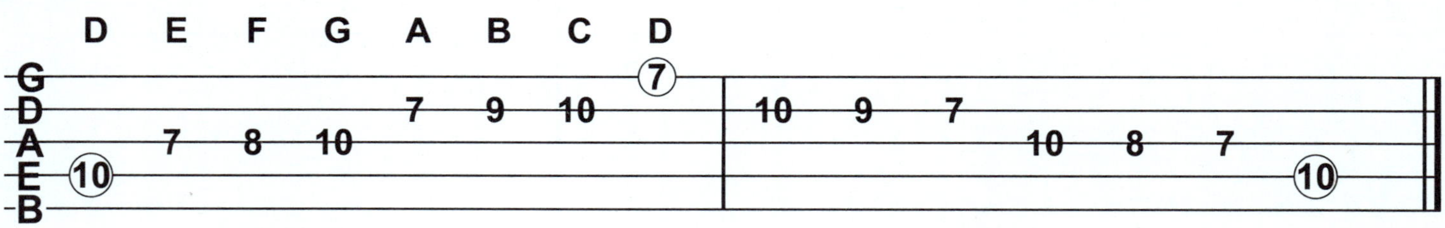

E Phrygian

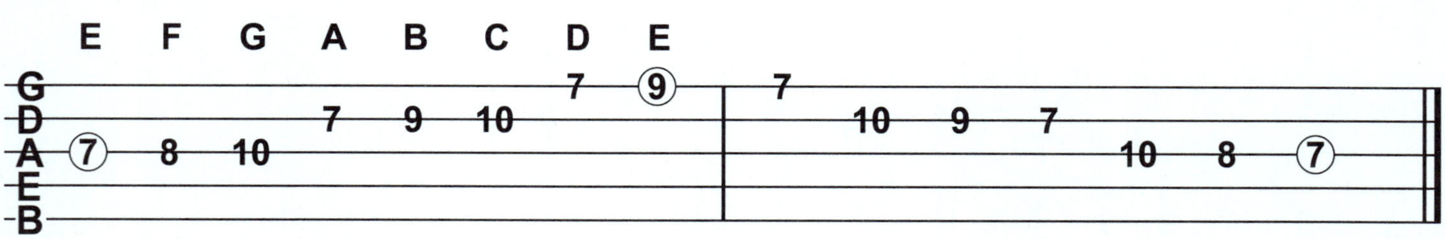

F Lydian

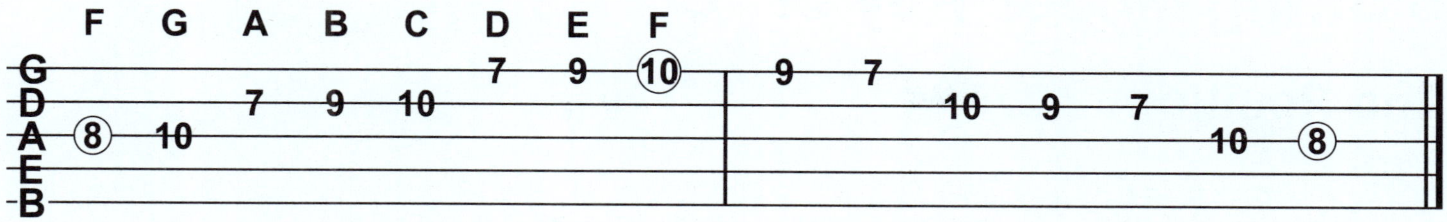

G Mixolydian

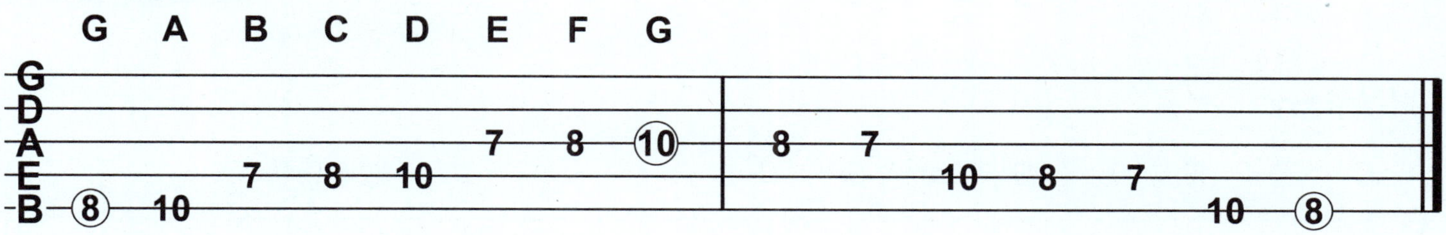

A Aeolian

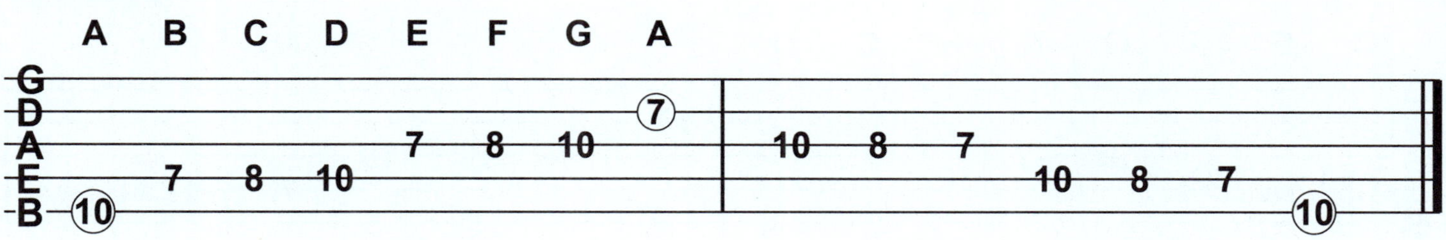

B Locrian

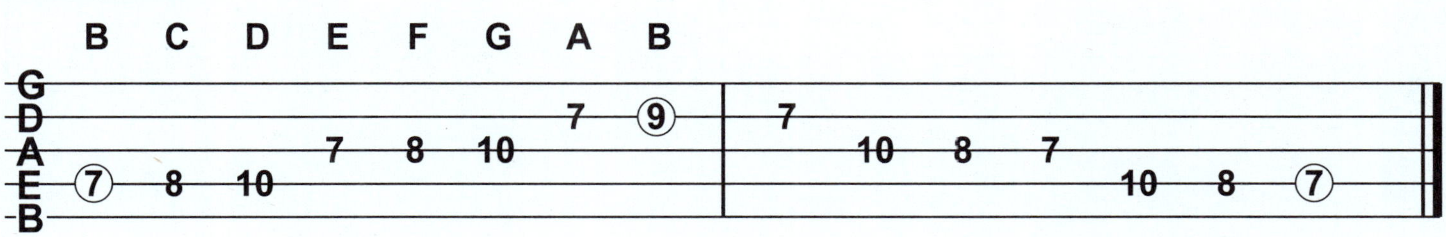

5 String Modes Key of “C”

2nd Position

2nd Position C Major Scale

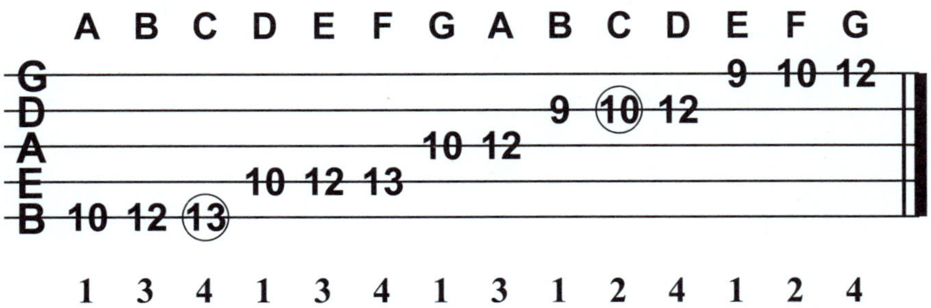

C Ionian

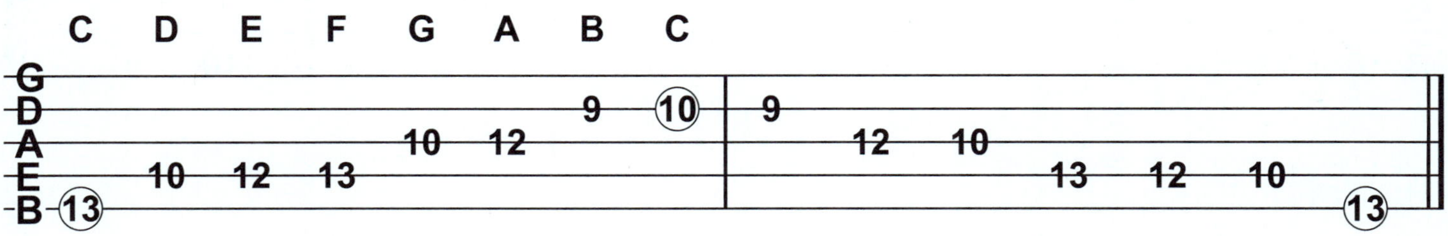

D Dorian

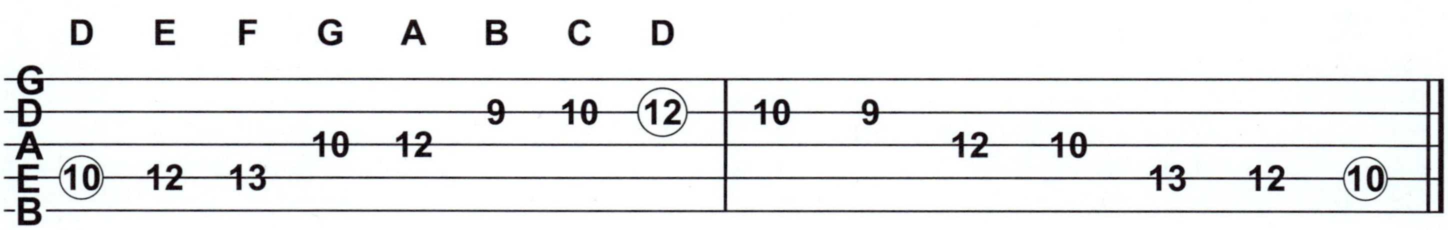

E Phrygian

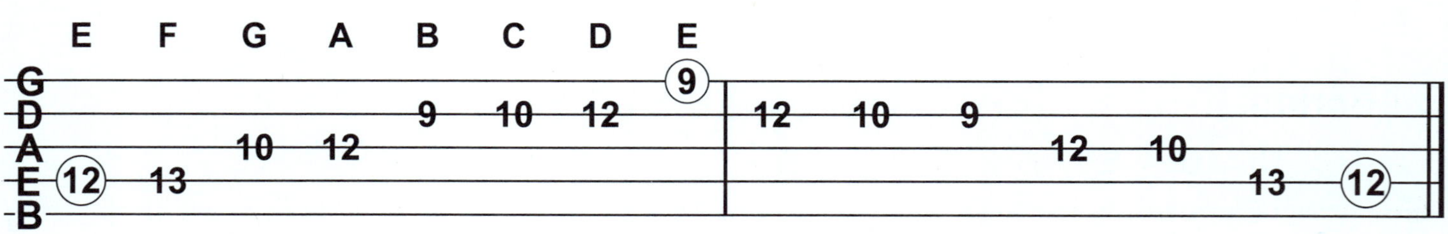

F Lydian

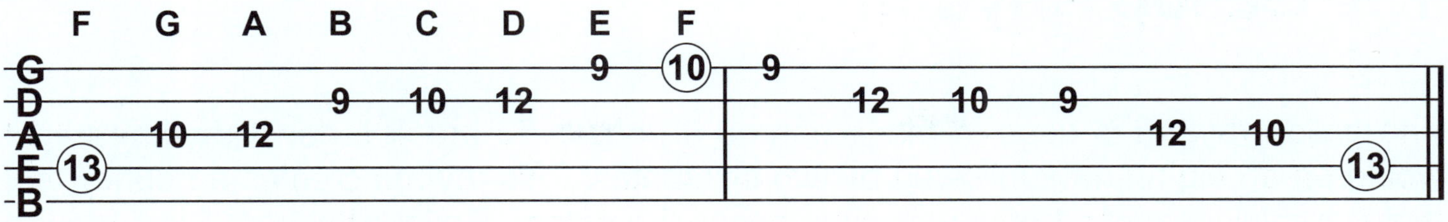

G Mixolydian

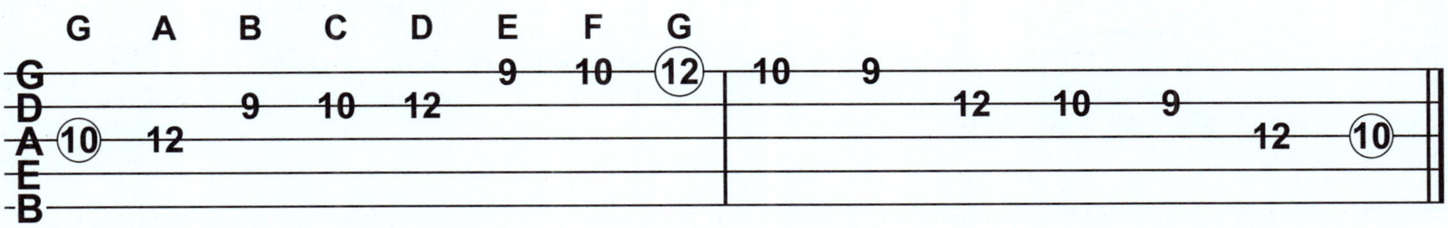

A Aeolian

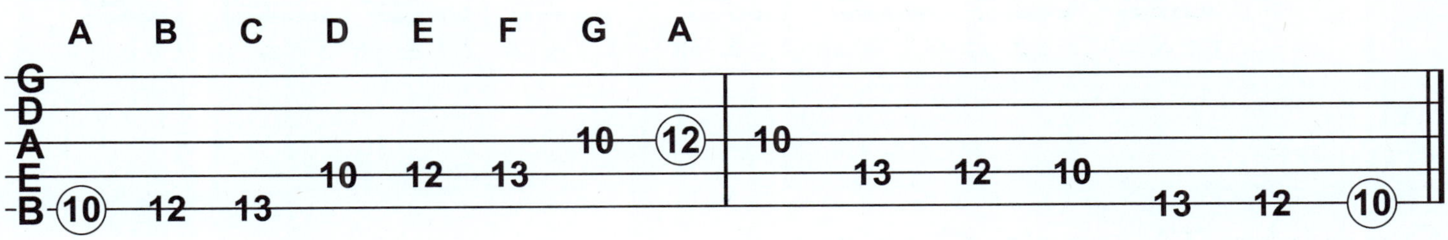

B Locrian

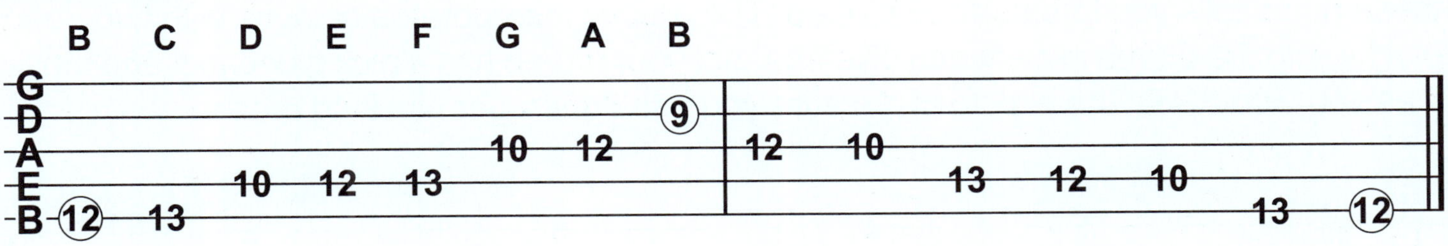

The Gallop Rhythm

The gallop rhythm is used in many genres of music. To break it down rhythmically it would be an eighth note followed by two sixteenths. This rhythm creates a bouncy feel that is reminiscent of a horse galloping; hence the name, "Gallop Rhythm." Play through the rhythm first with just the open E string below before you jump into the progression.

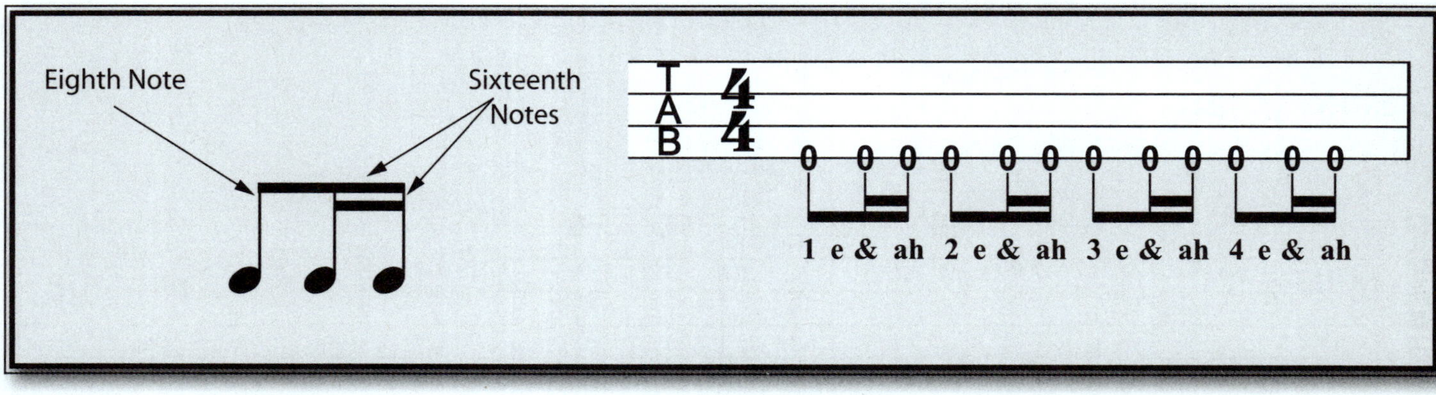

Now apply this rhythm to the entire progression below:

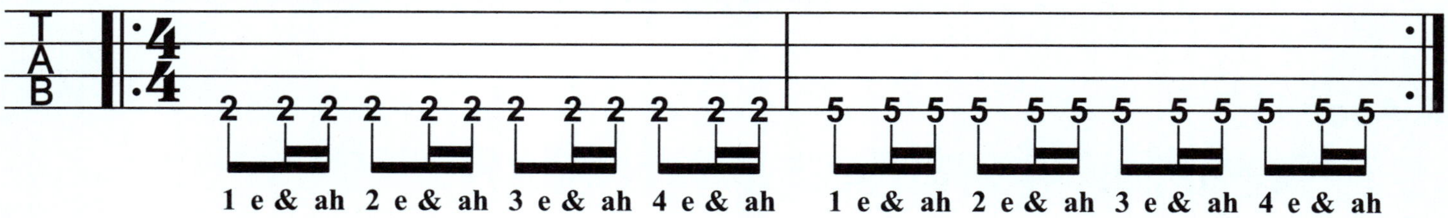

Double Thumb Groove

With this technique you use your thumb in the same fashion as you would use a pluck. Move the thumb in a down up motion to pluck the "x" deadened notes. The D and U below these notes tells you to pluck down or up. The groove incorporates octaves with two dead plucks with the thumb in-between. Pretend that your thumb has a pick glued to it and move it as you would with the pick to make sure you use the proper plucking motion.

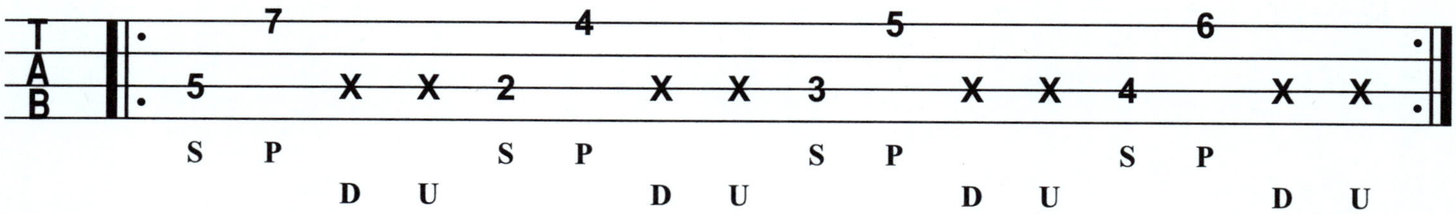

Slap Bass Pop Melody

This is a complicated bass line where you play the bass notes and a melody together. I wrote the chord progression notes above the staff so you can see the bass root notes. Pay close attention to which notes are slapped with the thumb and which are plucked with the pop technique. Once you feel comfortable playing this through from beginning to end play it with the backing track.

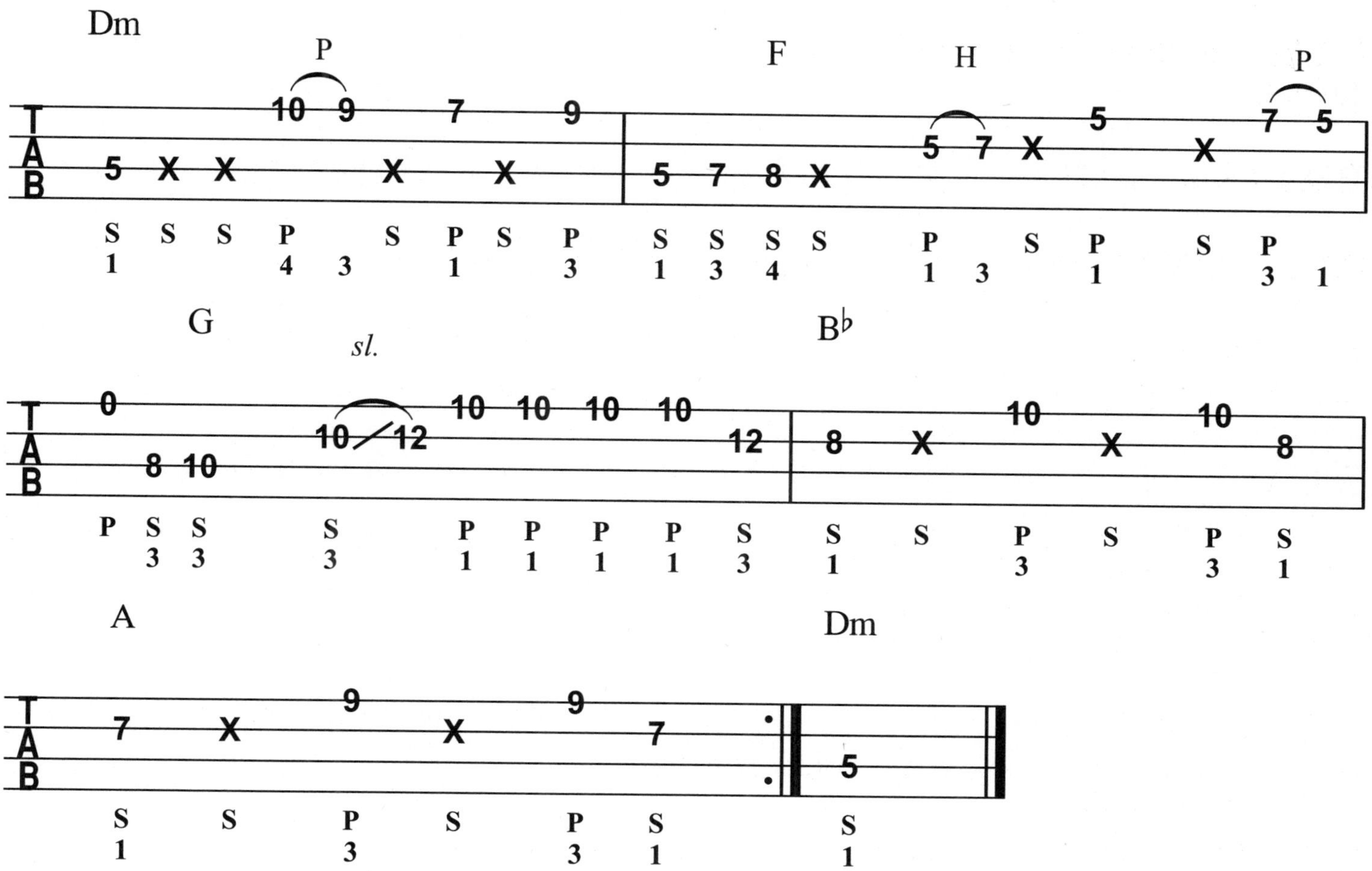

On the backing track after the first time through the progression there are variations added to the bass line. I encourage you to experiment and improvise to make your own variations.

Bass 2 Quiz #3

You're ready to take your next quiz now! Please review all the lessons in the previous section then go to page 4 to see where to take your quiz.

Musical Words

<u>Progression</u>: A series of chords that are played within a song.

<u>Accent</u>: A louder pluck or pick strum.

<u>Dynamics</u>: The variation of sound levels, louder and softer.

<u>Riff</u>: A short melody usually 2 or 4 beats long.

<u>5th Position</u>: The section of the bass spanning the 5th through 8th frets across all six strings.

<u>Triplet</u>: A group of three notes played in the time of two of the same notes.

<u>Natural Minor Scale</u>: The natural minor scale has the same tones as the major scale, but uses the sixth tone of the major scale as its tonic. This changes the semitones (half steps) between the second and third tones and the fifth and sixth tones creating a scale formula of Whole – Half – Whole – Whole – Half – Whole – Whole.

<u>Sixteenth Note</u>: A note having the time duration of one sixteenth of the time duration of a whole note.

<u>Syncopation</u>: Deliberate altering of the meter or pulse of a composition by a temporarily shifting the accent to a weak beat or an off-beat.

<u>Turnaround</u>: A short phrase at the end of a progression that brings the player back to the beginning of the song in a smooth transition.

<u>Arpeggio</u>: The Notes of a chord played separately.

<u>Octave</u>: An interval spanning seven diatonic degrees (eleven half-steps). An octave above C would be C.

<u>Root Note</u>: The tonic or fundamental note of a chord. The note which gives a chord or scale its letter name.

<u>Blues Tri-Tone</u>: The interval of a sharped fourth (augmented fourth, enharmonically spelled as a diminished fifth). This interval was known as the "devil in music" in the Medieval era because it is the most dissonant sound in the scale. This note is usually added to a minor pentatonic scale to give it a bluesy sound.

<u>Melody</u>: A succession of musical tones. It represents the linear or horizontal aspect of music.

Natural Harmonics: Chime like notes that are sounded by lightly touching the string above a point in the string length which divides the string into equal parts.

Natural Minor Scales

Key of "G" Minor

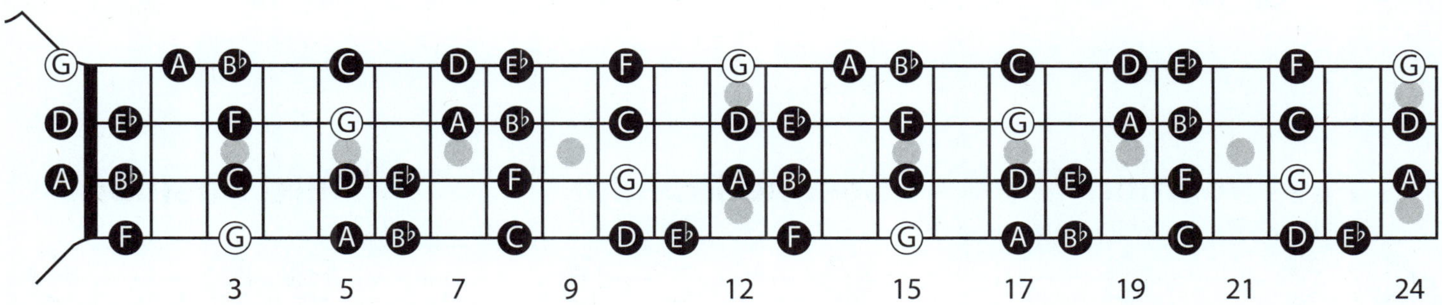

First Position

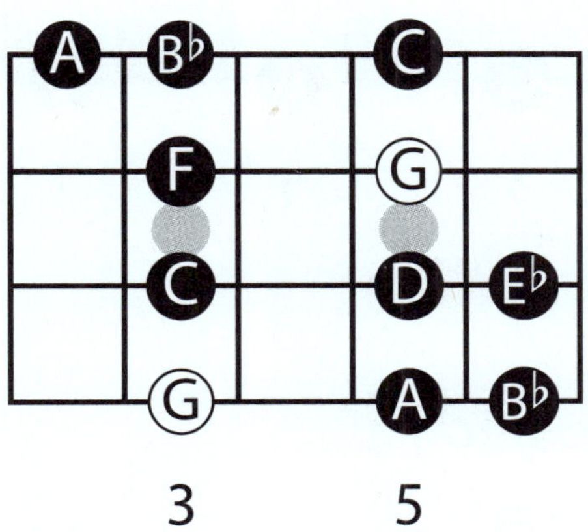

Second Position

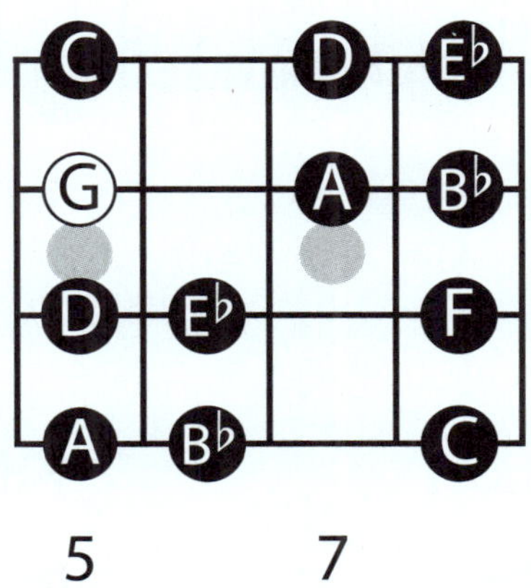

Third Position

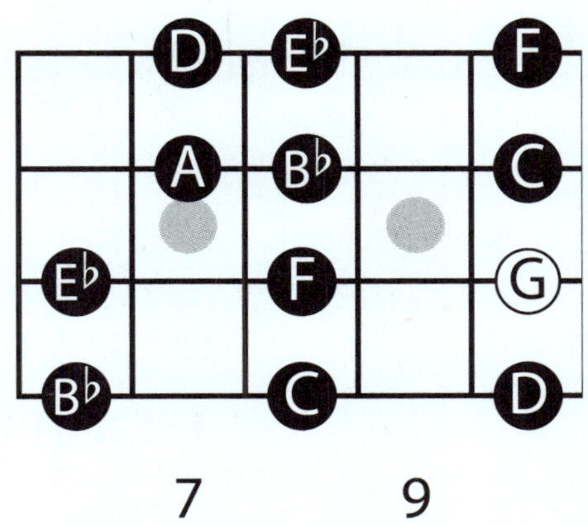

Fourth Position

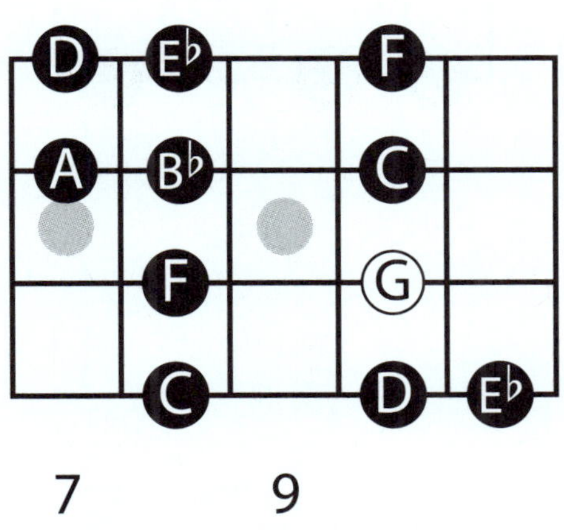

Fifth Position

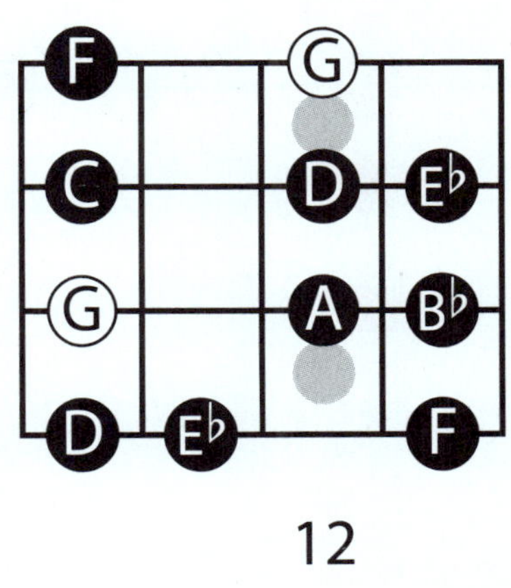

Key of "E" Minor

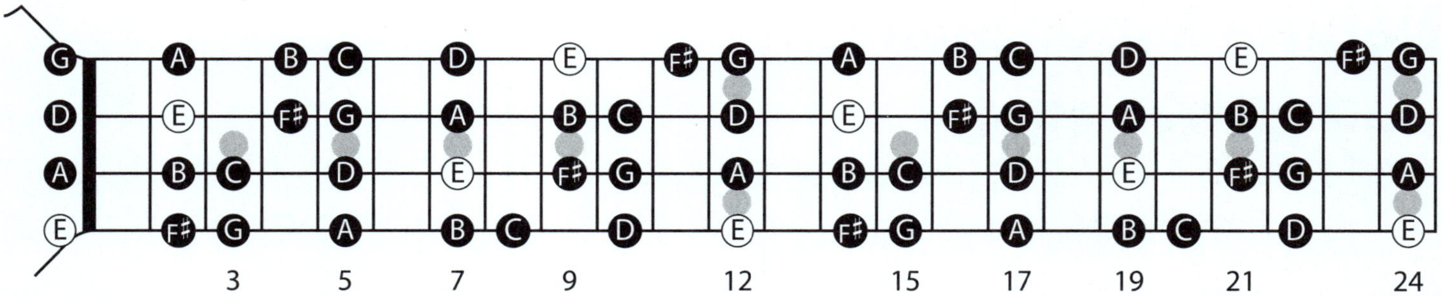

First Position

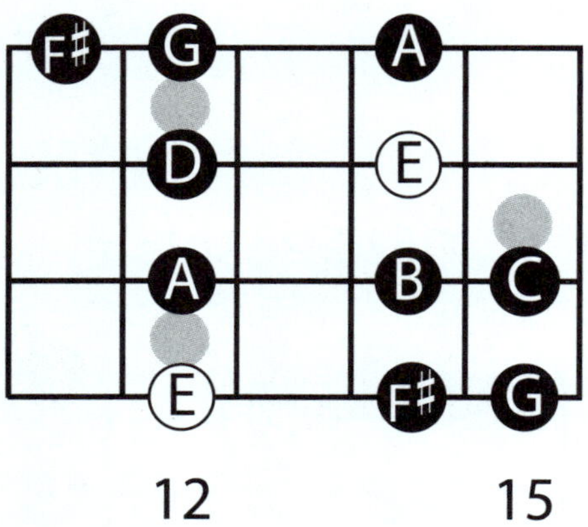

Second Position

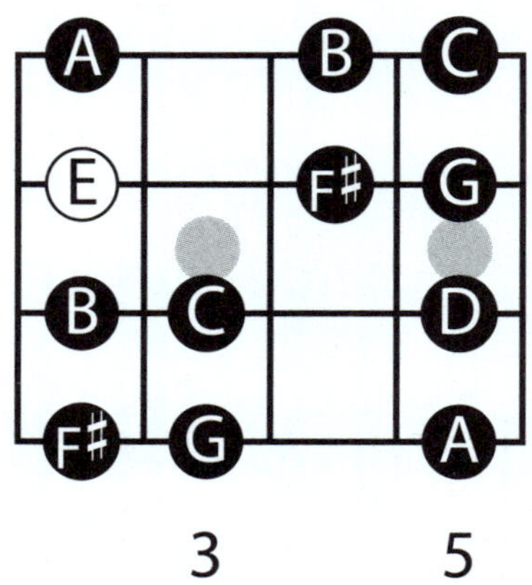

Third Position

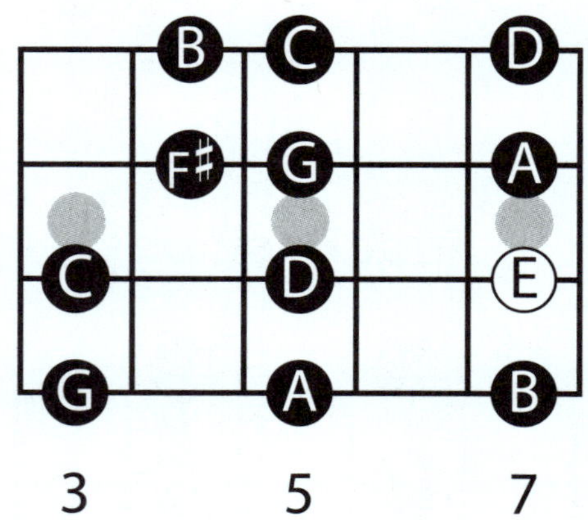

Fourth Position

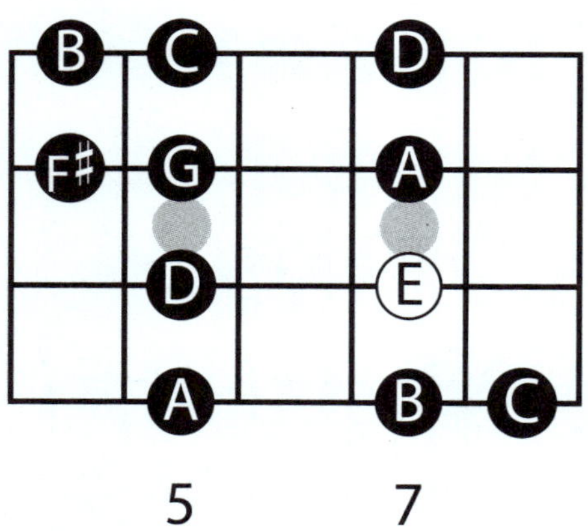

Fifth Position

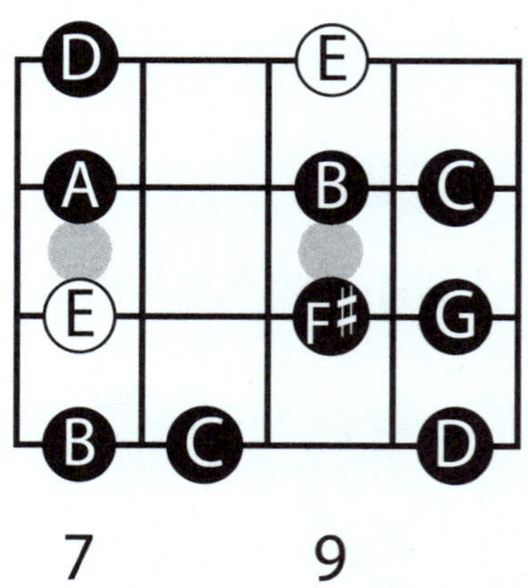

Key of "A" Minor

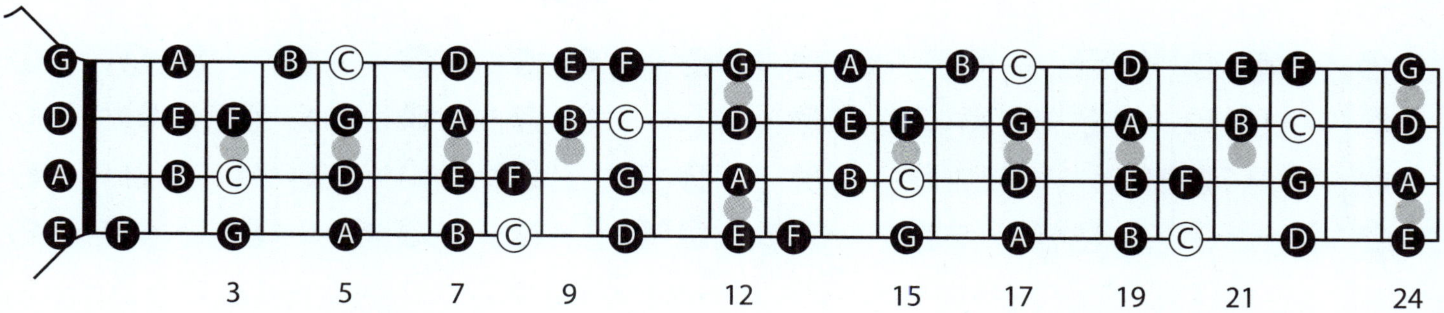

First Position

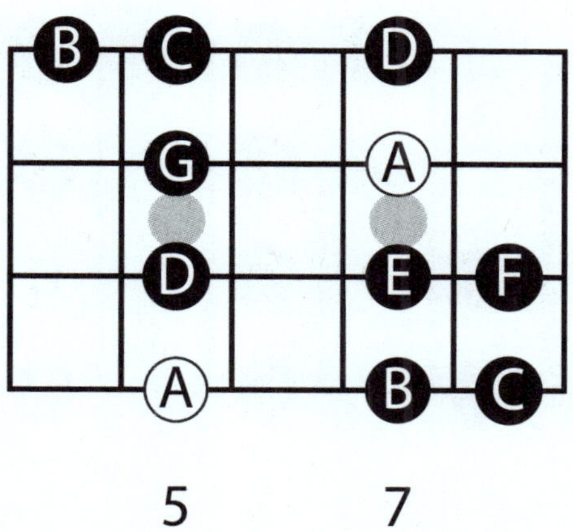

Second Position

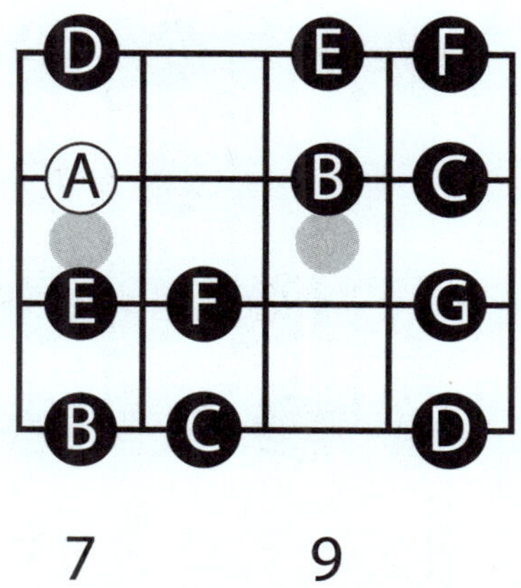

Third Position

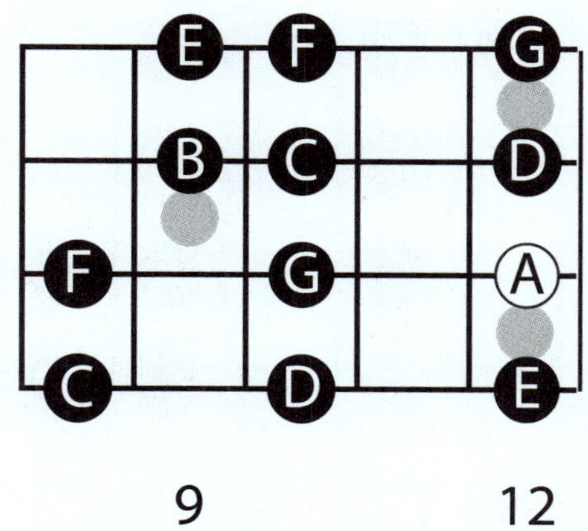

Fourth Position

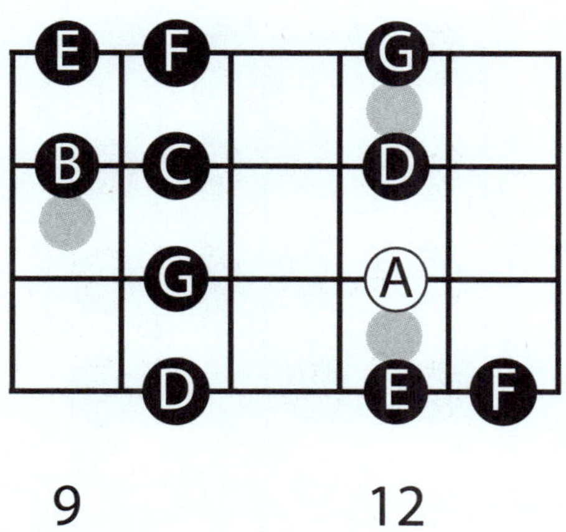

Fifth Position

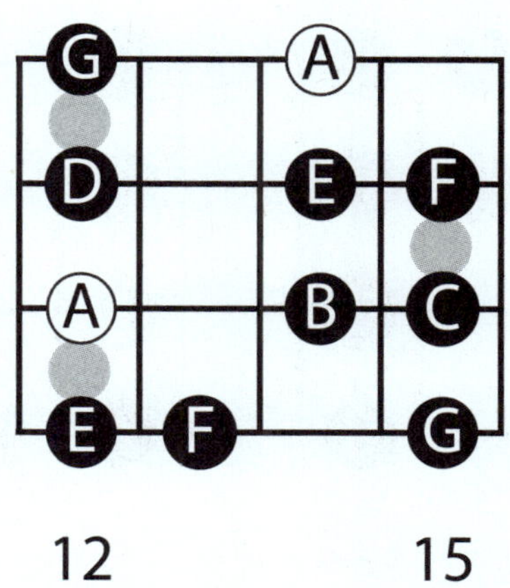

Key of "D" Minor

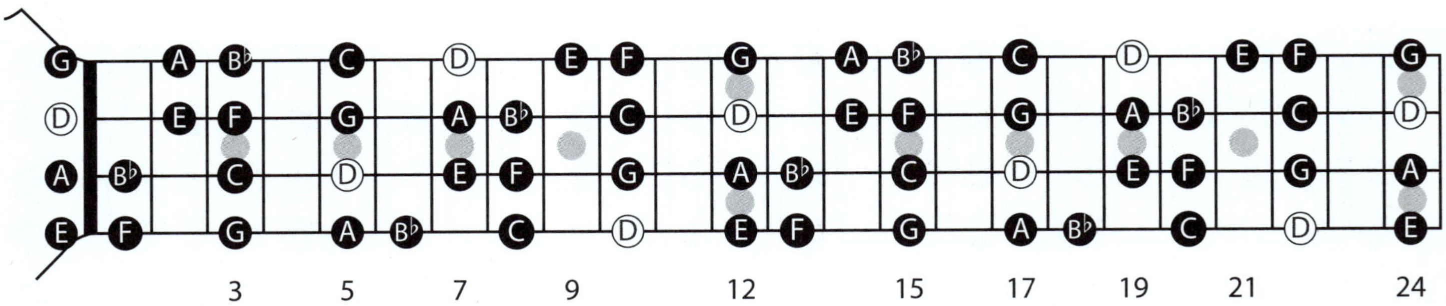

First Position

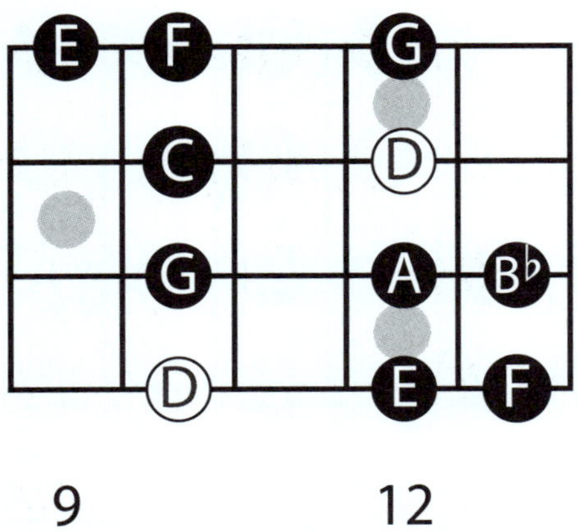

Second Position

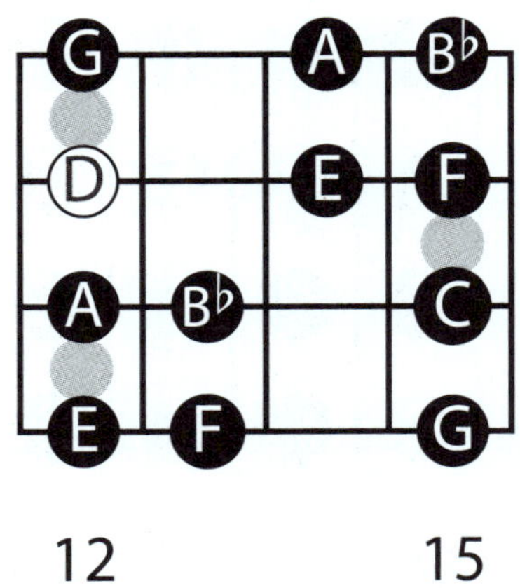

Third Position

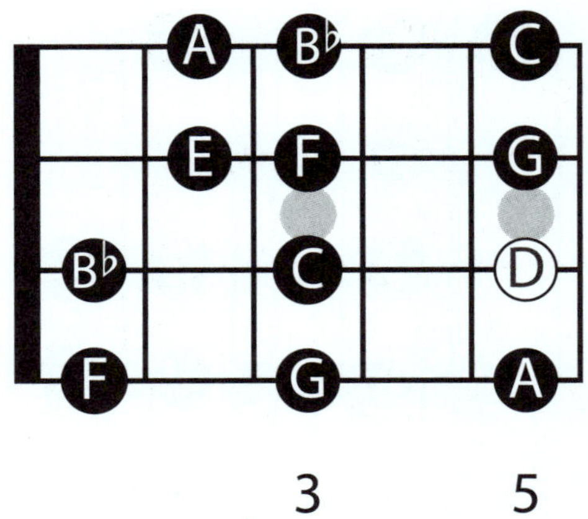

Fourth Position

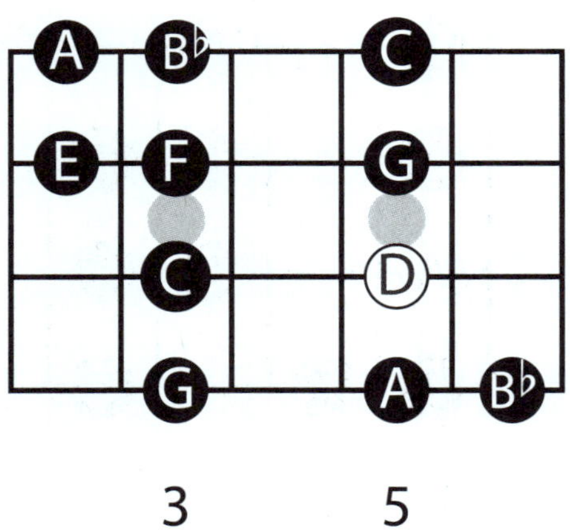

Fifth Position

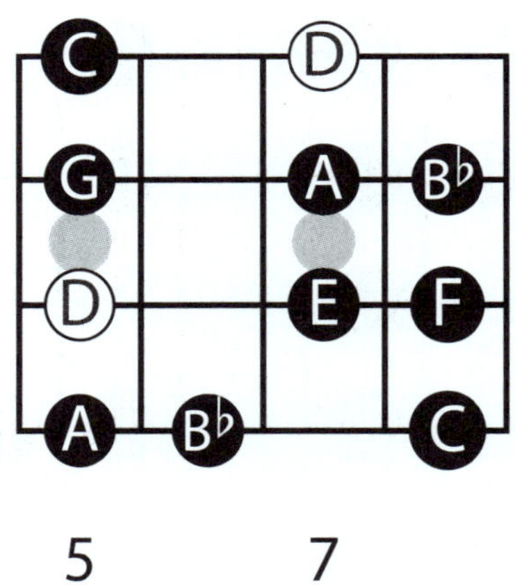

Blues Scales
Key of "A"

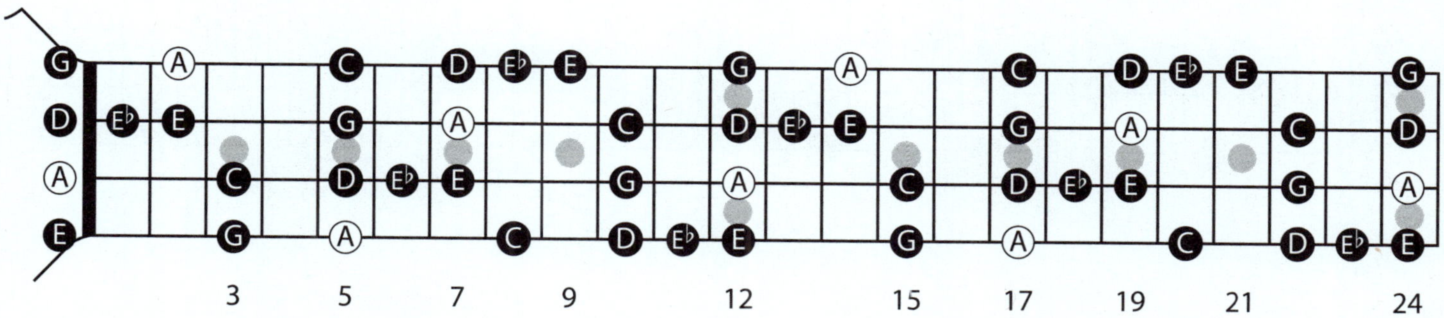

First Position

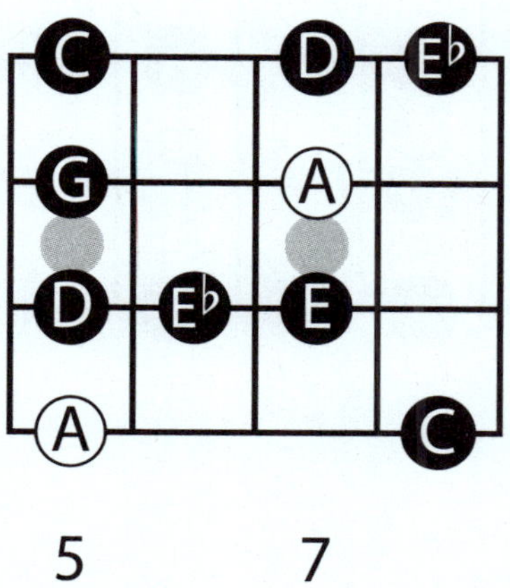

Second Position

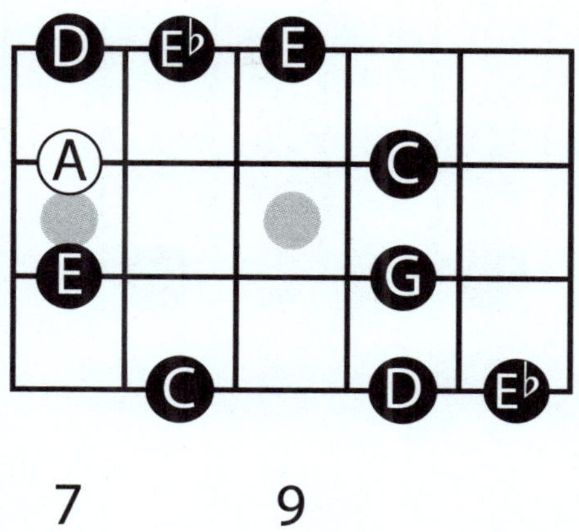

Third Position

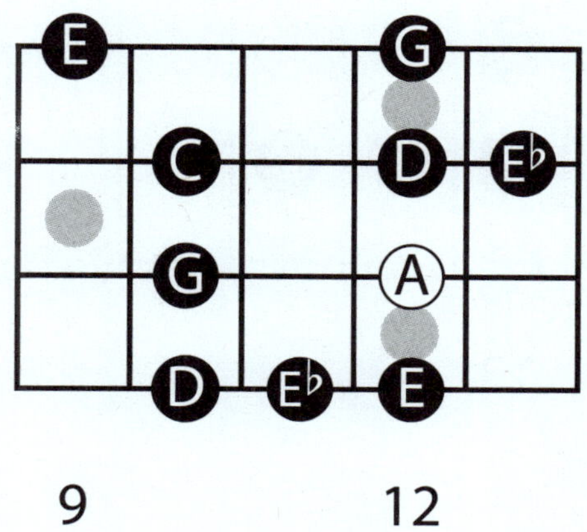

Fourth Position

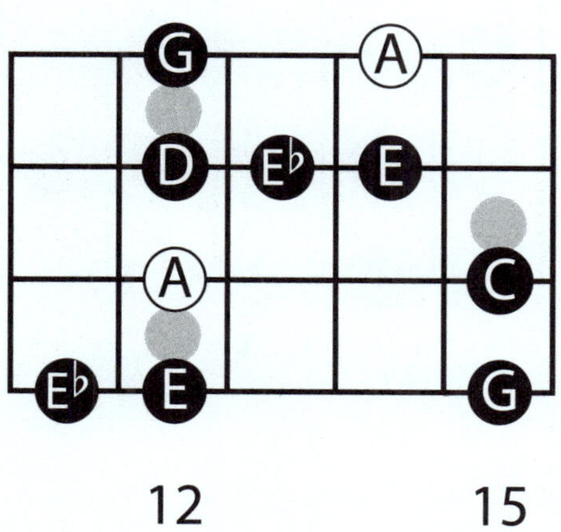

Fifth Position

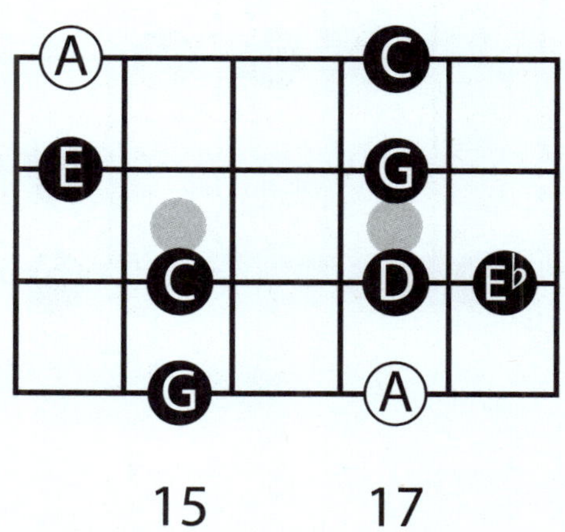

Key of "E"

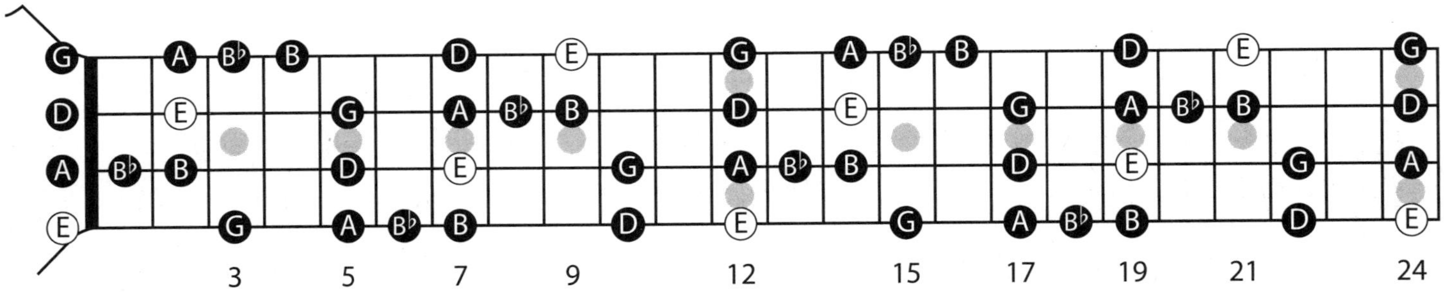

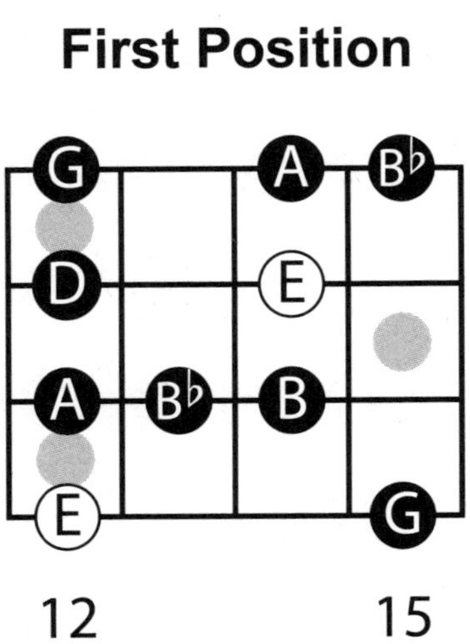

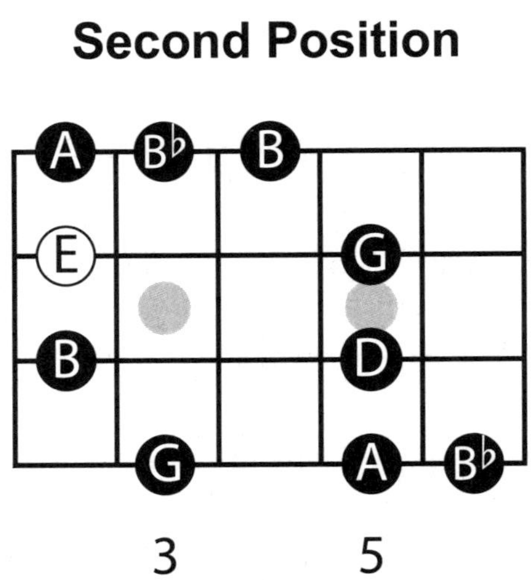

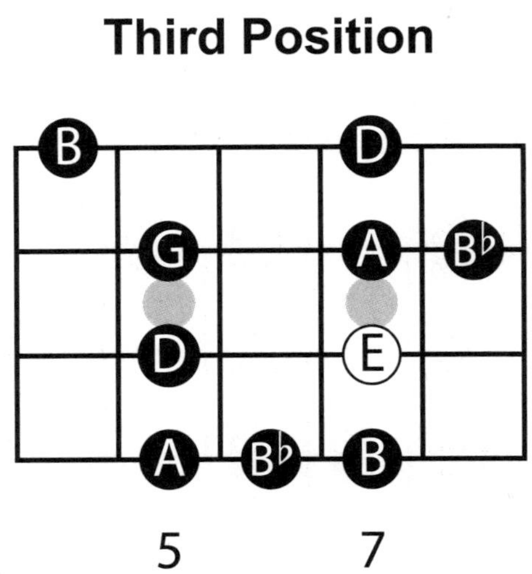

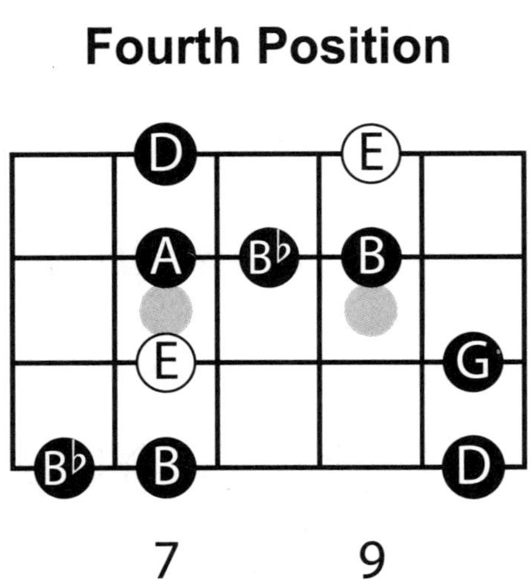

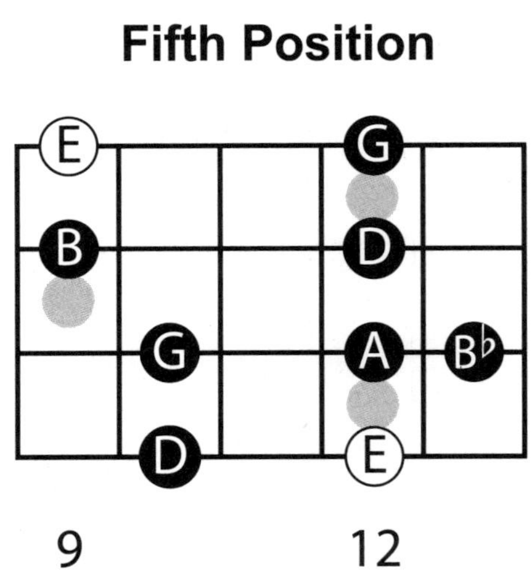

Key of "D"

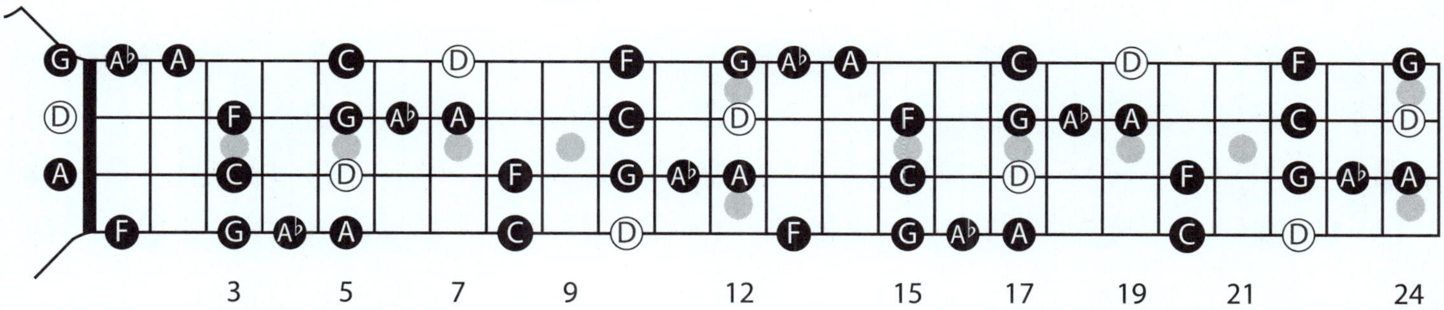

First Position

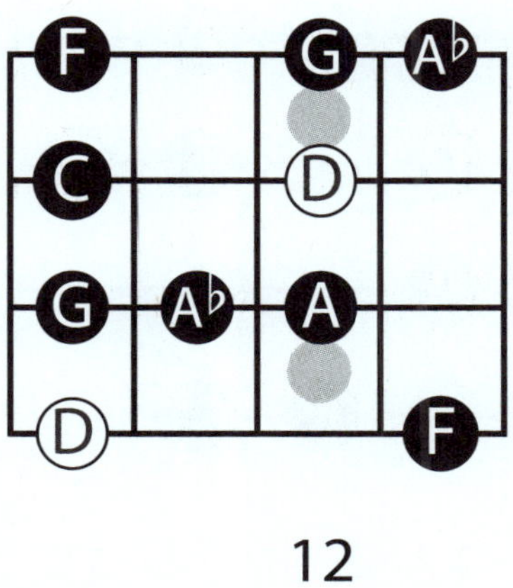

Second Position

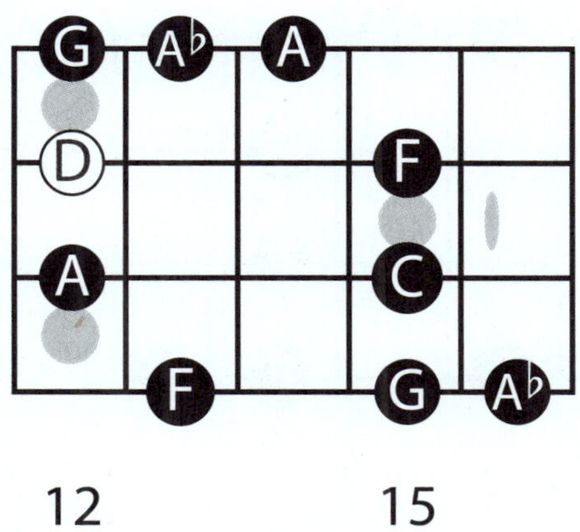

Third Position

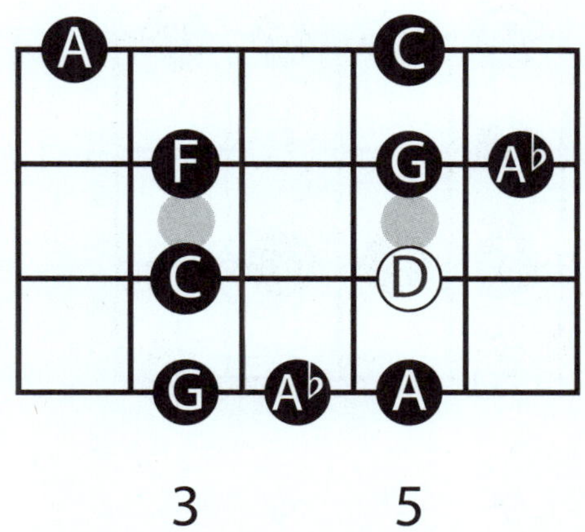

Fourth Position

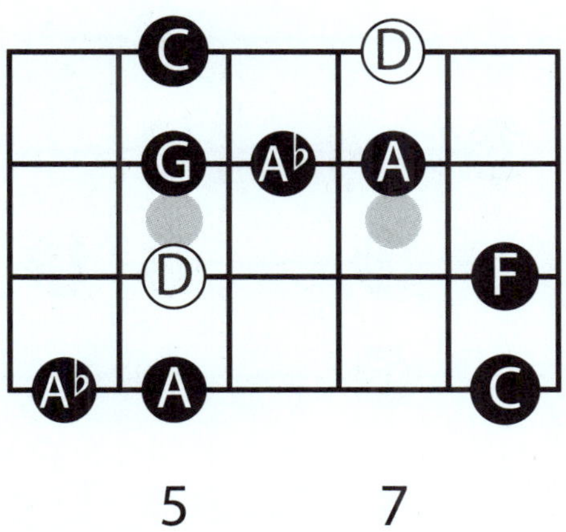

Fifth Position

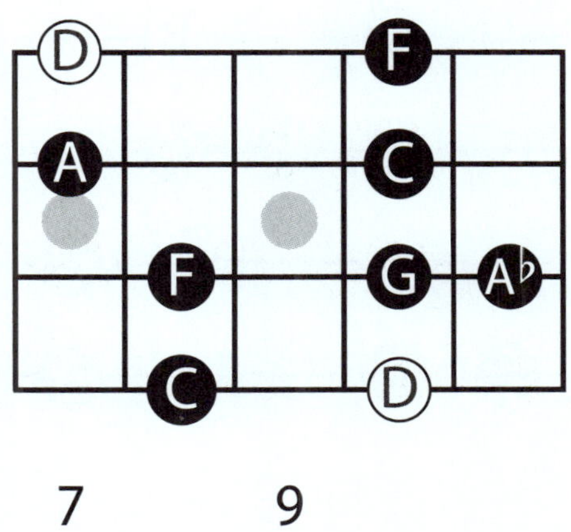

Key of “B”

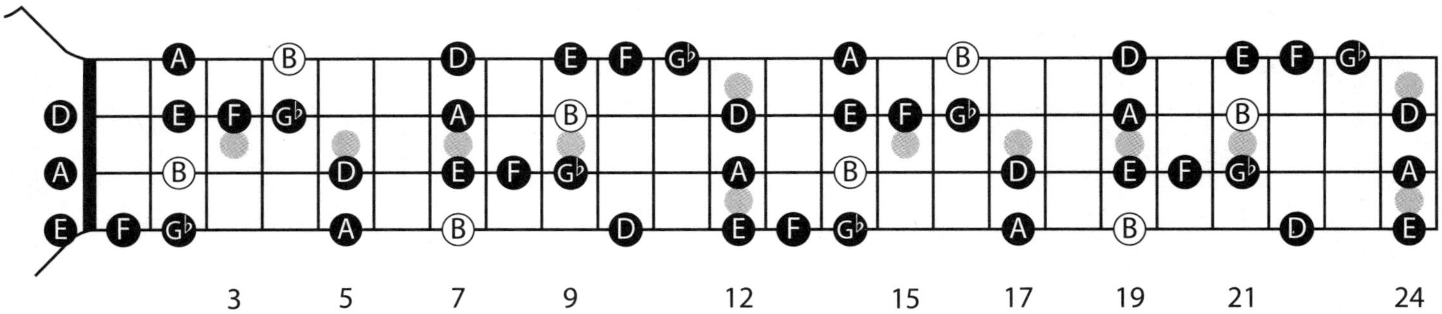

First Position

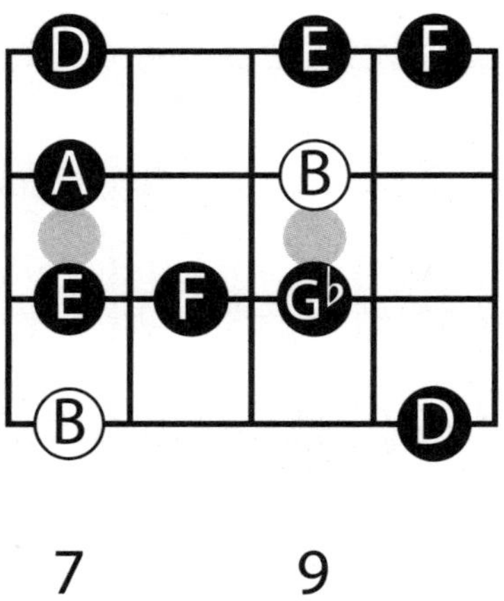

Second Position

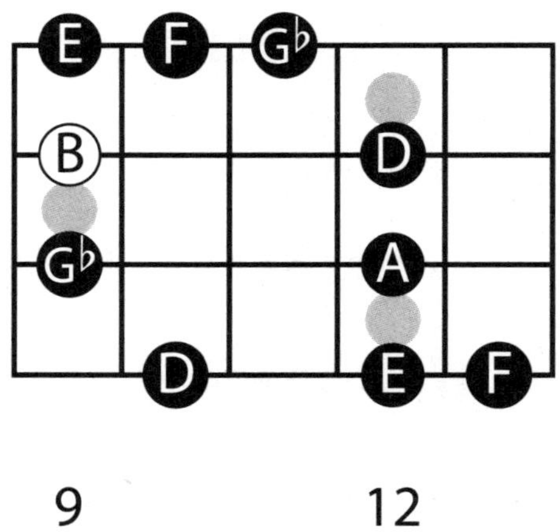

Third Position

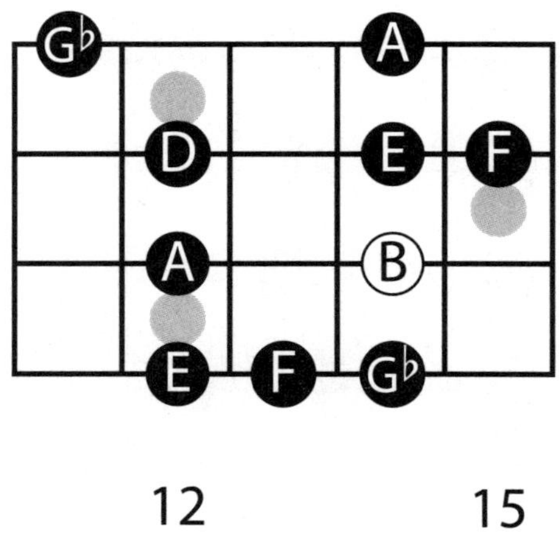

Fourth Position

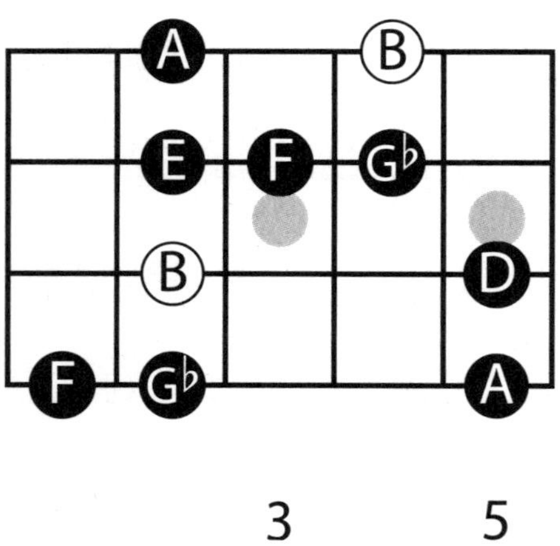

Fifth Position

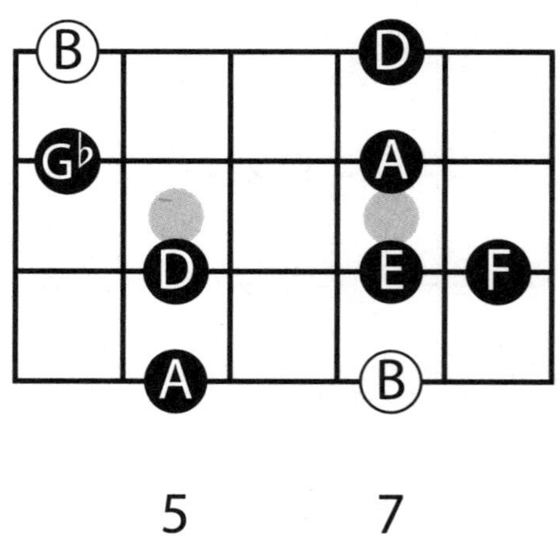

About the Author

John McCarthy
Creator of
The Rock House Method®

John is the creator of The Rock House Method®, the world's leading musical instruction system. Over his 25 plus year career, he has written, produced and/or appeared in more than 100 instructional products. Millions of people around the world have learned to play music using John's easy-to-follow, accelerated programs.

John is a virtuoso musician who has worked with some of the industry's most legendary entertainers. He has the ability to break down, teach and communicate music in a manner that motivates and inspires others to achieve their dreams of playing an instrument.

As a musician and songwriter, John blends together a unique style of rock, metal, funk and blues in a collage of melodic compositions. Throughout his career, John has recorded and performed with renowned musicians including Doug Wimbish (Joe Satriani, Living Colour, The Rolling Stones, Madonna, Annie Lennox), Grammy Winner Leo Nocentelli, Rock & Roll Hall of Fame inductees Bernie Worrell and Jerome "Big Foot" Brailey, Freekbass, Gary Hoey, Bobby Kimball, David Ellefson (founding member of seven time Grammy nominee Megadeth), Will Calhoun (B.B. King, Mick Jagger and Paul Simon), Gus G of Ozzy and many more.

To get more information about John McCarthy, his music and his instructional products visit **RockHouseSchool.com**.

T
A
B

T
A
B

T
A
B

T
A
B

T
A
B

T
A
B

TAB

TAB

TAB

TAB

TAB

TAB

TAB

TAB

TAB

TAB

TAB

TAB